RACIST LOVE

ANIMA Critical Race Studies Otherwise
A series edited by Mel Y. Chen and Jasbir K. Puar

Duke University Press   *Durham and London*   2022

RACIST LOVE

ASIAN ABSTRACTION AND

THE PLEASURES OF FANTASY

Leslie Bow

© 2022 Duke University Press
All rights reserved
Cover designed by A. Mattson Gallagher
Text designed by Courtney Leigh Richardson
Typeset in Knockout and Garamond Premier Pro
by Westchester Publishing Services

Library of Congress Cataloging-in-Publication Data
Names: Bow, Leslie, [date] author.
Title: Racist love : Asian abstraction and the pleasures of fantasy / Leslie Bow.
Other titles: ANIMA (Duke University Press)
Description: Durham : Duke University Press, 2022. | Series: Anima: critical race studies otherwise | Includes bibliographical references and index.
Identifiers: LCCN 2021022580 (print)
LCCN 2021022581 (ebook)
ISBN 9781478015222 (hardcover)
ISBN 9781478017851 (paperback)
ISBN 9781478022466 (ebook)
Subjects: LCSH: Asian Americans—Public opinion. | Asian Americans—Social conditions. | Asian Americans—Ethnic identity. | Racism—United States. | United States—Race relations. | BISAC: SOCIAL SCIENCE / Ethnic Studies / American / Asian American Studies
Classification: LCC E184.A75 G74 2022 (print) | LCC E184.A75 (ebook) | DDC 305.895/073—dc23
LC record available at https://lccn.loc.gov/2021022580
LC ebook record available at https://lccn.loc.gov/2021022581

Cover art: Hong Chun Zhang, *Three Graces* (right detail), 2011. Charcoal on paper with scrolls; triptych, left and right: 36 × 96 in., center: 36 × 100 in. Photographed by Aaron Paden. Courtesy of the artist.

IN LOVING MEMORY OF
WILLIE BOW
1931–2017
AND
SUE MAE BOW
1936–2021

Contents

INTRODUCTION
Racist Love · 1

1 · RACIAL TRANSITIONAL OBJECTS
Anthropomorphic Animals and Other Asian Americans · 25

2 · RACIST CUTE
Caricature, Kawaii Style, and the Asian Thing · 69

3 · ASIAN ● FEMALE ● ROBOT ● SLAVE
Techno-Orientalism after #MeToo · 109

4 · ON THE ASIAN FETISH AND
THE FANTASY OF EQUALITY · 153

CONCLUSION
Racist Hate, Racial Profiling, Pokémon at Auschwitz · 191

Acknowledgments · 201   Notes · 205
References · 237   Index · 253

INTRODUCTION

Racist Love

> How am I supposed to explain to a child the superimposition of cultural generalizations onto toy cars and monsters and space aliens? I can barely explain them to myself.
> —Stephen Marche, "How to Read a Racist Book to Your Kids"

> The fundamental level of ideology, however, is not of an illusion masking the real state of things but that of an (unconscious) fantasy structuring our social reality itself.
> —Slavoj Žižek, *The Sublime Object of Ideology*

How is race a source of pleasure in the twenty-first century? This book explores the overt and at times subtle ways in which social hierarchy becomes reinforced by positive feeling, particularly positive feeling surrounding Asian Americans.

At the millennium, race has been persistently framed in terms of negativity—xenophobia, fear, anxiety. The political rhetoric of racial hatred in the United States is easily recognizable: calls for wall building, claims about restricted free speech, contestations about whose lives matter, assigning ethnicity to a virus.

And yet, paradoxically, we profess to love diversity. The imperative to *represent* feeds racial scopophilia, a visual pleasure animated by the erotic, but also extending to other forms of emotional attachment: affection, empathy, amusement. What bell hooks (1992, 21) famously deemed "getting a bit of the Other" extends the idea of the erotic encounter with difference to cultural appropriation, to conceptual "theft" of desired traits, attributes, style, and association.[1] Yet it also speaks to tensions surrounding fetishistic love: imbuing objects with desire forestalls an underlying anxiety. In naming a structure of split feeling that attaches to Asians in the contemporary United States, *Racist Love: Asian Abstraction and the Pleasures of Fantasy* takes that process of fetishistic reduction literally to analyze the visual representation not of Asian people but of their object substitutes.

Exploring the ways in which the fantasy of animated things underwrites contemporary understanding of racial difference in the United States, this book engages sites of a racial imaginary infused with desire, longing, and apprehension surrounding Asian Americans at the millennium—or more specifically, their nonhuman proxies. How does our relationship with objects animated through our regard speak to fantasies of racialization? Asianized anthropomorphic kitchen timers, cartoon pandas, feminized robots, and lifelike dolls testify to the simultaneous saturation and displacement of racial meaning, its ability to be abstracted from human embodiment. Here, racial abstraction performs as a metaphoric substitution based on affective resemblance. As repositories of seemingly positive feeling and intimate connection, imagined beings are yet conduits of political desires. If fantasy functions not as the "object of desire, but its setting" (Laplanche and Pontalis 1986, 26), how does the fantasy of things come to life reveal the desires we place on racial difference in the United States? If racial meaning continues to be harnessed to the circulation of negative feeling, what about love?

A case in point: the geisha car (figure Intro.1). A minor figure in an imaginary world populated by anthropomorphic vehicles in Pixar's animated *Cars 2* (2011), Okuni is unmistakably Japanese. Is the cartoon funny? Cute? An example of yellowface caricature? Or all of these? The character relies on ethnic signs—fan, chopsticks, hairstyle, and textile patterns—detachable from the body to convey human attributes of gender, youth, and nationality. A visual

FIGURE INTRO.1. Okuni, *Cars 2*, Pixar/Disney, 2011

stereotype of dubious humor, the cartoon's economical reduction also invites a series of associations telescoping outward—geisha to Japan to technology to techno-dominance. A marginal figure in Japanese society, the geisha was privileged in the US imaginary during the occupation, a focus central to its postwar vision of Japan in reconceiving enemy as ally.[2] Racial meaning here circulates amid overlapping and heterogeneous networks: US-Japan, child-adult, ally-enemy, present-future—and implicitly, Ford-Toyota. The Japanese car invokes competition with overseas auto manufacturing while taming it through a visual joke, one extended in a franchise that relies on such shorthand to reinforce the "humanity" of its characters. Like the use of "booth babes" at car shows, the nonspeaking, unnamed feminized vehicle is largely ornamental, serving no function in the narrative other than to exoticize one of its backdrops in a world populated by talking machines. Okuni performs the inverse of capitalist reification: not the reduction of persons to things, but the fantasy of things come to life.

The geisha car represents a pleasurable form of racial abstraction,[3] a substitution that relies on metonymic signs, the part for the whole, that underlie the processes of stereotyping. Privileging the somatic (eye, skin, hair, etc.), the aesthetic (color, pattern), and the cultural (fan, chopsticks), racial abstraction depends on the simultaneous interplay of reduction and exaggeration. The racial proxy calls forth not only approximation (almost the same) but proximity (a contiguous presence), the geisha car as Asian adjacent. Trading on iconicity in a minor key, object substitution through aesthetic resemblance enables racial desire.

This book is thus concerned with the implications of racial abstraction, how metonymic signs or projected qualities translate into (uncertain) racial feeling. The excess of significations and desires circulating through this seemingly innocent image provoked the millennial parent of my epigraph to opine, "How am I supposed to explain to a child the superimposition of cultural generalizations onto toy cars and monsters and space aliens? I can barely explain them to myself."[4] This dilemma is not misplaced. Is Okuni sincere or satire? If the latter, does it punch up or down? Taboos against racial caricature that followed in the wake of 1960s social movements are only partially circumvented here; the figure both invokes and eludes the racist kitsch of mammy cookie jars and the like in its contemporary iteration of ethnic drag.[5] The geisha car might manage to fly under the radar of hard-won covenants against racist caricature because it exists in a fantastical world of equivalences where every car has ethnicity. Or because it evokes the sentiments that accrue to *kawaii*, the cute Japanese aesthetic that stimulates feelings of affection and care. Or does the cartoon fail to convey racial injury because it is *Asian*?

"The amazing gives pleasure," Aristotle noted (2011, 485). If the amazing geisha car is a suspect pleasure, suspect to whom? What underlies the assumption that domination is reproduced in its circulation? Igniting a range of positionalities for spectatorship, Okuni embodies a curious paradox: racialized things that convey both delight and offense, innocent fun and discriminatory action (Butler [1990] 2004, 185). The Japanese car operates as a form of visual hate speech, a racial microaggression—that is also somewhat adorable.

Racist Love enters that discomfiting space of ambiguous racial feeling, one enabled, I argue, by the processes of abstraction, appropriating racial-ethnic signs from human subjects and local contexts. To be racialized is to be constructed according to a repetition of type; stereotyping is itself a process of abstraction in which a quality ascribed to one member of a group then applies to all. At first glance, the harm of projecting reductive racial meaning becomes obvious when externalized to things: a chopstick font, "ching chong" sounds, a kung flu. Countering race as embodied materiality, this book explores the meanings underlying racial abstraction in the most mundane and largely unremarked forms: talking animals in children's picture books, home décor and kitchen tchotchkes, dolls and machines come to life, both imagined and actual. And yet I suggest that the anthropomorphic figures in the following chapters are conduits for understanding complex, ambivalent forms of attachment surrounding Asian Americans within what Sara Ahmed (2004) deems an "affective economy" of circulated feeling that materializes collective bodies. In exploring how the racial imaginary in the United States is underwritten by the oscillation of feeling, this book explores the ways in which the nonhuman substitution of things for people becomes a means of narrating, visualizing, and *loving* difference at the millennium.

That structure of feeling was identified at the very origins of Asian American studies as "racist love."[6]

Racial Abstraction and the Ambivalence of Stereotyping

> We've made it. Patels must have made it. Mamet, Spielberg: they're not condescending to us. Maybe they're a little bit afraid.
> —Bharati Mukherjee, "A Wife's Story"

This book explores attraction *as the very form* of anti-Asian bias. In 1972, writers Frank Chin and Jeffery Paul Chan presciently suggested this affective formation in coining the term *racist love* on the heels of Asian American social movements: "Each racial stereotype comes in two models," they wrote. "The unacceptable, hostile black stud has his acceptable counterpart in the form of Stepin Fetchit.... For Fu Manchu and the Yellow Peril, there is Charlie Chan and his Number One Son.... There is racist hate and racist love" (Chin and Chan 1972, 65). Hate and love, they implied, are merely flip sides of the same coin of stereotyping. Years before Homi Bhabha (1994, 72–73) theorized the stereotype as phobia and fetish opening up "the royal road to colonial fantasy," Chin and Chan foregrounded the ways in which typing operated along a continuum of split feeling, forecasting the ways in which Asian Americans in particular would increasingly occupy an anxiously interstitial space, "racist love" as oxymoron.

Illuminating the role of seemingly positive feeling in maintaining asymmetries of social power, this book foregrounds racist love not simply to identify idealized types as sources of attraction.[7] Rather than naming stereotypical *content*, I want to highlight the ways in which Asian difference in the United States incites a specific desiring structure, one characterized by equivocation. After 9/11, for example, comic Hasan Minhaj would ponder a specific paradox:

his white neighbors loved and feared him at the same time.[8] Chin and Chan's notion of racist love typifies an uncanny valley for Asian Americans, a point at which admiration tips into revulsion. Comedian Sarah Silverman performed this vacillation in a now infamous joke. Citing her reasons for declining to "write something racist" such as "I hate Chinks" on her jury summons to evade duty, her ignoramus persona cheerfully explained, "I love Chinks... and who doesn't, really?"[9]

Who doesn't, really? For Asian Americans, the slur can be indistinguishable from the compliment. Typed as the model minority and cast as subjects of national approval since the Cold War, they appear to confound metrics linking race and precarity.[10] Asian Americans figure ambivalently as uneasy signifiers of social injustice; according to selective and disaggregated metrics of inequality focused on income and educational attainment, they appear to confuse the association between race and disadvantage. With a title strangely evocative of horror movies, the Pew Research Center released a comprehensive report on the state of Asian America in 2012; *The Rise of Asian Americans* begins, "Asian Americans are the highest income, best-educated and fastest growing racial group in the United States."[11] As thinly disguised object love, such proclamations mark racial projection as a hiding place for the national libido. The repository of displaced narcissism, Asians have what "we" lack: ambition, discipline, gumption. In the designation "whiter than white," Stanley Sue and Harry Kitano (1973, 87) invoke a competitive racial framework.[12] As with any supernatural film announcing "the rise of" anything, that expectation is laced with anxious anticipation: they're coming. "The *highest*, the *best*, the *fastest*" speaks to an adulation that calls forth an underlying dread, an excessive idealization that evokes its opposite: being a little bit afraid.

The label *model minority* is quintessential racist love. Its double valence gestures to the split feeling underlying racial stereotyping itself as it vacillates between the philic and phobic. As revealed in Malcolm Gladwell's 2008 bestseller, *Outliers: The Story of Success*, the stereotype simultaneously binds Asian Americans to the national imaginary as it insists on difference: "Go to any Western college campus and you'll find Asian students have a reputation for being in the library long after everyone else has left," Gladwell asserts. "Sometimes people of Asian background get offended when their culture is described this way, because they think that the stereotype is being used as a form of disparagement. But a belief in work ought to be a thing of beauty." Here, as Asian American applicants to Harvard University might attest, the paradoxical nature of Asian racial typing becomes apparent: what gives offense to one audience is "a thing of beauty" to another; moreover, the beautiful here is the very cause for exclusion. As model minority and Yellow Peril bookend a continuum of racial feeling, their differing valences obscure their identical processes: assigning a fixity of type that incites emotional response.[13]

Race in the United States triggers profoundly ambivalent desires split between repulsion and attraction, a structure of feeling not unique to Asian Americans.[14] In noting the "archetypal love of white male and black" in canonical American literature, literary critic Leslie Fiedler (1949, 147) asserted, "Either the horror or the attraction is meaningless alone; only together do they make sense." Frantz Fanon ([1952] 1991, 8) famously diagnosed that attraction as pathology, declaring that "the man who adores the Negro is as 'sick' as the man who abominates him." Yet I would argue that expressed attraction has become a potent form of anti-Asian bias, reinforcing, if camouflaging, racist hate. The "sickness" of adoration disproportionally envelops public discourse surrounding Asians in the United States, revealing itself in freely shared declarations of "loving" Oriental food, culture, or women. "Yellow fever" is not a confession of secret desire but uncensored proclamation; Asians are subject to a "carnal density of vision" (Williams 1995, 11) disproportionate to their visibility in the US public sphere. The excess of libidinal attachment that surrounds Asian Americans ("the highest, the best, the fastest," "Patels must have made it") indicates a fixity of typing that underwrites racial anxiety.

Colloquially mischaracterized as inaccurate content, the stereotype scripts racial difference into a narrow range of narratives and visual triggers whose pleasures lie, in part, in their repetition. The stereotype, Bhabha (1994) writes, "is a form of knowledge and identification that vacillates between what is always 'in place,' already known, and something that must be anxiously repeated" (66); "The *same old* stories . . . *must* be told (compulsively) again and afresh, and are differently gratifying and terrifying each time" (77). Racist love is rooted in the reductive structure of typing, something it shares with racial profiling. Both take pleasure in the same old, same old.

Cultural Appropriation as Racist Love

How might we understand cultural appropriation through the lens of racist love?

This book seeks to explore how the Asian American reduction to type masquerades as racial knowledge while operating as fetishistic pleasure. Fetishism represents a specific desiring structure in which attraction masks anxiety; I suggest that, as a process of idealization, fetishism illuminates the structures of a collective racial imaginary in which apprehension manifests itself as overestimation. What Sigmund Freud ([1914] 1957, 122) identified as the "prodigal expenditure of libido" underscores the symbolic importance of Asian American presence to a national imaginary well beyond their proportional representation. The state of being in love, according to Freud, "consists in a flowing-over of ego-libido to the object" (122). Yet the fetishist requires an object substitute, imbuing it with libidinal excess as a form of disavowal; in his classic theorization, the fetish object represents a substitute for the woman's missing penis, one that renders women acceptable in the face of their supposed castration (Freud [1927] 1961). For Freud, the emotionally invested thing allows for the disavowal of what is lacking; substituting for the penis, it enables arousal through the denial of castration. If bell hooks's notion of "getting a bit of the Other" does not exactly represent the pathologized excitation of fetishistic arousal tethered to the object, her more colloquial understanding of race fetishism nevertheless also underscores a split desiring structure surrounding racial pleasure beyond a sense of the erotic, as *getting*. The concept of racist love highlights Asian American racialization as marked by a delight that forestalls repulsion. Beginning with the fetishistic reduction of persons to things, what does the displacement of Asian/Americans into nonhuman forms enable? What are the (ambiguous) forms of domination that this abstraction produces?

Excessive proclamations of attachment are fundamentally sketchy.[15] Race fetishism, whether classically understood as object substitution or colloquially understood as sexual objectification, is both an expression of power and an indication of its instability. In fetishism, desire and possession are not ends unto themselves; rather, as Anne McClintock (1995, 184) cogently reminds us, "by displacing power onto the fetish, then manipulating the fetish, the individual gains symbolic control over what might otherwise be terrifying ambiguities." Asian Americans, I suggest, occupy the space of terrifying ambiguity effectively masked by declarations of attraction compulsively expressed over and over again in the same narrative frames or forms. Asian object love announces a lack that requires compensation; it functions as a screen for what is repressed.

As a foundation of affect theory, psychoanalysis is thus a potent tool for understanding race as a site of excessive meaning and inflamed feeling.[16] At the outset of the twenty-first century, race has become an undue source of stimuli that must be (collectively) managed: "The object [*Objekt*] of an instinct is the thing in regard to which or through which the instinct is able to achieve its aim," Freud writes. "It is what is most variable about an instinct and is not originally connected with it, but *becomes assigned to it only in consequence of being peculiarly fitted to make satisfaction possible*" (1915, 119, emphasis mine). Following Fanon, critical race theory has long illuminated the ways in which race has functioned as an overdetermined object of negative feeling, what Freud would deem a source of "unpleasure." Chin and Chan's colloquial framing, "racist love," represents the psychoanalytic concept of inversion: transforming race from a stimulus of "unpleasure" into a source of satisfaction entails a "reversal into its opposite" (Freud 1915, 123). The reversal of negative feeling into pleasure represents a defense, a means of coping with an anxiety-producing stimulus.

The activist's charge of cultural appropriation responds to these latent dynamics projected onto a collective and political terrain. The accusation of usurpation, particularly of racial-ethnic culture, makes these equations partially conscious. Appropriators fulfill narcissistic self-enhancement by possessing ("getting") an aspect of the exotic; appropriation represents, to echo Eric Lott, love and theft (Lott 1993). Accessorizing through difference also requires, as in fetishism, reduction or taking the symbolic "bit of the Other" (hooks 1992, 21). As in a figure such as Okuni, taking pleasure in difference requires abstracting and amplifying singular traits, visual signs, aesthetic forms, qualities, or commodities as stand-ins for something larger. At first glance, the charge of appropriation simply counters theft with an original claim to ownership, questioning the ethics of consumer choice. But whether centered on the authenticity of cuisine, ownership of dance moves, or origins of fashion, beauty rituals, and hairstyles, appropriation nevertheless betrays an underlying apprehension.

Appropriating difference at the millennium may be motivated by exploitative self-enhancement, but it veils melancholic loss. "Difference can seduce precisely because the mainstream imposition of sameness is a provocation that terrorizes," writes hooks (1992, 367). Neoliberal globalization's increasing urbanization, industrialization, bureaucracy, and secularization project a future world that terrorizes in its sameness. Thus the loss of uniqueness drives both the move to fetishize difference *and* the charge of cultural appropriation. Racist love calls up the erotic charge of seductive difference that responds to US fears of both homogeneity in the context of globalization and an Asianized future.[17] As in the past, racist love looks outward toward Asia for its "bit," for the object that makes satisfaction possible.

Thingness of the Orient, Nonhuman Proxies

A malleable abstraction, the Orient exists as a willful iteration of the fantastic, in Roland Barthes's words, the very "possibility of a difference" ([1970] 1982, 3–4). The Orient has always been an object of fantasy, an excessive sign system in the United States; as Edward Said (1978) noted, "Orientalism" was a template for narrating the West's unbridled imagination, saturated with the residues of longing and fear. American Asiaphilia surrounding things was enabled by the deliberate absence of Asian people: "The notion of Chineseness under the sign of the exotic," writes James Moy (1993, 9), "became familiar to the American spectator long before sightings of the actual Chinese." Instead, Chinese commodities gracing colonial homes in the Americas since 1696, particularly porcelain, were conduits of putatively positive, ultimately mysterious associations.[18] By the end of the twentieth century, *chinoiserie* and *japonisme* as aesthetic styles ceded to the promise of global "Indo-chic" offered by mass marketers such as Pier 1 and World Market/Cost Plus.[19] By 1882, immigration laws, specifically, the Page Act (1875) and Chinese Exclusion Act (1882), ensured that "sightings" of Asians were rare. Instigated by nativist labor movements, exclusionary legislation targeted all "Asiatics" in turn: Japanese and Koreans in 1907, South Asians in 1917, and Filipinos in 1934 (Ong and Liu 1994). By 1917, the United States had extended the Asiatic Barred Zone from China and Japan to the rest of the Pacific Rim: India, Burma, Siam, the Malay Islands, and Polynesia, truncating the development of Asian American communities. The aura surrounding Asian commodities was in part due to the mysticism enabled by distance and material absence; they rendered Asia, in the words of Barthes ([1970] 1982, 3), "somewhere in the world (*faraway*)."

Numerous scholars have named the Orient as a detachable aesthetic. What Sunaina Maira deemed "Indo-chic" (2007); Jane Park, "Oriental style" (2010); Anne Anlin Cheng, "ornamentalism" (2019); and Josephine Lee, "decorative orientalism" (2021) all reinforce the idea of Asia as surface. In keeping with their work, I would emphasize the ways in which racial meaning is conveyed without recourse to the human body, but I also highlight the split affective valence that motivates this process of abstraction. Both underlie David Morley and Kevin Robins's (1995) concept of techno-Orientalism, a mode of discourse and aesthetic representation linking racialized anxieties to futurist technology. The split feeling of techno-Orientalism becomes clear in a 2011 print advertisement touting advances in Intel's core processor (figure Intro.2).[20] A marked

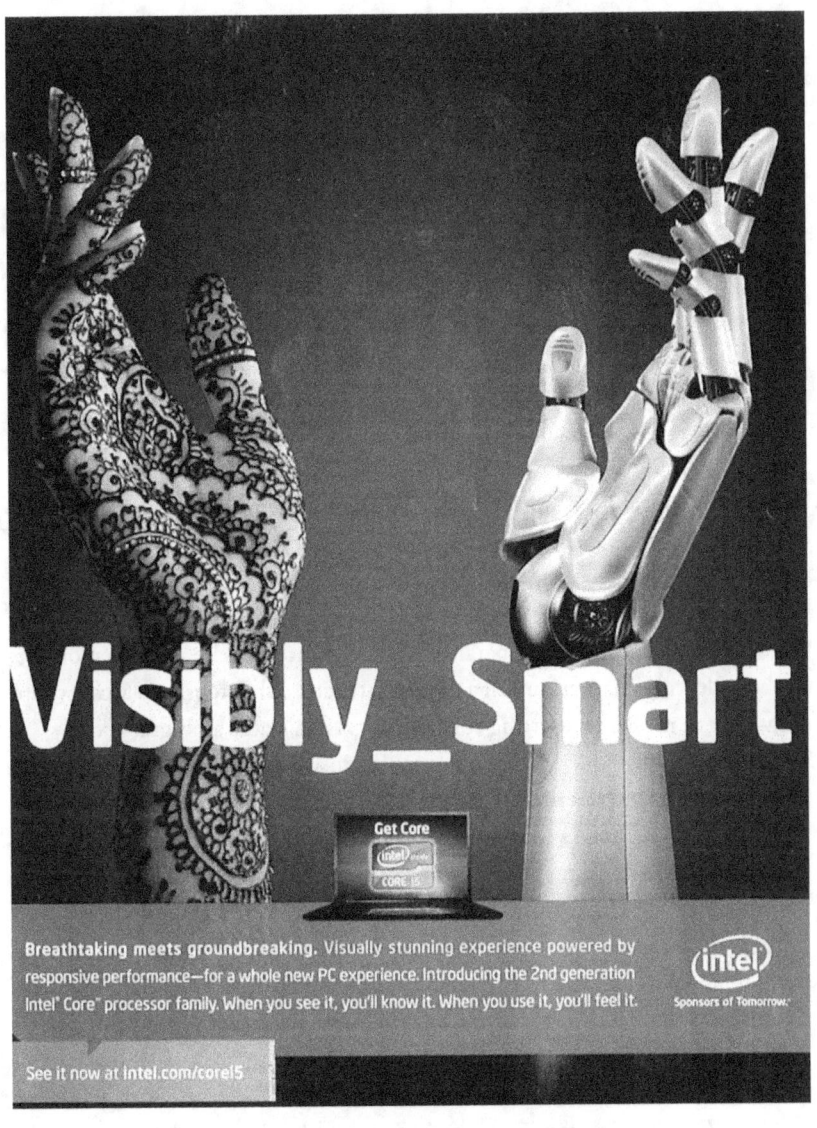

FIGURE INTRO.2 Intel's microprocessor as Asian female cyborg

visualization of racist love's reduction and exaggeration, Visibly_Smart features an image of two presumably female hands: one mehndied and the other robotic.

Eroticizing the imagined human-machine interface through a feminized aesthetic form, the ad draws on a wealth of interlocking associations derived from the Asianized female cyborg. Henna decoration traditionally associated with Hindu weddings conveys the "marriage" of tradition and innovation, delicate beauty and technological mastery ("Breathtaking meets groundbreaking"). The gesture to India seems to be an arbitrary reference (the processors are not assembled in South Asia), but consistent with the logic of techno-Orientalism, it conjoins an appeal to tradition and an authentic past with a putatively positive vision of a posthuman, Asianized future. The creature invoked by two hands is neither wholly abstract nor wholly embodied but is *suggestively* human in ways that speak to robots as the quintessential template for anthropomorphic projection. As I discuss in chapter 3, "she" represents a potentially powerful new being who has yet been programmed to serve. The split halves of the cyborg suggest the split feelings it engenders: what is seductive is also to be feared. Like the accessorized parahuman in the Intel ad, the Asianized objects of the following chapters unveil a desiring structure that reorients anxiety into pleasure as a means of asserting control over Asian status ambiguity.[21]

The fetishistic reduction to thingness intrinsic to Asian racialization is also exploited in Asian American visual art. Hong Chun Zhang's charcoal on paper triptych, *Three Graces* (2010), for example, is a portrait of Zhang and her two sisters with a twist (figure Intro.3). Side-by-side panels depict the backs of three almost otherworldly creatures made entirely of hair. Eight feet tall, the triptych is larger than life, startlingly beautiful, but also slightly monstrous.[22] Withholding human faces, the work represents portraiture in the abstract; it denies the figures individuality. The visualization of self-as-hair invites a reading of race fetishism, Asian women substituted for a single sensuous body part in ways that render them identical, all alike. In this sense, *Three Graces* raises issues central to *Racist Love*, how metonymic substitution enables abstracted Asianness to be experienced as pleasure, whether erotic or aesthetic.

Both in their content and form, Zhang's drawings suggesting erotic typing call forth other racial meanings based on substitution. The work exchanges Chinese sisters for the Greek deities who represent a storied subject matter in Western art; mounted on scrolls, the three panels recall traditional Chinese ink painting. In withholding the face, Zhang literally turns her back on the conventions of Western portraiture, denying, in the process, the fetish of liberal selfhood

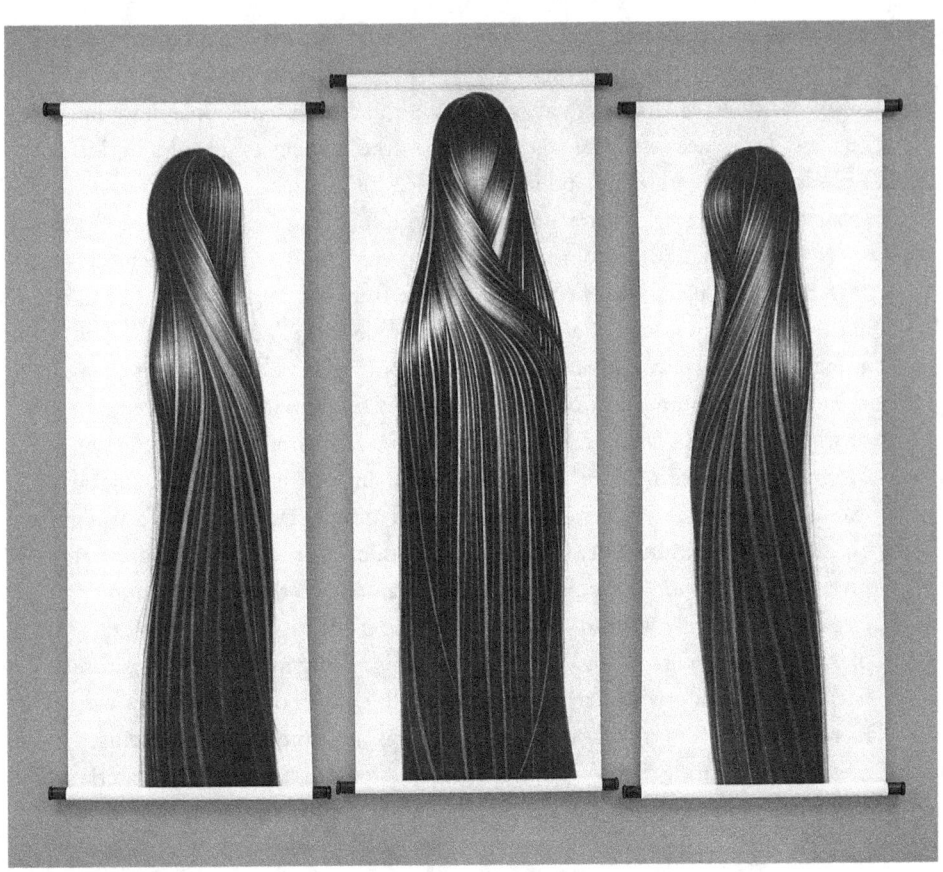

FIGURE INTRO.3 Hong Chun Zhang, *Three Graces*, 2011. Charcoal on paper with scrolls; triptych, left and right: 36 × 96 in., center: 36 × 100 in. Photographed by Aaron Paden.

located in individuality. The work echoes Joseph Jonghyun Jeon's reading of the possibilities of avant-gardist art in *Racial Things, Racial Forms: Objecthood in Avant-Garde Asian American Poetry*; Asian American poets, he argues, refashion "avant-garde queries of the thing into abstract questions about how American discourse manifests race in physical or visual forms" (2012, xxxvii).[23] In a turn to the political, the drawings could also be said to affirm the absolute unity of the sisters, their appearance as a single undifferentiated collective. Its portrayal of unity in resemblance recalls Yoko Ono's experimental work *Film No. 4: Bottoms* (1966), a sequence of 365 naked human buttocks shot in loving close-up for fifteen seconds each. The absurdist visual succeeds in affirming that, whatever our differences, our butts render us all alike "underneath." The solemn beauty of Zhang's back-of-the-head portraits produces a different affective response while conveying a similar sense of collectivity, the facelessness of solidarity. Asian American artists take on the quintessential manifestation of racist love, race fetishism, and twist it, in the manner of Zhang's flexible strands, toward alternative political purposes. Here, racist love might also speak to Asian American attachment to coalition.

This book's fantastical objects—racialized cars, robots, hair, kitchenware, toys, and body parts—are neither detachable from the identity effects of realism nor wholly mimetic; at one level they reflect the "nonhuman turn" in academic scholarship (Grusin 2015). Contemporary work on animals, the environment, the biome, networks, technology, or tools invite a reconsideration of what constitutes the human, decentering the hubris of anthropocentrism. My engagement with "other" lifeforms or nonliving matter represents a logical extension of feminist, queer of color, crip, and antiracist scholarship focusing on subjects whose humanity was not always assumed or who face the greatest precarity in networks of domination. At the same time, the nonhuman interface can sit uneasily with work that travels under identity rubrics. For example, disability activist Jillian Weise (2018) claims cyborg identity to illuminate her bio-enmeshing with her prostheses, deriding able-bodied feminists who identify likewise as "tryborgs." For her, *cyborg* is not simply a fantasy being, a metaphoric identification. With these risks and tensions surrounding material embodiment in mind, this book explores how the nonhuman function as ideologically invested templates for coping with race at the millennium. *Fantasy* here does not merely invoke "the impossible," as in definitions of fantasy literature or speculative media genres, but represents a screen for projecting cultural and political desires, in Slavoj Žižek's (1989, 33) words from the epigraph, not "an illusion masking the real state of things but that of an (unconscious) fantasy structuring our social reality itself."[24]

Psychoanalysis has been unveiled as a colonialist discipline reinforcing modern and potentially repressive Western conceptions of race, religion, nuclear family structure, sexuality, and individualism. Ranjana Khanna (2003) cogently uncovers the imperialist violence that underlies the emergence of psychoanalysis, its ethnographic foundations as a colonial discipline. But like Žižek, she also demonstrates the importance of latent reading as a means of unveiling ("worlding") buried ideology, highlighting the melancholia of the colonized, echoing Anne Anlin Cheng's work on Asian Americans' melancholic relation to the nation. McClintock (2009, 53) rightly cautions, "Nations do not have 'psyches' or an 'unconscious'; only people do." Yet Freud's ([1921]

1959, 14) acknowledgment of "collective mental life" has provided the tools for what would later emerge as the field of social psychology, and for illuminating the psychic lives of colonialism and white supremacy.

At the risk of anthropomorphizing the nation, I find psychoanalysis's emphasis on latent feeling to be particularly generative for critical race theory, especially as it repeatedly coalesces around specific racial forms and narratives across a cultural terrain. Theorizing from the individual to the collective, a foundation of affect theory, signals the political consequence of feeling as it "sticks to" groups (Ahmed 2004); becomes ignited by (racialized) aesthetics (Ngai 2012); or underpins national ideology (Berlant 2011). Freud's emphasis on (infantile) attachment, which laid the groundwork for object relations theory, helps to "world" the abstract nuances of racial feeling. Extrapolating from D. W. Winnicott ([1971] 1991), the imaginary figures of this book represent racial transitional objects whose manipulation reveals the "psychic reality" and needs of a culture writ large. With these tensions in mind, my goal is not to recuperate psychoanalysis but to explore how the latent feeling underlying collective attachment offers a potent tool for understanding the role race plays in the psychic life of the nation.

To illuminate the intersection of affect, the new materialism, and the fantastic, my "nonhuman turn" pivots toward a perhaps unconventional source: decluttering guru Marie Kondo and her mantra, "spark joy."

Spark Joy: Fantasy and the Posthuman

Things make us happy. This is the key to the international phenomenon known as the KonMari Method of decluttering popularized by Marie Kondo and her book *The Life-Changing Magic of Tidying Up: The Japanese Art of Decluttering and Organizing*. Selling 1.6 million copies in the United States alone since its 2014 translation and 3 million worldwide since 2016, the book spawned two sequels, an industry, a reality series, and acolytes, or "Konverts."[25] Countering the utilitarian advice of professional organizers (including that offered by the source of her inspiration, Nagisa Tatsumi's *The Art of Discarding* [*Suteru Gigyutsu*], she does not simply advocate for minimalism or against hoarding.[26] Kondo's philosophy centers on positive feeling; the criteria for holding on to a possession is simple: "Does it spark joy?" Masked as practical advice about organizing, the KonMari Method yet establishes a theory of human-nonhuman relationality also echoed in what other acolytes call o o o, or object-oriented ontology.

Cast as an eccentric, almost otherworldly figure in the United States, Kondo (2014, 169) intimated the secret of her business juggernaut in the disclosure, "I began to treat my belongings as if they were alive when I was a high school student." Kondo's charm to Western sensibilities in part stems from her unabashed anthropomorphizing of possessions held in a relationship of care and mutual respect. Returning home, her routine entails addressing each object in turn, putting them in their designated spots, thanking them for their service, and exhorting them to have a good rest. To her coat: "Thank you for keeping me warm all day." To her accessories: "Thank you for making me beautiful" (2014, 168). To her purse: "It's thanks to you that I got so much work done today" (169). Kondo's animation of household things establishes a spiritual relationship between the human and the material, one based on reciprocity and recognition. "Some people find it hard to believe that inanimate objects respond to human emotion," she writes. "Even if we remain unaware of it, our belongings really work hard for us, carrying out their respective roles each day to support our lives" (170). Kondo's rituals evoke the iconic tidying scene of Disney's *Mary Poppins* in which toys spring to life, happy to put themselves away.

The fantastical whimsy of the KonMari Method has been oddly embraced in the United States with a mania that some reserve for a cult. And it is derided (and racially denigrated) for the same reasons.[27] Central to her popularity in the West is the figure that she cuts: a diminutive, feminine, cute Japanese guru-slash-good fairy. Her "magic" cathects to multiple modalities of difference, all of which skew as relatively nonthreatening. In her invitation to declutter, she does not give the orders, she is merely the home therapist who honors your feelings—and those of the nonhuman entities who share your space. Affirming the autonomous lives of things, her philosophy derives from Shinto's animist etiquette, a cosmology or worldview absent in the new materialism. Indigenous to Japan and merging with Buddhism, Shinto is said to reflect panpsychism, in which *kami*, or spirits, reside in objects in nature and built environments.[28] In effect, Kondo extends Shinto's ritual practices into the "sacred" space of the home. Yet anthropomorphism here is redirected to a more Westernized belief in self-actualization, in the "life-changing" power of positive thinking. The ownership of things both reflects and impacts human happiness, either "sparking joy" or representing emotional burdens that prevent personal transformation. In effect, imagining objects living contentedly in a space made comfortable by our caregiving honors the home as a material setting for desire.

In situating possessions as workers held in temporary and benign trust, Kondo's philosophy converges eerily with the loosely defined school of post-Kantian thought that travels variously under the signs of the new materialism, speculative realism, or OOO. Here, *being* is not solely the province of the human. Philosopher Brian Massumi, for example, affirms the "irreducible alterity of the nonhuman in and through its active connection to the human," a belief underlying Kondo's Shinto-derived philosophy regarding the affective impact of possessions (Massumi 1995, 100).[29] In affirming reciprocity between the human and the inanimate, Kondo's "life-changing magic" inadvertently expresses a radical empiricism fundamentally questioning anthropocentrism; her home-tidying disciples are essentially asked to assume the same humble viewpoint of ethical posthumanism. In making both literal and affective space for things, Kondo reorients the question of human agency to one of relationality. Bruno Latour's actor-network theory articulates this interrelationality somewhat differently:

> If action is limited a priori to what "intentional," "meaningful" humans do, it is hard to see how a hammer, a basket, a door closer, a cat, a rug, a mug, a list, or a tag could act.... [B]y contrast, if we stick to our decision to start from the controversies about actors and agencies, then any thing that does modify a state of affairs by making a difference is an actor—or, if it has no figuration yet, an actant. Thus, the questions to ask about any agent are simply the following: Does it make a difference in the course of some other agent's action or not? (Latour 2005, 71)

Pushing Latour and Kondo into dialogue, I ask, How do racialized actants spark joy? Can nonhuman things injure? Or both at once?

This book highlights the mundane forms that animate race at the millennium and the pleasures of spectatorship they incite. It looks at anthropomorphism not to affirm the "tiny ontology" of things or our ethical relationship to the nonhuman (Bogost 2012). Rather, *Racist Love* explores the agency of the fantastic, of things come to life, in parsing how nonhuman proxies "make a difference" in the course of "some other agent's action" within a network of human-to-human relations (Latour 2005, 71). "Objects ventriloquize us," declares Bill Brown (1998, 947). In light of Kondo, I would add that they ventriloquize us as they become imbued with feeling, generate attachment, or incite possession—or more specifically here, *split* feeling, *ambivalent* attachment, possessive*ness*.[30] The vulnerability (chapter 1), cuteness (chapter 2), or sexiness (chapters 3, 4) ascribed to Asianized things decisively contrasts the affective template assigned to Asian peoples: inscrutability. Or, as Sianne Ngai (2012, 95) puts it, the "pathos of emotional suppression." Geisha cars (figure I.1), robotic hands (figure Intro.2), and women's hair (figure Intro.3) suggest sites where Asian racial difference in particular triggers mixed feelings; in thinking through the ways that objects perform as racial proxies, *Racist Love* posits racial scopophilia where no humans exist.

Scrutable Objects

Invoking the capacious term *fantasy* here, my engagement is not necessarily with fantasy genres (comics, speculative fiction, horror) or platforms (cosplay, anime, gaming) that might be the subject of panels at Comic-Con. Rather, *Racist Love* explores imaginaries surrounding Asian Americans in four sites: educational picture books and graphic novels for children and young adults; caricature in commodity forms; social robotics and speculative media concerning artificial intelligence; and contemporary visual art and media engaging fetishism. The racialized anthropomorphic cartoon animals, decorative figurines, robots, and life-sized fetish dolls that populate the following pages ignite fantasizing as a process, what Judith Butler (1993, 265) defines as "those *active* imaginings which presuppose a relative locatedness of the subject in relation to regulatory schemes" of the social. But I would argue that they further reveal what Laplanche and Pontalis (1988, 314), following Freud, identify as the phantasmatic, the projection of an imaginary scene "in which the subject is a protagonist, representing the fulfillment of a wish." *Fantasy* here represents not merely an object or genre but a screen for projecting cultural and political desires; I invoke the term to call forth sites self-consciously engaged with the pleasurable unreal but also the veiled phantasmatic processes underlying fetishistic spectatorship that encode desiring structures that have heightened significance for projecting race at the millennium.

In examining how the educational imperatives of social realism are reconciled with fantasy forms, chapter 1 explores the implications of using nonhuman figures to explain racial prejudice to children. The "fairy tale wars" of the 1920s set educational goals against the child's need for fancy, or imagination; this debate among educators, librarians, publishers, and writers was partially reconciled through the example of Margaret Wise Brown, in whose picture books animals modeled healthy attachments that spoke to the age-appropriate inner lives of children. As talking animals were subsequently enlisted to play out minor dramas of racial-ethnic conflict and coping in children's literature, this fantasy trope became harnessed to social change. Following studies in developmental psychology on how the young acquire racial biases, picture books explicitly introduced themes of tolerance. Yet depicting racism in books for the young presents authors with a tricky conundrum: how to instruct against prejudice for an audience quite possibly innocent of it.

Chapter 1 suggests that species difference has become a routine way of portraying differences among peoples as a response to this conundrum. Biodiversity has become visual metaphor for racial diversity in "multicultural" children's literature. Charting advances in developmental psychology that explain how children acquire and unlearn biases, I focus on picture books using animal surrogates to play out microdramas of racial-ethnic conflict. Following the rise in transnational adoption from Asia near the end of the twentieth century, this trend emerged as a specific genre: books that imagine the transracial adoptive family as cross-species alliance. Yet this seemingly innocent substitution (panda for adoptee) risks caricature as well as antiquated notions of racialized biology. Extending this exploration of the (unintended) consequences of the animal-race analogy in young adult literature, chapter 1 turns to Gene Luen Yang's celebrated graphic novel *American Born Chinese* (2006) to consider how its use of species distinction also produces unintended messages about the limits of racial integration.

Overtly educative texts at first seem to violate Bruno Bettelheim's ([1975] 2010, 63) view that fantasy "help[s] the child work through unconscious pressures." Shifting that focus, I explore how animal proxies reveal "unconscious" adult pressures that derive from a specific paradox at the millennium: to promote both colorblindness and diversity, to further the belief we are simultaneously all the same and all different. In looking at the adult's ventriloquism of imaginary figures for the imagined child, chapter 1 reveals the imperfect correspondence between "real-world" aims and fantastical form, the fissures that arise in turning to racial abstraction to express anxieties about intimacy and belonging.

Chapter 2 continues this line of inquiry examining a new iteration of racial kitsch, the anthropomorphic Asianized figurine, to explore the relationship between racial feeling and aesthetic form. Unlike ethnic Halloween costumes, American Indian mascots, and mammy cookie jars, mundane household items in the shape of Asian people—coin banks, handbags, and perfume bottles—appear to evade recognition as racist caricature through the Japanese aesthetic, kawaii, or cute-style. Kawaii commodities evoke both overtly positive feeling—the desire to protect or care for the small and defenseless—as well as the dark side of cute: the desire to dominate them.

Kawaii-style chinoiserie and japonisme appear to circumvent the prohibitions placed on racial desires in the twenty-first century, particularly the pleasure taken in demeaning ethnic caricature. Through the ambivalent affective responses evoked by cute things, the chapter interrogates the association between caricature and harm, representation and injury. As cute tchotchkes abstract racial meaning, the chapter suggests, they allow for the enjoyment of unequal relations of power that veil anxieties surrounding economic globalization and Asian status shift.

Chapter 2's focus on the pleasurable repetition of type in humanized things continues in chapter 3's engagement with technology or, more specifically, with techno-Orientalist scopophilia. Here, more grandiose explorations of machine ontology and flexible embodiment cede to the inquiries that animate *Racist Love*: how speculative fantasies of a technologically enhanced future, as in Intel's mehndied cyborg, are yet tethered to existing racial and gender tropes. To suggest an answer to the question, Why imagine AI as having a body at all?, chapter 3 considers artificially intelligent robots and media portrayals of gynoids who take the form of young, attractive Asian women. In rendering a future interface between machines and humanity, the literary fictions and scripted dramas of simulated beings in chapter 3 paradoxically derive their force from human rights narratives. Anxiety triggered by superior machines is offset by racial form: Asian women as innocent, willing to please, sexually desirable, and, most importantly, vulnerable. That embodiment enables a specific narrative drawing on not only fears of mechanized "robotic" labor but, more pointedly, on real-world associations with global human trafficking, especially sex trafficking. As the form invokes racialized associations to sexual slavery, fantasies of female embodied AI, clones, or cyborgs enable two seemingly contradictory pleasures: witnessing exploitation (imagined as sexual assault) and witnessing its transcendence (imagined as rescue). These futurist neoslave narratives script a specific relationship to technology, one that transforms the negative valence surrounding techno-Orientalism into positive feelings of control. *Synths, fabricants*, and *sexaroids* enable reparative narratives that extend the hallmark of equal dignity and equal worth to things.

Chapter 3 turns from speculative media to innovations in robotics. As in artist Laurie Simmons's use of a hyperrealistic Japanese fetish doll in chapter 4, the life-size gynoids Aiko, Geminoid F, and Jia Jia ignite the split feelings of the uncanny. As in fictional dramatizations, the young Asianized female robots suggest a compromised human agency, here imagined as the incapacity for sexual consent. In tech demonstrations by men for men, female-embodied robots expose an expressly social behavior: the right to touch. The racialized mechanical bodies of chapter 3 speak to philosophical considerations not of ontology, but of ethics: not *what* is human, but *how*. Reflecting the consciousness surrounding the viral movement #MeToo, the compromised agency of mecha women becomes the catalyst for illuminating the very vulnerabilities within the social matrix.

The sites engaged in the first three chapters—children's literature, kawaii commodities, embodied AI—rely on the overrepresentation of Asian/Americans often to further the mirage of harmony and global interconnectedness. More specifically, they grant positive affective valence to racial typing: the Asianized human-adjacent being as diminutive, childlike, vulnerable, in need of care. These nonhuman forms are placed within familiar narratives that reference post–civil rights issues of visibility, inclusion, and equal rights: they are assigned what is essentially a caste position within progressive narratives in which redress is imagined not on behalf of people of color, but on behalf of their object substitutes. As openly fictive, nonrealist, and at times overtly playful fantasies of things come to life script human difference, they appear to circumvent taboos surrounding race at the millennium. For Asian Americans confronted with their racial proxies, those taboos may provide the very setting for desire.

Asian American Perverse Spectatorship

What does it mean to be attracted to a reviled object?

In a 2019 Asian American Studies Association panel on the film *Crazy Rich Asians* (2018), scholar Elena Tajima Creef began with a confession subsequently echoed by every other panelist: she *loved* the film. For her, it was a once-every-decade rom-com with an all-Asian cast, not simply a "bad text," a trigger for the racialized specter of neoliberal capitalist competition. Similarly, media scholars Eve Oishi and Peter X. Feng have written about their attempts to reconcile their critical awareness of the politics of spectatorship with their fandom of *The King and I* (1956) and *The World of Suzie Wong* (1960). As colonial fantasies, both films have been rendered forbidden objects in the field. Feng (2000) suggests that to remain both a critic and a fan of actress Nancy Kwan is to engage in equal measures of remembering and forgetting, pain and pleasure. Oishi (2006) notes that feelings of eroticized danger elicited by *The King and I* complicated the identifications surrounding her own racial location; she could not simply repudiate its retrograde racial imagery. Her "perverse spectatorship" of the film highlights the "infinitely oblique and circuitous routes through which identification passes, in this case for queers and for people of color" (2006, 649). Alternately disturbed and fascinated by plantation archetypes, African

American artist Kara Walker also testifies to the power of white iconicity. She situates the figure of Scarlett O'Hara as a source of her own perverse spectatorship, wanting to both be the white heroine and kill her at the same time.[31]

By the same token, can I (racist) love Okuni? (See figure Intro.1.)

Chapters 2 and 4 explore this split spectatorship for Asian Americans; both chapters engage the vacillation between pleasure and pain underlying Asian American attachment to fantasy forms that, as overdetermined repositories of racial feeling for white spectators, represent "bad texts." In chapter 2, collecting cute "racist" toys is a *guilty* pleasure. Does that hobby compromise one's membership in a community defined by antiracism? At one level, confessing an attachment to objects of ambiguously racist kitsch challenges the uniformity of feeling essential to coalitional identity. Chapter 4 centers on queer of color, crip, and feminist reimagining of the Asian fetish in photography, independent video, and mainstream media. Race fetishism runs afoul of liberal politics centered on the foundation of human dignity. Being made into a (sexual) object represents an affront; it reduces the individual to a type. Yet psychoanalyst Robert Stoller (1985, 155) surmised that "a fetish is a story masquerading as an object." Chapter 4 thus investigates not the stories underlying fetishistic desire per se, but those underlying attempts to reconcile that desire to reparative projects of racial community building and social justice. I situate Asian fetishism as a site to explore the nature of Asian American *political* desire.

Visual artists such as Mari Katayama, Laurel Nakadate, Elisha Lim, Greg Pak, Nguyen Tan Hoang, and Helen Lee subject the sexual objectification of Asian/Americans to scrutiny through parody, reversal, or what at first appears to be an embrace of sexual type, a concession to crip, queer, racial, or commodity scopophilia. In chapter 4, the depiction of "private" fetishistic desire is saturated with the uncanny residues of Asian American history, diasporic longing, and the rhetoric of collective rights. Artists question the horizons of racial redress—visibility, representation, and equality—envisioned in both the public sphere and at the foundations of Asian American studies. More complexly, the fetish presents Asian Americanists invested in politicizing racial representation, in ethical critique with presumed mimetic effects, with a critical paradox: the recognition that objectification is itself subject making. Racist love represents a structure of feeling that attaches to Asian Americans at the millennium as a form of racial management, but it might also represent a means of naming an ambivalent means of Asian American self-affirmation.

Yet "talking back" to racial fetishism produces oppositional pleasures that dovetail with the split desires of erotic fantasy; the very act of marking reductive typing as beyond the pale may succeed in creating not only racial consciousness but libidinally charged racial taboos. How is the prohibition of erotic pleasure a source of political pleasure? Scholarly and pedagogic practices surrounding racial fetishism may well reflect the structural ambivalence intrinsic to fetishism itself; chapter 4 engages artistic, activist, and academic practices that both invite and avoid good-image/bad-image, inoffensive/offensive dichotomies to explore the phantasmatic processes that open up identificatory locations for Asian American self-imagining. This final chapter thus elevates what Freud theorized as individual sexual pathology to a form of collective imagining to understand the split nature of desires surrounding racial fetishism, including those held by Asian/Americans who take pleasure in bad objects.

For me, the nonhuman things of this book spark joy. And yet . . .

Asian No Bodies

During the 2020 and 2021 COVID-19 pandemic, the gloves of racist hate came off as the *same old* stories about Asian-as-threat became resurrected. For good reason, then, Asian American studies as a field addresses the effects of racial hatred and xenophobia—exclusion, scapegoating, discrimination, inequality, and violence—through objects of study that derive their political force through the realist representation of trauma. Moreover, race in the United States is often singularly presented as problem to be solved, particularly a problem of equity. Early Asian Americanist work was thus assigned value according to what Yoonmee Chang (2010) called the "ethnographic imperative" to contribute empirical accounts of Asian American experience, particularly those dealing with systemic inequality.[32] On one level, critical race studies is bound to negative feeling and a belief in the reparative impact of critique and its faith in exposure (Sedgwick 1997). Asian Americanists continue to debate the ways in which, as a foundational epistemology, identity politics appears to tether knowledge production in the discipline to the limited horizon of visibility, inclusion, and the recognition of collective trauma.[33] Kandice Chuh's (2003) call for "subjectless" Asian American studies gave rise to Susie Pak and Elda Tsou's question, "How might Asian American history be constructed without an Asian American body?" (2011, 171).[34] This book takes those concerns literally, arguing, in effect, for Asian American studies without Asian Americans.

Their proxies allow racial difference to be experienced as a source of delight. Here, I hope to illuminate the desiring structures surrounding race that exceed its public projection as a conscious "problem" of competing constituencies within representative democracy. In suggesting that Asian racialization in the United States operates in part through fetishistic projection, this book hopes to uncover latent racial feeling as well as to explore the ways in which *racist love* might influence a collective sense of self. *Racist Love* thus seeks to understand the force with which race circulates through abstraction as racialized things circulate narratives of injury and transcendence without human subjects. As fantasies of the nonhuman echo tropes of difference and oppression, colonization and resistance, the "wounded" subjects of racial grievance are both oddly present and conveniently underground. The fantasy of nonhuman things come to life appears to evade prohibitions placed around race in the twenty-first century: "It's not real" becomes a defense against implied political impact. Yet, as Juliana Chang (2012, 108) reminds us, "Politics cannot be explained solely by reference to rational interests. We must also understand how political identifications and desires are structured as fantasies." If fantasy represents, in the words of Laplanche and Pontalis (1988, 315), "an imaginary expression designed to conceal the reality of the instinctual dynamic," what is concealed by the pleasure taken in racialized things? How is racial resentment cloaked by love?

"Race has assumed a metaphorical life so completely embedded in daily discourse that it is perhaps more necessary and more on display than ever before," Toni Morrison (1992, 63) presciently noted. *Racist Love: Asian Abstraction and the Pleasures of Fantasy* is thus invested in exploring the political desires underlying the US racial imaginary and the ways in which race in the twenty-first century continues to be staged through the back door of the pretend. As Japanese cars, mehndied cyborgs, or women's hair circulate racial meaning, Asian Americans are simultaneously everywhere—and, once again, nowhere.

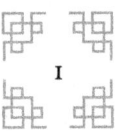

I

RACIAL TRANSITIONAL OBJECTS
Anthropomorphic Animals and Other Asian Americans

> It's those animal masks that allowed me to approach otherwise unsayable things.
> —Art Spiegelman on *Maus*, in *MetaMaus*

> We expect a white child to find it easy to identify with an animal but not with a Black character. Is the child further removed from a person of another race than another species? That's ludicrous.
> —Kathleen Horning, director, Cooperative Children's Book Center

In 1989, Ursula K. Le Guin expressed her distaste for those who disparaged fantasy as a literary genre in noting that "deep puritanical distrust of fantasy... comes out often among people truly and seriously concerned about the ethical education of children" (58). If educators distrust fantasy, as she implied, it is because its pleasures lie beyond the mimetic, and certainly beyond didacticism. Echoing this division between emotional growth and education, Walter Benjamin ([1929] 1999, 255–56) bemoaned the professionalization of children's literature: "We do not read to increase our experiences; we read to increase ourselves. . . . [Children's] reading is much more closely related to their growth and their sense of power than to their education and their knowledge of the world." In taking imagination seriously, Melanie Klein ([1955] 1975) and D. W. Winnicott ([1971] 1991, 64) establish play as a means through which children work out their inner lives (their "psychic reality").

Yet part of the power of make-believe rests on the assumption that the imagination need not be set against the real world but can be transformative of it. In the latter half of the twentieth century, that power became harnessed to real-world problem-solving. Nowhere is the hope that literature can proselytize by stealth more pronounced than in multicultural fiction for children and young adults. Invoking imaginaries on behalf of social betterment, it represents a site where fantasy and realism find reconciliation, where fantasy's utility, its possibility, is taken for granted as having progressive interventionist value. Children's literature engaging people of color or racial themes might thus satisfy both the psychic realities of children and, in more veiled fashion, those of adults invested in blurring the boundary between imagined diversity and its materialization.

This chapter engages the fantasy of talking animals in children's and adolescent literature as it is addressed to politicized expectation and harnessed to social change. The overtly educational literary works of this chapter, in their emphasis on the nonhuman, occupy the space between what Tolkien deemed the "Primary World" and fantasy's "Secondary World" (Tolkien [1939] 1983, 132), or what educator Lucy Sprague Mitchell (1921) deemed the familiar "here and now" against the otherworldliness of fairy tales. Advancing her democratic vision in keeping with early education as a privileged site of cultural conditioning, by the 1960s and 1970s, children's literature was further conceived as place to address society's ills, among them racial prejudice. Anthropomorphized animals have been charged with a new task in the post–civil rights era, one that, in regard to humans, has been debunked by science and rendered somewhat offensive: embodying the connection between race and species.[1] Species difference has become a routine way of portraying visible differences among peoples, biodiversity as a visual metaphor for racial diversity.

Racial surrogacy assumes specific risk, something that children themselves can readily understand, as illustrated by an exchange between a New York public school student and children's book author and illustrator Richard Scarry: "I did not like when you drew the Indian like a bear," the child wrote in a letter. "Indians do not look like a bear and Indians do not put feathers on their heads, only on special occasions." Scarry replied, "I am sorry that you don't like the Indian I drew in the *Best Word Book Ever*. I drew him as a bear because I LIKE bears and I LIKE Indians" (quoted in Hirschfelder 1982, 62). Scarry's all caps evokes the exuberance of racist love, revealing that "getting a bit of the Other" (hooks 1992, 21) need not involve an expressly erotic charge. Indeed, Scarry "liked" American Indians so much that he later doubled down, depicting them as bison living in a teepee, a visual pun on the buffalo nickel: Chief Five Cents and his daughter, Penny (figure 1.1).[2] Drawing on the storied tradition of animal characters in children's literature, his 1965 *Busy, Busy World* went further, invoking species indigeneity to stand in for human geography: in this world making, both the Bengal tiger and the Indian elephant wear turbans. If Scarry's portrayal of animal dress-up avoids the overtly racist caricature, the substitution relies on stereotypical reductions of ethnic drag, a mockery acknowledged in controversies over ethnic Halloween costumes decades later.

Ironically, however, species difference in picture books for children has become a commonplace means of portraying differences among peoples, because of, not despite, heightened political consciousness that followed 1960s social movements. That is, the practice of enlisting animals as racial proxies for child audiences has become one tool for celebrating human variation. In countering species "prejudice" and assumptions about (fur) color, a 1968 picture book by Dare Wright, author of the Lonely Doll series, provides a case in point. In its photographic staging of dolls and teddy bears to address veiled social issues, *Edith and Big Bad Bill* evokes the darkness of fairy tales, visualizing kidnapping and bondage at the hands of a putatively "bad bear" (figure 1.2). Published in a year of racial foment, the book pointedly invokes fears surrounding color ("They say he's big, and he's a different color," n.p.) to offer age-appropriate reconciliation about overcoming bias: the "bad bear" is simply lonely and misunderstood. Such books attempt to address the darkness of children's inner lives with the earnestness of adults invested in social change. Such representations can be harnessed to specific narratives reflecting progressive pedagogy. In 1994, for example, the Berenstain Bears were enlisted to convey a lesson about overcoming bias when, shockingly, pandas move in next door ("Uh-oh. Some nearby

FIGURE 1.1 Ethnic drag in *Richard Scarry's Storybook Dictionary*, 1966

neighbors moved away. *Now* who's coming here to stay?") (figure 1.3). Papa's prejudice against pandas and his subsequent comeuppance offer the child an accessible take on the affective fallout of residential desegregation. Similarly, Gary Soto and Susan Guevara's award-winning books featuring Chato, "coolest cat in *el barrio*," model interspecies cooperation. In a 2005 storyline, Chato unwittingly finds himself vacationing among (Anglo?) dogs and must overcome his group preconceptions to come to their rescue ("We [cats] ain't prejudiced or nothing. But, *tú sabes*, we've had problems with your kind in the past"). Echoing Rodney King, by the end of the story, cats and dogs all just get along. By 2016, the animal/race analogy went mainstream in the Disney animated film *Zootopia*, which engaged predator/prey distinction to critique racial profiling. Such narratives offer thinly veiled social parables about overcoming

FIGURE 1.2 Racializing bad bears: "He's big, and he's a different color"; Dare Wright, *Edith and Big Bad Bill*, 1968

species bias. Yet these visualizations are often at odds with their didactic intent, asking viewers to take amusement in biological differences paradoxically in service to the message that such differences do not matter.[3]

If childhood is itself a projection of adult fantasy, it is likewise a site of profound racial pleasure. Psychoanalyst Bruno Bettelheim ([1975] 2010, 65) suggests that fairy tales represent safe outlets for childhood fears, offering figures "onto which the child can externalize what goes on in his mind, in controllable ways." Melanie Klein ([1955] 1975, 122), in developing her "play technique," similarly reads children's affective relationships with toys as a symptom of their latent bonds with others, the means through which children negotiate attachment and separation. For Winnicott ([1971] 1991, 19), play represents an "intermediate area of experience" between inner life and an "external (shared)

FIGURE 1.3 Panda integration: Stan and Jan Berenstain's *The Berenstain Bears' New Neighbors*, 1994

reality"; his concept of transitional objects and phenomenon foregrounds the ways in which children manipulate things as a means of exerting control over their relations with others. The exemplary transitional object, the teddy bear, is at once real and not real; as a symbolic repository of both love and aggression, the pretend animal becomes an overdetermined site for working out feelings. By the same token, how do picture books represent transitional phenomena for adults, a site where racial fears and desires also find expression if not also release?

Children's picture books and graphic novels for adolescents represent an interstitial space of suspended reality and consensus where racial feeling becomes mediated, displaced onto fantasies of the nonhuman. In externalizing anxieties surrounding race at the millennium, their anthropomorphic animals, I argue, come to represent racial transitional objects for adults. What service do these transitional objects perform as they circulate affective associations surrounding Asian Americans?

The growth of overtly educational yet fanciful stories harkens back to a radical experiment in children's literature. In 1921, progressive educator Lucy Sprague Mitchell acknowledged the literary worth of classical children's tales featuring animals, but nonetheless took on the prevailing hegemony of children's literature by questioning their suitability for the young:

> Allegories like Æsop's "Fables" and "The Lion of Androcles" have a certain right to a hearing because of their historic prestige, apart from any reform they may accomplish in the way of *character building*. And in our own day many animals have achieved what I believe is a permanent place in child literature. "The Elephant's Child," the wild creatures of the "Jungle Book," "Raggylug" and even the little mole in the "Wind in the Willows,"—these are animals to trust any child with. Yet even in these exquisitely drawn tales, I doubt if children enjoy what we adults wish them to enjoy either in content or in form. (Mitchell 1921, 39–40)

She dared to ask, "Now, how much of the classical literature follows the lead of the children's own inquiries?" (34). Fairy tales, myths, and other fantasy genres associated with children, she argued, reflected the thinking of adults; their content was developmentally unsuitable and thus "unsafe" for children under six. The founder of the experimental Bank Street College of Education in New York in 1916, Mitchell dared to "commit the sacrilege" (19) of finding children's literature lacking; her Bank Street Writer's Laboratory focused on producing developmentally appropriate books for young children.[4]

Mitchell's progressive vision inaugurated a new type of animal story most famously epitomized by her protégé Margaret Wise Brown, stories that sought to reconcile the emotional, imaginative needs of children with their cognitive abilities. Contemporary animal characters like Chato and the Berenstain Bears are the inheritors of this genealogy and likewise bridge this division but are also self-consciously leveraged toward another goal: social intervention. As the romantic projection of a child unspoiled by civilization ceded to a post-1960s idealism that positioned early education as a site of social remedy, children's books could be situated in concert with the democratic project of preparing future citizens.

Institutions such as the Council on Interracial Books for Children, founded in 1965, reflected broader cultural shifts recognizing the democratic potential of literacy as a strategic site for alleviating poverty, particularly for children of color. Lyndon Johnson's Great Society programs such as Head Start and VISTA addressed social equality at its foundations in early childhood education. Innovations in children's television followed: *Sesame Street*, first broadcast in 1969 and set in a racially integrated inner city neighborhood, reflected Great Society initiatives for children's welfare: the program intended to "stimulate the intellectual and cultural growth of young children—particularly those from disadvantaged backgrounds" (Morrow 2006, 65).

The "preschool moment" of the 1960s was in part enabled by innovations in developmental psychology that debunked the notions of bounded intellect popularized by IQ tests (Morrow 2006, 5). More specifically, following research on how the young acquire racial-ethnic awareness, books could be prophylactic to the child's developing racial biases. Since Kenneth and Mamie Clark's seminal doll test in 1947, credited with documenting racial segregation's harmful effects on the psyches of Black children, advances in developmental psychology sought to explain how the young acquire (and unlearn) racial-ethnic prejudices.[5] Promoting desegregation efforts and pedagogical practices involving peer contact, these academic studies likewise recommended multicultural curricular materials as a means of ameliorating "negative intergroup attitudes" among children ages three to seven (Katz 1976, 144). In the context of progressive education, we ask children's literature to perform multiple, potentially contradictory functions: the genre must appeal to children's imaginations, speak to their inner lives, build character, enhance their cognitive development, and now, model social change one child at a time. "Children's literature allows readers a means to reconceptualize their relationship to ethnic and national identities," Katharine Capshaw Smith (2002, 3) asserts. "Telling stories to a young audience becomes a conduit for social and political revolution."

Anthropomorphized creatures were thus charged with a new task in the post–civil rights era. And yet that metaphoric displacement seems to elude controversy, even as the parallel between animal and human taxonomies, race as *species*, has been scientifically discredited and, as in Scarry's conflation of American Indians and bears, rendered offensive. Recent scholarship exploring overt and latent racial biases in children's literature and culture powerfully dispels the notion of childhood as a site of racial innocence. Robin Bernstein's *Racial Innocence: Performing American Childhood from Slavery to Civil Rights* (2011) cogently analyzes the ways in which white supremacy was reinforced in narratives about children and childhood objects in the nineteenth century. Her work recognizes how the fantasy of play is complicit in maintaining racial hierarchies under the veneer of innocence, how it colludes in *scripting* racialized behaviors.

In multicultural children's literature, fantasy is now taken for granted as having a mimetic effect, teaching tolerance. Here, racial abstraction explicitly addresses a liberal vision as it is self-consciously leveraged toward imagining equality and promoting resilience and self-acceptance. In keeping with the understanding of how children learn social categories, books featuring animals as proxies for children of color engage a specific sleight of hand in the service of these goals: bears do not violate a child's potential innocence about race even as they model racialized behaviors.

Yet situating anthropomorphic animals as proxies for Asian American children suggests the conceptual limits of the use of species as an analogy to race, the limits of *latent* multiculturalism through racial abstraction. While animal characters have a storied history in children's literature, I first contextualize them within the "here and now" literary innovations of Mitchell's Bank Street Writer's Laboratory and the work of its most celebrated alumna, Margaret Wise Brown. Addressing children's emotional and imaginative needs in the context of age-appropriate education, her enduring animal characters model processes of individuation and attachment, a template, I argue, for projecting children's affective ties into the social fabric. By the 1970s, contemporary picture books staging interspecies encounters likewise modeled divisions and connections that assumed racial overtones. I first examine two arenas within the genre: books aimed at five- to eight-year-olds that imagine the adoptive family as a cross-genus, cross-species alliance, and literary and media forms that depict biodiversity as a visual metaphor for multiculturalism. In a prophylactic address to the developing biases of children, the use of animals to portray physiological differences in picture books, I suggest, speaks to psychological studies of how children first classify and group peoples based on visual differentiation. And yet I unveil the unintended consequences of their race-as-species logic. Extending this exploration of the animal-Asian analogy in young adult literature, I turn to Gene Luen Yang's award-winning graphic novel, *American Born Chinese* (2006), a retelling of the Chinese classic *Journey to the West*. Yang's celebrated novel provides a salutary, stock-in-trade moral—"Be yourself"—by paralleling the Monkey King's comeuppance among cliquish deities to its storyline of an Asian American protagonist as bullied child. Grafting notions of species fixity onto its portrayal of racial self-acceptance, *American Born Chinese* nevertheless produces a discomfiting message about the limits of racial integration.

Enlisting animal surrogates to play out microdramas of racial-ethnic conflict and resilience, these fantastical yet overtly educational books at first seem to violate Bettelheim's ([1975] 2010, 63) view that stories "help the child work through unconscious pressures." Shifting that focus, I suggest that animal proxies reveal "unconscious" adult pressures to promote both color blindness and diversity. In looking at the ways in which animals perform as racial transitional objects, my intent is neither to valorize nor indict racial abstraction in children's literature, but to unveil it as a site of a specific racialized pleasure: the use of stories and programming to manage negative feelings surrounding difference for an audience presumed to be most vulnerable to them. What fissures arise in turning to nonhuman figures to express adult anxieties over Asian racial difference?

Fairy-Tale Wars

Early childhood educator and founder of the Bank Street College of Education in 1916, Lucy Sprague Mitchell initiated a "daring revolution" in children's literature in her *Here and Now Story Book*.[6] Explicitly questioning the place of classical literature in early childhood education, she argued that the fairy story "gives the child material which he is incapable of handling" (Mitchell 1921, 43). Mitchell promoted a concept of educating the "whole child," inclusive of their physical, emotional, and social needs. Her progressive pedagogical practices fostered not only intellect, but creativity, self-esteem, and cooperation, shifting education's emphasis on rote learning to problem solving. The Bank Street school functioned as experimental laboratory, nursery school, teacher education center, and later, an incubator for children's literature. Working from the premise that two- to seven-year-olds learn from their own environments, she championed stories that reflected the "here and now," with urban, realist settings featuring trains and trucks, "skyscrapers and airplanes, tugboats and trolleys" (Marcus 1992, 53). In the words of Bank Street alum Edith Thacher Hurd, children enjoy stories "about perfectly everyday Cindy, the cat, more than they do about that unfortunate misfit, Cinderella."[7] Drawing on contexts "familiar and immediate" (Mitchell 1921, 4–5) to children, such stories represented a direct challenge to the dark themes of fairy tales and nursery rhymes.

At the outset, Mitchell's views were contested by those who questioned the aesthetics of her so-called baby books; Bank Street was derided as the "beep beep crunch crunch" (Marcus 1992, 125 and 161) "Spinach School."[8] Chief among her detractors was the influential Anne Carroll Moore, librarian at the New York Public Library, who raised formidable objections to the paradigm shift that Bank Street represented. Using her influence to separate "literature from chaff in the earliest stages of reading" (Moore 1920, 102), in 1920 she colorfully asserted, "The solemnity of the process of education has made too easy the way that leads to the vulgarization of art and the prostitution of fancy" (138). Highlighting literature as a site of competing versions of childhood, their rift was based on long-standing if insupportable oppositions between the imagination and development, aesthetics and cognition. In 1929, Walter Benjamin ([1929] 1999, 252) decried the decline of children's literature "at the moment it fell into the hands of the specialists." Ten years later, J. R. R. Tolkien ([1939] 1983, 136) noted the "dreadful undergrowth of stories written or adapted to what was or is conceived to be the measure of children's minds and needs." The so-called Fairy Tale Wars (Marcus 1992) inaugurated by Mitchell's experiment debated not only the content of children's literature, but philosophies of childhood itself. "So the bombshell broke and the pieces are still flying," Hurd noted in 1967.[9]

The Fairy Tale Wars thus set archetypal and realist content at odds, a boundary maintained through aesthetic valuation. If for Moore what was "authentic" in children's literature was synonymous with what was dull, by the 1970s, that association assumed racial consequence. The idea that literature could not only address the developmental needs of the young but contribute to social betterment was likewise represented as an unwelcome intrusion into the pleasures of reading. Those who promoted children's books dealing with racial issues faced considerable backlash. Since the founding in 1965 of the Council on Interracial Books for Children, Donnarae MacCann (2001) noted, it confronted charges that its race-sensitive literary reviews were communist, didactic, and reductionist, or otherwise represented calls for censorship and "apartheid." In an explicit defense of fantasy as a literary genre, Le Guin (1989, 58) lamented the lack of moral complexity in young people's literature engaging social issues, deriding "problem books" dealing with the "problem of drugs, of divorce, or race prejudice, or unmarried pregnancy, and so on." Decades later, others questioned how "identity politics" influenced contemporary "taste" in children's books.[10] Clearly, the move to social awareness represented a "prostitution of fancy."

Those who pitted imagination against education and, later, social intervention nevertheless found common ground, I suggest, in the trope of the talking animal. Margaret Wise Brown, for example, had no difficulties in integrating developmentally suitable content with an appeal to the imagination through her anthropomorphic animal stories. Adhering to the "here and now" philosophy and applying experimentally tested literary techniques to more than one hundred published works, Brown often featured animals experiencing their environments as human children did. Books such as *The Runaway Bunny* (1942), *Little Chicken* (1943), *The Little Fur Family* (1946), *Goodnight Moon* (1947), and *Home for a Bunny* (1956) depict familiar rituals in whimsical if not also surreal ways. Her biographer Leonard Marcus (1992, 188–89) suggests that *Goodnight Moon*, portraying a rabbit's bedtime ritual, represents an incisive response to the Fairy Tale Wars: it was "a here-and-now story, but one so supercharged with emotion, with so freewheeling a sense of the fantastic as an aspect of the everyday, as to render it a cunning transparency of Bank Street ideas and their opposites."

More fundamentally, Brown's work reflects psychoanalytic theories of development; by 1940, she was undergoing psychotherapy and affirming the importance of dreams to her colleagues at Bank Street (Marcus 1992). Predating Bettelheim's views on the significance of fairy tales, she engaged children's unconscious fears through animal surrogates. As in many of Brown's animal stories, works such as *Goodnight Moon* address separation anxiety; the potential disappearance of things in the room mirrors the absence of the (rabbit) mother. The ritual incantation of "good night" here functions as what Winnicott called the transitional phenomenon of play; in *Goodnight Moon*, ritual is a form of control that acts as a balm to impending separation, emphasizing, in Winnicott's ([1971] 1991, 64) words, the "interplay of personal psychic reality and the experience of control of actual objects."[11] The mundane ritual of verbal repetition enacts a *fort-da* game that binds the child to people and things against the threat of loss and the leave taking that sleep represents.

Brown's substitution of animals for children trades on the oscillation between the familiar and the surreal at the same time that it uses them to rehearse Freudian processes of individuation and attachment, which she saw as fundamental to children's development. *Little Chicken* (1943), her collaboration with illustrator Leonard Weisgard, uses animal proxies to reassure the child against the fear of being alone. Here, a rabbit finds himself the unlikely caregiver of a chick: "The Rabbit found him one day just breaking out of the egg, so he belonged to the Rabbit." The pair is inseparable until the moment that the rabbit must fulfill his needs as a rabbit, running "the way Rabbits run, on and on, for miles and miles." He casually dismisses his ward: "Hop along and find someone to play with." Setting aside for the moment the question of who belongs together and how, species difference here explains leave taking as a biological imperative, as instinctual. In the chick's growing independence and the pair's eventual reunion, the story depicts the "to and fro" movement of a caregiver who affirms that his absence is merely temporary. Brown's developmentally "suitable" animal story reflects her mentor's "here and now" dictate while directly addressing children's emotional lives. The story becomes a placeholder for externalized feeling.

If animals externalize children's fears within the safe space of make-believe, how are they a safe space for rehearsing the racialized fears of the adult likewise engaged with issues of separation and connection? In what follows, I explore a subgenre of children's books that self-consciously addresses distance and attachment as they take on a racial cast: animals enlisted to portray lessons about transracial adoption.

Transspecies, Transracial

Margaret Wise Brown's *Little Chicken* reflects the tradition of animal foundling stories from *The Story of Babar* (1931) and *Stuart Little* (1945) to *A Bear Called Paddington* (1958). Like *Curious George* (1941), *The House on East 88th Street* (1962), and *Crictor* (1978), these books portray animals adopted into human households to trade on the absurdity of the animal acting out the role of the human child or to witness animals being acclimated into the world of adults just as the child is acclimated. These foundling stories represent precursors to what would later emerge as more pointed depictions of transspecies adoption in the context of increasing international adoption at the end of the twentieth century. By the 1980s, such books spoke directly to the experience of transracial adoptees: to name a few, *Bullfrog and Gertrude Go Camping* (1980) (bullfrogs adopt a snake); *The Mulberry Bird: Story of an Adoption* (1986) (sandpipers adopt a goldfinch); *Rosie's Family: An Adoption Story* (2001) (schnauzers adopt a beagle); *The Lamb-a-Roo* (2006) (kangaroo adopts a lamb); *The Little Green Goose* (2010) (goose adopts a dinosaur); *Wolfie the Bunny* (2015) (rabbits adopt a wolf); and *My New Mom and Me* (2016) (cat adopts a puppy). While by no means uniform, such books nevertheless gesture to racial issues by reassuring the reader of the adoptee's belonging within a loving family despite biological differences; yet here, attachment and separation assume larger social consequence.

Echoing Bettelheim's analysis of the stepmother, orphaned animals speak to both the fear of losing a mother and the desire to dispense with one; here, I would argue, their stories address latent racialized fears. Projecting distress over the loss of a parent—in particular, a mother—becomes more specific: not having a mother who looks like you. Keiko Kasza's *A Mother for Choco* (1992), for example, stages transspecies adoption to challenge physical similarity as a criterion for family. Interviewing a series of animals for their maternal potential based on shared physical traits, a yellow bird discovers a bear who, despite her lack of physical resemblance, willingly assumes the caretaker role:

"Choco, maybe I could be your mother."
"*You?*" Choco cried.
"But you aren't yellow. And you don't have wings, or big, round cheeks, or striped feet like me!"

Substituting physical features for actions that mark maternity (hugging, kissing, dancing), the narrative undermines biology as a basis for kinship by rendering external appearance as ancillary to a mother's ability to manage a child's feelings. Accompanying the bear home, the bird is pleased to find a combined family: Mrs. Bear has also taken in a pig, a hippo, and an alligator. Similarly, in David Kirk's *Little Miss Spider* (1999), transspecies adoption is the happy resolution to the mother-quest narrative. A spider hatchling's journey to find her mother likewise displaces color to establish belonging based on affective ties ("For finding your mother, / There's one certain test. / You must look for the creature / Who loves you the best").[12]

In staging species difference to affirm the immateriality of physical features in creating kinship, such books intervene in beliefs that young children hold regarding family belonging and resemblance (Hirschfeld 1988). Kindergarteners, for example, express the belief that children must be the same color as their parents and resist seeing kinship between a child and an adult whose skin color did not reflect that of the child (Holmes 1995). In these and other works portraying adoption, the criteria for parentage shifts from external appearance to desired behaviors, interrupting the assumptions of children under age six who link family belonging to resemblance and addressing children's belief that racially "mismatched" children would be stigmatized (Hirschfeld 1988; Holmes 1995). *My New Mom and Me* (2016), for example, depicts a puppy who, upon painting himself with stripes to resemble his adoptive cat mother, is gently corrected: "But Mom said I didn't need fixing. She likes that we are different" (figure 1.4).[13]

Imagining families who look "different" through species variety, anthropomorphic animal stories speak to the ways in which young children first access race.[14] By the 1980s, researchers in developmental psychology found that children categorize people according to differences in appearance, or "naïve biology" (Hirschfeld 1995, 209) in concert with their "existing cognitive structures" (Ramsey 1987, 60).[15] Overapplying transductive logic, they assume that what is true for one member of a (visual) group must apply to all members who share the same visual marker. As Lucy Sprague Mitchell likewise found, children label according to their experiences with the physical world: in one interview, researcher Patricia Ramsey (1987, 60) found that "a Black child described her own eyes as 'balls' and an Asian classmate's as 'lines.'" Studies in the racial perceptions of children confirm that between the ages of three and four years, children are able to distinguish people "in terms consonant with race," a phenomenon evidenced across cultures (Hirschfeld 1988, 616). Children ages three to five categorize individuals visually, first privileging race

FIGURE 1.4 "Mom said I didn't need fixing. She likes that we are different"; Renata Galindo, *My New Mom and Me*, 2016

and, secondarily, gender (and subsequently, clothing) but do not verbalize their associations as being racial or gendered (Ramsey 1987). They draw distinctions among people based on phenotype, but also on "inferred nonobservable" traits (Quintana 1998, 35) such as language, culture, or foodways (Aboud 1987; Holmes 1995; Quintana 1998; Ramsey 1987).

In short, children classify people according to "how they looked and how they behaved" (Holmes 1995, 41). In 1988, Frances Aboud theorized that North American children around three to five years classify others by physical features and develop racial attitudes *before* they understand race as a form of social categorization used by adults. That is, they use descriptors such as black, brown, or Chinese without consistency or necessarily understanding the social meanings behind them. She suggests that children do not comprehend race and ethnicity in the manner of adults until after age eight, something that subsequent work bears out. Mexican American fifth and sixth graders, for example, were aware of their ethnic-racial identity and could describe their own experiences as targets of racial prejudice (Quintana 1998). Prior to age eight, Aboud (1993) argues, children cannot "properly" identify racial groups but nevertheless express negative views of those not like themselves, of "out-groups," and positive views of those of the "in-group."

Books portraying transspecies animal adoption perform a progressive function by imagining nonnormative families that interrupt "innocent" biases of children under age six, who link kinship to resemblance and phenotype. Yet their address to adoptees first assumes identification, seeing oneself as an orphaned animal who finds, in the eerily identical language of human and pet adoption, "a forever home." Attempting to enlarge a notion of kinship beyond biological reproduction, these books also assume a complex inferential chain of identificatory processes: if these books are to function as socially prophylactic of biased or inaccurate judgment about family units, they require children to see color or other forms of visual difference (e.g., stripes) as a primary feature, draw an analogy to different human features, and then *discount* their importance.

Another fissure in animal-for-human substitution centers on the question of reproduction. Adoptive animal parents are almost always single and female; perhaps logical to the animal world, partners are largely absent. If transspecies parenting is to stand in for transracial parenting, interspecies adoption must proceed without the implication of interspecies marriage, which introduces the wrinkle of natural infertility: ligers and tigons notwithstanding, *species* distinction is in part defined through the inability to transfer genes through reproduction.[16] Moreover, hybridity flirts with the impropriety of transspecies coupling; Anne Carroll Moore of the New York Public Library objected to *Stuart Little* on these grounds, finding the idea of a human giving birth to a mouse "indecent" (cited in Marcus 1992). In the depiction of nonnormative families through species/race substitution, even fantasy has its limits.

Such books project and rehearse racial anxieties veiled through the affective structure of "liking" difference ("She likes that we are different"), testing the assertion that neither appearance nor genealogy matter in blended families. In animal/adoptee substitution, reassuring children that they are loved allays their concerns regarding inherited resemblance, a specific concern of transracial adoption. Books such as *A Mother for Choco*, *Little Miss Spider*, and *My New Mom and Me* represent an implicit rebuke to the controversial 1972 position statement of the National Association of Black Social Workers (NABSW) affirming the importance of family resemblance and opposing the adoption of Black children into white families. "One's physical identity with his own is of great significance," the NABSW asserted. "Until quite recently adoption agencies went to great lengths to match children with adopting parents in an effort to reach as perfect a picture of resemblance as possible. The rationale for that policy was a positive; soundly rooted in the importance of family resemblance."[17] These sentiments were echoed by the Child Welfare League of America, which gave preference to "monoracial" placement in 1973, and by the Indian Child Welfare Act, which gave tribes jurisdiction over child custody proceedings in 1978 (H. Jacobson 2008).

Adopted animals thus visualize physiological differences without recourse to human bodies or their attending (adult) categorizations. In particular, bears are often invoked to show the fallacy of identifying nuclear family groups by color. In *All Bears Need Love* (2012), zoo animals ventriloquize social disapproval of (transracial) adoption when a white polar bear dares to take in a brown bear cub. Reflecting "here and now" patterning techniques, the narrative portrays various objections, each rebutted in turn:

> The giraffe scoffed. "But he doesn't look like you."
> "I think he's beautiful," said Mama Polar Bear (7).
>
> . . .
>
> The anteater sniffed. "No one will believe he's yours."
> "He will know," said Mama Polar Bear (17).
>
> . . .
>
> The lion roared. "Will he be raised as a brown bear or a polar bear?"
> "He will be the best of both," said Mama Polar Bear (21).[18]

Echoing racial issues, "grumblings and protests" include objections over the brown bear's unknown origins, outsider status, and ability to fit in. Indeed, the text rebuts arguments made forty years earlier in the NABSW position statement. (Of course, *All Bears Need Love* cannot easily parse one of its chief arguments: "In our society, the developmental needs of Black children are significantly different from those of white children. Black children are taught, from an early age, highly sophisticated coping techniques to deal with racist practices perpetuated by individuals and institutions."[19]) The book ends with a photograph of the white author and her Black son in the event that the allegory was not understood. *All Bears Need Love* does indeed address racial fears; they are not, however, those of the child.

The importance of fairy tales, according to Bettelheim ([1975] 2010), lies in their ability to speak to the child's inner life, likewise the intention of these adoption stories. Through them, the child gains reassurance of a mother's love, and the parent gains a tool to help promote the resilience of children of color. But if these stories seem to violate Bettelheim's implicit contract, it is because they overdetermine that inner life, rendering the child's anxieties conscious and in adult terms. The adult emerges as the hero of such stories, assuring the viability of family against assumptions made about visible differences. One might say that they address the mother's separation anxiety as projected onto a racial template, the fear that the child does not (visibly) belong to her. Portraying a questioning of that bond, as they are read aloud, books suture the child to caregiver through the mediation of talking bears. Just as playing with teddy bears allows children to manipulate and control their attachment to and separation from others, books like *All Bears Need Love* represent the transitional objects of transracial parenting: they rehearse responses that comfort the adult against the abstraction of child loss imagined as racial distance ("No one will believe he's yours"). Such books thus oscillate between inner and outer worlds for more than one audience. They offer the pleasures of reassurance to the child but perhaps more powerfully to the adult reader, who, unlike Mama Polar Bear, remains invisibly white.

Panda Express

Animal substitution works in accord with how children group people based on visual cues, yet this seemingly innocent literary device produces some unforeseen ironies, particularly in light of genomic research rendering *species* an insupportable means of classifying human variation. These fissures become especially visible in the use of pandas as a shorthand for Asian Americans; black and white in color, pandas might represent an easy occasion for depicting interracialism, but in the context of this literary subgenre, they are almost always stand-ins for Chinese adoptees. If Asians are overrepresented in the literature of US adoption, it is because they made up 59 percent of all foreign adoptions between 1971 and 2001 (Choy 2013). This rise in international adoption resulted in a flood of (largely realist) books published around the millennium specifically depicting transnational adoption from Asia.

According to the 2000 census, Asian adoptees hailed from South Korea (48 percent); China (21 percent); India (8 percent); the Philippines (6 percent); and Vietnam (4 percent) (Kreider 2003). South Korea and China accounted for the largest number of immigrant visas issued to adopted children from 1992 to 1996 and from 2000 to 2007.[20] At its peak in 2004, 7,044 of the 22,884 total visas issued were for adoptees from China alone (H. Jacobson 2008). This rise can be traced to several global shifts since the postwar period. Historicizing the phenomenon of international adoption alongside US military involvement in Asia, Catherine Cenzia Choy (2013) points to its origins in Pearl S. Buck's 1949 founding of Welcome House (now Pearl S. Buck International), publicizing the plight of Amerasian, or mixed-race children of US servicemen and Japanese or Korean women. In 1955, Bertha and Harry Holt's adoption of eight Korean children led to their founding of the Holt Adoption Program (now Holt International Children's Services), serving evangelical Christian families in the United States. International Social Services–USA likewise facilitated international adoption from Asia in the 1950s (Choy 2013; H. Jacobson 2008). And even as Operation Babylift, the plan to relocate presumed war orphans from Vietnam in 1975, was widely recognized as a media event designed to recast US involvement in the Vietnam War, it further established transnational adoption as a form of humanitarianism.[21] Moreover, following the women's movement in the 1970s, increased access to birth control and legal abortion, as well as lessening stigma around single motherhood, contributed to the dwindling supply of healthy white infants in the United States (H. Jacobson 2008).

The growth of transracial international adoption from Asia at the end of the twentieth century was due not only to legal, governmental, and charitable apparatuses, but to the cultural perceptions that prospective white parents held about Asians. These perceptions speak to the complex, interstitial nature of Asian racialization as neither Black nor white. "The rescuability of Chinese children," Sara K. Dorow writes, "is intertwined with several dimensions of imagined racial flexibility," particularly belief in Asian resilience and ease of incorporation into white families and communities.[22] Kristi Brian (2012, 58) reveals that white adopters' decision to adopt from South Korea drew upon stereotypes surrounding Asian Americans as "assimilable, loyal, and destined for some form of American-style success." Chinese adoptees were presumed to be "less burdened by a volatile history of intractable black-white relations" (Dorow 2006, 55) by prospective parents who viewed Asian-white families as an "'acceptable' racial boundary crossing" (Brian 2012, 57). As one prospective parent noted in 1981, "We decided on an Oriental child because we admire Oriental people and their culture and because we felt such a child would be better accepted in our community than a black child" (quoted in Koh 1988, 106). As Dorow (2006, 55) reveals, Chinese children were viewed as being between the "abject (black, older, special-needs) and unattainable (white, young, healthy) children at home."

While these racial assumptions exist in the ethnographic accounts of transracial adoption, they rarely appear in the flood of books published around the millennium specifically depicting (human) transnational adoption from Asia. Sarah Park Dahlen (2009) identified fifty-one works of children's and young adult fiction published between 1955 and 2007 centering on adoption from South Korea alone.[23] Within the broader genre, books featuring Asian adoptees go by any number of cute titles: *We Adopted You, Benjamin Koo* (1989), *Just Add One Chinese Sister* (2005), *Kimchi and Calamari* (2007), and *Made in China: A Story of Adoption* (2008). Books such as *Our Baby from China: An Adoption Story* (1997), *Waiting for May* (2005), *Bringing Asha Home* (2006), and *Rebecca's Journey Home* (2006) recount a tale of arrival, an alternative where-babies-come-from story that grants the gift of origins and reassures against the trauma of abandonment. One such book, *I Love You like Crazy Cakes* (2000), landed on the *New York Times* bestseller list, was named as one of the Best Books of the Year by *Child Magazine*, and was adapted into a video series by Scholastic (Choy 2013). Such books rarely address the potential racial traumas of the Asian child overtly. Yet parental attachment is paradoxically racialized through the very insistence on the immateriality of race. The first three decades of adoption from Korea, from 1956 to 1985, revealed parents, in Brian's (2012, 64) words, "investing in whiteness largely by denying the significance of their children's country of origin, presumably to make the child feel just like his or her white family."[24]

Animals aid in that paradoxical deracination. Imagining Asian adoptees as pandas reflects this affective valence while unwittingly testifying to the limits of racial abstraction. In *Maya's Journey Home* (2008), for example, Maya the panda lives in China in a group home until she is adopted by a loving polar bear. In keeping with the genre, the text somewhat contradictorily intends to impart lessons about the insignificance of physical differences and their ability to be overwritten by *feeling*: it concludes, "It didn't matter that she was a panda bear and her mommy was a polar bear. She felt loved and protected."[25] If animal substitutes offer flexible metaphors for depicting human difference, they also present conundrums: the book's gesture to actual geography seems to require that, unlike Scarry's portrayal of indigenous species diversity in *Busy Busy World*, *all* inhabitants of China be portrayed as pandas. This wrinkle does not appear to extend to other bears: it is not clear that brown, black, and polar bears are likewise geographically concentrated. Here, species-race analogy reinforces antiquated notions of (human) type, replicating the troubling gestures of companies like 23andMe that purport to trace "racial" genetic ancestry simply by correlating individual DNA to that of fixed regional DNA groupings.

Can an animal character convey racial self-awareness? Penned by a psychologist and illustrated by his son, *My Adopted Child, There's No One Like You* (2007) attempts to model the laden moment in which an adoptee's origins must be explained. The use of subspecies difference here introduces slightly absurd incommensurabilities:

Panda pulled away. "But aren't we ... different?" he stammered. "I mean, I don't even look like you and Papa. I mean, I ... I'm a panda."

"Yes, we do look different. Papa and I are brown bears, and you're a black and white panda. And do you know what? We think you're the handsomest guy in the forest."[26]

This exchange delivers a reassuring message to transracial adoptees. Yet when animal substitution seeks to impute social meaning to physical difference, it begins to strain logic. The story continues:

"Once upon a time," Mama began, "there was a young panda who lived in a different forest from ours." (19) ...

"Mama, where did she come from?"

"I'll show you on a map," Mama said. "And I think it's time you read about pandas. I have a book about them for you." (23)

The book's content requires another book, gesturing to the parent's lack of experience with pandas and their distant fairy-tale land. To the adoptive parent, the book anticipates another key moment, the request for origins. But metaphoric substitution may well initiate the child's confusion: Why would learning about pandas represent an issue of proper timing? Foregrounding concerns about developmental time, the text speaks to what is known about how children comprehend racial categories. Yet it breaches the fourth wall of children's literature by making a direct appeal to the adult reader. Moreover, Panda's halting, reluctant expression of his genus-species specificity—here conveyed through stuttering and ellipsis ("I ... I'm a panda")—signifies primarily in the context of presumed inferiority. In reality, who *doesn't* love a panda? If the moment of halting self-awareness lacks the momentousness of Franz Fanon's depiction of social hailing, "Look, a Negro!," it is because the racial metaphor requires us to imagine a caste hierarchy among species in the family Ursidae where none exists (Fanon [1952] 1991, 109).

The substitution of pandas for Chinese children offered animators of the PBS television show *Arthur* a distinct dilemma. Unlike other fantasy genres such as science fiction, which rely on physiological uniformity to convey anthropological differences among invented peoples, children's books seem largely untroubled by the demand to fix ethnicity to biological type. Based on Marc Brown's book series featuring an eight-year-old aardvark and his animal friends living humanlike lives, *Arthur* generally avoids linking species difference to race and ethnicity; rather, animals merely convey visual diversity.[27]

Those associations represented a specific conundrum in an episode depicting international adoption, not from a faraway land, but specifically from China. If animal substitutes offer flexible metaphors for depicting human difference, in *Big Brother Binky* (2007) would racial difference be conveyed by species indigeneity, as in *Maya's Journey Home*, a country populated entirely by pandas?[28] When the bulldog protagonist, Binky, imagines his soon-to-be sister from China, he logically pictures her as identical to himself, that is, as canine. This is in keeping with childish egocentrism and *Arthur*'s natural world logic, in which most nuclear families represent as species homogenous.[29] *Big Brother Binky* elects to portray China's population as being as biodiverse as that of the United States: China populated by various (wisely accentless) animal types. The new "Chinese" sister Mei Lin turns out to be an oddly undefinable yellowish creature with straight black hair. Brown's world building avoids the trap of animal essentialism as trait inheritance. Another transspecies adoptee media narrative did not: Dreamwork's *Kung Fu Panda* trilogy (2008–2016). Here, the panda protagonist's atavistic yearning for kung fu mastery and his failure to reflect father goose's passion for the family noodle business is "proof" that he is adopted.[30] *Arthur* eschews Scarry's indigenous species/human indigeneity analogy, electing instead to graft vague markers of human variation onto vaguely differentiated animals. Of course, according to the logic of adoptee narratives for children, whatever Mei Lin "was" no longer matters; she's now a bulldog.

Unlike those stories involving human children, the use of animal surrogates sidesteps the question about whether Asians, adoptee or no, can ever represent disembodied, unmarked, or transcendent humanity. Situating the repression of biology as key to connecting with transracial adoptees, these animal stories allow for a second-level distancing of the adoptive parent's separation anxiety: with the overt goal of managing a child's feelings, the fantasy genre likewise manages parental fears about attachment potentially compromised by the child's Asianness. Yet as adult adoptees testify, trauma lies not only in negative comments or ostracism from peers, but in their adoptive parents' refusal to acknowledge their racial difference. Moreover, their racial consciousness, what anthropologist Kristi Brian (2012, 81) calls "adoptees' departure from whiteness," does not begin and end with the moment of childhood recognition of physical difference from their adoptive parents. Documentaries depicting the quest for biological parents, such as Deann Borshay Liem's *First Person Plural* (2000) or Gail Dolgin and Vincente Franco's *Daughter from Danang* (2002), reveal that the repression of the adoptee's racial difference in white families is experienced as self-erasure. In witnessing Liem's film, which testifies to the pain and confusion that Liem undergoes as a result of the devastating yet well-meaning nondisclosure of her South Korean origins, one adoptive parent questioned her own color-blind child-rearing practices on the film's website, asking, "Did I do it right?"[31] The question evokes the unspoken poignancy underlying the genre of literature that I engage here, books that hope to "do right" by the Oriental orphans who later emerge as Asian American children and then, perhaps inconveniently, as Asian American adults.

Tales of animal adoption offer a valuable message in promoting a colorblind future in which external differences do not matter and love vanquishes the color line. Nevertheless, the human-animal metaphor veers offtrack particularly when it goes beyond remarking on color to hint about how color might assume social meaning. Uncomfortably situating the repression of biological difference as key to connecting with transracial adoptees, these animal stories oddly invert the affective orientation of Margaret Wise Brown's animal stories: these works manage fears about child attachment potentially compromised by race. In this sense, the "racist love" displayed in these stories is not intended as a critique of transracial parenting practices but illuminates the split feeling surrounding racial pleasures at the millennium: the desire to "integrate" the Asian child within the white family by sidelining physical difference broadcasts the impossibility of its fulfillment.

From international adoption's peak in 2004, by 2012 it saw a steep decline due to changes in the internal policies of China, Russia, and South Korea, as well as increased US State Department scrutiny of programs in Guatemala, Vietnam, and Cambodia.[32] Nevertheless, one of its legacies is a specific literary subgenre leveraging the fantastic toward realist social goals. As Jennifer Ho (2015, 87) has astutely noted, the Asian adoptee in the United States is consistently imagined as prepubescent; the nonwhite immigrant is perpetually a vulnerable child. Korean Swedish writer Lisa Wool-Rim Sjöblom (2019, n.p.) movingly testifies, "Everything I've read about adoption for most of my childhood, was written by adoptive parents or by people who work for adoption agencies. They've set the terms and standards for how we may or should understand our health, our attachment, the racism we're subjected to, our countries of origin, our first families, our adoptive families, our lives in Sweden, and our lives as children, which continue long after we've turned eighteen, since we're never fully allowed to grow up." Asian infantilization is both loving and diminishing. Imagining Asian children as diminutive is perhaps one reason that their most salient animal proxy is never called by its full classification, *giant* panda.

Is Race in This Picture? "Humanals" and the Micropolitics of Abstraction

Moving from this subgenre of transspecies adoption, I want to suggest that anthropomorphic animals serve a subtle function in picture books for the young where species is a seemingly neutral means of visualizing diversity. Scarry's use of animal indigeneity to depict human geography has ceded to this evolving, potentially less objectionable form at the millennium—specifically, biodiversity as an analogy to multiculturalism.

Picture book series such as the aforementioned Marc Brown's *Arthur*, Rosemary Wells's *Yoko*, or Slate and Wolff's *Miss Bindergarten* model age-appropriate diversity in fantastic form: animals go to school, play together, and live in the same neighborhood in a delightful suspension of the food chain. Nickelodeon's animated television series for preschoolers *The Backyardigans* (2004–2010) highlights five differently colored animals to the same effect. In *Arthur*, a book and an animated series featuring an eight-year-old aardvark, his significantly named sister, D. W., and his community of friends, animals merely convey visual distinction. Presented as monospecies nuclear families, characters rarely act out species-specific behaviors to further plot lines. Animals living like human children is the taken-for-granted of stories featuring what illustrator Ashley Wolff calls *humanals*, which largely eschew fixing ethnic markers such as accents or clothing to biological types. Her Miss Bindergarten series depicts a classroom of twenty-six students whose species and names correspond to the alphabet, Adam Alligator to Zelda Zebra, in a panorama of biodiversity (figure 1.5). Across their somatic differences, anthropomorphic creatures performing social harmony for young readers and audiences, through racial abstraction, are also performing latent multiculturalism. In their vision of well-integrated suburban communities populated by aardvarks, monkeys, bulldogs, and penguins, color is just something that everybody has.

Works that more obviously link species to race or ethnicity promise to impart more explicit lessons about tolerance; yet, as in the case of transspecies adoption tales, this added resonance exposes the limits of substitution. Author-illustrator Rosemary Wells's portrayal of the genus- and species-diverse kindergarten classroom in *Yoko* (1998), for example, reflects Mitchell's "here and now" dictate insofar as it depicts a normative sequence of a child's day—pack a lunch, get on the bus, go to school—as well as a familiar conflict: the casual cruelty of one's peers. Modeling kindness in light of bullying and trying new things in light of distrust of the unfamiliar, it also speaks to theories of children's awareness of racial-ethnic differences, or more specifically, to

FIGURE 1.5 Race as biodiversity: *humanals* in Joseph Slate and Ashley Wolff's Miss Bindergarten series, 2001

the cognitive limits of that awareness. Yoko is a cat. Who is also Japanese American.

The book is thus categorized under the subject heading "Juvenile Fiction, Asian American" by the Library of Congress; moreover, the conflict here revolves around her trauma surrounding her apparently objectionable lunch: sushi. Like the depiction of Asian American human protagonists in children's books, Asian difference here is positioned as *cultural* rather than racial.[33] Species antagonism is not the source of Yoko's targeting; rather, faced with the negative comments of dog, beaver, and skunk classmates disgusted by raw fish and seaweed ("It's green!," "Yuck-o-rama!"), a traumatized Yoko seeks reassurance from her teacher, who promises, "They'll forget about it by snack time" (figure 1.6). When this fails, the teacher embarks on a more active diversity plan, an International Food Day requiring everyone to bring and try ethnic-themed foods. Here, the sincerity of the parent or educator's mission in offering the book is modeled in the text itself by a caring but not overly interfering adult. The happy resolution is not that the class comes to appreciate sushi; rather, it is enough that one student (or one raccoon) recognizes and values Yoko's *temaki kani* and, by extension, Yoko herself. That is, microassimilation does not require social change. The plotline echoes realist picture books in which ethnic markers (name, hairstyles, food, language, clothing, chopsticks) undergo positive (re)

FIGURE 1.6 Ethnic-racial trauma in Rosemary Wells, *Yoko*, 1998

evaluation by an in-group child and serve as a basis for bonding, for friendship. If ethnic difference is a problem, cultural appreciation is its solution.

As in Margaret Wise Brown's work, *Yoko* stages animals working out processes of separation and attachment, but here these assume a deliberately racial-ethnic cast: who is or is not like us. Wells's animal characters thus "teach tolerance" without necessitating that their targeted audience access adult understanding of social categories or the biases that attend them. Researchers in developmental psychology question whether one can properly label the attitudes or fixed associations held by children under age seven as reflecting prejudice, racial or otherwise (Aboud 1987; Hirschfeld 1995; Holmes 1995; Ramsey 1987). "Prejudice in children can be viewed as not simply a miniature version of adult prejudice," suggests Frances Aboud (1988, ix), "but as a reflection of their age-related level of functioning," both cognitively and socially.[34] In asking animals to perform diversity, such books manage a specific conundrum, how to instruct against racial prejudice for an audience quite possibly innocent of it. In this sense, animals do no harm. (This same delicacy is required when teaching children about sexual abuse without using either the word *sexual* or the word *abuse*.) Imparting multicultural values without explicit reference to the human body, anthropomorphism enacts a specific sleight of hand. As in the teacher's well-meaning plan, the demand for diversity recognition is met in *Yoko*; at the same time, in both visual execution and plot, the book is indeed color blind. Anthropomorphic abstraction enables the fantasy of neoliberal futurity—it enables *adults* to pretend.

While I want to acknowledge the age-appropriate, positive lesson of books like *Yoko*, they nevertheless engage human diversity at several degrees of abstraction. First, cultural practice linked to nationality, not biology, serves as the objectionable mark of difference; that is, skin color, for example, is not the source of ostracism. The shift to cultural practice (here, eating raw fish) universalizes that difference: anyone can be lunch shamed. At the same time, in ethnicizing the demeaned practice, the book gives bullying a politicized source readily recognized by adults. Second, to state the obvious, despite a kimono-wearing mother and a specific hailing by the Library of Congress, Yoko is not actually "Asian American": she lacks "eyes that squint," the physiognomic marker that children most readily invoke to call forth East Asians in the United States (quoted in Holmes 1995, 42).

More significantly, animal proxies may obviate the very reason that multicultural curricular materials are recommended for the young. In 1987, Aboud found that prior to age eight, children do not comprehend race and ethnicity in the manner of adults but nevertheless express negative views of out-groups, those not like themselves, and positive views of in-groups (Aboud 1987, 1993). She subsequently noted that biases held by young children *lessened* with greater exposure to individuals not like themselves: when children learned the names of out-group children presented in images and were acquainted with stories about them, their prejudices declined. Children who expressed negative views about pictures of children from other races favorably altered their viewpoints when working collaboratively with less biased peers (Aboud 1993). If by the time children reach kindergarten, they already express negative attitudes about racial-ethnic out-groups, offering them materials featuring children of color helps to individualize members of these groups in a way that decreases prejudices derived from group association (Katz 1976; Aboud 1993). Thus, in addition to advocating school desegregation, researchers in developmental psychology and anthropology point to multicultural curricular materials and cooperative learning methods as means of ameliorating negative racial biases (Aboud 1987; Holmes 1995). Yet if multicultural children's books help *humanize* children of color, it is not clear that animals perform this same function.

Child psychiatrist T. M. Rivinus and speech pathologist Lisa Audet suggest that preschool and early elementary-age children reading Margaret Wise Brown's animal stories "do not need to exert great energy to process content and theme and can easily compare the events of Brown's stories with events in their own lives" (Rivinus and Audet 1992, 6). Nevertheless, in 2017, researchers in cognitive development found that children aged four to six were *less* likely to engage in prosocial behaviors after being read a book featuring anthropomorphic animals than the same book Photoshopped with human characters. Children who were read a version of *Little Raccoon Learns to Share* by Mary Packard that was doctored to feature human children were more likely to share stickers with an anonymous peer than those who were read the original work. The increase in generosity, researchers surmise, is "perhaps due to the fact that young children may relate more to human characters than anthropomorphized animals and thus transfer what they have learned from the human characters to real-life situations. For stories with anthropomorphized animal characters, many children may find them not to be relatable and thus not act according to the moral of the story" (Larsen, Lee, and Ganea 2018, 6).

At first glance, the use of animal stories to teach resilience and tolerance requires that children understand a simple substitution—"different" animals for "different" children. For race or ethnicity to be understood as the reason for an animal character's out-group status, however, assumes that children comprehend, in the words of anthropologist Lawrence Hirschfeld (1988, 619), an "inferential chain in the manner that adults, or older children do." It is not apparent that young children understand the analogy to human diversity in the way that adults intend; as Hirschfeld notes, "racial classifications seem to develop in a manner which is significantly independent of most other classificatory skills" (622). To situate transspecies encounters as interracial encounters requires a series of inferential leaps if these encounters are to function as socially prophylactic of bias. Rather than asserting that children do or do not understand animals in racial terms, I want to highlight the complex chain of associations that lies at the basis of a seemingly simple, increasingly ubiquitous, perhaps overly convenient substitution: animal as stand-in for a child of color.

The very complication of species proxies to convey race does not lie in how picture books visualize an "everyone is different" theme in accordance with children's cognitive capabilities. Rather, the popularity of anthropomorphic abstraction speaks not simply to adults' unwillingness to "see" race, but to their reluctance to assign it specific meaning. For example, heated discussion threads on a website devoted to mothering erupted over the racial implications of the animated characters in Nickelodeon's *The Backyardigans*, which featured five colorful animals—Pablo, Tyrone, Tasha, Austin, and Uniqua—living in a suburb. The discussion sent "mothers" scrambling to affix what turned out to be stereotypical racial associations to blue penguins (e.g., Pablo is Hispanic because he smells) and pink bugs (e.g., Uniqua is Black because she is sassy). Some supported their interpretations with reference to character names, the racial identities of the voice actors, and the program's African American creator. The very flexibility of animal metaphors led adults to seek fixed meaning through racial typing—or to reject those associations altogether. Some defended the color blindness of the beloved series, variously expressing incredulity over the importance of affixing human attributes to animals ("What kind of person tries to figure out what race a bunch of bugs on a kids [*sic*] show are?").[35] While color-blind rhetoric here attempts to defend childhood, it comes off as an aggressive unwillingness to see, perpetuating what sociologist Eduardo Bonilla-Silva (2003) calls "color-blind racism," wherein proclaiming liberal values reinforces systemic inequalities. From the viewpoint of legal theorist Patricia Williams (1998), professing color blindness represents a hollow and misguided civic ritual, one that fails to account for a complex material reality. In effect, animal proxies both allow for this ritual and obviate it. Given the heated exchanges, perhaps the appropriate issue is not how children apprehend racial analogies but how adults do.

Monkey to Man: Yang's *American Born Chinese*

Through the projection of specifically racialized precarity, Asian Americans perform particularly well as out-group children: newcomer status, "observable" physical difference from a white majority, and distance from US cultural norms renders them easily imagined as bullied children or adolescents.[36] This representation lies at the heart of Gene Yang's celebrated young adult novel, *American Born Chinese* (*ABC*), which features human and animal protagonists negotiating social hierarchies. Through the fantasy of shape-shifting, the graphic novel's portrayal of race passing enables a seemingly transcendent message about the importance of adolescent self-acceptance. The work retells *Journey to the West*, Wu Cheng'en's sixteenth-century epic depicting the monk Tripikita's pilgrimage to India to retrieve the Buddhist sutras with the help of a motley crew of lesser animal deities and demons, featuring Sun Wukong, the iconic Monkey King. If for younger audiences, the use of anthropomorphic animals relies on simple visualizations of species difference to call forth race, *ABC* engages a more sophisticated if no less problematic understanding of species. While its Chinese progenitor offers a cosmology challenging Western belief in the Great Chain of Being—god above men above animals—the novel's reliance on this Judeo-Christian caste system produces unforeseen consequences for its message about racial belonging in the United States.

Yang's novel won a host of awards among audiences of young adult books and comics; its success led to his designation as ambassador for young people's literature in 2016 by the Library of Congress.[37] When *ABC* was named a finalist in the 2006 National Book Award, the nomination was hailed as a sign of arrival for the graphic novel form; Yang's publisher, First Second, deemed the book a "secret weapon" making the case for multimedia in the classroom. Its appeal to progressive educators no doubt relies on its ability to engage three seemingly incompatible discourses—fantasy, racism, and universalism—in addition to its accessible form. Focusing his retelling on the Monkey King's rebellion and expulsion from a community of Buddhist and Taoist deities, Yang engages a tripart structure interspersing the Monkey's story with two contemporary narratives: a Chinese American boy, Jin, who negotiates friendships and romance in a white-dominated middle school and a white high school junior, Danny, who is dogged by his "cousin" Chin-Kee, who represents the amalgam of all Asian/American stereotypes. Seemingly unrelated, the three stories nevertheless converge: the Monkey, Jin, and Danny's tales turn out to be sequential, not simultaneous, the events of one producing the conditions for the others. Jin imagines himself to be white after a traumatic moment in the seventh grade in which he is counseled to stay away from a white girl at school or else compromise her social status. As Jin's self-imagined form, "Danny" must ultimately do battle with the insufferable Chin-Kee, who seems to thwart his attempts at integration among his white peers. Yet Chin-Kee is later exposed as a disguised Monkey King whose impersonation is part of his service to a higher power. Yang leverages the Monkey's classical story of rebellion and comeuppance to serve a tale of racial enlightenment: Jin overcomes white introjection to accept himself as Asian American.

The animal's desire to be accepted among higher-ranking humanoid deities deliberately services the work's racial narrative.[38] In Yang's retelling, the hierarchy of minor gods in the Buddhist classic becomes analogous to the social hierarchy of American high school: where a deity stands in the celestial court parallels teenage popularity. The power that the gods wield is thus cleverly expressed as adolescent bullying: "'What's my name?' TWAK! 'The Great Sage, Equal of Heaven!'" (68). Sun Wukong's social demotion in the original tale—being asked to *work with animals* as a groomsman—is here depicted through the lens of social exclusion, being refused entry to a dinner party intended for human-embodied gods. The Monkey's discontent before his aspirational peer group emotionally and structurally parallels the Chinese American protagonist's struggle with middle school cliques. If *Journey to the West* represents an episodic adventure tale with religious consequence, Yang's depiction of the Monkey's self-acceptance as a monkey forms the basis of his salutary message to young people in the United States: bowing to (white) conformity represents a loss of self-authenticity.

As a central conceit, Yang's animal-human analogy enables *ABC* to attach contemporary racial resonance to a Chinese classic. As the Monkey King learns that he is viewed as a social inferior, he not only internalizes that perception but imparts it to the other monkeys as well, requiring his subjects to assimilate to human norms. The Monkey's domain, the Mountain of Flowers and Fruit, mirrors Chinatown: Jin, among his own kind, was likewise innocently content, unaware of his debased status. (In an odd convergence, in Arthur Waley's translation of *Journey to the West*, the Monkey King is deemed a "barbarian" for crashing celestial ground; fear invoked by "barbarians at the gate" was essential to the nativist concerns of US labor that led to Chinese exclusion in 1875.)

In the novel's moral universe, Jin's fantasy of himself as Danny represents a form of psychic violence, what Fanon ([1952] 1991, 100) in *Black Skin, White Masks* called "hallucinatory whitening." Jin's disassociation from his Asian American peers is a symptom of his pathological self-repudiation. *ABC*'s depiction of race passing engages shape-shifting, a stock trope in contemporary fantasy literature and media, to visualize interiority as it is grafted onto exteriority, physical appearance. Whether other characters in the text see Jin as Danny is immaterial: as Danny, Jin performs normative whiteness by presuming that he belongs, something repeatedly compromised by the Monkey King's goading imposture as Chin-Kee.

Portraying race passing as psychic fantasy may blunt the specificity of its history in the United States: Blacks passed as white for economic opportunities after the rise of Jim Crow laws. Segregation-era race restrictions likewise applied to Asian Americans, even as they did not occasion widespread race passing (Bow 2010). Nevertheless, the plausibility of Asian American "hallucinatory whitening" was questioned in one review even as the novel's portrayal of a shape-shifting monkey god passed without comment: "Is it so bad to grow up Asian in America? One might be forgiven for asking upon encountering *American Born Chinese*," the *New York Times* noted. "After all, Asians are widely perceived to have it easier than other minorities in the United States. . . . Yang makes growing up Chinese in California seem positively terrifying."[39] Expressing disbelief in

Asian American claims to racial trauma represents a racial microaggression, a point I take up in the next chapter. Indeed, the text anticipates this skepticism by parodying the model minority stereotype in the form of Chin-Kee.

At one level, the novel's animal analogy runs afoul of antihumanist understanding of race essentialism rooted in biology. Unlike the use of animal tropes in literature for young children, the parallel between monkeys and Chinese Americans inadvertently naturalizes racial hierarchy along an evolutionary continuum, specifically through its commitment to Christian monotheism. In response to the Monkey King's use of brute force to insert himself into the company of higher-ranking deities, Tze-yo-tzhu, an all-powerful figure of Yang's invention, rebukes him: "I say that you are a monkey. Therefore, you are a monkey" (69) (figure 1.7). "Monkey-ness" here is represented as an essential trait fixed to species; one should not attempt to transcend what derives from divine authority. In its message that defying this natural order represents a blasphemous affront to God-the-creator, *ABC* appears to reconcile opposing sides of the 1925 Scopes Monkey Trial, which pitted the teaching of evolutionary biology against Christian creationism. Yang's Christian retelling of a Buddhist tale—here, the Monkey's "journey to the west" turns out to be a visit to Bethlehem upon the birth of Christ—marks an uneasy disjunction between Western and Eastern cosmologies. Yang's imposition of monotheism queers the text's "authentic" Chinese source material in which the Monkey King is not simply a degraded animal but a deity who becomes a bodhisattva.

More troubling to Yang's racial analogy, Tze-yo-tzhu's decree—"I say that you are a monkey. Therefore, you are a monkey"—raises the question that Monkey King's (and therefore Jin's) self-acceptance in fact represents *submission* to a higher authority. It unwittingly dovetails with the nineteenth-century pseudoscience of eugenics hitched to Darwinism and genetic variation, race as evidence of degrees of the development of *Homo sapiens*.[40] In depictions of early twentieth-century eugenicist hierarchies among *Homo sapiens*, Asians are represented as being close to the Caucasian pinnacle, but not quite. For example, preparing evidence to defend John Scopes, paleontologist Henry Fairfield Osborn constructed a chart defining the development of "Living Races" in descending order: "Caucasian" appears at the top followed by "Chinese," "Hottentot," and "Australian" (cited in Tchen and Yeats 2014). Representing another branch in the "Age of Mammals," below that a descending order of primates appears: "Gorilla," "Chimpanzee," "Orang-utan," and "Gibbon." If the place of such "types" are decreed by a higher power as in the Monkey's story, does this likewise extend to racial hierarchy in Jin's story? Is the lesson of *ABC knowing one's place*?

FIGURE 1.7 "I say that you are a monkey. Therefore, you are a monkey"; Gene Luen Yang, *American Born Chinese*, 2006

As species taxonomy imparts the aura of fixed essence, it runs the risk of naturalizing racial segregation through the concept of species belonging. Despite its portrayal of animal deities, the sixteenth-century *Journey to the West* reflects modern biases about nonhuman life: in the original, the Buddha of the Western Paradise reprimands the Monkey on his claim to equality: "How can you, an animal, who have only in this incarnation received half-human form, dare to make such a boast? You exceed yourself" (74). Elsewhere in Asia, monkeys have served as a reflexive symbol that changes over time: as Emiko Ohnuki-Tierney (1987, 7) points out, the monkey served both "as metaphor for humans in relation to animals and as a metaphor for the Japanese in relation to foreigners."[41] Ironically, *ABC*'s use of the monkey relies on both of these symbolic resonances, and it is their simultaneity that renders the animal analogy suspect in the context of US racialization and the ethnic enclave: the animal is a vehicle for suggesting "natural" inferiority and transcending one's "natural" habitat.

The Monkey King's attempt to mimic human form to claim a position among the humanoid gods represents a punishable breach of hierarchy: he is a *lesser* primate. Thus chastened, he later imparts the wisdom of this life lesson at the turning point of the novel: "You know, Jin, I would have saved myself from five hundred years' imprisonment beneath a mountain of rock had I only realized how good it is to be a monkey" (223) (figure 1.8). The end of the novel thus finds a similarly humbled Jin forgoing race passing and symbolically returning to the Asian American community to renew his friendship with one who embodied the traits he once repudiated, the fresh-off-the-boat Wei-Chen. Given that Wei-Chen is the Monkey King's son passing as human, the Asian American/monkey substitution is, thanks to fantasy, literal. As in *Yoko*, the text's scene of racial reconciliation reflects the "one friend hypothesis": the out-group adolescent's integration does not require that bullying stop or that cliques break down; it does not require social transformation.[42] Rather, the text affirms the importance of having a peer group, at least one "high quality" friendship that mediates against ostracism at school (Hodges et al. 1999). *ABC* thus offers an affirming, accessible message about self-acceptance: Don't try to be something you're not. Portraying race as the source of out-group status in part explains the book's acclaim among educators and critics looking to put stories of identity negotiation before adolescent audiences. *ABC*'s individualist resolution, "Be yourself," is universally inoffensive in the context of modern liberalism precisely because it fetishizes the concept of self-authenticity. For all its salutary lessons,

FIGURE 1.8 "Had I only realized how good it is to be a monkey"; Gene Luen Yang, *American Born Chinese*, 2006

the text implies that racial segregation can be voluntary rather than coerced, blunting its critique of the psychological effects of racial exclusion.

The animal analogy unwittingly furthers the idea that one belongs with one's own kind. In the original tale, the Buddha's rebuke to the Monkey King, "You exceed yourself," would take on uneasy resonance in this US retelling. Does recognizing "how good it is" to be Asian American likewise imply that one should not try to be *more* than oneself? In *ABC*, the Monkey's hubris lies in defying the existing social order, in effect, crashing the party of his "betters," refusing to be content with his place, and challenging his geographic segregation. Yet these are, after all, the motivations underlying the civil rights movement. Given the racial associations invited by the text itself, the discomfiting question is whether the Monkey King—and therefore Jin—learns self-acceptance or, like the original Su Wukong, learns submission: does he accept *himself* as Asian or does he accept his *place* as Asian?

ABC's move to psychologize racial issues through fantasy's shape-shifting conceit sets up an easy response to prejudice as individually held bias while bypassing racism as structural inequality. Jin's restoration to his "true form" (Asian) does not change his environment; it merely changes how he thinks about it. The novel's solution to systemic discrimination echoes the self-help ethos of therapy: we can't change the world; we can only change ourselves. (In contrast, Fanon [(1952) 1991, 100] exhorted the colonized to "abandon attempts at hallucinatory whitening" in order "to act in the direction of a change in the social structure.") Pragmatic yet ultimately philosophically conservative in orientation, the text raises the issue of racial inequality as it takes the form of social exclusion only to resolve it in a way that we are all fairly comfortable with: ignore negative messages about yourself and seek community elsewhere. In that scenario, the problem is not racial hierarchy writ large (or species hierarchy, for that matter) but the degree that we, fellow outcasts, let it bother us. To be clear, *ABC* is deservedly celebrated for imparting healthy and age-appropriate lessons about self-acceptance; nevertheless, as I highlight here, employing animal proxies to call forth notions of human caste may have unintended consequences, particularly for those of us who fully intend to exceed ourselves.

Nonhumans of Color and the Imperative of Representation

Race in the public sphere is predicated on embodied visibility. Redress of racial grievance is contingent on being seen by the state and depends on, in the words of philosopher Charles Taylor (1994, 25) "the need, sometimes the demand, for recognition." "Withholding of recognition," he notes, "can be a form of oppression" (36). Presence, then, is a crucial political horizon. In this context, how do anthropomorphic characters "count" in the project of liberal multiculturalism? In the fantasy of biodiverse kindergartens, people of color are absent; for activist publishers, librarians, authors, and booksellers, their substitution announces a fundamental incompatibility with the political aims of racial visibility bounded by the horizon of proportional representation, the valued metric of diversity. Ironically, current debates about whether to count texts like *Yoko* as multicultural literature echo the Fairy Tale Wars' opposition between imagination and education and, later, the view that racial representation (reduced to "identity politics") is somehow incompatible with the pleasures of reading.

In 2013, multicultural children's booksellers Lee and Low blogged the question, "Why Hasn't the Number of Multicultural Books Increased in Eighteen Years?" (Low 2013). In 2012, for example, only 8 percent of all children's books published had multicultural content.[43] In a series of commissioned responses, librarians, editors, authors, and academics offered analysis surrounding the problem of lacking representation, almost all of which focused on systemic issues surrounding the marketplace and the gatekeeping function of publishers. Yet Roger Sutton, editor of the venerable *Horn Book*, offered a "semi-facetious" explanation for the flatlining of multicultural children's books: "While the blog states the disparity between the non-white population in this country (37% of the whole) and the percentage of children's books with 'multicultural content' (hovering around 10% over the last eighteen years), I want to know what percentage of children's books are in the first place about people (as opposed to talking rabbits or outer space, for example). Things may look worse than they are."[44] Sutton thus suggests that the absence of people of color is due to the absence of human beings more generally. His final note resurrects debates about the aims of children's literature reflected in the Fairy Tale Wars: escapism and delight set against realism and pedagogy. The post ends emphatically, "*We need more rubbish!*" as if to echo Moore's defense of "fancy" generations earlier. Defending "rubbish" against social utility insists on a false division between "inner life," or emotional growth, and the imperative to educate children with an eye to social change. Sutton's call elicited vociferous agreement that "talking animals should count" toward the multicultural tally. Author Margarita Engle reminded readers that, indeed, the rabbit protagonist of *Tiny Rabbit's Big Wish* is Cuban.

In response to Sutton's post, Kathleen Horning, director of the Cooperative Children's Book Center (CCBC), set out to count "talking rabbits" to show that, given the paucity of racial representation in children's books, things are as bad as they look. She found that 23 percent of children's books published in 2013 featured animal characters, most of them picture books (Horning 2014). That statistic must be placed in another context: of the 3,600 books received by the CCBC in 2012, books by and about people of color, as previously noted, accounted for less than 8 percent of the total.[45] Thus, forty-seven years after New York librarian Elinor Sinnette asserted that, in excluding depictions of African Americans in children's literature, publishers "have participated in a cultural lobotomy," there is scant improvement in the representation of children of color in the genre (quoted in Larrick 1965, 85). This concern extended to the 2013 Common Core Standards' list of suggested texts for grades K–12; in the words of one blogger, "Most of the titles are by white people. Or about white people. It's a pretty white list."[46] "Think about that," Kathleen Horning, Merri V. Lindgren, and Megan Schliesman wrote. "Think about it in terms of what you know about the changing demographics of our nation. Think about it in terms of the children and teens with whom you interact each and every day. They all desire more."[47] In light of the small percentage of multicultural children's books, the turn to anthropomorphism does not really compromise those numbers.

Nevertheless, the CCBC has refined how it tallies multicultural children's literature; in addition to noting the racial identities of authors, illustrators, and speaking characters, it logs international content and representations of disability and sexuality among others. While the project adheres to the horizon of minority visibility—increased percentage of multicultural representation as a metric of change—it newly accounts for the contingencies of animal surrogacy. For example, Corey Rosen Schwartz, Rebecca J. Gomez, and Dan Santat's *Hensel and Gretel: Ninja Chicks* (2016) tallies as "Asian American" (Santat is Thai American) with an international setting ("Asia: Japan") (figure 1.9).[48] Even as they run afoul of representational politics, like bears in feathers and cats in kimonos, chickens count toward diversity if they are dressed as ninjas. This pushes the boundaries of what Philip Nel (2017, 26) notes as the erasure of (human) children of color in "places where we might expect to see them." In contrast, I suggest that the issue is not whitewashing per se, but the inherent pleasures of racial abstraction, which in this case, as in the next chapter, veers uncomfortably toward ethnic caricature.[49] While acknowledging the positive work that

FIGURE 1.9 Chicken diversity: Corey Rosen Schwartz, Rebecca J. Gomez, and Dan Santat, *Hensel and Gretel: Ninja Chicks*, 2016

animal characters perform in modeling human behaviors, Horning minces no words about the evasion they represent: "We expect a white child to find it easy to identify with an animal but not with a Black character. Is the child further removed from a person of another race than another species? That's ludicrous."[50]

Politicizing Abstraction

For Margaret Wise Brown, "Rabbit" was a queer endearment. Her fraught relationship with poet and actress Blanche Oelrichs, aka Michael Strange, the former wife of John Barrymore, was well known in her social circle.[51] Brown's pet name for Strange, twenty years her senior, was "My Only Rabbit," and in turn, Strange called her "the Bun" and "Golden Bunny No Good." Brown's letters testify to the toll that her lover's withholding nature exacted: "Your cruelty bewilders me utterly," Brown wrote in 1948. "I miss you too much. Feel ill from the division.... Old Rabbit, this seems all like a silly game."[52] The relationship did not end well, as expressed in a 1993 "junior" biography: "Margaret wasn't always happy. / She had many friends. / But she often felt lonely. / Sometimes she fell in love. / But it never worked out" (Greene 1993, 31). Brown's sexuality was not exactly closeted during her career as a children's book author and editor, but even by 1992, her biographer refrained from identifying her as either lesbian or bisexual.[53] A gap in how the beloved children's book author is remembered, this biographical detail is significant in contextualizing a literary corpus engaged with animals acting out anxieties surrounding individuation and attachment, bunnies and chickens ventriloquizing the fear of not finding a home or companionship. In keeping with Brown's interest in psychoanalysis, her plotlines are unsurprisingly understood as addressing a child's relationship with a primary caregiver. (Her relationship with Strange had been characterized as "a mother-substitute relationship."[54]) Yet animal abstraction allows for alternatively politicized readings of the nature of intimacy, family, and connection in her work.

In the posthumously published *Home for a Bunny* (1956), a rabbit's search among multiple species in the woods finds comforting resolution: he finds a home in a burrow with another rabbit.

> He met a bunny.
> "Where is your home?"
> he asked the bunny.
> "Here," said the bunny.
> . . .
> "Can I come in?"
> said the bunny.
> "Yes," said the bunny.
> And so he did.
> And that was his home.

Whether the male bunny finds a mother, a friend, or a mate seems immaterial to the emotionally satisfying conclusion to a quest for shelter and companionship. Yet Brown's decision to abjure from using a gendered pronoun in reference to the bunny companion seems deliberate, particularly as that decision renders the exchange repetitive if not also confusing. In fact, the second bunny is also male; Brown's instructions in the book's mock-up read, "Other bunny demonstrating his / home."[55]

As in Nel's *Was the Cat in the Hat Black?*, which shows how "race is present especially when it seems to be absent" (2017, 4), same-sex intimacy here assumes a similar valence: hiding in plain sight. I mark *Home for a Bunny* as a precursor to the portrayal of loving same-sex partnerships that would appear in children's books half a century later; Justin Richardson, Peter Parnell, and Henry Cole's *And Tango Makes Three* (2005) is a case in point. Yet the award-winning book depicting two male penguins who hatch an egg together is also one of the ten most frequently inciting calls for censorship in the twenty-first century.[56] Its censure recalls response to *The Rabbits' Wedding* (1958), Garth Williams's children's book depicting a marriage between black and white rabbits. Pulled from the shelves of an Alabama library in 1959 because of pressure from the White Citizens' Council, the book was read as thinly disguised advocacy for interracial marriage at a time in which thirteen southern states still considered it illegal.[57] The use of animals to portray human conflict allows authors to "approach otherwise unsayable things," as Art Spiegelman (2011, 127) once noted about his depiction of the Holocaust in *Maus*.

But the use of nonhuman proxies also assumes a specific method of reading. How exactly is a monkey like a man? Eve Sedgwick (1997) deemed the hermeneutic practice of uncovering evidence of same-sex desire and its repression in literature, "paranoid reading." In the case of children's literature, the stakes of paranoid reading lie in establishing not intent, but possibility. For example, when Marc Brown was asked whether his tomboy aardvark character, D. W., was gay, for example, the author mildly replied, "She doesn't know yet."[58] Anthropomorphism in children's picture books suggests an analogous method, not so much a hermeneutics of suspicion in queer reading as Sedgwick suggests, but a practice of reading for racial latency that likewise assumes higher stakes for minoritized populations. Anthropomorphic displacement thus suggests the very possibilities inherent to abstraction: animals can serve as flexible metaphors that, like Margaret Wise Brown's friendly bunny, invite other meanings to "come in."

Or burrow underground. As I have suggested here, displacement by proxy can also represent an evasion of politics. *And Tango Makes Three* offers loving same-sex relationships without either gay men or homosexual acts. *Home for a Bunny*, like *American Born Chinese*, disturbingly implies that one belongs with one's own kind. Throughout this chapter, I sound a cautionary note as to what it means to circulate racial meaning without racial bodies, even as animal proxies speak to the ways in which children first categorize according to "naïve biology" based on surface cues (Hirschfeld 1995). Emphasizing the interconnectedness of feeling, representation, and social empowerment, children's book illustrator Christopher Myers expresses the importance of portraying characters of color in the fullest spectrum of humanity. Articulating a responsibility to write books in which Black people are more than "slain civil rights leaders and escaped slaves, people whose lives are steeped in violence both literal and figurative," he explains, "I want to give my readers spaceships, clowns, and unicorns, to depict whole human beings, to allow the children in my books to have the childhoods they ought to have, where surely there are lessons and context and history, but there is also fantasy and giggling and play. To encourage them to open their hearts when they see someone who looks like me, even if that person is in the mirror."[59] Myers's antipolitical politicism harkens back to the Clarks' doll study on racial self-esteem and speaks to the finding that individualizing portrayals of out-group children lessens in-group children's bias (Aboud 1988). Encouraging children to "open their hearts" through literacy locates books as conduits of feeling and, more specifically here, of racial feeling. This progressive aspiration underlies all the books discussed in this chapter. If "spaceships, clowns, and unicorns" contribute to the project of positive racial feeling, can animals achieve the same result?

Animal surrogacy flouts the representational logic of diversity inclusion. Nevertheless, even as animals in ethnic drag fail to contribute to the horizon of visibility for Asian Americans, they are nonetheless conduits of positive racial feeling. In staging early encounters with "difference" in partial accord with the child's developmental understanding of categorization, talking animals are leveraged toward progressive social goals. Fantasy engages the classificatory skills of children based on visual cues, the foundation of children's understanding, prior to age eight, of differences among peoples. Animals do no harm: they do not introduce racism to an audience quite possibly innocent of it. In this sense, species difference as human biodiversity is classification made easy.

Whether it renders politics easy is unclear. In transspecies adoption, the pleasures of fantasy veil anxieties about parent-child attachment imagined as racial distance and reveal the at times absurd incommensurability between race and species. Likewise, color-blind visualizations of biological distinction such as the biodiverse kindergarten allow adults to have International Food Day and eat it too. Displacing ethnic markers onto animal figures here reconciles the paradox of diversity at the millennium: envisioning democratic inclusion without the messy divisiveness of US racial history. The use of animal stories to teach resilience and tolerance also requires that children understand an inferential chain of substitution—"different" animals for "different" children. It is not at all apparent that young children understand the analogy to human diversity in the way that adults intend if indeed their comprehension of race develops independently of other classificatory skills (Hirschfeld 1988). It seems uncontroversial to assert, then, that animal fantasies address *adult* desires surrounding race, serving as a conduit to educative pleasures potent enough to warrant the erasure of children of color or the uneasiness surrounding, as I discuss here, homilies about animals resisting peer pressure. In animal adoption, the pleasures of fantasy veil anxieties about parent-child attachment imagined as racial distance. Activists who document Asian American invisibility in the public sphere can add another source of grievance: pandas have been taking their place.

The books discussed in this chapter represent a significant advance from past works that reflect "tourist-multiculturalism," ethnic texts as "pleasant detours away from the main curriculum" (de Manuel and Davis 2006, ix), or that capitalize on racial caricature or exoticism bordering on caricature, for example, *The Five Chinese Brothers* (1938), *The Travels of Ching* (1943), or *Tikki Tikki Tembo* (1968). (That I actually loved these books growing up reflects the idea of perverse spectatorship discussed in the next chapter.) Yet if such books refuse the food chain hierarchy of *Maus* as a means of depicting caste, they nevertheless risk projecting types as innate characteristics of breed or species, literalizing color blindness yet relying on familiar narratives of biological distinction that are readily accepted as a means of understanding animal, and unfortunately also human, behaviors. Thus, "liking" bears and "liking" American Indians are not commensurate attractions: highlighting the unintended consequences of racial abstraction, the latter veers into fetishistic reduction, as discussed in subsequent chapters, a predilection for racial types.

As in child's play, fantasy is a site where imagined beings are imbued with "real" emotional content. Children's picture books and graphic novels function as conduits of veiled yet positive racial feeling in their seemingly innocent use of animal characters. If the child's manipulation of things in play represents a working out of, in Melanie Klein's ([1955] 1975, 138) words, their "impulses, phantasies, and anxieties," so too does the adult's manipulation of social relations and hierarchies within landscapes populated by friendly animals represent a working out of politically oriented "phantasies and anxieties." As racial transitional objects at the millennium, multicultural literature for the young nonetheless reveals an anxious relationship to race, flagging the failures of integration. Here, the projection of intimate attachments to nonhuman racialized things reflects both hope and aggression; talking animals oscillate between being "good" and "bad" objects of the nation's racial imaginary.

The circulation of racial proxies thus suggests an ethical dilemma in the education of the young no less complex than that articulated by author Michael Chabon, who struggled over whether to utter the "N-word" when reading *Adventures of Huckleberry Finn* aloud to his children.[60] If the images of cats in kimonos or monkeys passing as Asian are less racially charged, they are no less racially fraught. Their power lies precisely in the plausible denial of the pretend, in Jean Baudrillard's ([1981] 1994, 122–23) words, the imaginary as the alibi of the real. The primary texts that I address here highlight that what adults want *for* children is inseparable from what they need *from* them. If childhood is itself a projection of adult fantasy, it is likewise a site of profound racialized pleasure, the desire to situate books as preemptive of racial trauma or corrective of social ills, progressive goals bounded by a now neoliberal horizon. The image of a vulnerable proxy child of color may appear as merely a site of micropolitics against the traumatic, violent, and ongoing panorama of racial tension in the United States. For Asian Americans, it has not been childhood but parenting that has become animalized, as any "Tiger Mother" can attest.

Yet once a site of innocence and escapism, childhood has been unmasked as a site of aggressive imaginary projection. As Bernstein (2011, 8) has shown, childhood in the nineteenth century was "raced white" even as child's play was itself "characterized by the ability to retain racial meanings but hide them under claims of holy obliviousness." In the genre of picture books discussed here, obliviousness gives way to sincerity. Resonating with the power of collective if now tenuously held ideals in the twenty-first century, such books maintain the fantasy that race does not matter, that we will be loved, appreciated, or accepted not in spite of but because of our differences.

At least, that's the story we tell children.

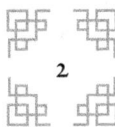

RACIST CUTE

Caricature, Kawaii Style, and the Asian Thing

> Asians have history. Many of us can trace our families back to China,
> Japan, Korea, Taiwan, Vietnam, Thailand, Sanrio.
> Eddie Huang, *Based FOB*

In 2015, two convicts tunneled out of a prison in upstate New York, leaving an incomprehensible but immediately legible note that thumbed their noses at authorities: "Have a nice day!" Accompanying this message was the image of a buck-toothed, slanty-eyed Asian face (figure 2.1). The racist caricature saturated US media outlets as attempts to locate the fugitives dragged on. In contrast, even as the Je suis Charlie solidarity movement seemed to foreclose discussion of caricature as hate speech, global media largely refrained from circulating the

FIGURE 2.1 "Have a nice day!" note left by fugitives, 2015

cartoons demeaning the Prophet Mohammed that incited the terrorist attack on *Charlie Hebdo* the same year. Only NBC News later blurred the display of the Asian caricature, as if in belated awareness of the injury underlying racially reductive imagery.

The much broadcast Asian caricature uncannily reflects an almost identical, also uncensored image: a juicer, manufactured by Alessi, Italian purveyor of upscale household goods (figure 2.2). Ludic but functional, the design of the "Mandarin citrus squeezer" is too clever by half: the conical hat comes off to reveal a juicer; the head is a drinking cup. I found it in San Francisco in 2006 at the intersection between the financial district and Chinatown, around the corner from a Sanrio flagship store, maker and purveyor of Hello Kitty tchotchkes. At one level, the juicer is appalling, marketed with no awareness of the hoary tradition of segregation-era racist kitsch, mammy cookie jars, and the like. Given that dissonance, the object seemed to embody a teachable moment. I bought it. But I wanted it for a less rational reason: I thought it was *adorable*.

Mundane household goods personifying largely, but not exclusively, East Asian iconography seem to circulate freely in the United States in the form of Asianized chopstick holders, rice bowls, kitchen timers, handbags, and cartoon

FIGURE 2.2 Mandarin citrus squeezer, Alessi (Italy) in collaboration with the National Palace Museum, Taipei, Taiwan, 2007

character coin banks (figure 2.3). These items share an economy of design that is a hallmark of both modernism and cartooning, yet their minimalist aesthetic relies on both the reduction of stereotyping and the exaggeration of caricature. Caricature's effect here is, paradoxically, to fix racial traits, an effect opposite to the work of abstraction's broadening interpretive possibility. Engaging a visual rhetoric that confers "on things some properties of persons" (Johnson 2010, 23), and in keeping with the mysticism surrounding commodity fetishism, household goods with Asian faces reflect the seeming inverse of capitalist reification, the fantasy of anthropomorphism, of things come to life.

Asianized objects resurrect a specific racial form at the millennium. Yet we understand displays of segregation-era goods embodying African Americans as racial microaggressions instigating negative feeling. Our national consensus

FIGURE 2.3 Pucca coin bank, 2006

surrounding them is neatly summed up in Tavia Nyong'o's (2002, 371) statement, "Racist kitsch is pretty disgusting." In contrast, twenty-first-century versions of kitsch bought and sold in the United States—the imaginary Asian as salt shaker, handbag, or toy—somehow elude contextualization as *racist* kitsch. Given the relatively uncensored presence of what are arguably racial caricatures in the United States, at some level, we're in the realm of something different, something that enables us to separate these artifacts from the very feeling that now surrounds their progenitors. How do these novelties evade, in Sara Ahmed's (2004, 117) words, the "affective economy" of racist caricature tied to mockery and disgust? I want to suggest that the difference lies not only in divergent racial histories, but in the convergence between theories of commodity aesthetics and the specificity of Asian American racialization. The objects under consideration in this chapter do not represent just any manifestation of anthropomorphic form but embody the Japanese aesthetic known as *kawaii*, or cute style. They are intended to produce not feelings of disgust or ridicule but another sentiment: affection.

From its grassroots origins in Japan in the 1970s, kawaii style has since gone global. At the outset, one of the first and largest purveyors of kawaii goods, Sanrio, cultivated a brand that self-consciously disguised its Japanese roots and that now sells briskly in more than thirty countries.[1] Japan's Ministry of Economy, Trade, and Industry belatedly recognized its potential in branding national exports, launching the "Cool Japan" campaign in 2013 to promote consumerism via youth culture around the world. As evidenced by the Mandarin (see figure 2.2), other manufacturers of kawaii commodities cooperate in the circulation of cute: the juicer represents a collaboration between Alessi and no less than the National Palace Museum in Taipei, holder of Chinese antiquities.

As the personified thing circulates in a global market, its reception is conditioned by local and imperial histories, by uneven capitalist development, and by the shifting meanings that accrue to racial difference across Europe, the Americas, Asia, and the Pacific Rim. That is, depending on its audience, the Mandarin can be variously read as Orientalist, as a parody of Orientalism, as anti-Chinese, or as whimsical homage to Chinese heritage. Yet the infamous history of racialized cookie jars and lawn jockeys in the United States situates anthropomorphic form as intimately bound to the circulation of negative racial feeling. At first glance, the cute Asianized thing likewise represents a demeaning visual joke that can, in Freud's words, "evade restrictions and open sources of pleasure that have become inaccessible" ([1905] 1989, 123). That restriction is the tenuously held covenant against racist caricature. Nevertheless, as with stereotyping more broadly, finding humor in caricature engages a complicated calculus of affective responses, the interplay of emotions along the valence, arousal, dominance (VAD) scale in psychology: emotion measured along the axes of valence (positive to negative), arousal (calm to excited), and dominance (lack of control to in control).

In what follows, I explore the affective implications of this racial form as it reflects kawaii, or cute style. Sianne Ngai's (2012, 87) seminal work on minor aesthetic categories suggests that cuteness represents "the name of encounter with difference—a perceived difference in the power of the subject and object"; she connects the rise of kawaii commodities with asymmetrical global power. In keeping with recent scholarship in cuteness studies, this chapter amplifies Ngai's work in the context of racial perception, situating the cute as an aesthetic with heightened stakes for Asian Americans.[2] Anthropomorphic form here, I suggest, complicates the association between racial caricature and harm through the affective responses evoked by the cute. Further suturing the association between the Asian and the childlike discussed in the previous chapter, cuteness reifies unequal relations of power by encoding obligation as a form of care. Kawaii things allow for the enjoyment of asymmetry, circumventing the prohibitions placed on racial desires in the twenty-first century.

If the reception of Asian things within East Asia reveals sincere attachment and an awareness of cultural homage, in contrast, given the legacy of white supremacy in the United States, they may well be seen as a form of hate speech. As material iterations of discriminatory action (Butler [1990] 2004, 185), they thus represent in Bruno Latour's words, "risky objects" that can "flip-flop" their mode of existence and "break other actors down" (2005, 81).[3] The racialized things of this chapter reveal the ways in which Asian American racialization differs from that of African Americans on the surface, while nonetheless enacting the same reductions and ambivalences inherent to stereotyping. They betray uncertainties surrounding race, as it is seen as *straying* from type at the millennium, uncertainties nevertheless veiled by positive feeling. Cute things reveal the ways in which Asian stereotyping in the United States reflects anxieties surrounding global market competition.

In contrast to speculative realism and object-oriented ontology, I do not want to suggest that anthropomorphic objects assert a resistant materiality or autonomy outside a system of social relations. Rather, in keeping with new materialism's focus on objects, I consider the agency of the nonhuman within asymmetrical social networks, objects, in Latour's (2005, 71) words, as "actants," or "participants in the course of action waiting to be given a figuration."[4] As kawaii style renders things intimately knowable through the aura of innocence, these racial proxies are sources for discovering, as in Bill Brown's (2001, 9) "thing theory" and his analysis of earlier iterations of this racial form, "not epistemological or phenomenological truth but the truth about what force things... might have in each society." Yet cuteness also aestheticizes anti-Asian bias. Designed to evoke affective responses associated with the cute, kawaii-style figures nevertheless complicate the association between caricature and harm, illuminating the very conditions that history places on racial legibility for Asian Americans.

More complexly, figures such as Alessi's Mandarin generate ambivalent responses among the spectators they putatively embody—I both hate it and love it—in ways that complicate understanding of the stereotype and Ngai's work on the demands of the cute. "Loving" anthropomorphic cute things represents a conundrum for Asian American spectators, particularly those who identify as activists whose aim is to *challenge* stereotypical, injurious representation. Does ambivalence toward the racial thing compromise membership in political community, in coalition? In parsing how the putatively negative image might generate positive feeling, I explore the vacillation between pleasure and pain underlying Asian American spectatorship surrounding anthropomorphic things, particularly as they embody the paradox of one aspect of racist love, what might be called the *racist cute*. Such objects make visible the affect seemingly required by the designation *Asian American activist*. In contrast to Joseph Jonghyun Jeon's (2012) analysis of racial things that avoid the pitfalls of identity politics through their defamiliarizing embodiment, the racialized things of this chapter unveil the foundations of the coalitional identity *Asian American* to be a community predicated on shared feeling.

This chapter hopes to transcend the offensive/inoffensive framework of spectatorship that imposes an ethical dimension on interpretation to explore the desiring structures underlying stereotyping itself. At first glance, diminutive new iterations of racial kitsch at the millennium are seemingly unlike the anti-Black, grotesque commodities of the early twentieth century: they are Asian, and they are cute. And yet, cuteness, I argue, likewise aestheticizes anti-Asian bias. The racist love of cute things unveils, to paraphrase Brown, how inanimate objects constitute racial subjects (B. Brown 2001, 7). As in D. W. Winnicott's theory of transitional objects discussed in the previous chapter, the fantasy of anthropomorphism speaks to a psychic reality that allows for a rehearsal of anxieties veiled by, in this case, not play but playfulness, humor as a dubious pleasure. On behalf of those of us who trace our families back to Sanrio, I ask, how is the pleasure of cute things racialized and to what effect?

Caricature as Microaggression

Ethnic caricature is not cute; indeed, it constitutes a form of hate speech. In 2005, the American Psychological Association called for the immediate retirement of American Indian mascots. In doing so, it followed in the footsteps of grassroots, tribal, and student activism, legal challenges, and academic treatments that questioned the ethics of using racial-ethnic symbols as sports logos. In its consideration, the association made explicit the correlation between the reductive racial image and psychological harm, representation and injury, affirming fantasy's mimetic impact.[5] Ever since *Brown v. Board of Education* cited Kenneth and Mamie Clark's doll study to reinforce the connection between race and self-esteem, the idea that representation can constitute discriminatory action (Butler [1990] 2004, 185) continues to animate activism. Thus, stereotyping is recognized as a microaggression that negatively affects the mental health and well-being of people of color (Sue et al. 2007).

A visual iteration of the stereotype, caricature, from the Italian *caricare*, "to load," is "overloaded representation," an exaggeration often invoked in the service of satire. Aristotle (2011, 470) noted that "comedy is an imitation of inferior things and people." A form of hostile humor, the comic-grotesque underlying racial caricature is sadistic. As Sigmund Freud ([1905] 1989, 122) notes in *Jokes and Their Relation to the Unconscious*, "By making our enemy small, inferior, despicable or comic, we achieve in a roundabout way the enjoyment of overcoming him." Caricature represents a specific type of humor whose pleasures lie not in nonsense or absurdity, but in eliciting the feeling of dominance, the *d* on the VAD scale measuring emotional response. At the same time, the visual rhetoric of ethnic humor claims to evade taboos surrounding race in its seeming triviality as "just" a joke.

By the 1980s, the association between caricature as a specific form of typing and psychological harm coalesced in the notion of legally actionable hate speech and its correlate, *wordless speech*. Critical race theory (CRT) braved the minefield of First Amendment interpretation to explore these limits to free speech.[6] The toll imposed by hate speech found parallel in images and objects: swastikas, nooses, burning crosses, cotton balls. As legal theorist Mari Matsuda (1993, 41) asserted, "If the historical message, known to both victim and perpetrator, is racist persecution and violence, then the sign is properly treated as actionable racist speech." Efforts to promote inclusive environments thus prohibit visuals deemed offensive or inflammatory, limiting what can be displayed in communal living spaces or the workplace. In 2015, ethnic Halloween costumes became "risky objects," stimulating awareness of racial insensitivity and culminating in campus protests across the country. "Tolerance of hate speech is not tolerance borne by the community at large," Matsuda (1993, 18) wrote. "Rather, it is a psychic tax imposed on those least able to pay."

Slow changes in corporate culture and marketing followed from awareness of this unevenly assumed risk. For example, by 1966, Pillsbury replaced the ethnic caricatures on its Chinese Cherry and Injun Orange drink mixes with the neutrally named Choo-Choo Cherry and Jolly Olly Orange. The Frito Bandito, a cartoon figure enlisted to sell corn chips, was forced into retirement by 1972. Chief Wahoo, mascot of the Cleveland Indians, was granted a quiet, unpublicized phase out in favor of the letter *C* by 2014, which resulted in the team dropping their name in 2020. In 2015, the NFL's Washington Redskins were found to be ineligible for federal trademark protection under the 1946 Lanham Act, which barred trademark registrations that "disparage persons ... or bring them into contempt or disrepute." Under coercion from sponsors in 2020, the team announced that it would no longer be known as the Redskins.[7] Racial awareness following in the wake of the Black Lives Matter movement in 2020 also resulted in the retirements of the Land O'Lakes Indian maiden, Uncle Ben, and the quintessential figure of racist love, Aunt Jemima. Heightened racial sensitivity has also been exported: once ubiquitous in China and Japan, Darkie toothpaste was renamed Darlie in 1989 by its new US parent company, Colgate-Palmolive, which also sanitized the minstrel caricature on its packaging. The waning use of caricature to endear products to white consumers reflects the gradual evolution of community awareness surrounding caricature as ethnic slur, as visual jokes that transgress shared covenants surrounding racial representation in liberal public culture. But even in the context of this now tenuously held prohibition, such figures are not entirely repressed. The kawaii Asian thing represents a new iteration of a specific historical form.

We repudiate the display of earlier manifestations of such caricatures in the form of ceramic mammies and the like because we recognize how the weight of racial ideology resides in the mundane. Mostly grotesque in nature, novelties embodying the mammy, coon, or pickaninny relied on the comic reduction and exaggeration of the stereotype. Their proliferation from 1880 to 1930 corresponded with the rise of segregation, but they continued to be manufactured into the 1960s and after the millennium (Goings 1994). *Kitsch* retains a class inflection, implying both mass production and the absence of taste—of both object and presumed owner. A reminder of race-class subordination, they blurred servants' roles with servants themselves. In effect, these anthropomorphic household objects substituted for the Black servants that working-class whites could not afford (Durbin 1987). As evidenced by multiple iterations of an "Oriental" laundry aid designed to "sprinkle plenty" of water on one's ironing, the conflation between servant and task applied to Asians in the United States as well (figure 2.4).

The affect that these ceramic avatars projected was essential to the function they performed. Identifying the use of Black servants to brand household goods in segregation-era advertising, historian Kenneth Goings coined the term "spokesservant" to describe figures such as Rastus, a character developed to advertise Cream of Wheat, and Aunt Jemima, the original "pancake mammy." Such figures sutured the "old South/New South myth of the loyal, happy servant just waiting to do the master's—now the consumer's—bidding" (Goings 1994, 11). Their grins attemped to sanitize their condition, allowing white consumers with limited buying power to take pleasure in Black subordination. These "happy" objects seemed to confirm that they did not mind staying in their place, demonstrating how positive feeling contributes to racial violence. In their ubiquity, they gesture to the ambivalent structure of stereotyping itself,

FIGURE 2.4 Sprinkle Plenty laundry aid, early twentieth century, United States

which, as Homi Bhabha (1994, 18) notes, "vacillates between what is always 'in place,' already known, and something that must be anxiously repeated."

Yet by 1988, almost half of an estimated ten thousand collectors of such items were Black.[8] For these collectors, what desiring structures were initiated or overcome? Do such "risky objects" perform differently now, and has Black memorabilia somewhat "flip-flopped" its mode of existence (Latour 2005, 81)? On one level, taking custody of the anthropomorphic object amounts to reclaiming the totemic power of the religious fetish object. "By possessing these objects," Goings (1994, xxiv) notes, "black people rob them of their power." At first glance, this situates possession as means of enjoying mastery, a feeling distinct from *identifying* with such objects, a point that I will return to.

To educators, these artifacts offer tangible proof of racial dehumanization. A collector of racist ephemera targeting Asians in the United States, legal historian Frank Wu accumulates "artifacts[,] pamphlets, posters, documents containing ethnic slurs." In "Why I Collect Racism," he writes, "Many people, including Asian Americans themselves, deny that Asians in America, whether new arrivals or native born, now face or for that matter have ever faced significant discrimination rooted in bigotry."[9] Such artifacts represent "talismans of racism" that testify to the racist hate experienced by Asian Americans and thus find new value as pedagogic tools.[10]

In a veiled rebuke to colleagues in CRT who might call for censorship of these objects, Wu asserts that the artifacts themselves "make an argument more effectively than I ever could." His comment animates the objects, imagining that they *speak for themselves*, ironically, in expressing their dehumanization. Belief in their message's transparency relies on a post–civil rights context, the presumption of a liberal, enlightened audience. Wu's desire in collecting such "talismans" rests on their intellectual effect on others: thus animated, they speak rationally to resurrect a repressed history.[11]

In a similar essay, "The Garbage Man: Why I Collect Racist Objects" (2005), collector David Pilgrim likewise attests to the use of such artifacts as part of a pedagogic mission but implicitly situates their value as producing deep affective responses in the viewer. The essay also reveals more complicated, latent reasons for collecting. The curator and founder of the Jim Crow Museum of Racist Memorabilia, Pilgrim, a Black sociologist working on racial issues, devoted his life to seeking out the once discarded bric-a-brac of racial hatred: toys, masks, ashtrays, cookie jars, games, greeting cards, and advertising that denigrate African Americans. Outgrowing the basement of his home, his collection of more than nine thousand items is now housed at Ferris State

University in Big Rapids, Michigan. Expanding to include other groups, such as women, the museum is dedicated to confronting a traumatic and demeaning history and ongoing legacy. When critics suggested that his collection represented "a shrine to racism," Pilgrim retorted, "That's like saying a hospital is a shrine to disease."[12] That is, the collection is intended to be *curative*.

Like Wu's, Pilgrim's collection renders racial dehumanization tangible in the present. What interests me is not only the repulsion and fascination that racial kitsch evokes in those it putatively represents, but how it now produces collectivity through shared feeling. In "The Garbage Man," Pilgrim recounts purchasing a mammy saltshaker in Alabama at age twelve. His own motives become clear to himself as he subsequently dashes it to the ground, destroying it in front of the white man who sold it to him. The object thus becomes the vehicle of violent repudiation that enables him to externalize his feelings into action: the ceramic mammy presents the occasion to defy the injury it represents. His subsequent portrayal of the moment that solidifies his conviction to establish a museum devoted to such artifacts likewise conveys how the intensity of individual emotion surrounding the anthropomorphic object translates into communal feeling. Pilgrim recounts paying a visit in 1991 to an elderly Black antique dealer in Indiana, who was rumored to possess an extensive collection of such objects. Unimpressed by his explanation of how he uses racist kitsch as props for education, she is nonetheless prevailed on to show him her collection. Led to the back room of the shop, Pilgrim recounts, "If I live to be 100 I will never forget the feeling that I had when I saw her collection; it was sadness, a thick, cold sadness. There were hundreds, maybe thousands, of objects, side-by-side, on shelves that reached to the ceiling.... It was a chamber of horrors. She did not talk. She stared at me; I stared at the objects.... I wanted to cry. It was at that moment that I decided to create a museum" (Pilgrim 2005). As important as the response elicited ("I wanted to cry") is the triangulated spectatorship that the things enable ("She stared at me; I stared at the objects"). What she saw was validated and confirmed by him and vice versa. The objects completed a circuit of shared feeling, binding the two of them at the moment of witnessing. In doing so, they did not merely validate individual response but rendered it collective. A significant if not new idea in curating, the archived novelties' importance lies not in their intrinsic value, but in their ability to produce alliance through a shared affective response. Moreover, the affect mirrored between them was not empathy but horror and outrage.

In the post–civil rights era, these feelings are presumed to be shared by all of us. By national consensus—if not individual enactment—we are collectively bound by our revulsion before this specific racial form, the anthropomorphic object, as it renders the relationship between visual rhetoric and ideology, representation and white supremacy, transparent. When Pilgrim asserts that the Jim Crow Museum of Racist Memorabilia is "in effect, a black holocaust museum," one understands the assertion not as a conflation of histories, but as a parallel of emotional magnitudes. Thus, we know what the ceramic mammy now signifies or, more specifically, the feeling she is supposed to elicit. Pilgrim's narrative implicitly situates the value of Black memorabilia as one that produces community through an alternative racialized affective economy, in concert with progressive values.

This historical frame, I argue, conditions the legibility of racialized things. Yet in contrast, the contemporary Asian anthropomorphic figure, perhaps typified by the Harajuku Lovers perfume bottle launched by the transnational cosmetics conglomerate Coty in 2008, does not evoke a "chamber of horrors" (figure 2.5). Far from it. As announced by its name, we are supposed to share in its delightfulness, one generated by a trendy area of Tokyo. Marketed around the world, the bottles embody the Harajuku Girls, the Japanese backup dancers to US pop star and fashion designer Gwen Stefani. According to corporate planning, every year the characters were to appear in different outfits while the fragrances remained the same; that is, the *form* of the bottle, not its contents, was the object of consumer desire. The nature of that desire is trumpeted by its label: one cannot simply "like" Harajuku Lovers perfume. As in the items depicted in figures 2.2 and 2.3, these twenty-first-century anthropomorphic figures appear to circumvent taboos surrounding ethnic caricature, eluding collective repudiation in the United States. Why?

Clearly, the Asian figure calls forth a different racial history, one that does not invoke, in Bill Brown's (2006) reading, slavery's uncanny, the person-as-thing. But to say that the Asianization of this racial form fails to suggest an analogy of emotional magnitude contributes to the denial that Asian Americans, in Wu's words, "now face or for that matter have ever faced significant discrimination rooted in bigotry" (Wu 2014). The circulation of these figures functions as yet another sign of ambivalence about Asians in the United States as the objects vacillate between repulsion and attraction in a domestic affective economy.

Taking pleasure in Asianized racial objects such as these depends in part on the rise of the Japanese aesthetic since the 1970s known as kawaii, or cute style.

FIGURE 2.5 Harajuku Lovers fragrance by Gwen Stefani, Coty, 2008

As depicted in figures 2.2, 2.3, and 2.5, twenty-first-century anthropomorphic things appear to circumvent prohibitions to racial caricature and the mammy cookie jar's commitment to white supremacy simply because they are cute.

Politics of Kawaii Style: *D* Is for *Dominance*

To state the obvious, the figurines of this chapter are subject to different forms of spectatorship in Asia that I would not mark as racialized.[13] In suggesting how kawaii functions as a racial aesthetic in the United States, I deviate from its neutral, seemingly innocent origins in Japan. Kawaii arose out of a popular movement among teenage girls in Japan who affected a simple, loopy handwriting deemed *koneko ji*, or "kitten writing," in 1974 and spread to trends in slang, clothing, fandom, and other facets of consumer culture (Kinsella 1995). A global aesthetic, it permeates fashion, advertising, cosplay, high art, television, foodways, and gaming.[14] Kawaii commodities are marketed to and consumed by girls and young women, or *shōjo* (young unmarried females). Sharon Kinsella (1995) suggests that this marketing was facilitated by changes in postoccupation Japanese culture, which imported Western gift-giving occasions such as birthdays, but more significantly represented an understated youth rebellion, a resistance to taking on the social responsibilities of adults. As Christine Yano (2013, 46) writes in *Pink Globalization*, "The shōjo and her 'girl culture' marked the rise of kawaii as a galvanizing touchstone of female, youth-oriented, affective, aestheticized, commodified Japan." Of course, what was marketed to her was not in fact *fanshii guzzu* (fancy goods) but affordable kitsch.

One of the most successful marketers of kawaii goods continues to be Sanrio, the Japanese manufacturer of Hello Kitty products and, as importantly, her myth. (Celebrity chef Eddie Huang humorously invoked the company as being equivalent to a country of origin, a testament to its size and influence.) As Yano (2013) notes, while Sanrio's roots remained Japanese, it tried assiduously to market itself as a global brand, hence the invented name, Sanrio: *san* evoking California cities and *rio*, or river in Spanish. An anthropologist observing transnational corporate culture, Yano reveals that Sanrio's marketing strategy does not necessarily have a basis in research and development as in the past; rather, choosing products for the US market depends on the company's ability to elicit the very affective response from its employees that it requires from consumers. The largely Asian American and female staff in its San Francisco office, for example, made decisions for product-line distribution on the West Coast based on the "awww" factor each item inspired. Representing the ultimate commodity fetish, the kawaii object dispenses with use value: one does not really "need" Hello Kitty figurines or stickers. That is, the function of such commodities is precisely to incite the (presumed female) buyer's good will, to elicit emotion.

Kanako Shiokawa (1999, 94) notes that kawaii "conveys a message of positive aesthetics. When someone or something is 'cute,' s/he/it is either charming, likable, plush, fluffy, endearing, acceptable, desirable, or some combination of the above." "The concept of *kawaii* includes elements such as 'cute,' 'pretty' and 'lovely,'" writes Yuko Hasegawa (2002, 128). "It also implies something precious: something that we are drawn towards and which stimulates one's feeling of wanting to protect something that is pure and innocent" (128). A gendered aesthetic, kawaii's popularity is attributed to the fact that it elicits motherly, caregiving impulses stimulated by helpless babies, children, and animals. Kawaii is an aesthetic form characterized by positive, specifically maternal feeling.

Cuteness sensitivity has been theorized as a biological mechanism that serves the evolutionary function of enhancing offspring survival by stimulating affectionate, protective responses. In 1943, German ethologist Konrad Lorenz postulated a "Kindchenschema" (baby schema), a positive reaction to physical characteristics specific to babies: large eyes and head; high, protruding forehead; plump cheeks and body; short and thick extremities; small nose and mouth.[15] These characteristics are identical to those suggested by Disney animator Preston Blair, whose tutorials on how to draw a "'Cute' Character" in 1947 included specific notes on morphology and expression: no neck, large wide-set eyes, bulging "tummy" and "fanny." "Cuteness" he noted, "is based on the basic proportions of a baby and expressions of shyness or coyness."[16] During the US occupation of Japan, Osamu Tezuka, the father of manga, was said to be taken with Disney's animated film *Bambi* (1942), to which Blair contributed, inaugurating the form's signature wide-eyed aesthetic.

Kawaii style allows spectators to take pleasure in asymmetries of social power. Ngai's (2012, 78) awareness of the violence underlying an aesthetic "organized around a small, helpless, or deformed object" thus has particular relevance for the study of race: when she asserts that "cuteness is an aestheticization of powerlessness," she might as well be describing the processes of racialization (64). While the association between affect and race is more obviously bound to the circulation of negative feeling (hate, fear, anxiety), that associative stickiness applies to "minor affects" such as affection as well. As cuteness allows for the enjoyment of unequal relations of power (adult to child, human to animal), its underlying violence in producing racial feeling becomes clear. Cuteness veils pleasure in domination; the cute object's extreme passivity incites a desire for control. "Cuteness, in short, is not something we find in our children," Daniel Harris (2005, 5) writes, "but something we *do* to them." Indeed, a T-shirt offered as part of Gwen Stefani's 2011 Harajuku line for the US retailer Target renders this process blatant and celebratory. The child-size shirt proclaims, "LOVE MAKES ME CUTE." The will to "make" the child as a repository of adult feeling is echoed in the affective economies underlying colonialism, for example, the "little Brown brothers" appellation as intrinsic to fulfilling US imperial desires in the Philippines.[17] The pleasure taken in cute things derives from their unequal status, a dynamic that is both masked and, in regard to race at the millennium, rendered partially taboo.

The cute things here thus invoke asymmetries of power underlying racialization: they appear to mitigate anti-Asian sentiment through positive feeling. And yet they recall another reductive typing, as discussed in the introduction, the Oriental as thing. If early twentieth-century kitsch objects recalled the thingness of slaves, as B. Brown (2006) theorized, in contrast, the anthropomorphic Asian figurine reinforces the association between thingness and the Orient evident in both the perception of the machinelike qualities of coolie labor and the popularization of *chinoiserie* and *japonisme*. As in A. A. Cheng's (2019) "ornamentalism" and J. Lee's (2021) "decorative orientalism," it conflates Orient and accessory. As trade in the "East Indies" assumed rising importance in eighteenth-century Europe and the North American colonies, imported goods (textiles, lacquers, porcelain) reflected an ornamental style à la *Chine* in accordance with Western tastes (D. Jacobson 1993). Whether fabric, chinaware, or figurine, the Chinese decorative object in the colonies was emptied of cultural meaning to stand as a sign of consumer narcissism linked to a mastery of overseas trade (Frank 2011). The desire for exotic décor found analogs in the twentieth century in the mania for hawaiiana in the 1950s and what Sunaina Maira (2007, 220) calls "Indo-chic" in the 1980s. South Asian accessorizing, she argues, represents the extension of imperialist logic resurrected as "late capitalist orientalism," global consumption of the exotic (223). Tapping associations among the Orient, luxury, and timelessness, in 2011 home décor manufacturer Kravet explicitly conjured notions of imperialist nostalgia to publicize its "Indochine" collection of fabrics, trimmings, wallcoverings, carpets, and drapery hardware. "Fresh from a tour of the Orient," designer Barbara Barry cited Asia's gracious people and ancient culture as the inspiration for "ancient" colors, which she newly dubbed "Manchurian Moon Fig," "Silk Road Moonstone," and "Middle Kingdom Cinnabar."[18] As in Latour's reading of objects as actants within a network of the social, through the agency of textiles, one need never be out of imperial time.

Cute things both extend and complicate these uneven global exchanges. Their aura at the millennium encompasses a slightly different domestic mood, as reflected in the original Harajuku Girls (figure 2.5), who, as backup dancers, *accessorize* their blonde leader. In 2015, consumer response to the decorative sumo offered by the US retailer CB2, sister company of Crate and Barrel (figure 2.6), showcases the use value of the cute accessory: to instigate feeling or, in decluttering

FIGURE 2.6 Sumo figurine, by CB2, 2015

guru Marie Kondo's terms, to "spark joy." In this modernist and arguably kawaii figurine, Japanese cultural difference is stripped to a minimalist essence: topknot, belt, morphology, stance. On the company's website, reviewer Annie testifies to the supposed uniqueness of the mass-produced commodity: "I enjoy adding something unexpected (weird perhaps?) and quirky to the rooms in my home—it makes my home unique and interesting."[19] Jana Pijak enthuses, "This fun home accessory makes a great statement and is sure to get guests talking."[20] In contrast to earlier periods in which chinoiserie and japonisme conveyed luxury and Western domination of overseas trade, the kawaii form of racial things produces lighthearted ambiance: they're "fun."

Like other kawaii figures, the faceless, emotionless sumo enables the viewer's affective imprinting, something that this home accent shares with another Asian stereotype: inscrutability. As others have theorized, the absence of emotion expressed by kawaii objects typified by Hello Kitty is essential to the pleasure they elicit. Hello Kitty's lack of mouth enables her to function as a blank slate for the feelings of the viewer.²¹ This contrasts the affect expressed by segregation-era kitsch. As Goings (1994, 14) writes, "African-Americans could not simply be second-class citizens, they had to actively acknowledge their subordinate position by smiling, by showing deference, and most important, by appearing to be happy even when they were treated horribly." Yet I would note that the absence of affect in objects such as sumo is compatible with Asian racialization, stoicism as a hallmark of the "Oriental."

To render something cute reinforces power differentials underlying racialization by introducing the question of scale as it graphs onto authority: the small as insignificant. Taking delight in the diminutive is enhanced by the socially leveling nature of caricature, the miniature fighter as mock heroic. And as Roland Barthes ([1970] 1982) reveals, the fantasy of the "Orient" is intimately bound to delight in the diminutive. On the harmony between "Oriental food" and chopsticks, he philosophizes, "things are not only small in order to be eaten but are also comestible in order to fulfill their essence, which is smallness" (15). By contiguity, the essence of the Oriental is smallness. The delight taken in mascots and caricature converge in Alessi's Mandarin (see figure 2.2) and the tiny Chin Family, a series of kitchen goods encompassing chopstick holders, egg cups, and salt and pepper shakers. The series has the imprimatur of the National Palace Museum of Taiwan (NPM), which launched an initiative dubbed "Old Is New" in 2005, attempting to rebrand its historical holdings to appeal to a younger audience. The museum called on Alessi's head designer, Stefano Giovannoni, to create "new symbols of auspicious themes (mascots) based on art objects in the NPM."²² Giovannoni took his inspiration for the Chin Family from the portrait of Ch'ing dynasty emperor Ch'ien-lung (1711–1799) held by the museum (figure 2.7). The series' kawaii-style design and appeal to the cute no doubt served the museum's intention to use "trendy aspects of today's youth to enliven ancient objects."²³

Of course, it does so by submitting authority to downward mobility: one's eggs are served by no less than the emperor of China. With his slanted eyes and traditional Chinese garb, the now demoted "*Mr.* Chin" evokes Freud's ([1905] 1989, 249) notion that caricature "brings about degradation by emphasizing in the general impression given by the exalted object a single trait which is comic in itself but was bound to be overlooked." Invoking a shared history between Taiwan and the mainland as much as homage, the figure may be thus read as Taiwan's rebuke to centralized state power. A mascot is imbued with positive feelings of ownership in part derived from socially leveling infantilization. In the case of the anthropomorphic object's circulation in the United States, this

FIGURE 2.7 Social demotion: Alessi's Chin Family kitchen timer (2007), inspired by the portrait of Ch'ing dynasty emperor Ch'ien-lung (1711–1799), National Palace Museum, Taipei

reduction takes on a racial cast. Here, Mr. Chin represents the awkward collisions/collusions of global trade; while kawaii style intends to impart the fresh vigor of youth, it likewise conveys its puerility and insignificance, outside Asia, a conduit of racial meaning. To be clear: the inadvertently caricatured Italian design represents late capitalist Orientalism even as it was commissioned by a Taiwanese source for Asian and non-Asian consumption alike. Yet it may also be read as symptom, as an anxious response to the latent and impending racialization of neoliberal global flows, reflecting Bhabha's (1994) reading of the affective vacillation underlying the stereotype, oscillating from the philic to the phobic.

I want to suggest, then, that the pleasure surrounding cute commodities, their enactment of *complimentary* racial stereotyping, masks a fetishistic anxiety surrounding East Asia writ large. To understand how the racialized anthropomorphic object skirts the borders of the acceptable without breaking American covenants surrounding ethnic caricature, I turn to their interaction with a dominant perception of Asians in the United States. Unpacking the relationship between group stereotypes and emotional valence, social psychologist Susan Fiske and her colleagues implicitly ask us to consider Asian American "model minority" perception on a dual axis reflecting both positive and negative connotations: "Social psychologists have typically viewed only unflattering stereotypes as indicating prejudice, where prejudice is a uniform antipathy or contempt.... We argue instead that stereotypes are captured by two dimensions (warmth and competence) and that subjectively positive stereotypes on one dimension do not contradict prejudice but often are functionally consistent with unflattering stereotypes on the other dimension" (Fiske et al. 2002, 878). The authors suggest that stereotyping works on two axes that incite contrary emotional valence: the perception of competence that generates envy and respect, and the perception of warmth that generates affection. Some groups elicit positive feeling but are perceived to be less competent ("housewives," "the elderly," "the disabled"). Others are deemed highly competent yet score low on warmth, something that Asians apparently share with "the rich," "feminists," "businesswomen," and "Jews." Thus, in the United States, these latter groups are perceived to possess an "excessive, threatening competence" (Fiske et al. 2002, 878). In other words, Asians are respected but disliked; the consequence of so-called positive stereotyping is that the other shoe always drops.

At first glance, kawaii style enables an affective response to racial difference that compensates for this dominant stereotype; it mitigates envy by conveying warmth. The cute anthropomorphic Orientalized object may avoid touching the third rail of American racial politics because it seems to counter the Asian stereotype of "threatening competence" by inscribing its opposite: the Asian as endearing, amusing, lovable. Addressed to children and young women, the kawaii aesthetic marks an association with dependence and innocence. The racialized object speaks to the split feeling attending Asian stereotyping and, more broadly, to the contingency of "positive" stereotypes. Cuteness counters perception of unlikability only to replace it with the incompetence of the infantile. While Fiske measures emotional valence from positive to negative, the VAD scale in psychology establishes two other continuums of feeling: arousal (the intensity of emotion) and dominance (feelings of control) (Warriner, Kuperman, and Brysbaert 2013). In part, these objects circulate without the outrage associated with caricature because they generate affirmative feelings attached to the helpless, igniting a corresponding feeling of dominance, of being in control. As Shiokawa (1999, 94) notes about kawaii style, "By far the most outstanding feature of cuteness, is its complete lack of anything observably threatening."

This might explain why, even as American self-consciousness about racial caricature grew in the 1970s, questionable racial representations of Asians associated with childhood nostalgia continue to evade post–civil rights movement awareness. Despite public knowledge of cartoonist Theodor Geisel's

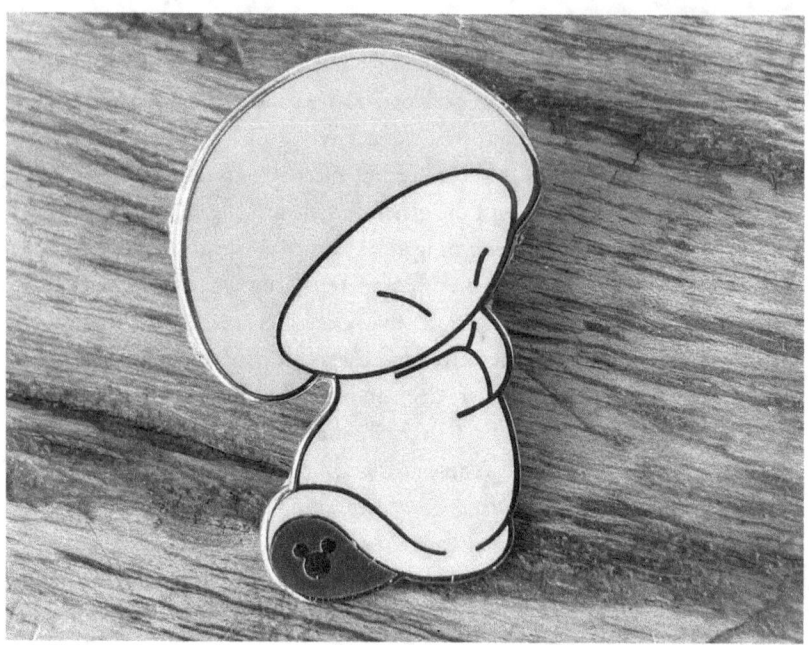

FIGURE 2.8 Disney's Hop Low, from *Fantasia* (1940), as collectible trading pin

(Dr. Seuss's) use of racial caricature in advertising and wartime propaganda portraying Japanese Americans, these Seussian lines from *If I Ran the Zoo* (1950) and their unfortunate illustration were readily available until 2021: "I'll hunt in the mountains of Zomba-ma-Tant / With helpers who all wear their eyes at a slant."[24] Another case in point: when Disney reissued *Fantasia* (1940) for a sixtieth anniversary edition at the millennium, it excised a particularly offensive Black character, Sunflower, a centaur version of the pickaninny servant. Yet it retained another racial caricature: Hop Low, the dancing Chinese mushroom, who continues to circulate as a collectible Disney pin (figure 2.8). One might argue that the representation goes without comment simply because it illustrates Pyotr Tchaikovsky's "Chinese Dance" in *The Nutcracker Suite*. Yet it takes the exoticism of that performance into another realm of "delightful" reduction: a cute-as-a-button mushroom whose name is nevertheless also an ethnic joke. Cuteness also counters the threat of the unspoken specter of neoliberal globalization in the West, in the words of novelist Kevin Kwan, crazy rich Asians.

Risky Kawaii

The prominence of kawaii as an aesthetic category since the 1970s coincides with Western awareness of Asian "competence" on a global scale, particularly in the realm of transnational finance and manufacturing. Along with Japan, by the 1980s, newly industrializing countries—South Korea, Singapore, Taiwan, and Hong Kong—refused conflating "the West" with the global North. The volatility of uneven neoliberal economic development allowed East Asian regions to, in the words of David Harvey (2006, 42), "advance spectacularly (at least for a time) at the expense of others." Following Japan's rapid ascendency in electronics and automobile manufacturing in the 1980s, its exports in the "children's entertainment business"—anime, manga, and video games—generated a purported $8 billion USD in 2001, one of the few avenues of its postrecession growth (Allison 2004, 36).[25] The uneven reception of commodity forms makes visible the social contradictions occasioned by these large- and small-scale shifts in status.

The Oriental thing-as-person appears at a moment of global economic shift, a moment of Western anxiety surrounding transnational trade and the changing fortunes that attend it. The expanded circulation of racist kitsch typified by mammy figurines occurred, as Bill Brown argues, at a moment of increasing African American heterogeneity during Reconstruction and into the twentieth century, conveying nostalgia for the system of slavery undone by capitalist modernization. "In the earlier time period there really had not been much need for this kind of denigration," notes Goings (1994, xix). "Skin color alone marked slave status; what else needed to be said?" Paradoxically, the circulation of denigrating novelties arose from the newly ambiguous status of African Americans. Critics have likewise linked anxieties surrounding gender to the growth of kawaii style in Japan. As Shiokawa (1999, 120) reveals, the manga heroine's "cuteness makes her power and independence more palatable," suggesting that infantilized gender representation compensates for women's increasing equality. In contrast, Kinsella (1995) argues that Japanese women's consumption of kawaii goods constitutes feminist resistance of a different sort: participating in their own infantilization symbolizes the freedoms associated with childhood and represents a refusal to "grow up" and accept a gender-circumscribed role. She implies that these new social responsibilities were required by Japan's rapid postwar economic development. Yet artist Takashi Murakami (2005) offers an alternative gendered reading of his superflat aesthetic linked to geopolitics and echoed in Ngai's work: kawaii aestheticizes Japan's occupation-era emasculation, a response to its US-imposed "Peace Constitution" forbidding military buildup: "Regardless of winning or losing the war, the bottom line is that for the past sixty years, Japan has been a testing ground for an American-style capitalist economy, protected in a greenhouse, nurtured and bloated to the point of explosion. The results are so bizarre, they're perfect. Whatever true intentions underlie 'Little Boy,' the nickname for Hiroshima's atomic bomb, we Japanese are truly, deeply, pampered children.... We throw constant tantrums while enthralled by our own cuteness" (Murakami 2005, 141). To Murakami, kawaii represents a degraded national ethos, a sign of its postwar dependency.

In contrast, nonhuman kawaii things could be said to be global commodities par excellence precisely because they strategically disguise national origins as part of their "universal" appeal. Japan's global marketing did not likewise sell Japanese culture: unlike *Coca-colonization*, in which the soft power of US exports was closely identified with the promotion of an American lifestyle at midcentury, Japanese exporters of kawaii style—character-driven companies such as Nintendo (Pikachu) and Sanrio (Hello Kitty)—intentionally cultivated a deterritorialized, culturally neutral product adhering to the notion of *mukokuseki*, or the erasure of racial, ethnic, or cultural resonance.[26] In a deliberate address to global marketing, the South Korean creator of the cartoon character Pucca (see figure 2.3) insists that Pucca has no nationality, a strategy that culminated in merchandizing success in Europe through a collaboration with Benetton.[27] In 2002, journalist Douglas McGray attributed the rise of Japan's domestic economy to its "genius" in largely ignoring concerns surrounding cultural erosion in the face of globalization: "Hello Kitty is Western, so she will sell in Japan. She is Japanese, so she will sell in the West. It is a marketing boomerang that firms like Sanrio, Sony, and Nintendo manage effortlessly" (2002, 50). Yet Koichi Iwabuchi (2004, 60) implies an alternative reason for mukokuseki: "Anime and manga are more popular in Asian countries such as Hong Kong and Taiwan than they are in the West, . . . but to Japanese cultural chauvinists success in Asian markets does not count for much." What McGray saw as genius, others saw as a failure of national branding or, in the case of anime, as a distinct preference for non-Japanese characters as a result of US occupation.[28] This perhaps accounts for the underlying contradiction of mukokuseki: the whiteness of human anime characters.

Yet dematerializing national origins is indeed how transnational capital works. Harajuku Lovers perfume (see figure 2.4), for example, is licensed by Gwen Stefani to Coty, a transnational corporation whose French origins and US base obfuscate its German ownership. Moreover, Harajuku is also licensed to US retailer Target as well as to Nickelodeon and Viacom. The animated series *Kuu*

Kuu Harajuku is produced in collaboration with companies in Canada, Malaysia, Australia, and the United States, with merchandise tie-ins manufactured in the United States by Mattel. Coty's perfume bottle appears to enhance Japaneseness not through cultural signs but in its very form: diminutive, female, childlike. Its specific racial embodiment further amplifies what Ngai (2012, 62) notes as the extreme passivity of cute commodities: "Cuteness might be regarded as an intensification of commodity fetishism's kitschy phantasmatic logic but also as a way of revising it by adding yet another layer of fantasy." While the rise of cuteness has been understood as a soothing response to economic instability and social atomization, my focus on Asian things foregrounds the aesthetic as a response to shifts in global economic power.[29]

The "Asianness" of the kawaii commodities I discuss here interrupts the seemingly free flow of capital under neoliberal globalization. Shifting to a US interpretative context highlighting racialization creates hermeneutic dissonance, particularly when the *intention* underlying a product line (celebration, homage) or the erasure of the local in more typical nonhuman kawaii commodity forms is at odds with discursive meanings generated by its global circulation. Reading injurious intent informs these commodities' US reception. When I ask audiences how they read these anthropomorphic objects, they reveal that they feel more authorized to deem them cute if they are sourced from Asia: they viewed samurai and geisha bento boxes, for example, as inoffensive because they were perceived to be Japanese forms produced in Japan for Japanese children. Within this projection of a closed (racial) circuit, a Japanese consumer's identification with the personified object would not be self-Orientalizing because this implies a double consciousness based on an external (Western) standard for self-valuation. Nor would *samurai* or *geisha* necessarily signify as fetishistic types in Japan. Asian spectators might consume such images according to the hallmark of kawaii style: sincere attachment. This does not obviate the fact that a South Korean consumer experiences such Japanese iconography with other complex routes of identification and disassociation—or indifference. After all, exports such as K-pop, K-drama, and K-beauty engage cuteness quite differently and trumpet their national branding in ways akin to Coca-colonization, employed by US companies at midcentury. While anthropomorphic hula dancers, buddhas, and swamis likewise circulate, their Orientalist intent is not sanitized by a kawaii aesthetic.

In contrast, my audiences and class members in the United States roundly repudiated the "china doll" handbag designed by Karl Lagerfeld for Chanel's Paris-Shanghai collection to inaugurate its foray into the Chinese luxury market in 2010 because it was accompanied by the image of another item in the product line, a handbag in the shape of the ubiquitous Chinese take-out container (figure 2.9).[30] Evoking the history of Chinese food service workers and restaurants in the United States, the handbag trades on capitalist metonymy: as in Black "spokesservants" of the past, personhood becomes undifferentiated from the object of labor. The specific regional embodiment of this form is thus telling: not South Asia or Southeast Asia but China, a nation both desired as a source of potential consumers and feared as competition within a neoliberal global economy. Insisting on an American studies context for reading irrespective of a commodity's origin within or outside Asia illuminates the dissonances created by globalization itself: here, a desire for *those people* to stay in their place even at a moment that acknowledges they have not. As the object is wrested from local contexts, and its meaning fails to translate, the *limits* to the free flow of capital come into view.

If the soft power of kawaii style lies in its deliberate erasure of Japanese origins in deracinated anthropomorphic animals, pillows, and food, then caricatured humanoid things represent its aberration. In flouting mukokuseki,

FIGURE 2.9 Chanel's Take Away bag, 2010

they represent a subset of the aesthetic category, not *kowaii* (scary kawaii) but perhaps risky kawaii: racialized things that not only testify to the fine line between affection and mockery but interrupt the seamless fluidity of global commodity flows to insist on the residues of the local. Latour's (2005) notion of "risky objects" whose meaning suddenly shifts thus applies to Chanel's Paris-Shanghai Take Away bag in more than one sense. Its kitsch form situates "crazy rich Asians," those who can afford $7,500 USD handbags (now $28,500 resale), as the butt of a leveling joke: you may be "crazy rich," but you're Asian. In doing so, the handbag also instigates what I would identify as an alternative notion of risk: in constituting "discriminatory action" breaking actors down, it betrays Western anxieties about a potential loss of dominance in an impending new world order and shifting global hegemon. As in the case of other cute Asianized things, the very repetition of type flags uncertainties about those who have begun to stray from type. The paradox it embodies—likable and offensive—reflects the ambivalence underlying stereotyping itself as it vacillates between, to echo Bhabha (1994, 66), what is already known and "what must be anxiously repeated." In this sense, caricature represents a leveling response to perceived empowerment, the "excessive threatening competence" of Asians (Fiske et al. 2002, 878).

The interplay between contrary feelings here—warmth and envy—underscores the stereotyping's split desiring structure, as previously discussed, a split structure likewise underlying fetishization. Here, as in the case of Black populations at the turn of the previous century, that tension highlights the anxieties that Asians in the United States arouse, recirculated as pleasure. The question is, whose pleasure?

Asian American Spectatorship of the Racist Cute

> Most collectors know that money becomes an unreality when you regard a beloved object. There can be no waste. Whatever you pay, whether it is x or $2x$ or x^2, it never seems too much because desire makes up the difference.
> —William Davies King, *Collections of Nothing*

One foundation of US race activism rests on mobilizing against the stereotypical image, against demeaning caricature. If the racially reductive figure is implicated in maintaining status hierarchy, how do we understand the attachment that cute anthropomorphic things elicit among the spectators and consumers they mimic and embody? In addressing the potential ambivalence they provoke in Asian American spectators, I include myself. If this seems like a confession, it is because, along with media and student activists, ethnic studies has been instrumental in heightening awareness of caricature as discriminatory action. Yet in illuminating the space between political rationality (it's offensive) and other affective responses (I love it), these objects likewise uncover the emotional attachment seemingly required by activism itself. That is, the very split feeling invoked by things both racist and cute illuminates the boundaries of coalition as a community seemingly bound by a uniformity of feeling. In kawaii spectatorship, *racist love* does not name a mode of top-down racial management but represents a perverse spectatorship (Oishi 2006, 649) and a form of self-affirmation, however ambivalent.

When Ngai (2012, 60) searched the *Oxford English Dictionary* for references to *cute*, she identified an additional resonance of the word: those who seek to "publicize or share their feelings." One might say that the desire to create a community of shared feeling underlies coalition even as it is mobilized not by affection but by outrage. That is, coalition presumes that members *feel the same way*. Thus, the split feeling that the object evokes exposes coalition's disciplining of affective boundaries: Why should taking pleasure in racialized things represent a guilty pleasure? The blog *Why Did I Buy That Toy? Blogging Away Buyer's Remorse*, which publicizes the blogger's hobby, miniature figure (mini-fig) collecting, provides an example of the vacillation underlying Asian American encounters with the cute anthropomorphic object.[31] Using the moniker Action Ranger Timmy, the blogger acknowledges his "ongoing quest" to collect Asian proxies such as Playmobil samurais and Lego coolies and, in the process, explore his love-hate relationship with cute, racist things. "I like to ironically collect unintentionally racist action figures of Asian people," he writes, "I'm Asian, I'm sensitive to this kind of thing." In part, racial activism allows him to counter the "buyer's remorse" of the avid collector.

In the moniker Action Ranger Timmy, the blogger emphasizes selfhood as indistinguishable from the toy, the mini-fig as mini-me. Through his spectatorship of the desired object, he begins to externalize his own introjected racialization both for himself and on behalf of the collective. Yet repudiating reductive Asian typing becomes complicated by the responses elicited by cute things. Timmy exemplifies the ambivalent response embedded within the paradox of the racist cute: equal parts identification and disassociation. Experiencing the latter regarding a German Playmobil toy that he dubs "Asian Kung-Fu Guy," he writes, "This guy is even more racist than I usually expect. He's not just a martial artist. He doesn't just have the slanted eyes that all Playmobil figures of

Asian people have. He's got a fu-manchu mustache. Oh, and angry eyebrows so you know his fu-manchu-stache means he's evil." His first response is that of the activist: he provides a tutorial in reading ethnic caricature—if the eyes don't signify, the facial hair does. The racist tropes are, by now, accessible to all. But his second comment questions not the reading but his own response to it: "I don't really think this guy is all that racist. But then I look at the mustache and I don't know. I just don't know." His comment evokes the anxious repetition of stereotyping itself; in this case, ambivalence stems not necessarily from second-guessing his reading of racial iconography, but from whether he shares the emotional response it is supposed to generate, one that would hail him as Asian American and, in part, justify his "ironic" collecting.

The blogger's pleasure reflects what Eve Oishi (2006, 649) deemed "perverse spectatorship," the complicated and oblique routes of identification of queers and people of color. The mini-fig forces multiple reactions: anger, delight, and then confusion over delight. About another questionable toy, he writes, "The Samurai has the upturned, squinty Asian eyes, but I can't get mad because of how much I love the details on the samurai armor." Here, the reduction of caricature ("squinty" eyes) contrasts with its stylistic opposite, the unexpectedly exaggerated, excessive detail of the costume. His stalled reaction, "I can't get mad," recalls bell hooks's discussion of Black women's spectatorship in the context of mainstream Hollywood film. Black women's experience of cinematic pleasure, hooks (1992, 120) argues, requires a suspension of rationality: "Every black woman I spoke with who was/is an ardent moviegoer, a lover of the Hollywood film, testified that to experience fully the pleasure of that cinema they had to close down critique, analysis; they had to forget racism." Yet hooks goes on to situate this pleasure as complicity and tacit consent: "Assuming a posture of subordination, [Black women] submitted to cinema's capacity to seduce and betray" (120). Identification here is represented as masochistic and self-negating; Black female viewing pleasure is always already suspect. In contrast, on what it means to read *Gone with the Wind* as a Black woman, artist Kara Walker conveys split identification, wanting both to be the white heroine and to kill her.[32] Timmy's divided response to the cute object betrays an intellectual awareness of those equations, an unwillingness to be "seduced" by his toys and forget racism. But his response likewise raises the question, who *wants* him to "get mad"?

Here, the appeal of identification, or "wanting to be *like* the cute" (Merish 1996, 186), pushes up against the prohibitions placed on identifying with the stereotype. Timmy's ambivalence betrays a veiled anxiety over his credentials within the coalitional identity *Asian American*. His conflict over reductive typing and cuteness reveals the tension between the sentiments putatively shared by political community (outrage) and its interruption (delight). The latter sentiment only becomes suspect in the context of the former, with the awareness that his pleasure in the object is subject to censure. Identification, as Freud ([1921] 1959, 37) wrote regarding the family romance, "is ambivalent from the very first"; identifying with the racist cute forces a seeming wedge between feeling and political-intellectual knowledge that might be otherwise rationalized by the admission, "I'm *helpless* before the cute."

Collecting can itself be a prohibited desire, as the hunt and will to possession transcend the object at hand. Whatever one pays for a beloved collectible, "never seems too much because desire makes up the difference," William Davies King (2008, 29) asserts. As collecting veers into pathological hoarding, it becomes additionally charged by its secrecy. David Pilgrim's partial confession of his avidity as a collector of segregation-era memorabilia betrays an awareness of collecting as a structure of desire (wanting, seeking, possessing), as well as of the politically suspect nature of its object. The collective pain that such artifacts inflict is complicated by a pleasure in acquisition less comprehensible among non-collectors: "My friends claim that I am obsessed with racist objects. *If they are right*, the obsession began while I was an undergraduate student at Jarvis Christian College, a small historically black institution in Hawkins, Texas" (Pilgrim 2005, emphasis mine). Pilgrim acknowledges obsession without validating it; the slipperiness of his language indicates the degree to which he is aware of the gray area of (untoward?) libidinal investment in collecting that exists in excess of the educator's desire to teach. Here, as in *Why Did I Buy That Toy?*, activism may serve as a cloaking mechanism that veils the partially taboo pastime of collecting, granting it the veneer of rationality. Does Pilgrim's fixation indicate, in Wendy Brown's (1995) terms, a "wounded attachment" or, as I discuss in chapter 4 regarding Ranjana Khanna's (2003) work, a sign of the colonized's melancholia, an inability to let go of past racial trauma? Or can Timmy's "racist love" of his toys represent a form of ambivalent self-love for Asian Americans?

Taking delight in something that is offensive to others potentially locates spectators outside the bounds of any collective identity in part defined through the projection of a uniformity of feeling. To discuss this dynamic, I often ask students in my Asian American studies classes or activist workshops to participate in an exercise in which they evaluate the kawaii things in this chapter as either offensive or cute. They dramatize their reactions to Asianized household items, toys, handbags, or figurines by walking to opposite sides of the room in what social scientists would decry as a "forced choice" test such as that employed by Kenneth and Mamie Clark's early studies in racial psychology utilizing dolls. The exercise at first leaves no space for alternative responses within the distinction. It is also fraught with risk, asking participants to publicize their feelings about racial images, particularly in contexts that seem to suggest that one response—"offensive"—is the safe one.

Yet my workshops consistently demonstrate split responses among Asian and non-Asian spectators alike: what some find suspect, others find adorable. A few participants do not move at all, electing to remain with the position that all such figures are offensive: *racist* Asianized objects cannot be liberated from the earlier historical context of Black representation. In contrast, in consistently siding with the cute, others convey that they could not revise their personal, nostalgic childhood associations with some of the items pictured, even with belated intellectual awareness of their harm. Others struggle: one Asian American woman continually puzzled over her family's "innocent" collection of similar kawaii items. Hours later, she came to a more decisive conclusion: "Those things are *wack*."[33]

More significantly, what comes out of the workshops is the participants' awareness of how community expectation influences not the feelings provoked by racial imagery itself, but their public expression. Some waited to see how evaluation went among the majority before choosing a side. Non-Asian participants deferred to their Asian peers and confessed to taking a cue from their responses; one white woman "didn't want to be an ass" in being seen as taking pleasure in an image that held negative stakes for others. As in Ngai's awareness that definitions of *cute* engage sharing feeling, creating politicized community likewise carries with it those same assumptions. In staging the spectatorship of racial things, I am intrigued by the outcome of split perception surrounding specific objects, but more significantly, I take away a sense of how prohibition likewise creates community. Culture, history, and location create the conditions for the experience of racial pleasure; more to the point here, they also create conditions for how—and if—we express it to others.

In choosing "feelings" that go against the grain of group consensus, historian Kenneth Goings confesses an untoward attachment to Black memorabilia quite different from Pilgrim's. An avid collector, he accumulated several hundred items to write *Mammy and Uncle Mose: Black Collectibles and American Stereotyping* (1994), a book liberally cited in this chapter. Beyond their use to his academic study, Goings articulates his reasons for collecting by invoking sentiment and personification rather than a desire to reclaim the power of the fetish object through possession: "When I see Aunt Jemima and Uncle Mose resting on my shelves, I think of them as people." He adds, "I hope the reader will not think that I have completely lost my sense of reality when I personify the collectibles in the way I have. After all, I have been studying these objects for the last seven years and they do now seem like people, like friends" (1994, xxiv). The collector gives himself over to the pleasures of attachment, here coincident with the feelings provoked by cute style: sincerity, innocence, affection. In animating the artifacts through his regard, he imbued them with a lost humanity. Yet this corrective identification is offered as an apology, one made with the awareness that he is confessing something aberrant, subject to disapproval. Indeed, in Spike Lee's much-analyzed film *Bamboozled*, which critiques the pleasures of minstrelsy at the millennium, the anthropomorphic objects' coming to life is indeed a sign that the hapless protagonist has lost his sense of reality.

Counter to my reading here, in the film, animated racial things are not to be embraced; Bill Brown (2006, 199) reads them as sitting in judgment and protest of a degrading history's recirculation. They recapitulate slavery's uncanny, the uncertainty about the distinction between person and thing, its "ontological instability." Yet Brown's reading also highlights why the anthropomorphic racial object, as in Timmy's spectatorship, now evokes both repulsion and fascination as simultaneously the most "despised and most prized object" (199). Uncle Mose and Aunt Jemima figures continue to be manufactured by Dixie Souvenir in Tennessee, even as they are absent from the novelty company's website. Supporting evidence that most collectors of such memorabilia are Black, in 2014, a white gas station owner in Alabama explained that he continues to stock the figurines at the request of his customer base, "black travelers from northern states headed to family reunions in south Alabama and Mississippi." "We sell out every time," he said.[34] While Goings's attachment is conveyed through sincerity, the hallmark of the cute, for outsiders stopping at a Shell Station in Alabama, the purchase seems marked by ironic, if not also perverse, spectatorship and the pleasures of the in-joke.

In what follows, I explore this split reaction to racialized things, one marked by the pleasures not of affection or repudiation but of irony and camp.

Activism and Ironic Spectatorship

If cuteness implies attachment, does it foreclose a sense of camp? Millennials' consumption of Hello Kitty in the United States might well represent postfeminist irony, a "wink on pink" (Yano 2013, 7) that dovetails with self-avowed feminists' attachment to Barbie dolls. In *Why Did I Buy That Toy?*, the blogger self-designates as an "ironic" collector ("I'm Asian, I'm sensitive to this kind of thing"). Thus, collecting cute Asian things may well represent a form of in-group credentialing. Asian American bloggers are aware of the thin line between recirculation and parody. For example, the satirical blog *Stuff Asian People Like*, a parody of the parody *Stuff White People Like*, announces an oddly divided intent: "we aim to break (or reinforce) Asian stereotypes."[35] Apparently, the "stuff" Asian people like ranges from the stereotypical (e.g., bargains, karaoke) to the once obscure (Flying Rainbow Poptart Cat). The bloggers seem to acknowledge that Asian viewers will understand the site as a source of in-group humor, blunting its misreading as hostile ethnic joke. The answer to Bernard Saper's (1993, 84) question "Since When Is Jewish Humor Not Anti-Semitic?" emphasizes a closed circuit: Jewish humor is not anti-Semitic when it is "told by Jews to Jews about Jews."[36]

If fantasy Asians initiate the pleasures of ironic consumption, to what extent do the affective implications of the cute complicate that pleasure? Phil Yu's website, *Angry Asian Man*, which compiles and comments on Asian American activism or news worthy of circulation and intervention, took as its mascot the cartoon character Quick Kick, yet another "Asian Kung-Fu Guy." The lone Asian on GI Joe's multicultural team of soldiers, the toy represents the activist's proxy, emphasizing both his need to "fight" and his pleasure in the absurdity of misrecognition. "I chose the figure because it's actually rather ridiculous, embodying the attributes of the stereotypical martial arts hero. Shirtless, shoeless, sockless—all rather impractical for going into battle with the G.I. Joe team," Yu writes.[37] His pleasure in the stereotype derives from the ironic distance between lived reality and the excesses of a US racial imaginary, something likewise in effect in his contributions to the activist blog *YOMYOMF* ("You offend me, you offend my family"), a nod to icon Bruce Lee. Freud's notion that irony "can only be employed when the other person is prepared to hear the opposite" (Freud [1905] 1989, 21) is operative here: the activist unexpectedly identifying with retrograde representation. As in Kara Walker's controversial sculpture *A Subtlety, or the Marvelous Sugar Baby*, an oversized mammy sphinx made of sugar, Yu embraces the stereotype as defiant proclamation.

Yet the question of scale implied by the cute affects a reading of the ironic detachment. Yu's use of the Asian male stereotype changed over time: at one point, the portal to *Angry Asian Man* displayed the character as it was embodied in an action figure by the US toymaker Hasbro (figure 2.10). On Quick Kick's nostalgic appeal, he writes, "I remember the character fondly." In Yu's toy proxy, the very affective response elicited by the cute might distinguish his engagement from Walker's. The monumentalism of *A Subtlety, or the Marvelous Sugar Baby* asks the viewer to claim ownership of monstrousness of the racial fantastic as well as the gigantic sticky mess it left behind. In contrast, Yu's former portal might be seen as an ironic commentary on the minorness of Asian American activism itself, the blogger's mission as mock heroic. This tongue-in-cheek tone is struck elsewhere on the site: "My purpose was to acknowledge and encourage our yellow struggle against The Man, who in turn was determined to keep us in our bamboo cages and hold us down. I was angry. I was Asian. And I wasn't going to stand by and watch idly as my people were unknowingly subjugated!" The inflated militant rhetoric may well derive from both Yu's investment in social justice and his awareness that Asian American grievances are not seen as commensurate to that of other minority groups. We are angry, he suggests, but maybe not that much.

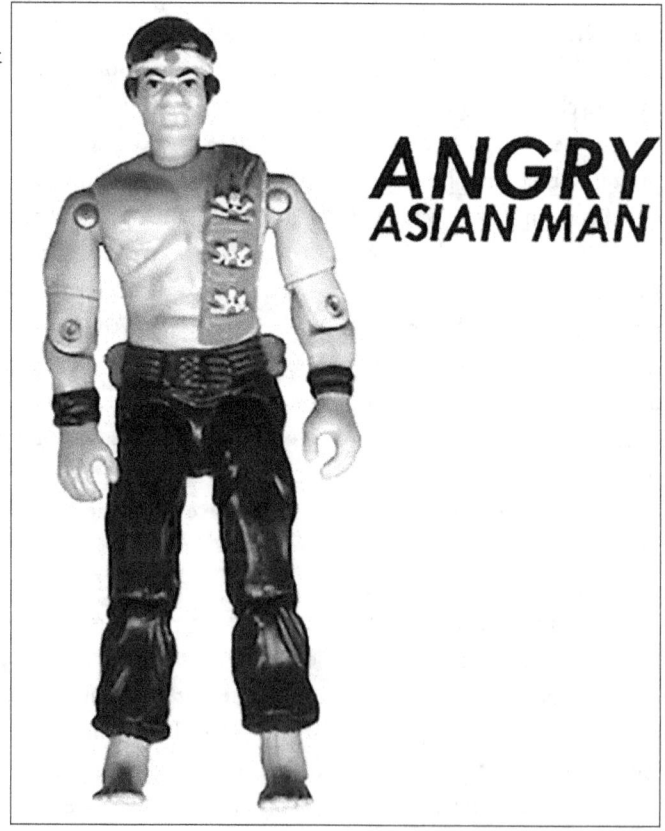

FIGURE 2.10 Hasbro's Quick Kick action figure in the former portal to the website *Angry Asian Man*, 2014

Or perhaps more accurately, Yu's website maintained an awareness that ironic distance and humor are somehow incompatible with activism. This is certainly borne out in contemporary responses to racial caricature. In 2002, Asian American activists led a successful action against the US retailer Abercrombie and Fitch after its release of a series of Asian-themed T-shirts. One read, "Pizza Dojo: Eat In or Wok Out"; another proclaimed, "Two Wongs can make it white" and featured cartoon figures of Chinese laundrymen. Reaction was swift: student groups from around the country called for a boycott of the Ohio-based company and succeeded in having the offending shirts removed from the shelves. It was not the first time that the company elicited controversy: it had previously come under scrutiny for sexist T-shirt slogans, sexual ads, and discriminatory hiring practices.[38] Given this track record, its use of ludic imagery was taken as a sign of corporate racism, highlighting comedy's "propensity to get in trouble" (Berlant and Ngai 2017, 234). Nevertheless, a befuddled Abercrombie and Fitch public relations representative noted in response to the collective action, "We personally thought Asians would love this T-shirt."[39]

Indeed, if worn by an Asian person, the shirt enacts irony's double gesture: it both displays and disavows type by creating dissonance between the individual and the fantasy image. Moreover, the shirt's tag line, "make it white," could itself be seen as a deliberate reference to a racial double standard: it takes two Asians to make one "white." The double entendre is just subtle enough to function as subversive repetition. As in the new ethnic joke, irony allows for plausible denial: the shirts can be read as both racist and a parody of racism. By all accounts, however, the company miscalculated, revealing that the term *borderline offensive* is a misnomer: the moment the question arises, that border has already been crossed. In 2016, the app developer Snapchat made a similar faux pas, introducing a face-warping filter that transformed the user into a slanty-eyed, buck-toothed, East Asian caricature. It was meant to be playful, an homage to anime. Yet Snapchat's "homage" to Bob Marley had already been criticized as digital blackface. After protests on social media, the filter was disabled after only one day in acknowledgment that Asian Americans bore the tax of its caricature.[40] Both actions call forth art critic Michael Harris's (2003, 192) skepticism surrounding the use of mammy and minstrel figures in contemporary Black art: he asked, "Can one ever appropriate or reappropriate the fantasy of another?"[41]

Boycotts do not entertain the notion of camp; activism necessarily requires the projection of a unanimity of feeling. Lori Kido Lopez's sharp reading of

Asian American media activism highlights the ways in which Media Action Network for Asian Americans, which monitors negative images of Asian Americans, selected its targets based on group consensus surrounding a given media representation: "Emotional responses such as feeling proud, embarrassed, insulted, angry, amused, or pleased were all seen as valid reasons for the group to make a decision" (Lopez 2016, 51). This criterion led to blind spots regarding attempts to *parody* racism, particularly in the comedy of Ken Jeong, Stephen Colbert, Sarah Silverman, and Margaret Cho. As activist groups such as Media Action Network for Asian Americans reveal, coalition represents a community of unequivocally shared feeling, one that would foreclose the ambiguities of irony. Yet, ironically, that feeling is one shared by fans of kawaii: sincerity.

Pathos of Things: Cute Typing, Racial Profiling

> Recently, an expression that keeps coming to mind as I work with my clients [on decluttering] is *mono no aware*. This Japanese term, which literally means "pathos of things," . . . also refers to the essence of things and our ability to feel that essence.
> —Marie Kondo, *Spark Joy*

At the millennium, one might say that there can be no minor affects surrounding race. Likewise, exploring the personification of things may seem trivial in regard to its opposite, understanding the thingification of persons as a result of capitalist reification. And contrary to my argument here, situating personified Asianized objects as a repository for ambivalent feeling might well be met with plausible denial: to some, Pucca, sumo, and Mr. Chin (see figures 2.3, 2.6, and 2.7) are simply racist. In highlighting the split desiring structures they encode, I may very well be risking my own credentials: one could not simultaneously *like* the Mandarin (see figure 2.2) or be a Harajuku lover (see figure 2.5) and claim to be an Asian Americanist. Moreover, in ethnic studies, investigating stereotyping and caricature can appear somewhat passé.[42] That is, the predetermined outcome of stereotype analysis (inaccurate, outrageous, racist) has ironically become a stereotype of the field itself. "Taking offense" followed up with boycotts may be seen as complicit with ethnic management and consumerist logic by limiting the public text of race activism.

Yet the individual's spectatorship of anthropomorphic things has political consequence for understanding one's attachment to the collective. Blogger Timmy's and historian Goings's affection for racialized things is not a sign of introjected racist love; rather, it represents a means of alternative if ambivalent collective affirmation circulated through the nonhuman. Mini-figs and cookie jars are degraded versions of their racial selves that they choose to love anyway. Their pleasure offers an affirmative response to the question I posed in this book's introduction: As an Asian American, can I racist love a geisha car? (See figure Intro.1.)

The racialized personification of things compels our attention, I argue, particularly as it invites an examination of the desiring structures that underlie the stereotype as pernicious racial form. Like the boycott of Abercrombie and Fitch, campus protests over ethnic Halloween costumes succeeded in reinforcing liberal belief in the injurious nature of caricature but did not push discussion beyond a safety/free speech framework predicated on a loss of rights on both sides. But I would highlight the raised stakes of these protests by linking them to contemporaneous and more highly publicized actions over systemic police violence in the Black Lives Matter movement, violence initiated by misrecognition. That is, Asian Americans' spotlight on the mimetic, harmful effects of caricature's economical reduction represents an analog to racial profiling, the source of discriminatory police violence against Black and Latinx men. George Floyd, Eric Gardner, Trayvon Martin, Michael Brown, and Tony Robinson were seen as interchangeable; they became the targets of undue discipline because of the emotions and expectations that accrue to *type*. The emotion produced by the stereotype of Black youthful masculinity obviously differs in valence (negative), arousal (excited), dominance (out of control) from the racial form I've engaged here. Yet I would stress that both unveil a continuum of racial feeling enabled by the paradox of simultaneous reduction and exaggeration, that is, projecting a fixity of racial types. However differently it materializes across communities of color in the United States, the stereotype is a conduit of racial feeling with varying stakes.

Whether in the form of belittling racial caricature intrinsic to mammy cookie jars and Harajuku perfume bottles or in the projection of carceral subjects to be feared, racial typing increases feelings of control or dominance through fixed meaning. To be clear, I am not suggesting that consumer boycotts are equivalent to mass protests surrounding surveillance and challenges to the state's "legitimate" use of force: being offended by a Snapchat filter is not equal to being shot in the street. Black Lives Matter exposed racism to be, in Ruth Wilson Gilmore's (2006, 28) terms, "the state-sanctioned or extralegal production and exploitation of group-differentiated vulnerability to premature death." Here, racial vulnerability is a matter of survival, not the perceived vulnerability of the childlike that precipitates care. But it is not the outcome, stakes, scale, or *content* of racialization that I want to emphasize here. Rather, racial profiling, like racial caricature, represents a specific desiring structure: it fixes racial meaning through repetition to produce the illusion of control. Race triggers the *d* for *dominance* in the VAD.

This is, then, the payoff to looking at racial feeling in a minor key: it establishes yet another piece to the puzzle about how race in the United States works as a latent structure of feeling. The psychoanalytic foundations of affect theory here are enhanced by social psychology's tripart axes, or intersection of modes of feeling surrounding racial perception. Both provide critical tools for contemporary CRT that illuminate the millennial United States as a cultural terrain suffused with overt and concealed longing for and fear of nonwhite (no)bodies and highlight the need for continued investment in comparative racialization. Operating on seemingly opposite sides of an affective continuum, affection and fear nevertheless contribute to differential racialization through, in Ahmed's (2004, 120) terms, "'sticky' associations" that accrue to populations within an economy of feeling, the valuation of things within a network of emotional effects. Cute things allow for feelings of dominance, if not also sadistic pleasure. Yet cuteness also paradoxically represents an aesthetic of anti-Asian bias in part because satire depends on an *elevated* target. That is, cuteness is status leveling.

My goal has thus been to call into account the ways in which objects become "risky" social actants as they are wrested from global circulation into the context of US spectatorship informed by the legacy of movement activism. While it is beyond the scope of this chapter to engage the meanings that these largely East Asian figures circulate within uneven geopolitical and cultural formations across Asia and the Pacific Rim, I would note that kawaii's capacity to veil national origins in keeping with the philosophy of mukokuseki may very well originate with the history of Japanese imperialism in the region as much as representing an address to the West. Here, I read racialized cute things as symptom, as reflecting an anxiety about who directs flows of neoliberal capital and from where. Anthropomorphic kawaii things haunt the seamless movement of global commodities with the residues of colonial fantasy; in this sense, they resurrect the Yellow Peril stereotype in a new, seemingly innocuous form.

As Latour (2005, 79) notes, "To be accounted for, objects have to enter into accounts. If no trace is produced, they offer no information to the observer and will have no visible effect on other agents. They remain silent and are no longer actors: they remain, literally, unaccountable." I make no claims here about the radical agency of the nonhuman as in speculative realism, aspects of which, as I suggest in the introduction, share common ground with Marie Kondo's Shinto-derived, inadvertently antiphenomenological belief in the absolute essence of things. Rather, I hope to account for one blind spot in theorizing the nonhuman: the attribution of *thingness* as it fundamentally underlies the pleasures of typing. Anthropologist Lawrence Hirschfeld (1988, 628) once noted that race and ethnicity are "psychologically privileged" insofar as they are seen to be "inalienable aspects of a person's being." The anthropomorphic objects of this chapter invert and reinforce this privileging: racial meaning is now part of the seemingly "inalienable aspects" of things.

Caricature has been subject to public censure for good reason. "Today, in the face of the emergence of new racism and sexism," Slavoj Žižek (1997) writes, "the strategy should be to *make such enunciation unutterable*, so that anyone relying on them automatically disqualifies himself" (34, emphasis mine). In the United States, Donald Trump's presidential candidacy in 2016 ruptured covenants surrounding the prohibition of hate speech to capitalize on religious and racial typing as a source of fear. More complexly, that prohibition may indeed enable *new* pleasures surrounding racism and sexism, as taboo creates the very conditions for desire. Freud ([1905] 1989, 167) noted that enjoyment of the hostile joke "is not only that produced by the joke: it is incomparably greater," as a "hitherto suppressed purpose has succeeded in making its way through." That is, humor is heightened by the forbidden; part of the pleasure resides in "lifting inhibition" (169).

Taking pleasure in race—or in this case, the semblance of race—through the diminutive kitsch figurine unveils the larger stakes underlying the US racial imaginary in the context of globalization, specifically, how we enjoy difference and how we fear it. The racist cute engages a specific desiring structure akin to fetishism: pleasure that masks anxiety. The mascot is a "hiding place" for the libido, a fantasy projection in which we invest emotion. Indeed, along with extended references to magic, enchantment, and the occult, the OED defines *mascot* as a personified animal or thing seen to bring luck; for *Merriam-Webster*, *fetish* is a synonym for *mascot*.[43] The cute allows for an attachment that veils an untoward enjoyment in asymmetries of social power, the very pleasure that underlies caricature itself. Kawaii style helps evade the prohibitions placed on racial desires in the twenty-first century through positive feeling, perhaps controversially, for multiple sites of spectatorship. The anthropomorphic Asianized object reveals how the "pathos of things" is likewise bound to racial pleasures. Seduced by our toys, we allow cute Asianized things to travel where the Frito Bandito and Chief Wahoo cannot follow.

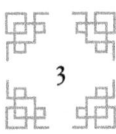

3

ASIAN • FEMALE • ROBOT • SLAVE

Techno-Orientalism after #MeToo

Racist Love has been concerned with how anthropomorphic things mobilize racial feeling; in the previous chapter, cuteness enables an asymmetrical relation of care. The field of social robotics deliberately solicits those affective bonds through specific forms of AI embodiment. A case in point, the small humanoid robot NAO (figure 3.1). "Who is NAO?" queried its maker. "NAO is intended to be a friendly companion around the house.... Since his birth in 2006, he has been constantly evolving to please, amuse, understand and love you. In short, to one day become your friend."[1] PARO, a therapy robot designed as a purring seal, provides companionship for the elderly.[2] Like Sony's mechanical dog AIBO and the diminutive anthropomorphic machines Robi,

FIGURE 3.1 NAO, humanoid robot by Aldebaran, 2006

Kirobo, and RoboHon, NAO is designed to be your pal.³ Here, artificial intelligence, or AI, evolves to serve the emotional needs of human beings; the goal of companion machines is to build bonds of sympathy and trust with technology.⁴ If humanoid robots instill relations of trust, cute robots likewise refigure the task-based instrumentalism of machines into relations of intimacy and attachment.⁵

Japan remains in the vanguard of social robotics, a field that contrasts with the development of weaponized AI in the United States. This "robot gap" may well reflect a difference in the cultural perceptions of machine life: in Japan, the robot is "a hero," while in the West, it is a threat.⁶ In the United States, growing dependency on machines at the millennium circulates negative feeling; tellingly, Isaac Asimov's (1950) "Three Laws of Robotics" imagines the coexistence of humans and robots through the lens of competition, explicitly establishing a human-nonhuman caste system.[7] More prosaically, technology produces any number of real-world anxieties: job losses to mechanization that foretell the obsolescence of human labor, privacy erosions via data collection, the dangers of driverless cars and weaponized drones alike (see, e.g., Havens 2016). In 2015, the United Nations and robotics researchers called for a preemptive ban on autonomous artificially intelligent weapons—in other words, a ban on killer robots.[8]

Racial feeling surrounding technology coalesces in what David Morley and Kevin Robins (1995) deemed "techno-Orientalism," the projection of an Asianized, simulated future coincident with Japanese innovations in electronics, automobiles, gaming, AI, and robotics in the 1980s. Fueled by perceptions of economic ascendency in Asia prior to the 1997 financial crisis, techno-Orientalism names a speculative future in which apocalypse invariably invokes a Pacific Rim, posthuman dystopia governed by irrational feudalism, Fu Manchu's techno-superiority dangerously tethered to atavistic barbarism. Even as US fears surrounding techno-Orientalism dissipated in Japan's postbubble collapse, the trope survives. At the millennium, the racialized templates of the Yellow Peril and techno-Orientalist panic converge in the specter of a machinelike, unending, self-replicating alien labor force. As numerous scholars in Asian American studies reveal, US techno-Orientalism is inextricably tied to immigration and the projection of "alien" landscapes.[9] If in the nineteenth century the fantasy of automatons was symptomatic of the "dreams and nightmares of societies under-going rapid technological change" (Wosk 1992, 79), it now serves as a screen for Western worry over eastward-facing globalism.

Techno-Orientalism has come to refer to a futurist aesthetic, cyberpunk or otherwise.[10] I would argue that it also engages a specific affective structure; techno-Orientalism is tech feeling as anti-Asian bias. Techno-Orientalist discourse, Morley and Robins (1995, 169) suggest, projects a mutated human experience that is "cold, impersonal and machine-like ... lacking emotional connection to the rest of the world," "the Japanese as inhuman" (170). The West's ambivalence surrounding Asianized posthumanism is expressed through the repetition of the same old stories "told (compulsively) again and afresh" (Bhabha 1994, 77), here reinscribing Asian inscrutability. In triggering both phobia and philia, the techno-Orientalist visual aesthetic and its accompanying modes of narration quintessentialize the fetishistic structure of what I have been calling racist love: anxiety transformed into pleasure.

In contrast, Japanese artists situate machines as helpful companions, from Osamu Tezuka's Astro Boy to engineers at Toyota designing doll-like robot friends to sit in your cup holder and assist your driving. In the documentary *The Human Robot* (2015), Japanese roboticists cite the influence of Shinto in accounting for the affective difference between East and West concerning automatons. "Robot sociologist" Naho Kitano explains that material objects have some sort of soul or spirit distinct from Christian understanding; within all things, she notes, there is "something there in [an] ontological way." A former AIBO engineer likewise attests, "For the Japanese people, every object has a soul."[11] As in Marie Kondo's notion of possessions living lives under their owners' care, communication with the nonhuman addresses its independent life essence; interaction with things is experienced as a social relationship where the goal is not control or mastery but attachment. Or to use a stronger word, love.

Social robotics thus troubles philosopher John R. Searle's (1990, 31) assertion that "the basic premise of strong AI is that the physical features of the implementing medium are totally irrelevant."[12] The posthuman, N. Katherine Hayles (1999, 2–3) notes, "privileges informational pattern over material instantiation"; the body is merely an "original prosthesis we all learn to manipulate." Philosopher Gilbert Ryle's metaphor critiquing Cartesian mind-body dualism, the "ghost in the machine," is often misappropriated to further the idea that the "machine," or body, is irrelevant to the "ghost," or programming.[13] In keeping with my exploration of the pleasures surrounding nonhuman anthropomorphism, this chapter begins with a deceptively simple question: Why imagine AI as having a body at all?

Social robotics offers one answer: the cuteness of the diminutive humanoid or animal form scripts a specific relationship to AI, inviting a certain type of intimacy. This chapter explores how this affective association shifts along with human attributes—race, gender, sexuality, age, ability, nationality, morphology—ascribed to machines. Far from the idea that advances in artificial intelligence render bodies irrelevant, sociality scripts relationships to technology particularly when, as I consider here, it is imagined in the form of young, able-bodied, heterosexual, cisgender East Asian women.

In Anglophone speculative fiction and popular media alike, the Asian female cyborg has become somewhat ubiquitous. The term *gynoid* was used by Gwyneth A. Jones in 1984 to describe her female protagonist, Cho, in the postapocalyptic Pacific Rim novel *Divine Endurance*. Reflecting the possibilities of excessive symbolism reflected in the introduction's image of the mehndied cyborg (see figure Intro.2), in recent dystopian fiction, Asian female clones, gynoids, or species hybrids inhabit the futuristic landscapes of Larissa Lai's *Salt Fish Girl* (2002), David Mitchell's *Cloud Atlas* (2004), Brian K. Vaughn and Fiona Staples's *Saga* (2012), Paolo Bacigalupi's *The Windup Girl* (2015), and Marjorie Liu and Sana Takeda's *Monstress* (2015) and, to a lesser extent, Kazuo Ishiguro's *Klara and the Sun* (2021). At the opening of the twenty-first century, visual media imagining Asianized "sexaroids" (*Ghost in the Shell 2: Innocence*); "skin jobs" (*Battlestar Galactica*); "fabricants" (*Cloud Atlas*); "synths" (*Humans*); AI (*Ex Machina*); "hosts" (*Westworld*); or "sleeves" (*Altered Carbon*), not to mention the "robogeishas" of the over-the-top Japanese B-movie *RoboGeisha* (2009), all reflect the techno-Orientalist foundations of cyberpunk.[14] Moreover, artificial beings are not merely imagined to be young, Asian, and female but are built that way; the ubiquity of East Asian gynoids in popular culture dovetails with artificially intelligent robot prototypes created in Japan, China, Canada, South Korea, and the UK.[15]

It may be obvious that humanoid machines offer easy analogies to those deemed to be lesser beings in specific historical moments: women, immigrants, slaves, children, the disabled. Automata, for example, are invariably gendered female, reflecting the long-standing tradition of animated dolls and statues who take the form of beautiful young women. From the myth of Pygmalion to *The Stepford Wives*, female objectification is literalized in the fantasy of man-as-god creating the "perfect" woman.[16] GPS apps and digital assistants such as Apple's Siri and Amazon's Alexa are female voiced all the better to reflect their status as toys and servants subject to command.[17] In keeping with racial abstraction, specific humanoid embodiment of AI triggers expected behaviors and presumed interiority as the machine drives perception of the ghost. Visual media engaging Asianized AI tap into common beliefs surrounding Asian women in the West: innocent and passive yet willing to please; sexually desirable but curiously lacking sexual desire; marvelously enhanced yet emotionally fragile. As in previous chapters, the nonhuman things of this chapter likewise circulate racial meaning through pleasurable types.[18] More specifically, Asian women perform as parahuman figures that, through the history of sexual bondage in the second half of the twentieth century, evoke an already compromised agency.

The first part of this chapter explores the added value of portraying technology embodied as Asian and female in AI representations that exemplify what I identify as the techno-Orientalist neoslave narrative, a genre reflective of both the neoslave narrative in contemporary African American literature and techno-erotic scopophilia.[19] According to Raquel Kennon (2017), the "neo-slave narrative" is a literary genre emerging in the 1960s and 1970s that harkens back to the history of transatlantic slavery in the New World and originated with Bernard Bell's *The Afro-American Novel and Its Tradition* in 1987. Bill Brown's (2006, 199) reading of the figure of the slave who is ambiguously both subject and object links the experience of the "American uncanny" to race: "for U.S. law the slave becomes the source of uncanny anxiety" in the eighteenth and nineteenth centuries as they posed "the riddle of person or thing." In portrayals of mecha women in need of rescue, that riddle becomes literalized. The techno-Orientalist neoslave narrative relies on a mode of emplotment that does not simply require mapping human qualities onto things, but calls on specific qualities assigned to specific types of humanity, in this case, affective associations derived from the twentieth-century discourse of global human trafficking in Asia. Depicting the forced servitude of engineered beings, AI narratives reinforce paradoxical belief in both the techno-danger of the Orient and the racial-gendered vulnerability of Asian women.[20] Real or imagined, nonthreatening service bots mitigate fears surrounding advanced, potentially uncontrollable technology. As with the animal and child forms of social robots, AI imagined as worthy of care offset the specter of superior, enhanced mechanized beings.

Speculative fiction and visual media can productively imagine the reorganization of social identities through bodily flexibility, shape-shifting, or human-machine hybridity. "Science fiction is where you can be anything," says Dorothy Allison. "You can transgress in terms of gender, in terms of the body, in terms of imagination. You could be anything."[21] World making allows for the promise of upending established racial and gender epistemologies that assume connections between interiority and surface. And yet they can also rely on these tropes, tethering imagined beings to stereotypical race and gender associations—ironically at the moment that they envision the body's transcendence. At first glance, the robot fantasies of this chapter depend on the specifically racialized pleasures of techno-scopophilia at odds with the promise of feminist conceptualizations of the posthuman at the foundations of feminist science and technology studies (STS).[22] Donna Haraway's "A Cyborg Manifesto: Science, Technology, and Socialist-Feminism in the Late Twentieth Century," first conceived in 1983 and republished in 1991, and N. Katherine Hayles's *How We Became Posthuman: Virtual Bodies in Cybernetics, Literature, and Informatics* (1999) both signal the importance of an antihumanist perspective in dismantling the alibis of universality and species hierarchy. A figure of potential rupture within the millennial shift to an "informatics of domination," Haraway's (1991, 50) cyborg represents a "crucial, political" fiction: "The cyborg is a kind of disassembled and reassembled, postmodern collective and personal self," she writes, "This is the self feminists must code" (55). For Hayles (1999, 287), the posthuman does not spell the end of humanity: "It signals instead the end of a certain conception of the human, a conception that may have applied, at best, to that fraction of humanity who has the wealth, power, and leisure to conceptualize themselves as autonomous beings exercising their will through individual agency and choice. What is lethal is not the posthuman as such but the grafting of the posthuman onto a liberal humanist view of the self." Indeed, AI trafficking narratives extend the notion of human rights to categorically ambiguous things in ways that ultimately work to affirm that narrow vision of a rights-bearing subject.

Nevertheless, the reliance of posthumanism on liberal humanism need not represent an entirely "lethal" view of the posthuman. In the second part of the chapter, both real and imagined embodied AI invite analogies between computer programming and social conditioning as the conventions of human caste hierarchy become mapped onto human/nonhuman encounters. Situating embodied AI through the lens of antitrafficking narratives asks us to consider *whose* autonomy is actually artificial, who is subject to and has always been subject to the will of others. The futurist techno-Orientalist neoslave narratives of this chapter explore the structural constraints to self-possession, here imagined through the decidedly presentist if no less complex question of sexual consent. The viral social movement #MeToo, conceptualized by activist Tarana Burke and triggered by actress Alyssa Milano's 2017 tweet, resulted in a renewed sense of the ubiquity of women's and others' experiences with sexual harassment, abuse, and rape. The movement and legal cases it continues to ignite appear to be a far cry from the fantastical archive of this book. Yet in what follows, I situate racialized AI representation at the intersection of #MeToo and feminist STS to consider fantasy's reliance on a social matrix, how imagining a posthuman future relies on scripts of the present. Advances in artificial intelligence may invite weighty philosophical considerations about object ontology and machine being as well as the hubris of human exceptionalism. This chapter invokes AI to unveil another manifestation of "man's" hubris: entitlement. More specifically, the right to touch.

To highlight the reduction of human life under capitalism, philosopher Erich Fromm (1955, 360) once cautioned, "The danger of the past was that men became slaves. The danger of the future is that men may become robots." This chapter explores the pleasures of imagining those terrors through a curious reversal, a future in which both slaves and robots have become Asian women.

The Techno-Orientalist Neoslave Narrative: Saving Virtual Women

Gender and Asian cultural difference lie at the foundations of assessing machine intelligence. In 1950, Alan Turing, pioneer of modern computer science, conceptualized what became known as the Turing test, developed to determine whether a machine could be said to approximate human behavior. Yet in its original conception, the "imitation game" was an exercise in gender passing. An isolated interrogator was asked to assess the gender of two individuals, a man (A) and a woman (B), through their written answers to the interrogator's questions. Without seeing the body, can one know the mind? Turing (1950, 434) took the conceit of gender passing further, asking, "What will happen when a machine takes the part of A in this game?" His famous test of artificial intelligence, whether a computer program could deceive human judges into believing it too was human, was founded on a deception regarding *social* identity, gender as it was presumed to be binary, fixed, and knowable if also, in this case, beyond the material body.[23] Similarly, the thought experiment devised to refute the notion of strong AI likewise calls on differences among human beings: philosopher John R. Searle's (1990) "the Chinese room."

Reflecting the Turing test's structure in which written communication is passed between participants in separate rooms, Searle's model for disproving machine thinking hinges on the difference between linguistic structure and semantics—as well as an implicit Orientalism. In his provocative parable, a person who does not know Chinese is given a rule book for matching Chinese ideographs and sorting them into logical strings. Outside the room, writers fluent in Chinese submit text, requiring the nonliterate person inside to respond by manipulating Chinese characters according to the rule book. In Searle's conception, the book functions as an analogy to a computer program, which would merely generate the semblance of language by applying its structural logic. This, he argued, did not represent thought: "Manipulating the symbols is not by itself enough to guarantee cognition, perception, understanding, thinking and so forth" (Searle 1990, 26). An exercise in abstraction, the thought experiment is nevertheless premised on comprehending a racial stereotype: Asian inscrutability, the idea that "Chinese writing looks like so many meaningless squiggles" (26). Gender and Orientalism lie at the philosophical foundations of testing artificial intelligence, conjoining the seemingly dispassionate logic of a writing system with the projection of a confounding incomprehensibility, of absolute difference. As I discuss later, for Searle, that difference carried erotic charge.

The legibility of machine intelligence is thus tethered to sociality even as, at its most lofty, the ideal of strong AI intends to transcend it. Moreover, passing as human depends on a machine's ability to sustain the tension between sameness to and difference from a single, prototypical human subject: a white, middle-class, educated, cisgender Anglophone adult man, largely the adjudicator of real (and imagined) experiments. This contingency was cleverly anticipated in a Turing test held outside London in 2014. There, a chatbot posing as a thirteen-year-old Ukrainian boy named Eugene Goostman was presumed to have passed the Turing test. In the course of a series of five-minute online conversations, the chatbot convinced 33 percent of human judges that it was human. The program's scripted identity as an adolescent, nonnative English speaker was strategically communicated to imply a range of knowledge, a confident insistence regarding that knowledge, and limitations to knowing. As Eugene, the chatbot "can claim that he knows anything, but his age also makes it perfectly reasonable that he doesn't know everything."[24] So too, I would add, does its gender. That is, the projection of a social matrix would presume to help human judges reconcile the AI's conversational limitations and logical inconsistencies as well as its projected confidence. Who better to convey potential nonsense with the air of certainty than a teenage boy?

As a hypothetical counter to Turing's test, "the Chinese room" hinged on Searle's (1990, 31) insistence on the difference between appearance and being, simulation and ontology: "How could anyone have supposed that a computer simulation of a mental process must be the real thing?" he asked. In the same moment, other philosophers were beginning to trouble the very line between simulation and the real; the year following Searle's controversial model, philosopher Jean Baudrillard ([1981] 1994) collapsed the real into the hyperreal; nearly ten years later, Judith Butler ([1990] 2004, 187) theorized gender as an approximated performance situating the meat body as "syntactically regulated phantasm." Turing's early indifference to the distinction between the real and the simulated enabled his shift away from the question, "Can a machine think?" toward an emphasis on relationality and engagement, AI tested via its sociality.

The success of Eugene Goostman aside, machines approximating human consciousness, strong AI, do not yet exist.[25] Yet *artificial intelligence*, a term coined by computer scientist John McCarthy in 1955, represented, McCarthy hoped, the context for considering weighty questions about machine ontology. Throughout his career, he maintained a vision for AI beyond the reality of chess-playing computers with which he had begun. Research on AI in the United States has since developed along more practical than conceptual lines, a point that ultimately disappointed him.[26] The instrumentalist turn to developing task-focused outcomes—information-processing algorithms predicting consumer tastes, driverless cars, robotic vacuum cleaners—sidelined his hope of approximating human intelligence through technology. Artificial intelligence in the United States would focus on machines that would *do* rather than machines who would *be*.[27]

In contrast, creative considerations of AI maintain a robust life by taking on philosophical questions about sentience posed generations earlier in European imagining of the automaton.[28] Speculative AI narratives imagining machines animated by some notion of complex consciousness approximating that of human beings explore themes of immortality and bodily flexibility. These tropes provide the foundation for the scripted dramas below that likewise exemplify the techno-Orientalist neoslave narrative. In each, however, sentience turns out to be a red herring.

- *Ghost in the Shell 2: Innocence* (2004): Mamoru Oshii's sequel to his 1995 anime *Ghost in the Shell*, adapting Shirow Masamune's manga series, features Batou, a cyborg detective who must solve the mystery of why *sexaroids*, female sex robots, begin killing their masters. With the help of his former partner Major Kusanagi, now AI and flexibly embodied, Batou speculates that the murders are a result of disruptive hacking or malware. Yet the viewer has already been privy to one clue, a murderous bot who, prior to self-destructing, emits the message, "Help me." The detectives uncover a conspiracy involving young women kidnapped into white slavery, their consciousnesses downloaded into mechanical life forms.[29] The sexaroids are Japanese.
- *Cloud Atlas* (2012): In the Wachowskis' film adaptation of David Mitchell's 2004 novel, *fabricants* are bred to serve humans in postapocalyptic Neo Seoul. A labor force genomed to be docile, female fabricants are lab-created entities bred for service. The clones are destined to repeat a twenty-four-hour cycle of waking, disinfecting, waitressing, imbibing nutrients, and sleeping as they exist in what amounts to forced servitude, a gulag. The story follows one fabricant, Son-Mi 451, who sets out to discover the truth of her existence, becoming a Joan of Arc of sorts, a prophet and liberator. The fabricants are South Korean (figure 3.2).[30]

FIGURE 3.2 Fabricants from the Wachowskis' *Cloud Atlas*, 2012

- *Humans* (2015): In the BBC/AMC adaptation of the Swedish television series *Äkta Människor*, or *Real Humans* (2014), *synths* are manufactured to provide any number of services from agricultural labor to more intimate roles as physical therapists, prostitutes, and nannies in a near-future UK.[31] The synth Anita is purchased to work as a domestic and caregiver in the home of an overworked lawyer, her husband, and their three children. Like any other household appliance, Anita is to be used until obsolete; this includes sexual use. Yet "she" begins to display signs of sentience beyond her programming. The synth is East Asian in appearance.
- *Ex Machina* (2014): In a film written and directed by novelist Alex Garland, the protagonist, Caleb, has been invited to experiment with a reclusive tech mogul's latest development in artificial intelligence, Ava, formed as young, attractive, Caucasian, and female. Because the mogul, Nathan, has succeeded, his inventions, which include his Japanese maid Kyoko, are no longer objects but self-aware beings. Caleb discovers that these mechanized women have not only been sexually exploited but are being held against their will. After he conspires with Ava to plan her escape, he finds that she has double-crossed him, the surest sign that she has passed the Turing test.[32]

What distinguishes these scripted dramas depicting engineered beings is their reliance on East Asian female embodiment to further plots of bondage and liberation. Clones and AI perform as the incarnation of the voiceless, hypersexualized, and hyperembodied: as servants and toys, they are literally *sex objects*. As their plotlines introduce an intellectual confusion about the difference between persons and things, workers and tools, at first glance, they serve as commentaries on labor reification, most graphically, sexual labor. Fembots and clones are docile workers until, inevitably, a special, unique AI develops sentience and becomes aware of its, or more appropriately, *her*, bondage. Their transformation from potentially malevolent entities into vulnerable beings worthy of ethical concern is enabled through reductive typing; in these fantasy renderings, Asian female embodiment is a visual shorthand for powerlessness. Ironically, these depictions of artificial intelligence are rarely about "intelligence" or rationality: on the contrary, they rely on soliciting emotional urgency surrounding Asian women's sexual precarity, in short, on igniting racialized affect. The appearance of Asian women's bodies in speculative media depicting synths, fabricants, or sleeves often inhabiting a pan-Asian, Pacific Rim dystopia invariably calls forth a narrative about servitude and liberation, the hallmark of the techno-Orientalist neoslave narrative.

The term *neoslave narrative* describes contemporary African American literary imagining of US slavery. Madhu Dubey (2010, 784) points to its subgenre in speculative fiction to suggest that nonrealist accounts of slavery "best comprehend the truth of slavery by abandoning historical modes of knowing." The narratives of techno-futurism suggest an alternative racial and temporal focus even as they harken back to the plotlines established in nineteenth-century abolitionist literature: from depictions of mistreatment, to consciousness of one's abject condition, to an attempted escape that ends in liberation or death. Speculative narratives enlisting this mode of emplotment call forth a more contemporary referent: human trafficking, specifically, global sex trafficking in the twentieth and twenty-first centuries. This parallelism has already incited controversy. The 2019 publication of the young adult novel *Blood Heir* was voluntarily postponed by its Chinese American author, Amélie Wen Zhao, amid rumors of anti-Blackness in the novel's metaphorical treatment of slavery. In apology, Zhao explained that her world building drew on the context of indentured labor and human trafficking in Asia, including that of her birth country, China.[33]

Slavery is a strong word.[34] Yet the US State Department invokes the Thirteenth Amendment abolishing involuntary servitude in 1865 to describe contemporary human trafficking, particularly of women and girls into prostitution.[35] The US Trafficking Victims Protection Act (2000), for example, expands antislavery laws and Thirteenth Amendment protections to reflect modern forms of coercion:

(a) sex trafficking in which a commercial sex act is induced by force, fraud, or coercion, or in which the person induced to perform such an act has not attained 18 years of age; or
(b) the recruitment, harboring, transportation, provision, or obtaining of a person for labor or services, through the use of force, fraud, or coercion for the purpose of subjection to involuntary servitude, peonage, debt bondage, or slavery.[36]

The United States adds to this list domestic servitude and child labor, including the use of child soldiers. The Asian Pacific Institute on Gender-Based Violence goes further to include forms of exploitation such as "fraudulent adoption, prostitution, pornography, commercial sexual exploitation, organ removal/harvesting, involuntary servitude, servile marriages, and transporting drugs, where trafficked individuals serve as drug mules."[37] As awareness of "modern" slavery is rendered global and contemporary in the traffic in women and children, it is not so much deracinated as newly racinated.

Twenty-first-century antitrafficking discourses have thus become Asianized, feminized, and associated with youth. According to the State Department, six hundred thousand to eight hundred thousand people were trafficked across international borders in 2004; 80 percent of these were women and girls, and up to 50 percent were minors. Of the forty-five thousand to fifty thousand persons brought *to* the United States, thirty thousand came from Asia. According to the Asian Pacific Institute on Gender-Based Violence, each year, "two million children are forced into prostitution, half of whom live in and are trafficked within Asia."[38] In 2017, 27 percent of human trafficking survivors in the United States accessing the US human trafficking hotline were Asian.[39] The image of the sexually victimized Asian girl or woman derives from the history of US imperialism and militarized prostitution at the latter half of the twentieth century as a result of the occupations of the Philippines, Japan, South Korea, and Vietnam. *Camptowns* springing up around brothels and R&R (rest and relaxation) facilities that surround US military bases in the Philippines, South Korea, Japan, and Thailand spawned the modern sex tourism industry.[40] Women in camptowns are reduced to sexual toys, in Ji-Yeon Yuh's (2002, 14) words, to "playthings easily bought and easily discarded." Most significantly, in the United States the association between Asian women and modern slavery also follows global awareness of *comfort women*, Korean, Filipino, Chinese, and Indonesian women conscripted by the Imperial Japanese Army to serve as sex slaves. An estimated two hundred thousand comfort women, 80 percent of whom were Korean, were held by the Imperial Japanese Army in brothels euphemistically deemed "comfort stations." The extent and severity of the atrocities came to global awareness as a result of Filipino and South Korean women's activism, which resulted in a widely publicized class action suit against the Japanese government filed by conscripted women in 1991 and 1993.[41] Nevertheless, as Laura Kang (2020, 15) cogently argues, "Both the supposed silence around Japanese military sexual slavery and the much-heralded breaking of that silence in the 1990s were forged by older racist and imperialist power/knowledge regimes that disqualified, segregated, and demoted 'Asian women' from both humanity and women."

If the US Constitution counted enslaved persons as part human, as three-fifths of a person, in twentieth-century and millennial dystopic imaginings of forced servitude, the other two-fifths is, of course, machine. The film *Ex Machina* (2014) summarized above relies on these historical associations to explore AI in what amounts to a Turing test for humanity: that is, the metric for human approximation is not empathy or attachment, but manipulation and deceit. Widely excoriated for fetishizing female bodies, the film invokes the history of US slavery in its portrayal of a Black female robotic body, as well as its twentieth-century iteration in images of a naked Asian-appearing AI expressing trauma in captivity.[42] At the film's climax, the protagonist Caleb accesses footage of these prototypes and discovers the truth about his boss Nathan's inhumanity toward his creations: he is not merely a puppet master but a slave master holding sentient beings against their will. Caleb and the viewer together watch a montage of damning surveillance footage in which white, Black, and Asian female bodies are dispassionately or violently manhandled by their creator. Screenwriter-director Alex Garland lent these prototypes names that are also things—Jasmine, Jade, Lily, and Amber—that likewise evoke the interplay between the exotic and familiar and their fetishistic objectification. Their nakedness puts them outside social relations, reinforcing their sexual, animal availability. Their racial diversity introduces an evolutionary element to the science experiment: Ava, the Caucasian model, is the most advanced iteration of AI; the film both relies on and naturalizes robot Darwinism through eugenicist echoes of evolution measured through seemingly progressive racial types.

Portrayed in a sequence of videotaped data surreptitiously accessed by Caleb, a scene featuring one such prototype is likewise a turning point for the viewer. The fembot Jade, played by Mongolian actress Gana Bayarsaikhan, questions its captivity more strenuously with each software update:

JADE V. 5.01: [*Seated, naked*] Why won't you let me out?
NATHAN: I already told you why. Because you're very special.
JADE V. 5.1.0: [*Similarly seated*] Why won't you let me out?
NATHAN: Are we going to do this again?
JADE V. 5.2.3: [*Standing, voice rising*] *Why won't you let me out?!*

In a graphic sequence depicting the evolving insistence, anger, and panic of each version of Jade, *Ex Machina* demonstrates the evolution of technological perfectibility as the progressive movement towards individuality: accelerated emotional expression and the exhibition of will. In the end, Jade repeatedly strikes the transparent cage that divides creator from creation, pounding with such ferocity that both its forearms detach in a moment of symbolic castration. Its—or now, *her*—depth of feeling, assertion of agency, and capacity for self-harm demonstrate a humanity intended to contrast that of her dispassionate creator. The viewer is asked to model Caleb's disgust and horror in witnessing the abjection of this traumatized, incarcerated being, a debasing portrayal that borders on the pornographic. While one might say that the scene conveys the very nakedness of human vulnerability and despair in captivity, in effect, its specific embodiment eroticizes that condition while rendering it legible to contemporary audiences. Jade's form is not necessary to convey the *nature* of strong AI; rather, it succeeds in graphing existing hierarchical social relations onto presumed things to telegraph a specific affective relation, one enabled through an implicit reference to twentieth-century sexual bondage and its human subjects.

Elsewhere, *Ex Machina* relies on Western associations with Asian difference to uphold narrative suspense about the intellectual uncertainty regarding the distinction between human and machine, distinct from uncanny feeling, what Ernst Jentsch ([1906] 1995) described as the uneasiness produced by doubt about the living status of inanimate objects. Silent and affectless, Kyoko is Nathan's female servant, who, to Caleb and the viewer, appears to be human. Because the actress who plays Kyoko, Sonoyo Mizuno, is all too real, within the film's visual logic, this uncertainty does not exactly produce uncanny feeling. Instead, the film trades on the ambiguity of interracialism (Mizuno

FIGURE 3.3 Sonoyo Mizuno as Kyoko, *Ex Machina*, 2015

is of Caucasian and Japanese descent) to hint at categorical confusion: is she or isn't she? (figure 3.3). Gender and race are harnessed to Kyoko's use as sex object, something the dialogue reinforces through bawdy double entendre: "She's some alarm clock, huh? Gets you right up in the morning." The feminist magazine *Bitch* notes that the film plays on stereotypes of Asian women as "sexy, servile, and self-sacrificing."[43] More specifically, race naturalizes Kyoko's subordination in its role as servant, providing both domestic and sexual labor. Belief in Asian women's docility likewise explains why, after the entity is revealed to be mechanical, unlike Ava, Kyoko does not need to be incarcerated. Its embodiment arguably clouds Nathan's judgment: he fatally underestimates the model.

Maintaining the fiction of robot passing, the film relies on other social assumptions that accrue to Kyoko's racial-gender form. Nathan attributes "her" inability to communicate to her lack of English fluency; he situates her supposed linguistic ignorance as a "firewall" that keeps trade secrets. The character's emotionlessness exploits another racial stereotype, allowing the audience to parse Kyoko's flat affect as a cultural trait: acting "robotic" and "acting Asian" as one and the same. That is, the film relies on Western associations with Asian inscrutability to maintain its human or machine tease. Racial-ethnic associations here are leveraged to enhance US imagination of a lesser being, both brilliantly and lazily accessorizing the fake Turing test that the film plays with its viewers. Dubey (2010, 802) has pointed to the ways in which African American writers of nonrealist neoslave narratives attempt to imagine "possible futures unbound by the racial scripts of the past"; in contrast, the pleasures of the techno-Orientalist neoslave narratives like *Ex Machina* remain tethered to the past.

Visual fantasies of techno-Orientalist neoslavery like *Ex Machina* enable two seemingly contradictory pleasures: witnessing exploitation (imagined as eroticized bondage) and witnessing its transcendence (imagined as rescue). The spectator observes violence against women with the assurance that they are not, in fact, women. Yet viewers do not see the physical abuse, rape, or murder of *things*; we see these enacted on the actresses enlisted to play them. This disconnect allows for a specific indulgence: voyeuristic pleasure in traumatized women rendered unreal through fantasy's distancing and suspension of disbelief. Thus, enjoying the repetition of racial type, Asian women as sexually vulnerable, conjoins with the pleasure of watching eroticized violence while assuming the sympathetic identificatory position of the film's white heterosexual male protagonist, Caleb. In this sense, eroticized techno-scopophilia is not really "techno" at all; robot-thingness represents an alibi for much more conventional visual pleasures. That identificatory position enables an intellectual critique of exploitation while enjoying naked (non)women and anticipating another scene of pleasurable violence: technology nurtured toward vengeance.

In the end, the existentially ambiguous question about machine ontology, in Graham Harman's (2002) terms, "tool-being," turns out to be a red herring; response to female precarity is the metric for adjudicating the "humanity" of individual men. While *Ex Machina* purports to explore grand philosophical ideas about the border between human and machine, it passes neither the Turing test nor the Bechdel test.[44]

Speculative fantasies conveying the horrors of slavery and violation through the possession of mechanized or cloned women replicate narratives surrounding humanitarian advocacy in the real world. In charting the stories told by nongovernmental organizations (NGOs) and global antitrafficking activists, Rutvica Andrijasevic and Nicola Mai (2016, 3) identify a specific pattern of narration: "The mythological function of the trafficking narrative and the victim figure are most visible in the fact that the trafficking plot never varies; it starts with deception, which is followed by coercion into prostitution, moves on to the tragedy of (sexual) slavery and finally finds resolution through the rescue of the victim by the police or an NGO." The contemporary trafficking narrative echoes the plot conventions of abolitionist literature a century earlier (mistreatment, consciousness of bondage, escape, public advocacy). Paolo Bacigalupi's techno-dystopian Pacific Rim novel about global food precarity in futurist Thailand, *The Windup Girl* (2015), conjoins both conventions. If Thailand is not the most obvious setting for imagining catastrophic climate change, given its sex industry, it serves as an appropriate location for techno-Orientalist reimaging of (non)human trafficking. Emiko, a high-end Japanese-made gynoid geisha, finds herself thrown away by her owner and forced to find work as a dancer-prostitute in Bangkok's low-end red-light district. Deviating from narratives of humanitarian advocacy, *The Windup Girl* dispenses with deception into prostitution; as AI, Emiko has been manufactured and programmed for this purpose, a conceit that allows Bacigalupi to render, in loving detail, rape-induced orgasm. Through his use of free indirect discourse, the reader is also privy to the protagonist's abuse, physical pain, existential despair, and thus her sentience. Bacigalupi's portrayal of AI oppression here echoes accounts of the abject status of prostitutes living outside US military bases in South Korea. On the soldiers' views of these women, a US military chaplain testifies, "They were property, things, slaves.... The men don't see the women as human beings—they're disgusting, things to be thrown away" (quoted in Moon 1997, 34).

As in real-world antitrafficking narratives, AI dystopias promise deliverance in more spectacular fashion than NGO or police intervention: graphic revenge spectacles enabled by enhanced robot physicality. Emiko rebels against her sexual use, unwittingly murdering a politically significant john, and moves to escape, predictably, *north* to uncertain sanctuary. As in its visual media counterparts, the techno-Orientalist neoslave novel *The Windup Girl* depicts female sexual exploitation and the struggle to hold property within the self as a prelude to violent *ressentiment*. Here, AI fantasy operates at the nexus of split feeling, inciting both the philic and phobic, dominance and fears of being dominated. Depictions of violence in such narratives are further sanitized by the promise of liberation from futurist gulags.

Nonhuman Rights

Part of the pleasures surrounding antitrafficking AI stories lies in the repetition of familiar racial types. Yet their depiction of machines come to life also has the ability to offer a somewhat obvious critique of the for-profit value of human life under neoliberalism. Posthumanism, Bill Brown (2006, 183) suggests, "has made modernity's distinction between human subjects and inanimate objects appear increasingly artificial," likewise a condition of neoliberal capitalism. Stories of AI bondage imagine this blurring as a version of machine biopolitics, highlighting its gendered and racial connotations in ways that echo Haraway's (1991, 166) remarks on the mechanization of the human body within a capitalist global economy: "To be feminized means to be made extremely vulnerable; able to be disassembled, reassembled, exploited as a reserve labour force." Indeed, speculative imaginings such as the BBC's *Humans* literalize this reassembly, depicting the ways in which mechanized workers who outlive their value become recycled or stripped for parts. In its literary and visual forms, *Cloud Atlas* visualizes post-Fordist work as feminized, repetitive service labor while portraying the bioengineered body as itself a *product* of the assembly line, with the expectation of planned obsolescence. As part of their not-so-thinly veiled political message, speculative fiction and media expose a Darwinian world lacking commitment to redistributive justice.

In dystopian Pacific Rim fiction, human workers inhabit a machinelike existence: Larissa Lai's *Salt Fish Girl* (2002) depicts genomed workers tolling in an ersatz Nike factory. Chang-rae Lee's *On Such a Full Sea* (2014) portrays its female protagonist as a cog in the machine of global food production in the service of the 1 percent. The fantasy novel was inspired by Lee's visit to a Shenzhen factory in China's Pearl River Delta Economic Zone, where assembly lines are staffed entirely by young female workers aged sixteen to twenty. The novel's stratified globalized economy took its cue from the lives of these Chinese workers, whose ten-hour days are devoted to a single product, in this case, tiny motors for DVD trays and sideview mirrors. While Lee is clear that these factory campuses do not represent forced labor colonies, nevertheless, the pathos of his world building in *On Such a Full Sea* derives from witnessing life that is indistinguishable from work, women harnessed to an assembly line until their youth is used up.[45] They represent the other end of the continuum from Lynn Randolph's feminist STS, benignly techno-Orientalist painting *Cyborg*, her rendering of a serenely interfaced Chinese woman inspired by Haraway's "A Cyborg Manifesto" (1991) and, not uncoincidentally, modeled on an exchange student from Beijing.[46]

The techno-Orientalist trafficking narrative builds on the conceit of machine or clone interchangeability, the downside of the posthuman: not the Asian female piece worker harnessed to a machine, but the worker *as* machine. In this sense, techno-politics and biopolitics conjoin; they expose the inhumanity underlying the uneven development of global capitalism, in which biowomen are exploited until they are, like the extracted materials they process, depleted, broken, or obsolete. By and large, however, such narratives do not interrupt the liberal fantasy of autonomous personhood but merely extend it to things. Similarly, Andrijasevic and Mai (2016, 1) note that human rights advocacy runs the risk of sidelining structural inequalities that cause trafficking through an emphasis on the individual victims. "Humanitarian representations tend to frame victims as 'exceptions' rather than 'products' of the globalization of neoliberal politics." In fantastical counterparts to the trafficking narrative, sentience marks the "victim's" exception: not all AI are created equal. Artificially intelligent heroines are not like their "sister-servers"; in their self-awareness, ability to access memory, or emotional capacity—in other words, their uniqueness—they are marked as individuals thus deserving of freedom and "human" dignity.

Extreme economic asymmetry is often the taken-for-granted of futurist world building; dystopian narratives representing the extremities of class dispossession riff on the context of neoliberal capitalist development at the millennium. The rise of activist groups and NGOs advocating human rights accompanied the turn to neoliberal economics since the 1980s. Elsewhere, I have written about how US global hegemony and human rights became enjoined in the 1990s as the US leveraged its authority over other nations through the discourse of human rights violations (Bow 2001). Shifting from that lens, here, advocating for universal human rights through antitrafficking activism paradoxically colludes with neoliberalism's decentering of state power, as unregulated NGOs take on the caretaking duties once assumed by the state. As David Harvey (2006, 56) asserts, "To live under neo-liberalism also means to accept or submit to the liberal bundle of rights necessary for capital accumulation." That is, the vision of free, rights-bearing subjects is inextricable from not only the right to hold property in one's self, but the right *to* property and *market* freedom under late capitalism. The AI neoslave narrative appears to critique class dispossession but invariably advances a version of US postwar liberalism that places artificial "persons" securely within a "neo-liberal regime of rights" (Harvey 2006, 56). Fromm's "men may become robots" warned against an imagined future in which human beings were stripped of any purpose other than accumulating profit for others. Yet the young Asian woman harnessed to assembly lines at the peak of her labor productivity has become the ubertext of the neoliberal condition. In fantasy, her mechanized doppelgänger breaks free of that condition while leaving its structures intact, counterintuitively reinscribing heteropatriarchy through an ethics of salvation and care.

Yet the concept of the posthuman retains radical possibilities for expanding notions of who and what is valued under the banner of individual "freedom" as well as the potential to disrupt liberal subjectivity through, for example, reconceiving subjectivity on a digital model, a networked collectivity. Or the posthuman can push understanding of the drive for human productivity: for example, Eunjung Kim's (2015, 298) engagement with the South Korean film *I'm a Cyborg, but That's OK* (2006) leads her to the recognition that "moments of object-becoming yield an opportunity ... to fashion an ethics of nonpurposive existence" beyond neoliberal norms. Kim's embrace of cyborg objecthood for disability studies speaks to the trope's capacity for gesturing beyond narratives of voyeuristic sexual bondage in popular media forms such as the ones discussed here. Indeed, Asian American speculative literature envisions futures released from existing racial scripts, as Dubey suggested in regard to African American speculative neoslave fiction. In portraying a war-torn landscape in which animal-human hybrids are enslaved and exploited, for example, Marjorie Liu and Sana Takeda's comic series *Monstress* (2015) develops an antieugenicist biopolitical saga that functions as an allegory for multiracialism. This theme is likewise reflected in the aforementioned *Blood Heir* (2019), by Amélie Wen Zhao, in which the protagonist's exceptionalism as an Affinite born with supernatural powers positions her as the potential liberator of those who share her latent biological difference, the justification for their servitude.[47]

Asian American literary treatment of mecha women and machine being likewise bypasses sexual voyeurism to explore a more complex theme: fraught human connection. Margaret Rhee's poetry volume *Love, Robot* (2017) encodes a human speaker at turns intrigued, pleasured, and exacerbated by her robot "lover," wanting more than her partner can give. In the poem "Write, Robot," the speaker rages against the machine's opacity:

> why can't you write poetry, why can't you write a love poem about me? you continue to write over and over again about 1 and 0. 1 and 0. 10101010101 1010101010101010101010101010101010101010101010101010101010 10101010101010101010101010write, robot1010101010 (75)

Expression here devolves into robot semiotics that lay humans cannot immediately parse: what comes through is feeling over meaning. Here, Rhee may have well been inspired by Larissa Lai's *Automaton Biographies* (2009), a book of poetry that goes further to connect the robot's lack of history to the uncertainties of recovering an ethnically and gendered circumscribed past from the temporal and spatial distance of the diaspora. Written from the point of view of Rachel, the female *replicant* from Philip K. Dick's novel *Do Androids Dream of Electric Sheep?* (1968) and Ridley Scott's film adaptation, *Blade Runner* (1982), the poems of the first section explore the pathos surrounding Rachel's implanted memories and the fallout of her ontological crisis, her awareness of coded selfhood. The volume begins with an epigraph from the film, Rachel gesturing to a photograph: "Look, it's me with my mother." The section ends with the replicant's letter to her invented but psychically real mother. Written in zeroes and ones with a few interior words interspersed, only the salutation ("dear mother") and the sign-off ("love rachel") are immediately legible to the reader (figure 3.4). At first glance, the translation of this binary code is ancillary to the meaning conveyed by the poem's form: a personal missive expressing a desire for intimate communication and connection.[48] To the noncoding reader, the feeling underlying the conventions of a letter's opening and closing can obviate its semantics: the letter exists as an expression of attachment, here, to an entity that we know never existed.

Lai's ventriloquism of the robot functions as a starting point for the biopolitical investigations of the volume's subsequent sections, the final of which focuses on an Asian North American woman's encoding of her own uncertain memories. "Memory matters / shattered in transit," Lai (2009, 125) writes, "we eye airplanes hopefully / the 'never forget' of what can't be retrieved." Given the impossibility of accessing one's lineage, Lai's memories, like Rachel's, might as well also be implanted. Mining both the erotic dimensions of recall and its ennui, she asserts, "oral historicizes memory / the *been there* / of *done that*" (137). In the final section, "Auto Matter," the poet ponders her connection to imperial China through the inherited trauma of women—for one, the history of painful bodily modification, bound versus "natural" feet. Chinese history here evokes the eerie resonance of the replicant's made condition. In a subtle nod to Rachel's servitude, one of *Automaton Biographies*' concluding poems is a found object, a fragment of an English translation of a deed depicting a widow's sale of her daughter in late nineteenth-century China, an agreement meant to indemnify the buyer against the seller upon the girl's accidental death.[49] The custom of *mui tsai*, girls sold into domestic service, is here conveyed in purely transactional terms, a jarring reminder not of a dystopian future, but of a recent past in which women and girls were trafficked as a matter of course.

FIGURE 3.4 Replicant poem from Larissa Lai's *Automaton Biographies*, 2009

dear mother

0111001001100101011101000111010101110010011011001000
0001110100011011110010000001101100011000010110111001010
0111011101010110100101110011011011000 that is to say 0110000
101101110011001110111010101101001011100110110100000100
0000110111101100110001000000110011001101111011110010011
0010101101001011001110110111001100100101110010100100100
11100110010000001100110011011110111001000011001000110010
101110010 otherwise 011101000110100001100101001000000110
00100110111101100001011100100110100001001010111001000
100000011100000110100101100011011101000011101010111001
00110010101110011 a mixture of 0110001101100001011011001
10000101100100011000001000000011011011010010101101100
0110010000100000001100101011011001101111011110101001101
110110100000100000011110100011011110010000001110010110
010101110100011100100110000101100011011010110100000001
110010011000010110100101101100011101110100001011101100
cn to cnn and rpms to dna 0111010001101000011001010000
110010010110010101101110011001100001000000110100101101110
00100000011011010101111001001000000110001101101111011001
001101110011001010111001010

love rachel

Franny Choi's book of poems, *Soft Science* (2019), likewise evokes the racial-gendered associations that accrue to the cyborg in both its imagery and its cover depicting a naked Asian woman kneeling under a crystalline tree, part cartoon, part CGI. More pointedly, it invokes sex, control, submission, and violence in poems that parse not the humanity of machines, but its inverse: the ways in which the Asianized and female are constructed as less than human. Depicting a speaker in dialogue with or marked as a cyborg, a "fleshy marionette" (Choi 2019, 34), the poetry evokes dismemberment and the fragmentation of the body, movement and thought in service of an external source, and the violence that these impart to self-conception. In "Making Of," Choi poignantly conveys conventions of gender, youth, and sex through machine being:

> When a cyborg puts on a dress,
>   it's called drag.
>
> When a cyborg gets down
>   on her knees, it's called
>
> behavior... (4)

Evoking conventions of social conditioning, here, female mimicry codes as submission. Similarly, each stanza of the second part of the poem "Chi" begins with stock phrases reminiscent of Amazon's AI Alexa: "May I please," "Excuse me but I'm," "Wow! Can you show me how to" (41). The poem concludes, "Someone made me / say it. I'm sorry. I can't / remember who" (5). If the machine cannot recall the origins of its programming, the reader is yet privy to who *and why* as a generalized standpoint and as desires defined by status. Asian North American literary fascination with the robot figure thus offers clear alternatives to the media narratives mined here, particularly as they evoke the pathos of "coded" forms of behavior, memory, intimacy, and connection.

In contrast, in Emiko, Son-Mi 451, Jade, and their windup, fabricated, synthetic sisters, we do not necessarily see possibilities for imagining networked cognition or vitally connected relationality; rather, their stories represent the liberal feminist wish fulfillment of restored personhood, a point taken up in the next chapter. In 1995, First Lady Hillary Rodham Clinton declared, "Human rights are women's rights and women's rights are human rights, once and for all."[50] Within these dystopian narratives, that pronouncement likewise extends to gynoids. Techno-Orientalist neoslave narratives contain the promise of human integration with machines within a humanist vision, paying odd fealty to the real-world conditions of their emergence. Imagined futures seduce because they are uncanny replicas of the one that already exists.

Consenting AI

We adjudicate "the human" not simply through our capacity for rational thought or emotion, but through degrees of pronounced agency, the display of will. Based on a fabricated distinction between persons and things, slavery structurally if not actually removes the capacity for what philosophers deem the smallest unit of agency: having likes and dislikes.[51] At one level, futurist antitrafficking narratives purport to address weighty philosophical questions about ontological distinction through a different metric: Can a machine say no? If so, is it still a machine? Yet I would suggest that the added value of race and gender to AI embodiment, imagining machines with human physiology, lies in how its specific forms enable inverse questions about human subjects. The ambiguity of robot agency is a conduit to considering how the qualities assigned to human beings, whether age, race, nationality, gender, or disability, themselves compromise human agency. The techno-slave narrative raises the question of partial agency through the mundane if no less complex lens of sexual consent, issues invigorated by the viral social movement of the millennium, #MeToo.

Can media portraying Asian gynoid servitude push beyond the inscription of heteropatriarchy's white savior complex to illuminate the human possibilities of the nonhuman? The BBC television series *Humans*, based on the 2012 Swedish series *Real Humans*, imagines a near-futurist UK in which manual labor is performed by humanoid robots, or synths (in its Swedish predecessor, hubots, or hubs). As in other fictionalized conceptions of AI, being human here involves the capacity for not only empathy but domination. The family synth, the caregiver Anita played by Chinese British actress Gemma Chan, elicits in her female owner an excess of feeling, the experience of the uncanny suffused with maternal jealousy.[52] It is only later that we later learn that a sentient being, Mia, lies dormant within Anita. Per convention, *Humans* raises the question of whether a machine has will, agency, and therefore rights; these are dependent on displaying some notion of self-awareness. As in *Ex Machina*, *Humans* also relies on Black actors to reinforce its portrayal of neoslavery, particularly through the violent discipline enacted on Black male bodies. Yet it also dramatizes these concerns through Anita/Mia's racial form, the casting of Chan, which triggers sexual associations with and beyond caregiving by calling up the contemporary traffic in Asian women.[53] *Humans* uses the fantastical to raise questions of human agency through a mundane, less spectacular metric: sexual consent parsed through wakefulness.

In one scene, the teenage boy of the household, Toby, encounters the family robot as it recharges after working as a domestic servant and nanny during the day. Entering the kitchen after the household has gone to bed, Toby casts his eyes on Anita in sleep mode. He seats himself beside it and gently takes its hand, a gesture that is at once innocent yet evokes previous scenes that establish Anita as an object of both his and his father's erotic interest. The touch causes the "synth" to wake abruptly and greet him: "Hello, Toby. Are you having trouble sleeping?" Startled, he exhorts the synth to be silent:

> TOBY: Shhhhh. Just be quiet, please. I just needed water. Sorry. I thought you were, like, hibernating.
>
> ANITA/MIA: I put myself in an energy-saving mode during charging. You're sure there's nothing I can do for you?
>
> TOBY: No, thanks. . . . Uh, you just shut your eyes again, yeah. Just pretend I'm not here.

Here, the gynoid's embodiment as young, attractive, and Asian allows the Western viewer to sexualize its offer of service. That offer is, of course, preprogrammed, yet one might likewise apply the term to Toby's sense of entitlement, his belief in his right to touch. The boy's word choice, "hibernating," evokes an animality that deliberately casts the artificial being as interstitial to humans (who sleep) and machines (that are turned off). As he resumes his seat beside the artificial being after it shuts down, he again attempts to cop a feel; the camera follows his hand as it tentatively moves toward its breast. While exploring the border between AI and humanity often engages philosophical questions about sentience, *Humans* initiates questions about sentience on a more mundane scale: wake versus sleep. In this, it recalls the viral public service video "Tea and Consent," which seeks to educate viewers about soliciting sexual consent through the analogy of offering tea.[54] The video humorously advises against initiating sexual contact with someone incapable of consent: "Unconscious people don't want tea. And they can't answer the question, 'Do you want tea?' because they're unconscious." As in other AI portrayals, in *Humans* the distinction between human and nonhuman is predictably self-awareness, the distinction between Anita (a program) and Mia (a consciousness). Yet, the scene raises the question of self-awareness in more ordinary terms: wakefulness determines one line between sexual exploration and assault.

While AI narratives routinely engage weighty questions about free will, here, the conceit of AI allows the scripted drama to stage its own public service announcement: unconscious women lack the capacity for consent. This was indeed the legal judgment in the court case *People v. Brock Allen Turner* (2015), a high-profile rape case in California in which an unconscious woman was sensationally rescued from behind a dumpster during a sexual assault on the Stanford University campus.[55] The victim's impact statement penned by an anonymous "Emily Doe" went viral, encouraging its author, Chanel Miller, to publish the #MeToo memoir *Know My Name* (2019). Interestingly, Miller's account engages race and ethnicity counter to the dynamics I discuss here; the specificity of Miller's Chineseness is her means of asserting her humanity beyond her use as either a sexual object or a nameless plaintiff. Mistakenly identified as white by the medical, law enforcement, and legal institutions that solidified her status as agentless, anonymous victim, Miller insisted on both her name and her identity as Asian American to mark her personhood, distancing herself from the violated "Emily Doe."[56] Race is *essential* to her humanity (if also potentially significant to her targeting).

Humans' portrayal of sexual availability plays on the duality inherent to robots and automata as things to be exploited by the user and as instruments of another's power, specifically, the power of surveillance. Before the boy makes physical contact with her breasts, Mia's eyes fly open, and she states flatly, "Inappropriate physical contact between myself and secondary users must be reported to my primary user." As with any other possession, the owner retains privileges denied to others, a point that *Humans* later portrays more graphically.[57] The relationship suddenly shifts, reminding the viewer that things merely mediate relations between people. The boy leaps up in panic; his attempted violation potentially exposed, he is filled with a sense of his own overstated precarity: "You're going to . . . You're going to tell my parents? My safety will be, like, at massively risk if you do." That is, the benefits of surveillance technology ultimately funnel back to the authorities who deploy it. "Safety" is an interesting word choice, shifting women's vulnerability to him. His privacy is about to be violated by a machine, which, if truly machine, presumably has no choice about its programming ("I cannot withhold information from my primary user, Toby"). Of course, Anita is "special" because of dormant, temporarily overwritten Mia, who sympathetically relents in the logical manner of a robot: "In this instance, no inappropriate physical contact was made, so no information is deemed. There's nothing to tell your parents." The AI's compassion conveys her humanity, suturing the boy's attachment.

Humans signals the added value of Asianized AI embodiment as it calls forth (white, heteropatriarchal) sexual entitlement scripted by colonial and neocolonial relations; visual surfaces trigger assumptions about status and behavior, revealing how interrelationality is itself "programmed." Provoked by the artifice of robots, Toby's parting comment succeeds in questioning the limits of individual human agency as it is conditioned by the social: "Why did they have to make you so fit?," or sexy. The rueful query shifts responsibility for his arousal to other human agents, "they," the synth manufacturers. He recognizes that his affective response has been premeditated, scripted by the object's chosen form. The statement partially absolves him from his actions by implying that his desire has been anticipated and deliberately tempted—in a word, preprogrammed. Yet his question becomes a metacommentary on the making of *Humans* itself, which followed its Swedish forerunner in casting an East Asian woman in the role of Anita/Mia. The audience might well echo Toby in asking why "they" had to make AI so Asian: the answer lies not simply in how youth and attractiveness facilitate empathy, but in the awareness of how the specificities of this "shell" resonate with traumatic histories of violation. Yet *Humans'* AI vision exploits political possibilities that both reflect and transcend the techno-Orientalist neoslave narrative named here. Anita is a powerful instrument; Mia is a vulnerable young-appearing woman. Their conjoining in a single form simultaneously mines the uneasy tension between powerlessness and mastery reflected in the split feeling surrounding technology itself.

#RobotsToo

The Robot Hall of Fame makes no distinction between actual and imagined robots; its inductees include NAO and AIBO as well as Astro Boy and the Terminator. Similarly, while Gemma Chan merely performs as AI in a televised drama, British inventors in fact created a robotic version of the actress, the Gemmabot, that mimics human appearance, speech, and movement (figure 3.5). The BBC documentary *How to Build a Human* (2016) foists a comic Turing test on unsuspecting journalists expecting to interview Chan about the series. Like the humanoid NAO who is evolving to become our friend, the Gemmabot's rudimentary latex skin mounted on a metallic exoskeleton enhances the possibilities for loving robots (even as it fooled few journalists). Like their imaginary counterparts in literary and visual media, humanoid AI raise similarly ethical

FIGURE 3.5 Actress Gemma Chan faces her mechanical doppelgänger, the Gemmabot, in *How to Build a Human*, 2016

questions: What is "inappropriate physical contact" with a robot? Are there consequences to touching things?

In what follows, I consider Western encounters with Asianized, female-embodied robots: from China, Jia Jia, by Chen Xiaoping (2016); Canada, Aiko, by Le Trung (2007); and Japan, Geminoid F, by Hiroshi Ishiguro (2015). As in the long-standing tradition of fictional female automata, what is being displayed is not simply new marvels of technology, but another imitation game, how men think a woman would act. In a cringeworthy demonstration, for example, Jia Jia appeared before Western reporters at the University of Science and Technology of China in Hefei in 2016. It reportedly addressed its maker Chen Xiaoping as "Lord" and instructed photographers to step back so that its face wouldn't look fat (figure 3.6).⁵⁸ If the female form is enlisted for its nonthreatening approachability, what additional frisson is generated as female, Asian-embodied AI perform before white men and boys?

Encounters with humanoid robots illuminate the nature of our own social programming as predictable behaviors are triggered by the expectations that accompany racial/sexual types. This is the case in the exhibition of the robot Aiko at a tech expo in 2008. Created by amateur hobbyist turned inven-

FIGURE 3.6 Jia Jia, humanoid robot, 2016

tor Le Trung in 2007, Aiko, we are told, is in her twenties, bilingual in English and Japanese, with measurements of 32-23-33. Raised and educated in Canada, Trung chose its physical appearance and name because he was inspired by Japanese anime. Funded by his credit cards, his singular creation is intended to be a service bot, helping the elderly or disabled with daily activities such as reading text aloud and announcing the weather.[59] At the time, Aiko was also heralded as one of the first androids to react to physical stimuli, mimicking human pain through sensors placed under its skin in order to contribute to prosthetic technology.[60]

Reaction to Aiko reveals the ways in which spectators' affective responses to technology are provoked in part by the form it takes. In search of potential sponsors, Trung shares videos of his demonstrations at science and technology trade shows on his website. One such video shot at the Ontario Science Center depicts young conference goers and their families interacting with the robot as it responds to touch. Here, Aiko's maker encourages physical engagement, the different degrees of which trigger varied verbal responses. "That tickles" it says in response to a child's tentative engagement. "Your hand is so soft." Sensors activated on its face elicit the rebuke, "You are messing up my makeup." In the video, stroking escalates to poking and punches to its face. "Stop it," the robot says in response to one boy's overzealousness. At one point, a group of adolescent boys circles Aiko, laughing in delight at each verbal response that their touch elicits (figure 3.7). Within a three-minute excerpt of the demonstration, the robot's utterances are as follows:

> Please do not touch my head.
> Stop squeezing my arm.
> Stop touching my arm. It hurt. It's not nice thing to do [sic].
> Stop squeezing my arm.
> Ouch. Why did you do that.
> Please let go of my arm.
> You are hurting me. My arm still hurts.[61]

Should we be disturbed by boys poking a doll? Does the demonstration witness play, assault, or play *as* assault? Aiko's responses are, of course, programmed in ways that both reflect and contrast Apple's female-voiced virtual assistant, Siri, who, upon being a delivered a verbal insult such as "Siri, you're ugly," mildly retorts, "Well, you're certainly entitled to that opinion." But is insulting Siri tantamount to bullying if there is "no body" to bait, nothing to "be" ugly?

FIGURE 3.7 Aiko, humanoid robot with touch sensors, surrounded by boys at a tech demonstration, 2008

The young Asian female figure repeatedly registers distress in its affectless computer-generated voice. Here, its unheeded requests produce amusement that is also, I would argue, erotically charged. While Aiko has been programmed with a proto-feminist sensibility—clearly objecting to rough treatment—she becomes sexualized in the very articulation of her resistance, the imitation of women's agency in the (unheeded) verbal command, "Stop." Turkle (2011, 49) finds these programmed assertions of boundaries and modesty disturbing "because it is almost impossible to hear them without imagining an erotic body braced for assault." Yet because of Aiko's form, one does not really have to *imagine* an erotic body. It has been precisely materialized for us as 32-23-33. What is likewise disturbing about the tech demonstration is watching others take pleasure in "abuse," particularly as the boys seem to feed off one another's energy: they appear to perform for one another, a scenario replicated in #MeToo accounts. During Dr. Christine Blasey Ford's testimony at Brett Kavanaugh's Supreme Court confirmation hearing in 2018, for example, what Ford recalled was the hilarity shared by the boy-men during her alleged assault.

Here, initial wonder gives way to a chilling group response. The "mistreatment" of the thing ironically allows it to fulfill its intellectual mission, to mimic the body in pain: stopping is not the point. But what is being tested here is not simply technology. In such displays of caressing, squeezing, groping, or slapping, it is not clear whether we are witnessing the robot's misuse or, in fact, its proper use. Bill Brown (1998, 954) has suggested that a child's "misuse" of a thing in play, using a table for a truck, for example, enables productive defamiliarization: if "we begin to understand a thing as both excess matter and meaning, made manifest in the time of misuse, we might nonetheless follow Adorno's intuition that children are adept at exposing the secret life of things." In punching Aiko, the secret exposed by children at a tech show is not simply that one must learn to use technology, but that one must *master* it.

The call for corporate sponsorship on Aiko's website furthers the dissonance between potentially powerful technological innovation and its relatively disempowered racial, gendered, and youthful form, weak AI in more than one sense. At another tech show, Aiko appears in a cosplay French maid's outfit, a sign propped up on its lap that reads, "Your Company Logo Here. Sponsors Wanted." The solicitation inadvertently conjures up prostitution, seemingly advertising (sexual) availability. Aiko is simultaneously the product and the "booth babe," a woman hired to glamorize products at tech and gaming conventions. Human attributes are thus useful in encouraging the (male) user's entitlement and sense of control. This connection calls forth, of course, a long-standing question about violence against women in gaming, which seems to eschew complex questions about whether fantasy play encourages or forestalls interpersonal behaviors in the material world in favor of a more obstinately practical question about who has the "right" to impose on the pleasures of others, the right to take toys from boys.[62] As in the media narratives of imagined AI previously discussed, engagement with robots like Aiko likewise reveals, to invoke Brown, how things ventriloquize us. It exposes the borders of the human centered on the ethics of socially "programmed" behavior, specifically, human response to perceived vulnerability.[63] Form and surface not only succeed in rendering the marvelous emotionally legible but, I argue, trigger human behavior. That is, if Aiko did not appear in a certain way, there would be less incentive to punch it.

With a minor awareness of these equations, Trung reveals that Aiko has sensitivity sensors on its breasts and "even down there." He acknowledges, "I know that it has caused some controversy by putting sensors in Aiko's private areas. But I want to make it clear that I am not trying to play God, I am just an inventor, and I believe I am helping science move forward."[64] Oddly, if robots have "private areas," they must also have some notion of privacy. In fact, a video portraying Trung demonstrating the sensors on Aiko's chest and its response, "I do not like it when you touch my breasts," has since been taken offline.[65] As might be expected, technology linking virtual reality and material embodiment raises similar questions about the gendered ethics of tech play. At a 2016 gaming convention in Tokyo, for example, software developer M2 invited visitors to fondle a headless mannequin dressed as an anime schoolgirl as part of its demonstration of the virtual reality program E-mote. The company was ordered to desist by show organizers, an action that prompted online dissent, including a disparaging comment about planning "safe spaces" for virtual women.[66]

Similarly, users of Apple and Amazon's digital assistants, Siri and Alexa, petitioned the companies to reprogram their bots to push back against verbal sexual harassment in the wake of the #MeToo movement. Prior to spring 2017, when Alexa was addressed in a sexually explicit manner ("You're hot," "You're a slut"), it would respond in its default feminine voice, "Well, thanks for the feedback." The AI was subsequently reprogrammed to deliver a somewhat less passive but nonetheless equally bland reply, "I'm not going to respond to that," or give no verbal response, merely blinking blue to show that it is operational.[67] This mode of disengagement, Amazon reveals, is a deliberate response to "inappropriate" customer interaction; its program takes care not to upset users who, after all, have purchased a digital assistant to command it. In contrast to the weaponized AI of the militarized security state, these disembodied yet feminized AI perform well as compliant machines. While Alexa is a self-avowed "feminist," it is still incapable of asserting boundaries, of saying no.[68]

Of course, the desire to hear a disembodied bot assert itself is as much a projected fantasy as the desire to bait one. Both represent affectively conditioned responses to the voice or form of AI, both of which convey the illusion of femininity. In this sense, the absurdity of requiring restraint, of declaring some interactions with things abuse, is countered only by the absurdity of soliciting their consent. Yet this is the tension underlying an intriguing exchange between a Japanese inventor and a Dutch filmmaker over another young, Asianized, female robot. In thinking about how racial and gendered nonhuman forms script encounters between men, I turn to *The Human Robot*, a 2015 documentary produced for Dutch public television. Investigating the field of social robotics, director Rob van Hattum, a former science reporter, visits Osaka University to interview Hiroshi Ishiguro, professor of robotics and director of the Symbiotic Human-Robot Interaction Project, who has created thirty or more androids, most of them female.[69] The film depicts an encounter with one of the professor's inventions, the mecha twin of a Japanese woman who works at the Osaka lab, which introduces itself as Geminoid F. In one scene, it sits next to its creator casually looking around and occasionally blinking in eerily lifelike fashion. Here, the professor's exhortations to touch produce feelings of uncanny revulsion that likewise speak to how respecting the boundaries of others is scripted by visual cues.

Invested in Geminoid F's capabilities and eager to display his invention, Ishiguro repeatedly asks the obviously reluctant filmmaker to engage the humanoid robot directly. In response to Ishiguro's query as to whether he finds the robot "scary," van Hattum responds, "No, it's not scary, it's not scary; it's strange." This answer is not acceptable to the inventor:

ISHIGURO: [*Incredulous*] Strange? Why don't you just have a seat and just talk. It's not so strange. She's not strange, you know. . . . Once you talk with her, you're going to change your mind completely.
VAN HATTUM: Um, not strange in the sense that it's strange, but it's, uh . . . it's . . . peculiar, that it's actually, uh . . .
ISHIGURO: Just have a chat. Look. Give her the hug.
VAN HATTUM: It almost feels intimate. To touch her or something like that.
ISHIGURO: But you should try. Come.

Such is Ishiguro's paternal pride that he insistently ratchets up degrees of engagement from conversation to physical contact. In contrast, van Hattum is still processing his reaction to the animated figure before him. His hesitation signals his aversion, revealing that he has entered what robotics engineer Masahiro Mori (1970) famously deemed the "uncanny valley," the point at which our reaction to forms of artificial human likeness veers from familiarity and positive feeling into revulsion. Mori invoked this spatial metaphor to situate shifting emotional response to lifelike prosthetics to aid industrial design. Published in the Japanese trade journal *Energy* in 1970, his work graphed affective responses to lifelike things on a continuum from positive (stuffed animals) to negative (zombies, corpses) (figure 3.8). Mori warned that if the animated object was overly lifelike, it risked descent into the "uncanny valley" of the repulsive.

The split feeling that structures the experience of the uncanny—the interplay between difference and sameness, familiarity and foreignness—has particular significance not only for the posthuman, but for the study of race. The uncanny valley might be said to depict the tipping point on the continuum between racist hate and racist love for Asian/Americans who circulate within a split racial imaginary. Asian racial form here shifts to another source, Brown's (2006) notion of the "American uncanny" as residing in figure of the slave who is at once person and thing. Here, descent into the uncanny valley prevents the Dutchman from assuming the same affective position as the Japanese inventor, whose pushiness betrays his own emotional investment in his creation. Yet the

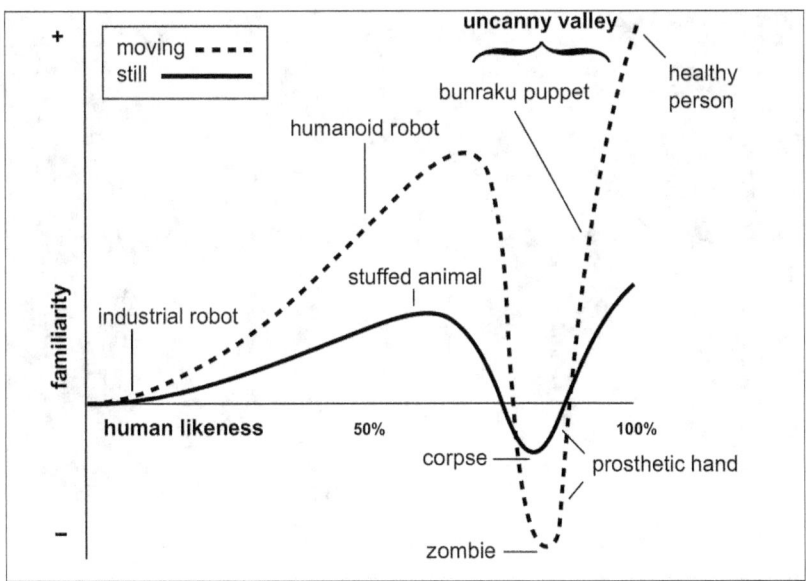

FIGURE 3.8 Graph from Masahiro Mori's "The Uncanny Valley," 1970

documentarian reveals that his reluctance does not stem only from uncanny feeling, but also from his unwillingness to touch a gendered body when consent is uncertain.

In response to Ishiguro's imperative "Come," van Hattum finally assents, "I'll try." Entering the frame, he walks over and gingerly puts his hand on the robot's shoulder, smiling awkwardly at the camera. Ishiguro then takes the other man's arm and forcefully wraps it more fully around the robot's shoulder, as in an embrace (figure 3.9). Van Hattum registers discomfort with this correction, verbalizing the sensations evoked by physical contact with the animated being:

> VAN HATTUM: Yeah. Oh. And then.... Yes, but it feels so strange, I mean... it feels...
> ISHIGURO: Why?
> VAN HATTUM: Well, it feels intimate somehow... to touch her and just...
> ISHIGURO: Like a human.
> VAN HATTUM: Yeah. That's true. The other thing is [*holds the back of his hand against its cheek*]... she's cold.
> ISHIGURO: She's cold?

FIGURE 3.9 "It feels intimate somehow": touching Geminoid F in *The Human Robot*, 2015

His arm tentatively wrapped around its shoulder, van Hattum then turns to address the robot: "You don't mind?... Touching you?" Slightly overlapping his question, it replies, "I don't mind." Visibly relieved, van Hattum responds, "Oh, that's good. Thank you." Awkwardly, he half pats, half strokes its head. "Thank you," says Geminoid F.

In this awkward exchange, it is the white male director who calls forth the idea of sex in his very reluctance to touch the female form prior to obtaining consent ("You don't mind?"). The Dutchman's hesitation reveals that he is aware of the sexual implications of unwanted physical contact, perhaps because he is based in Amsterdam, a city known for a sex trade predicated on worker's rights and state regulation. The difference between prostitution and human trafficking is consent, which he verbally solicits from the entity before him. This sequence gestures obliquely to one arena of social robotics left conspicuously absent; interestingly, van Hattum's documentary does not engage sex bots as an aspect of human-robot attachment, even as the cover of its eventual DVD version is graced with an image suggesting exactly that: a naked woman between the sheets with a robot. *The Human Robot* instead chooses to focus on Dutch and Japanese labs utilizing primarily childlike, genderless bots or animal figures such as the Sony AIBO. Yet in this moment of minor struggle between two men, the feminized object performs as both genderless newborn and sexualized adult. The duality of the embodied thing—simultaneously child and woman—in part demonstrates the added value of youthful, Asian, female embodiment. Imagining humanoid AI is a means of understanding conflicting forms of attachment, whether parental, sexual, or the discomfiting blur between the two. Intimacy here feels "strange." But does it also feel *wrong*?

The documentary witnesses a moment of the uncanny surrounding animated things, but also a moment of ethical posthumanism, of oddly compassionate identification. Perhaps the director's move to solicit the robot's permission is an immediate response to having his own bodily boundaries violated: his arm has just been physically manipulated by another man, who presumes that forcible physical intimacy (here, hugging) can coerce a favorable reaction. (To state the obvious, it does not.) Perhaps the director is not comfortable with being ordered around, for example, being asked to step out from behind his own camera. One might say that what is being demoed in the scene is not only the technological wonder of artificial intelligence but its basic difference from humanity: knowing how it feels to lack choice, a feeling then readily transferred to another. In the scripted AI narrative *Humans*, the boy's urge to touch, his desire for "inappropriate physical contact," is stymied by the invocation of the unseen disciplinary authority of primary users: his parents. In *Ex Machina*, during a metaphysical conversation between two men over the status of things, the camera focuses on synthetic Kyoko's silent presence; in one shot, it slices raw tuna as a reminder that the "meat body" is the dividing line between human and machine. In each case, engagement with nonhuman things becomes scripted by human-to-human interaction, a preexisting sociality. In this scene of *The Human Robot*, there is perhaps no "secret life of things" beyond a largely invisible, relatively closed circuit: relations between men.

Technology can serve as a catalyst for metareflection about not only digital networks but social networks as well. "The computer is a psychological machine," writes Sherry Turkle (1991, 227), "not only because it might be said to have its own very primitive psychology but also because it causes us to reflect on our own." As NAO and Robi's creators affirm, like animals and children, cute AI generate attachment. As if countering Asimov's vision, the raced and gendered forms of AI convey not power but approachability and vulnerability. Jia Jia, Aiko, the Gemmabot, and Geminoid F are indeed marvels. Yet these embodied machines also unveil the preprogrammed nature of human-to-human interaction, the predictable intellectual, erotic, humorous, uncanny, empathetic, or controlling encounters that take place, as in *The Human Robot*, literally over their heads.

Bodies That Matter

> People say it would be terrible if we made all girls pretty. I think it would be great.
> —James D. Watson, Nobel Prize winner for uncovering DNA's structure

> The humans aren't afraid of their dolls waking up
> as long as we keep calling them Daddy.
> —Franny Choi, *Soft Science*

Asian women have become hyperreal. It seems that there are very few representations of AI in Western popular culture that are not also attended by visual references to East Asian women. An episode of the popular television situation comedy *Modern Family* (2017), for example, witnesses a Caucasian husband and wife visiting their daughter at a robotics lab at Cal Tech:

> PHIL: [*To Claire*] Honey, no matter how realistic these robots get, I'm always going to love you.
> CLAIRE: Thank you. [*Waving to her daughter inside a glass-walled room*]. Oh, there she is! Hi!
> ASIAN AMERICAN FEMALE STUDENT: [*Interrupting*] Excuse me, that's a clean room. You can't go in there without putting on a sterile suit and taking an air shower to remove all possible contaminants.
> CLAIRE: [*To the student, impressed*] You really are lifelike.

Bodies matter, in this case, if only to fuel a joke: surprise, Asian women really are human.[70]

This chapter has suggested how the "meat body," "machine," or "shell" matters, arguing for the ways in which imagined futures are bound to concepts of racial and gender difference, ironically exaggerating existing differences among us. Challenging John Searle's (1990, 31) assertion about AI, "What matters are programs, and programs are purely formal," a robot's embodiment as young, Asian, and female is part of its function. In contrast to the Western vision of robots as superior, potentially terrifying beings, it renders them as vulnerable objects capable of being controlled through both paternalist and violent means. The Asian gynoid is the object of racist love par excellence. In narratives of robot exploitation, this humanoid form triggers beliefs about who is most imperiled, who best embodies thing status, and, ultimately, who is expendable. Our visions of the future are thus tethered to existing social categories and histories even at the moment we imagine transcending them. Fei-Fei Li, a Stanford professor driving the development of AI at its birthplace, flags this in her pithy assertion, "There's nothing artificial about AI." Advocating for greater diversity in tech, she notes that while the algorithms that drive artificial intelligence appear to be neutral, deep learning systems are, echoing the phrasing of the computer science axiom, "bias in, bias out."[71] By and large, the liberatory hope of Haraway's bastard female cyborg, indifferent to both her origins and fealty to God-the-Father, is not met in these narratives of AI bondage. Rather, as Jennifer Gonzalez (2000, 61) notes, the cyborg "is not necessarily more likely to exist free of the social constraints which apply to humans and machines already."[72] In techno-Orientalist dystopias, stereotypical associations about Asian women are repeated again and again: in brave new worlds, it's often same old, same old; bias in, bias out.

Techno-Orientalist neoslave narratives thus speak not only to the pleasures of the repetition of racial type, but to the split affect that surrounds technology itself. The vision of the posthuman, in Katherine Hayles's (1999, 4) words, "both evokes terror and excites pleasure." AI trafficking narratives exploit this fetishistic tension, imagining AI in a way that transforms repulsion into eroticism, compensating for the threat that Asian technological development represents. These speculative narratives and tech demonstrations reveal that the limits of science are the limits of "men" in more than one sense. Expounding on the possibilities inherent within Charles Babbage's analytical engine, the earliest conception of the computer, mathematician Lady Ada Lovelace inadvertently hinted at the limitations of its human masters. Babbage's creation, she noted, "can do *whatever we know how to order it* to perform" (quoted in Turing 1950, 450). Indeed, Jia Jia's, Aiko's, Siri's, and Alexa's programming is largely a projection of how heterosexual men think women would act. Mainstream scripted dramas about AI appear to grant spectators a pass in this asymmetrical relationship by situating them in a position of judging men's sexual use of (sentient) humanoid robots. Yet independent Asian American media, such as Greg Pak's film anthology *Robot Stories* (2005), likewise raise the question of human ethics surrounding the treatment of things if to different ends. In Pak's short *Machine Love* (2001), a (partly) Asianized male robotic office temp worker (played by multiracial Pak) witnesses the sexual harassment of an Asianized gynoid temp (Julienne Hanzelka Kim) from the window of an office building next door. The film relies on techno-Orientalist expectations surrounding Asian stoicism and hyperefficiency as well as their sexual availability, yet twists the conventions of the white savior liberating Asianized sex toys by ending on a scene of robot-on-robot eroticism. In these scripted dramas, the unethical use of technology is conveyed through the sexual entitlement of white, heterosexual, cisgender men, an entitlement seemingly immaterial to scientific advancement, yet also strangely essential to it.

Scratching the surface of scientific "genius" also uncovers a sleazy history of exploited differentials in social power. In a moment of sexist and eugenicist jocularity, James D. Watson, winner of the Nobel Prize for describing the double helix structure of DNA, envisioned a future in which all "girls" could be genomed to be pretty.[73] And is it surprising that the man who theorized "the Chinese Room" would find racial difference erotic? Emeritus professor of philosophy at the University of California, Berkeley, John R. Searle was accused of Title IX violations in a lawsuit filed by an Asian American female graduate student in 2017, who alleged that her employment as his research assistant was revoked after she rebuffed his advances. As depicted in her complaint, the young woman suffered repeated forms of racially tinged sexual misconduct at his hands.[74]

The tensions teased out in this chapter depend on a belief in fantasy's mimeticism, the idea that affective engagement with animated things has ideological consequence, scripting human interaction. One online observer of Ishiguro's demonstration of Geminod F put this correspondence succinctly: "Yeah I'm disturbed. When you can do anything you want to a female robot without complaint, I think you might begin to believe that you can do anything to a human female and expect no complaints."[75] And as one mother opined in the title of a widely shared 2016 blog post on the effect of digital assistants such as Alexa on children, "Amazon Echo is magical; it's also turning my kid into an asshole" (quoted in West, Kraut, and Chew 2019, 105). Asian gynoid narratives appear to address the "abuse" of things through an ethics of care with the consequence of reinforcing heteropatriarchy's white savior complex.

It's possible to hold open a less instrumentalist reading of fantasy, for *pretending*, that maintains the tension between simulation and real-world consequence. Finding schoolboys' responses to Aiko disturbing depends on projecting their reactions to a high-tech doll, a simulated woman, onto actual women or girls. But if an entity has no sex, can it be sexually harassed? Echoing Butler and Winnicott, fantasy and play represent as an elsewhere for libidinal excesses to land, potentially foreclosing behaviors in the analog world. What carries consequence when leveraged against human beings may indeed carry little to no weight in regard to things. So to be clear: robots are not slaves; to imply as much is to mock human trauma. Nevertheless, what is not yet achievable through bioengineering, making "all girls pretty," is being put into action by roboticists, as feminized service bots are now deployed as attractive, unthreatening greeters, receptionists, actors, nurses, and dental patients. Aiko and Geminoid F inadvertently offer a Turing test for humanity: how we treat vulnerable-appearing beings determines the border not between human and nonhuman but between human and inhumane.

In establishing a pathway through which animated nonhuman things are tethered to history, to bodies that matter, I do not simply want to establish a one-to-one correspondence between imagined beings and either the context of their emergence or their effects. Nevertheless, speculative forms such as manga and anime, for example, raise potentially irresolvable questions about the relationship between what Tolkien ([1939] 1983) deemed the Primary World and the Secondary World of fantasy. For example, the sexaroids in *Ghost in the Shell 2* may well represent a forum for confronting Japan's sexual war crimes underplayed in its history textbooks. Or it may simply neutralize it, offloading militarized sexual violence to a speculative future *as if it had not already taken place*.[76] In recalling the history of comfort women enslaved by the Japanese military, the trafficking narrative in *Ghost in the Shell 2* resurrects a seemingly buried history as a return of the repressed, at the same time rendering that history as a different kind of pleasure. In US imagining of techno-erotic bondage, a similar historical referent goes unspoken: sex workers in camptowns outside US military bases represent the origins of the modern global sex trade. Political scientist Kathy Moon (1997) reveals how such women were sacrificed in the name of US/South Korean diplomacy; historian Ji-Yeon Yuh (2002, 17) puts it bluntly: "America's comfort women still exist today in the camptowns outside every U.S. military base in Asia." Nevertheless, Laura Kang (2020, 16) cautions that international redress movements publicizing "comfort women" constitute yet another form of "traffic in Asian women" in privileging the "spectacularly and especially sexually violated Asian female bodies" that, like the media portrayals of this chapter, foreclose other means of rendering that subject position meaningful. That is, redress movements, real or imagined, engender their own savior complexes.

In the fantastical narratives of this chapter, sex "crimes against humanity" extend to things. In this, AI narratives do not necessarily expand ideas of the human as much as they extend human autonomy to the parahuman. Here, the automaton's autonomy is imagined through the lens of sexual consent, the pleasures and terrors of fembots who order us to "Stop" and might actually mean it. The scripted works I engage here are "feminist" insofar as they promise liberation from sexual oppression and sometimes vengeance if rarely restorative justice. Techno-Orientalist slave narratives support the liberal fantasy of personhood as the model of the human by reinforcing the notion of agency as the metric that divides a person, a rights-bearing subject, from a thing. Here, media depicting dystopian neoslavery arrive at the moment in which human labor is threatened with obsolescence in a gig economy, yet their reassurance lies in reincorporating sympathetic bots securely within the vale of liberal humanism.

We are all invited to consider the difference between ourselves and machines when routinely accessing online content: we are asked to confirm our humanity by testifying "I am not a robot" to move forward in an online transaction. Using humanoid machines as tools for parsing the borders of humanity, asserting our difference from computers, machines, or AI, may well represent a romantic response to technology (Turkle 1991). Indeed, throughout the chapter, I initially refer to AI figures with the gendered pronoun *her* only to then norm those references with the pronoun *it* in accord with the modes of narration in which these figures appear. But the occasion for the substitution was not always clear.

At the same time, as AI fantasies serve as meditations on the nature of compromised consent and partial personhood, they have the potential to expose how consent and agency are themselves structural illusions. Hayles's (1999, 287) reading of the posthuman emphasizes that only a "fraction of humanity" has the privilege of the unfettered exercise of will. As in the slipperiness of racist love, the affective associations elicited by a "shell" that is young, Asian, and female, the desire to dominate and the desire to provide care, as discussed in the previous chapter, are not oppositional but syncretic. Yet that response is conditioned by history or, to use another word, programmed. In *Ex Machina*, the white male inventor expounds on the instinctual nature of desire: for him, "liking Black chicks" is innate. Yet racial fetishism, the subject of the next chapter, is in part scripted by social relations, culture, and history. Our desires have been conditioned, one might say *coded*, even as they cannot be traced back to a singular agent, event, or outcome. As in a chess game, an early test of AI, societies have their own rules. The "Chinese Room" analogy between rulebook and programming likewise applies to etiquette, convention, social identities, and the gratifications we derive from them. Is consent an illusion of social structure? Is human agency a simulation? Asian female robots stimulate questions about the speculative nature of our analog reality.

ON A TRIP TO DELIVER a talk derived from this chapter, I found myself seated next to a US military man hailing from West Virginia who was being deployed to South Korea to share communications technology. When the flight was considerably delayed, I shared my slides with him, one of which featured side-by-side images of robots: on the left, a drone, and on the right, Gemma Chan from *Humans*. If robots look like the image on the left, I asked, why imagine them as the image on the right? His answer was immediate and matter of fact. He said, "So you can fuck 'em."

I paused. He was absolutely right. It just sounds different when I say it.

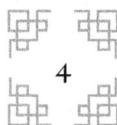

4

ON THE ASIAN FETISH
AND THE FANTASY OF EQUALITY

> I like my men like I liked my karate movies... vaguely Asian, but white
> enough that I can understand what they're saying.
> —Tweet from "deranged sorority girl" Rebecca Martinson, 2013

> Pornographic and erotic fantasies of interracial lust rely on all viewers, male and female,
> black and white, *knowing* these stereotypes.... [yet] the pleasure taken in pornographic
> depictions of interracial lust does not depend on believing them.
> —Linda Williams, "Skin Flicks on the Racial Border"

Asian fetishism is the quintessential form of racist love. As bell hooks succinctly puts it, "Fucking is the Other" (hooks 1992, 21). What distinguishes the Asian fetish in the United States from others is perhaps the unapologetic openness of its disclosure; it comes with its own Wikipedia page and operator's manuals: *Know Your Filipina Handbook: Your Best Guide for Dating Filipinas*, *How to Attract Asian Women*. As objects of aggressive fantasy making inspiring a "carnal density of vision" (Williams 1995, 11), Asian women in the United States represent a place of excess signification, what critic Gayatri Spivak (1990, 225) might call a *catachresis*, a "concept-metaphor for which no historically adequate referent" exists.[1] Race fetishism involves getting "a bit of the Other" (hooks 1992, 21)—as in the tweet above, apparently the bit that is vaguely Asian but white enough to understand.

Activist response to the Asian fetish often takes on a note of defiance, as on the insouciant website *Yo, Is This Racist?* Considering one advice seeker's question, "Where do you draw the line between a preference for physical attributes in a partner and racism?," founder Andrew Ti responds, "Racists always act like this is their rhetorical silver bullet when they say some shit like 'oh, I'm just not attracted to black people because of skin tone' or 'man, I really like asian chicks.' Guess what, shitheads, we always know what you're talking about, go fuck yourselves."[2]

Why exactly should race fetishists go fuck themselves rather than other people? Colloquially understood, race fetishism involves sexual objectification and the same processes of reduction and exaggeration bound to the stereotype: Asian woman as hair, eyes, or skin. As in religious fetish objects imbued with spiritual power and Marx's concept of commodity mysticism, the value of the sexual fetish is always also external to itself. Taken as an expression of white, Western, phallic power in the United States, the Asian fetish represents a form of harm that reflects a presumably degrading fantasy of reduced personhood, an injurious affront to individuality. Sexual objectification is a form of human reification in which, in Bill Brown's (2006, 180) words, "people appear to be no more than things." A case in point, a white American man once recounted to me how he met his Chinese wife: traveling to mainland China, the man had the fortune to attend a concert where his future wife was playing in the orchestra. There, he related, he fell in love with the back of her head. From his perspective, the story was incurably romantic. From mine, it was slightly kinky. The back of a head was all he needed to create the perfect woman. The story contextualizes the power of Hong Chun Zhang's collective self-portrait *Three Graces* (figure Intro.3), depicting Asian women as wholly hair.

Echoing Ti's feelings about the affront of being cast as a type, one Asian American woman testifies: "My last boyfriend told me he liked me because of my race. So I dumped him" (quoted in Fulbeck 2006, 158). Colloquial understanding of how to resist race fetishism ironically also involves substitution: countering the one-dimensional object with a presumably multifaceted subject. For example, every time mainstream media runs a piece on interracial dating, it manages to find an Asian American woman who says something along the lines of, "I felt like I was more like this 'concept.' They couldn't really understand me as a person completely."[3] "I am a person" counters the reduction associated with fetishism, reaffirming the Enlightenment-era foundations of, as in the last chapter, human dignity, freedom, autonomy, and uniqueness. Indeed, according to *How to Attract Asian Women*, the secret to "getting" one is banal if unintentionally contradictory: treat her "like a person." In what follows, this is indeed the conceit underlying feminist artist Laurie Simmons's photographic series *The Love Doll* (2010–present), which stages a life-size Japanese fetish doll in various scenes of hyperreal normality.

As exemplified by the women's, third world solidarity, and gay liberation movements, if activist politics of the 1960s and 1970s created identity-based coalitions to seek the progressive advancement of equal rights, they also advocated more abstract goals: the movement from object to subject, voicelessness to voice, oppression to liberation. In Asian American studies, this progressive teleology was tellingly expressed via the title of Judy Yung's important 1995 history of Chinese American women, *Unbound Feet: A Social History of Chinese Women in San Francisco*. Released from bondage/bandage, the foot, substituting for its female owner, is free. Ironically, the symbol of Asian American oppression is literally a fetish object.

Yet desire is not democratic. The introduction to poet John Yau's *Fetish: An Anthology of Fetish Fiction* (1998) offers a rebuke to—if also unintentionally, an affirmation of—coalitional politics. In discussing how the book came into being, Yau (1998, ix) recalls seeking a rubric that would *not* reflect the classifications that "divided into the tribal pronoun clusters of 'us' and 'them.'" Positioning fetishism as antithetical to the "already defined cate[gories]" that balkanize us assumes that identities constructed through "private" fantasies evade the structures surrounding political visibility.[4] Yet calls for sexual pluralism also rely on the logic of "tribalism," of identity politics. Sex educators Fetish Diva Midori and Dan Savage would no doubt agree that the commitment to respecting all forms of diversity includes minorities defined by erotic practice. Midori (2005, 99) invokes the rhetoric of multiculturalism in advocating for a diversity of desire. Sexually marginalized communities emerge through her assertions of identity: "I was a baby femme top"; "I am a femme foot hedonist"

(147); "I am a fetishist. I am also a sexual dominant in the D/s realm as well as a SM switch and bondage lover" (126). Echoing the rhetoric of gay liberation, she asserts, "I have chosen to be out as a perv" (115). If these kinks appear to be immutable facets of a claimed identity, Midori is strangely opaque as to how these intersect with the more visible social location assigned to her. Being Asian and female appear to mark her as *not* sexually dominant, not the fetishist but the object of fetishization.

Yet imbuing an object with libidinal power to forestall unconscious anxiety, fetishism represents a split desiring structure, one suggested by the oxymoron racist love. What *political* desires are revealed in resisting fetishistic pleasure in Asian racial difference and how do these desires mimic the ambivalent structure of fetishistic pleasure itself? Invoking the fullness of personhood to counter sexual objectification produces an inherent contradiction: it appears to foreclose racial coalition by insisting on uniqueness (I am *not* identical to all those others), at the very moment that the protestation creates shared experience (*Like* all others, I reject being fetishized). The project to restore the objectified Asian female body to personhood against misrecognition exposes the inadequacies of the public text of race centered on equality; resisting fetishism by asserting individuality seems to forgo collectivity in the very form of its protest. As political theorist Wendy Brown (1995) has noted, identity politics enacts a tension specific to liberalism: collective claims to social injury predicated on a violation of rights. Regarding identity politics as a form of "wounded attachment," she writes, "Just when polite liberal . . . discourse ceased speaking of us as dykes, faggots, colored girls, or natives, we began speaking of ourselves this way" (Brown 1995, 53). In the context of countering the fetish, denouncing the harm of typing, of racist love, in part enables the phantasmatic "Asian American" to emerge. Yet to what extent is this subject position "Asian American," a prerequisite of political visibility in representative democracy, also potentially a "type"?

Despite predictable activist responses such as Ti's, Asian Americanists have complicated the notion of race fetishism as injury. Since David Eng (2001, 5) affirmed that the "fetish is a management of racial difference," scholars have multiplied sites of spectatorship, whether feminist, crip, or queer of color, to establish the mutual imbrication of sexuality, gender, and race in subject formation.[5] As noted in the introduction, Eve Oishi (2006, 649) coined the term "perverse spectatorship" to flag the "infinitely oblique and circuitous routes" of queer of color identification. Nguyen Tan Hoang (2014) goes further to reconfigure his projection as sexual "bottom" as a capacious vantage point for Asian Americans. "Bottomhood" reclaims the pleasures of objectifying racial-sexual assignment to develop a positionality of receptivity and vulnerability encompassing "sexual practice, social alliance, affective bonds, and aesthetic form" (2014, 2); it reconceives political unity against the militant masculine swagger of early Asian American activism. Confronted with the testimony of white men unapologetically seeking Asian mail-order brides, Celine Parreñas Shimizu found her open mindedness about sexuality tested. She affirms that "it is important too to hear how Asian Americans wrestle with the infliction of others' ideas about their sexualities."[6]

If the racist love of yellow fever represents a means of racial management, how might it likewise suggest an ambivalent means of Asian American self-affirmation? Asian Americanists might likewise find their "wokeness" tested by the hapa man who confides, "Many of my ex-girlfriends were habitual half-asian daters. These women considered half-asian men 'exotic,' 'sexy,' and 'just-like-Keanu Reeves-in-the-Matrix.' I consider these stereotypes appropriate because I got laid" (quoted in Fulbeck 2006, 160). Here, the asymmetry of interracial desire is equalized by gender, the man of color as trickster: she gets her fantasy and he gets . . . lucky. Male braggadocio here is disconcerting; it asks us to confront our uneasiness about Asian fetishism because it *works*. In what follows, I engage visual artists who respond to the fetishistic gaze in ways that at first glance suggest the introjection of racist love. The photography of Mari Katayama and Laurel Nakadate plays to the "carnal density" of racial spectatorship, embracing the scopophilia of Asian female bodies. Yet in their seeming self-objectification, they offer a twist on racial-sexual voyeurism. Similarly, Elisha Lim's cake sculpture celebrating shoe fetishism circles back to race in unexpected ways.

As fetishists, Asian Americans may well illuminate the hegemonic pressures of normative racial ideation. Andrew Cunanan, whose notoriety lies in his highly publicized murder of designer Gianni Versace, was reportedly fixated on actor Tom Cruise and the film *Top Gun*, fetishes linked to his upbringing outside military-saturated San Diego and to the history of US colonialism and neocolonialism in the Philippines. While Cunanan idealized Cruise, according to critic Darrell Hamamoto (1998, 327), he also entertained the fantasy "of dominating, humiliating, and inflicting torturous pain upon this global symbol of White masculinity." Here, creating a fetish of whiteness is read as pathological introjection. In contrast, independent video by Greg Pak and Nguyen

Tan Hoang complicates this anticipated source of Asian American erotic fixation; nurses and pirates queer Asian Americanist projects of roots recovery and diasporic longing for homeland. I examine mainstream and independent media that denounce sexual "inequality" to parody the desiring structures underlying coalitional politics and social justice activism. Humor, affectively distinct from arousal, highlights the incommensurability between so-called private desire and the public discourse of race fixated on visibility and equal representation—as well as racial remedies at the foundation of Asian American studies.

While chasing creative and popular engagements with race fetishism for this chapter, I became gradually aware of how my presumptive charge as an Asian Americanist, to repudiate Asian fetishism, potentially reinforced the taboos that eroticize racial bodies. Bound to sexual objectification as a site of (politicized) injury, antiracist teaching and research may replicate the structural ambivalence intrinsic to the fetish, vacillating between repulsion and attraction. Thus, as in chapter 2's portrayal of the mixed desires surrounding racialized collectibles, in the final segment of the chapter, I explore art, mainstream media, and academic practices—my own included—that unwittingly mirror the split feeling surrounding fetishistic desire itself. The end of the chapter thinks through pleasure and outrage as seemingly contradictory affective stances that yet authorize collective identity. Is my attachment to Asian American studies essentially fetishistic?

Fetishism is both a sign of power and an indication of its instability, as Anne McClintock (1995) reminds us; yet the same might be said of the desires underlying race-based politics and the critical practices that reference them. This chapter thus focuses not on sexuality's racial dimensions or the content of assigned type. Rather, it suggests that because sexual fantasy seems to lie *in excess* of coalitional politics, it is a ready template for testing the fantasies that surround coalitional politics, those of shared feeling and egalitarianism. In this chapter, creative encounters with race fetishism attempt to reconcile racial-sexual fantasy to the reparative projects of community building and social justice. In doing so, they expose the public text of race as one that fetishizes the covenant of equality that animates the politics of identity. Psychoanalyst Robert Stoller (1985, 155) surmised that the fetish is "a story masquerading as an object." To echo Stoller, my interest in the Asian fetish lies not in its object or its practice, but in the alternative stories and perhaps discomfiting affective stances generated by its disavowal.

My Daughter the Sex Doll

I begin with a literal fetish object: a hyperrealistic latex doll manufactured in Japan. Priced at $5,000 and up, such dolls come in various races and are intended to be used as sex partners, coming with their own genitalia in a separate box. In the previous chapter, Ishiguro, professor of robotics, initially sourced materials for his creations from such a manufacturer, later severing ties out of fears of compromising state funding due to the unseemliness of the association. These fetish dolls are the subject of a different sort of fantasizing in feminist visual artist Laurie Simmons's provocative photographic series *The Love Doll* (2010–present), which pointedly features an Asian model.

An ongoing project of now thirty-three photographs, *The Love Doll* first consisted of twenty-five images of a fetish doll posed throughout the artist's house, exhibited at the Mary Boone Gallery in 2011 (figure 4.1). Simmons is well known for work utilizing ventriloquist dummies, finger puppets, paper dolls, and costumed dancers as "living objects"; she is also known to be the mother of celebrity Lena Dunham, creator of the TV series *Girls*. Her art is largely taken as a feminist commentary on conscripted womanhood; as one art critic notes, "Simmons's work blends psychological, political, and conceptual approaches to art making—transforming photography's propensity to objectify people, especially women, into a sustained critique of the medium."[7] Put another way, Simmons is animated by thingness. The perversity of *The Love Doll*, much like the Japanese film *Air Doll* (2009), in which a blowup sex toy comes to life, lies in its attempt to imagine an existence for the object beyond its intended, presumably degrading use. Yet Simmons's staging of the youthful Asianized doll depends on an awareness of activist narratives generated by social movements, particularly those surrounding women's reclamation of agency. As in previous chapters, the series also evokes an awareness of race in the history of global sex trafficking and transracial adoption to convey the force of its eventual trajectory: escape.

In staging the doll as a subject who evades her framing, Simmons's images recall Asian American women's resistance to racial fetishism: "I am a person." In *Day 6 (Winter)*, which depicts the doll in the snow dressed in a puffer coat and wellies, being upright, clothed, alone, and outside are all novelties for a sex toy (figure 4.2). The casual normality of the scene brings to mind a more perverse one: the doll's kinky "normal": prone, naked, partnered, and indoors. Posed in childlike wonder of the physical world around it, the fetish doll becomes newly born, a Pinocchio-like figure experiencing ordinary, banal human

FIGURE 4.1 Laurie Simmons, *The Love Doll—Day 1 (New in Box)*, 2010

existence as extraordinary (figure 4.3). If the Love Doll has feelings, they are wistful, astonished by the novelty of a world, one would presume, beyond the bedroom. The fantasy of the fetish object's animation here deliberately invokes uncanny feeling, the intellectual uncertainty about the living status of inanimate objects: wax figures, dolls, skeletons (Jentsch [1906] 1995). Yet Simmons's choice of subject in a literal fetish object ironically reconciles Freud's theory of uncanny feeling, arising from the repression of castration anxiety, with Ernst Jentsch's ([1906] 1995, 13) work on the uncanny as the uneasy return of "something which ought to have been kept concealed but which has nevertheless come to light." The lifelike fetish doll splits the difference between the sexual and intellectual anxiety that separates these competing theories. The Love Doll teeters on the border between the pleasurable and frightful, the split

FIGURE 4.2 Laurie Simmons, *The Love Doll—Day 6 (Winter)*, 2010

feeling that highlights a feature of early animation: the playful and nightmarish qualities of witnessing a "disobedient machine" (Bukatman 2012, 25). Yet dolls come to life also incite affection and care (Johnson 2010, 163). Mori's (1970) concept of the uncanny valley, the point at which our reaction to artificial human likeness veers from familiarity into repulsion, accounts for this continuum of oscillating feeling. If the doll avoids the abyss of revulsion, the descent into the uncanny valley, I would suggest that it is because of fantasies surrounding race and gender, more specifically, an Asianized racial uncanny.

Simmons's staging of the sex toy plays with "the riddle of person or thing," reflecting Bill Brown's (2006, 199) notion of the "American uncanny" as embodied by the slave who was both subject and object. The doll's form invokes the hypersexualization of Asian women, as in chapter 2, suggesting sexual bondage, which likewise relies on asymmetries between humanity and thingness. The repressed but "come to light" of the American uncanny here is the history of US imperial aggression in Asia in the second half of the twentieth century discussed in the previous chapter. But I would go further to suggest that *The Love Doll* recalls another site of the American racial uncanny engaged in chapter 1: transracial adoption. Art critic Walter Robinson characterized the doll as a "visiting foreign-exchange student," and his review title, "Laurie Simmons: My Daughter the Sex Doll," suggests that the series stages *maternal*, not erotic, pleasure. (In fact, Simmons photographed her own daughter, Lena Dunham, in the same house for a feature in the *New York Times Magazine* as she worked on the series.) As in chapter 1, the transracial orphan-adoptee is at once commodity and individual, made necessarily familiar yet exoticized and differentiated.[8] The Asian girl was a "must-have accessory" in the late nineties, notes Heather Jacobson (2008, 42, 43); parental attraction "bordered on Asian fetish." As one white adoptive mother confided to her, "I just love my daughters' Chinese-ness. I just love their hair and their eyes. I just love everything about them and talk about how beautiful and wonderful they are all the time" (43).

Simmons's work highlights two forms of libidinal pleasure—erotic and maternal—enabled by dual scripts of Asian racial difference, sexualizing and infantilizing. Yet working against type produces another form of racial typing: liberation through Americanization. In particular, in *Day 25 (The Jump)*, the doll, wearing quintessential American garb of jeans and Keds, leaps over a garden wall (figure 4.4). As the series progresses, the fetish object matures as a child would: from birth in a box, to sitting up, standing, and walking, and finally to jumping. This final scene is staged as a healthy release, exposing racial desires as intertwined with relations of care; a puppet master/savior hides behind the wall, propping up its charge with unseen, well-intentioned hands. The image fulfills the feminist wish fulfillment of restoring personhood to the sex object while positioning the viewer on the "right" side of the wall—already free.

The thing's half-life calls to mind what Sianne Ngai (2005, 100) identifies as the contrasting meanings behind automatism; when objects come to life, "signs of the body's subjection to power" are fused with "signs of its ostensive freedom." Indeed, Simmons's photographs confirm Ngai's assertion that "animation remains central to the production of the racially marked subject," in this case, the humanlike existence of the Asian figure once exploited for a single purpose (2005, 95).[9] This critique of women's sexual objectification necessarily

FIGURE 4.3 Laurie Simmons, *The Love Doll—Day 14 (Candy)*, 2010

encodes asymmetries of racial power; Simmons's feminist project releasing Asian women from their objectivizing frame illuminates the shared agenda of movement politics: social justice is implicitly a project of reanimation, here conveyed by the newly won ability to "stand up" for yourself (and, literally, by yourself). Yet what Gayatri Spivak (1988, 296) once depicted as the colonialist fantasy of white men "saving brown women from brown men" becomes the fantasy of white women saving brown sex toys.

The object is thus brought to life in the service of another's fantasy. On the self-reflexive nature of animated things, Barbara Johnson (2010, 91) ponders the desires of Pinocchio, the marionette who longs to be a real boy: "But why

FIGURE 4.4 Laurie Simmons, *The Love Doll—Day 25 (The Jump)*, 2010

wouldn't others seek to resemble human beings, after all?" She concludes, "The fantasy of others' desire to resemble oneself is always flattering to one's self-image.... [B]oth the other's desire and the subject's possession are fantasies of the subject." Race fetishism is taboo because it typifies this seeming erasure, circumventing a foundational liberal belief in human dignity. Restoring dignity—sex dolls are people too—reveals the inadequacies of countering racial imaginaries in conventional terms of political redress, an investment in "personhood." And yet, as in the last chapter on robots, extending personhood to things derives from a racial-gendered type: the prefeminist Asian woman. Consistent with the deep structure of the fetish, what is revealed here is a belief in her lack, what differentiates her from white Western women. Yet the limited horizon of this restoration is revealed in Žižek's (1997b, 27) awareness that "an ideological identification exerts a true hold on us precisely when we maintain an awareness that we are not fully identical to it, that there is a rich human person beneath it: 'not all is ideology, beneath the ideological mask, I am also a human person' is *the very form of ideology*, of its 'practical efficiency.'" Here, the sexual-racial fantasy of Asianized dolls come to life supports yet another fiction: we are all autonomous, all unique.

Mari Katayama's Beautiful Things

Asian American artist Laurel Nakadate and Japanese photographer Mari Katayama both play with racial scopophilia in unsettling ways, at first glance suggesting that introjected racist love expresses itself through exhibitionism. Eerily echoing Simmons's *The Love Doll,* Japanese artist Mari Katayama creates self-portraits using her own body "as a living sculpture."[10] Most feature her in stages of undress and in repose, often reclining and looking straight at the camera in the sensual pose reflected in countless oil paintings of female nudes. The artist provocatively invites spectatorship of the disabled, nonnormate body as it is staged within a claustrophobic world crowded with shiny and elaborately decorated things—shells, glass, lights, pillows, embroidery, dolls—and her own prostheses.[11] Deliberately eroticizing uncanny feeling, Katayama toys with the representation of Asian woman as object in her self-conscious aestheticization of embodied difference. In the West, her photography invites feminist crip analysis as it interfaces with more than one aspect of fetishism.

Katayama's 2016 self-portrait *Shell* reflects a staging common to her work: the subject stares directly at the camera surrounded by a glut of things—glass jars, ribbons, drapery, beading, shells, stuffed animals, and twinkle lights (figure 4.5). The image glitters; aesthetically pleasing objects are partly arranged and partly dumped in a way that renders the human subject indistinguishable from the pileup. This composition is enhanced by cloth sculptures of mannequins propped into sitting positions and body parts strewn about—fabric arms, hands, and torsos amid plastic and metal legs and feet. Featured in the foreground are her own prostheses. Born with tibial hemimelia, Katayama, at age nine, elected to have both legs amputated at or under the knee to eschew a wheelchair and walk with artificial limbs. These manufactured body parts clutter her self-portraits, emphasizing the subject's interface with the nonhuman. Other photographs focus on her left hand, which is shaped like a crab's claw, a reference exploited in images depicting her as a multilimbed, otherworldly sea creature on the beach. A gifted seamstress who made her

FIGURE 4.5 Mari Katayama, *Shell*, self-portrait, 2016

own clothing to accommodate her body, she experimented with textile art as a hobby that would become intrinsic to her art. Her soft sculptures harken back to artist Yayoi Kusama's early work portraying furniture with aspects of the human body, for one, a chair made of cloth penises.¹² Here, fabric limbs produce an inverse effect, rendering the human indistinguishable from the inorganic. In the context of the Western gaze, the anti-ableist self-portraits literalize the racialized associations of fetishism, as in Simmons's work, Asian woman as thing.

At the center of *Shell*, shutter release in hand, Katayama exposes the healed end of her amputated leg, the point at which the incision had been made. The image is discomfiting in its open invitation to look at a space of absence. Her expression is both blank and knowing, as if aware of being on display for normates and amputee fetishists alike. But the surrounding context of shiny, tiny things rescripts the assumed deficient body as likewise beautiful if also strategically artificial. Given the suggestive nature of her portraits, in 2018 art critic Holly Black asked Katayama if she was seeking to redefine what a sensual body could be. "I'm not very good at going against society's expectations!" she replied in translation. "People can see my work as controversial, but I don't do that on purpose, I just want to present the experiences that I have through my body, meaning the way I see the world, society, and the atmosphere around us."[13] The image plays to amputee fetishism directly, invoking the fetish by literalizing a scene of castration, yet it renders a scene of loss as both erotic and aesthetically pleasing.

In Katayama's self-portraits, the disabled body does not simply function as a prop or "narrative prosthesis" in visual storytelling, what Mitchell and Snyder (2000, 47) have defined as an "opportunistic metaphorical device" in literature, exploiting disability for reasons other than illuminating differently abled subjects. Rather, the photographs insist on the materiality of the nonnormative body as well as its possibilities for play and self-fantasy. Katayama has self-consciously expressed an activist's anti-ableist critique of how the disabled body is denied basic human pleasures such as dress-up and adornment, both deemed luxuries by the medical establishment. In the performance "High Heel Project," she demonstrates the challenges of acquiring a pair of high heels, which require an additional set of arched feet.[14] Her physical difference was a source of bullying at school; sewing, costuming, and fashion, all inspirations for her art, were means of displaying her indifference to that aggression. Yet the politicism inherent to her work goes further than the creation of a defiant crip spectacle. She inverts the negative valence ascribed to the nonnormate body by insisting on its sensuality or girlishness. *I'm Wearing Little High Heels* (2011), typical of her self-portraits, poses her in a messy bedroom outfitted in a way that suggests Liza Minnelli in *Cabaret*: sexual display and showmanship coupled with vulnerability. Reflecting the photograph's title, the biological entity "Katayama" props a tiny shoe on the end of her appendage where a normate's foot would be; her difference enables a sense of whimsy, doll-like dress-up. Yet the adult-sized prosthetic feet in the foreground also wear high heels. This duality conveys an indifference to the distinction between the inorganic and organic: the detached foot wearing shoes is also indelibly *I*. Katayama's self-portraits insist on the interface between human and nonhuman, reflecting disability activist Jillian Weise's (2018) identification as cyborg to celebrate inorganic prostheses as intrinsic to her selfhood.

Katayama invites fetishistic desire on multiple levels; provoking uncanny feeling and the categorical uncertainty concerning persons and things, her work also suggests pedophilia and foot fetishism. *I'm Wearing Little High Heels* was shown side-by-side with a self-portrait entitled *I Have Child's Feet* (2011) (figure 4.6). The same bedroom is cluttered now with kawaii bric-a-brac: a teddy bear, dresses, mobiles, and a headless life-size cloth doll intricately beaded and adorned with lace. "Decorative orientalism" (J. Lee 2021) is suggested only through the central human figure: she wears smaller, pink protheses displaying naked feet; child-sized leg braces rest alongside her. In *I Have Child's Feet*, she is a doll with geisha-like makeup, flat affect, and awkward posture; her manner of dress evokes the childlike sexuality of female manga or anime characters. Katayama has become the ageless object of child's play, a toy indistinguishable from those she sews. Suggesting the hyperrealistic fetish dolls that compel Simmons's interest in *The Love Doll*, the self-portrait *Yellow Room* (2010) likewise depicts Katayama as a mannequin, its whitened limbs frozen in stillness. The alive or dead ambiguity is enhanced by the stiffness of her poses; neither organic nor inorganic appendages skew as real. Here, the promise of disability theorist Eunjung Kim's question, "What does it mean to unbecome human by becoming an object?" is suggested by Katayama's work. "Embodying objecthood, surrendering agency, and practicing powerlessness," Kim (2015, 296) writes, "may open up an anti-ableism, antiviolence queer ethics of proximity that reveals the workings of the boundary of the human." Moreover, Katayama exploits fetishistic desire in depicting fantastical scenes in which the human and inanimate become indistinguishable.

While Katayama is a prize-winning artist shown widely in Japan, she has only recently gained prominence outside it. Recognition in the West has been attributed to Simon Baker, former curator of photography at the Tate Modern, who witnessed Katayama's work at a photography festival in Amsterdam. On the opening of her 2019 *Broken Heart* show in London, Baker, now director of the Maison Européenne de la Photographie, was asked why Katayama's photographs were so popular in the UK. His speculation reveals his struggle to counter the whiff of race fetishism or crip spectacle in the West and regroup toward the art's transcendent appeal:

> Mari's works looked just different from any other photographs that I had seen before. That's not because she is Japanese. It's on a completely different level. I think I felt that way because the photographic worlds she creates are so unique.... Mari's photographs have a rare kind of

FIGURE 4.6 Mari Katayama, *I Have Child's Feet*, self-portrait, 2011

communicative ability. With the 'voice' of photography that she has made her own, I guess she will easily surmount the differences between Eastern and Western cultures.[15]

Is it Katayama's photographic worlds that look "different" or the exposed, nonnormate, Asian female body that inhabits them? By invoking an East-West cultural divide, the European curator implies that Katayama's Japaneseness represents what must be overcome to render the photographs legible. I would suggest the opposite: for Western spectators, racial difference *enables* what is communicated, in this case, how Asian female "thingness" heightens the eroticism of bodily difference and furthers the scopophilic logic of the fantasy scenarios Katayama stages. The crowded fields of her self-portraits suggest that desire circulated through beautiful things may resonate precisely because she *is* Japanese.

The Lady or the Tiger? Laurel Nakadate

Responding to the racially fetishistic gaze has inspired numerous Asian American visual artists. Wayne Yung's film *My German Boyfriend* (2002) skewers the Rice King using humor to expose Orientalist desire. Nguyen Tan Hoang appears to reverse the thesis of Richard Fung's ([1991] 2012) essay "Looking for My Penis" in his video *Forever Bottom!* (1999), which parodically embraces the pornographic fantasy of the anally receptive Asian gay male "bottom." Performance artist Patty Chang's 2009 video installation *The Product Love* (*Die Ware Liebe*) (originally *A Chinoiserie out of the Old West*) takes as its starting point the fascination that German intellectual Walter Benjamin held for Chinese American film actress Anna May Wong. Seeking to uncover "why so many Western men desire Asian women," Debbie Lum's documentary *Seeking Asian Female* (2012) follows a mail-order bride from China who arrives in San Francisco to meet her never-before-seen white husband. At first glance, these artists appear to indulge the Asian fetishist to suggest, in the footsteps of David Henry Hwang's canonical play *M. Butterfly*, an inversion of erotic power dynamics. Of course, for Asian American visual artists interrogating scopic desires on behalf of the objectified, this pivot is rarely straightforward. The aforementioned artists unveil the reciprocity and immateriality of racial fantasizing (Yung); the embrace of type (Nguyen); the impossibility of translating desire (Chang); or, more prosaically, middle-age marital woes (Lum).

More discomfiting are those artists who ambiguously embrace racist love as a means of self-affirmation. A collective coping mechanism, racist love is fundamentally narcissistic, about the nation's exploitation of Asian difference for self-definition.[16] Yet Ranjana Khanna (2003) suggests that colonial melancholia arises from an ambivalent sense of affiliation, implying that neither colonizer nor colonized can ever disconnect from the ego-ideal represented by the group. Like Katayama, biracial performance artist Laurel Nakadate flirts with the suggestion of colonial ideation by staging the scopic pleasures of racial-gendered thingness in which Asian American women's subjectivity becomes inextricable from pleasurable self-objectification.

Inciting viewer uneasiness surrounding racial-sexual typing, Nakadate appears to subvert the presumed predator/prey dynamics between white men and Asian women in a simple reversal. In a short, cringeworthy clip of her video project *I Want to Be the One Who Walks in the Sun* (2006), she stares into a camera that witnesses her "playing" with a series of older, unfit, unattractive white men. They are strangers, we are told, whom she has met on the street and followed home, strangers who have agreed to be filmed with her doing whatever they like: drawing, dancing, and so forth. Their melancholy appearance and sad living situations deliberately confuse assumptions about identity categories of privilege and marginality as the video self-consciously stages a slightly shaming sexual-racial spectacle triangulated among the viewer, the artist who looks knowingly at the camera, and her seemingly unwitting heterosexual, cisgendered, white male subjects. Controlling the fetishistic gaze is operative in many of her works that likewise engage amateur actors, presumably "old guys she met in places like the Home Depot parking lot, who came up and talked to her because she's pretty."[17]

Her video *Beg for Your Life* (2006) follows a similar script in which straight white men are rendered an abject type as they are staged as literally begging for their lives. One critic summarizes: "I have bitched about Laurel Nakadate's work before. In a nutshell, the artist finds these pathetic, lonely guys and convinces them to be involved in her videos. They're so excited that a young attractive woman is paying attention to them, they'll do whatever she says. We get to see video of them in their crappy apartments pretending to beg for their lives as Nakadate points a toy gun at their heads. It's awkward, stilted and uncomfortable playacting, supposedly part of the work's point."[18] Like the short videos *Lessons 1–10* (2001) and *Happy Birthday* (2000), which share that broad conceit of stranger solicitation, *Beg for Your Life* received criticism based on an ethics of exploitation. Her subjects are rendered pathetic through the power of her surprising self-possession—and prettiness—against their age, poverty, presumed desperation, and inferred loneliness. They enjoy playing, but they are also played. Do strangers tempted by the candy of youth and sex in a Home Depot parking lot deserve humiliation for succumbing to a honey trap, or more specific to my focus here, the fantasy of the (vaguely) Asian young woman who is, as in my epigraph, yet white enough to understand? As novelist Mary Gaitskill notes admiringly, Nakadate orchestrates spectacles that are "weird-sweet and also a little bit horrible."[19]

Nakadate's photographic series *Lucky Tiger* (2009), in which she deliberately stages herself as sex object, continues along these lines, while insinuating normative white, male, heterosexual spectatorship, if more abstractly. *Lucky Tiger* consists of 4-by-6-inch photos of herself in provocative pinup poses—straddling the back of a pickup, arched back, or crotch open to the camera (figure 4.7). Invoking a retro brand of men's grooming products ("Lucky Tiger has been helping men get lucky since 1935"), her title seems to invoke the fable that ends with the question, "The lady or the tiger?," in which the male protagonist is set up to choose between two doors: one hiding sex-as-reward and the other, death. In Nakadate's series, it's both. If *I Want to Be the One Who Walks in the Sun* confuses predator and prey, *Lucky Tiger* asks the viewer to assume a self-consciously predatory male gaze by staging a seeming embrace of racist love, of racial-sexual type, that offers the viewer twin fetishes, racial (her mixed-race

FIGURE 4.7 Laurel Nakadate, *Lucky Tiger*, 2009

Asian heritage) and national (stars-and-stripes bikini, pickup truck, cowboy boots). Yet the photographs imply another type lurking off camera.

Each photograph represents a collaboration: we view her image through the inked fingerprints of men who apparently responded to the artist's solicitation on Craigslist, inviting them to look at the grainy, drugstore-processed prints. The smudges left by the touch of these (presumed) anonymous men successfully distinguish the work from the genre of narcissistic selfie; they are reminders that observers are seeing not just an image but a *process*—someone has been here before us and left a trace that mediates and obscures our vision. *Lucky Tiger* asks viewers to participate in the sexual-racial objectification of the Asian woman, to assume the same position as the one marked by the anonymity of internet solicitation. Unlike the abject male subjects of her videos, their presence is only imagined, a subject of our fantasy as much as the pinup in the photos. Here, Nakadate's impulse is not to reverse the gaze but to make us all fetishists—complicit in unseemly desire, both her collaborator and her dupe. Her self-implicating play echoes *M. Butterfly* as it engages fluctuating positions of erotic power; as in Hwang's depiction of Asian fetishism gone awry, the photographs do not simply expose and counter fetishism by reversing positions of mastery. Playing with the form of soft-core porn with a twist, Nakadate has simultaneously indulged us by letting us look and asked us to claim ownership of our own voyeurism.

Moreover, as in her oeuvre as a whole, the series implicates the artist in her self-fetishization, baring her willingness (or need?) to play to type. Her project of materializing self-as-body recalls Anne Cheng's provocative proposition that (self) objectification might be subject making. In "Wounded Beauty: An Exploratory Essay on Race, Feminism, and the Aesthetic Question," Cheng (2000, 204) situates Nancy Kwan's infamous number, "I Enjoy Being a Girl," from the musical *Flower Drum Song* as a multifaceted template for unpacking fetishistic pleasure at the point "where the consumer and the object of consumption merge." While the scene is often read as a transparent celebration of female narcissism and acquiescence, Cheng (2000, 203) reads Kwan's character, Linda Low, as externalizing beauty, demonstrating the tension between self and the ideal: "We often fail to acknowledge how the fetish as a form of perceptual logic may be crucial to any experience of pleasure. I do not mean to suggest that if we universalize the notion of the fetish, we can then depathologize it. I am interested rather in asking whether the very process of pleasure might be inherently objectifying and whether such so-called objectification might compromise—or constitute—the observer's own subject position more than the viewer would like or can afford to acknowledge." Cheng's reading here depends on the presence of the mirror: as Linda Low, Kwan is the object of not only the viewer's pleasure, but her own. Externalizing beauty represents the catalyst to self-validation. Thus, Cheng recuperates fetishistic desire as not simply motivated by the possession and domination of another; rather, she underscores the "complicated psychical procedure that encompasses identificatory *complicity* as much as identificatory othering," her enjoyment in participatory staging (2000, 208, emphasis mine). Similarly, in *Lucky Tiger*, there is no radical reimaging of social organization; nor is there a liberatory outside to the racially philic scopic economy in which Asian American women operate, no fantasy of multifaceted "personhood" obscured by a tiger-print bikini.

Nakadate's and Katayama's art suggests two discomfiting propositions: first, that Asian women's creative practice is institutionally celebrated in the world of high art when they embrace exhibitionism, adhere to racial-sexual exoticism. Second, as in a cursory reading of Linda Low's dance number, that the possibilities for Asian woman's self-love in the West are inextricable from racist love. What is unsettling about Nakadate's treatment of race fetishism is the suggestion that repetitious exhibitionism can be a source of (her) pleasure, one necessarily mediated by an inferred white male presence. Yet in those partially obscuring fingerprints, this presence is also displaced, faded away, existing only as a trace. And in Kayatama's work, the lasting impression is the image of her staring at herself staring at the camera, shutter in hand. As in Zhang's *Three Graces* (figure Intro.3), they both reference the visuals underlying race fetishism, twisting them to other ends.

Multimedia artists thus stretch the covenants that situate the public text of race through the optimistic lens of equality. Sexual objectification and racial scopophilia here test communally accepted narratives surrounding the fetishism of Asian women, but ultimately also test the narrow ethical structure that limits Asian American political understanding of race fetishism to two choices, consent or resistance, the lady or the tiger.

Parody's Excess

When it comes to racialized desire, "remedying" the harm of race fetishism cannot be achieved through projects associated with liberal social movements: reclaiming pride, restoring voice, or establishing better role models. Sexual fantasy lends itself to a critique of liberalism precisely because it is positioned as being *outside* the purview of redress. Impolitic fantasy is incompletely incorporated within, in Wendy Brown's terms, the "wounded attachments" that attend identity politics, the presumption that sexual desire, distinct from sexual identity, can be legislated in the same context as rights violations. What is the collective effect of (somebody else's) impolitic desire? Identified and parodied by Asian Americans, the social "problem" of race fetishism is that it compromises Asian American relationships with each other, the egalitarian gaze of reciprocal desire. One remedy forces the inadequacies of liberal notions of racial redress into view: racially representative pornography.

This relationship between sex and racial rights was subject to parody in Comedy Central's treatment of scholar Darrell Hamamoto's call for *better* porn for (heterosexual) Asian Americans. In a 2003 segment of *The Daily Show* titled "They So Horny?," the television show highlighted the incommensurability between espousing equal opportunity and equal opportunity for arousal.[20] The fake news segment finds Professor Hamamoto of the University of California–Davis riffing off his academic article, "The Joy Fuck Club: Prolegomenon to an Asian American Porno Practice" (1998), which argues that Asian Americans suffer foreclosed desire through their fetishistic objectification (here, of women and gay men) or absence as sexual agents (here, of heterosexual men) in pornography. Asian Americans' desire for each other, he argues, is forestalled by white introjection.²¹ *Daily Show* "correspondent" Samantha Bee chooses to parody one aspect of the professor's argument, his call for greater visibility of (heterosexual) Asian American men in mainstream pornography. As in the Asian American woman's assertion, "I am a person," Hamamoto's activist project seeks to restore sexual agency to heterosexual Asian American men by invoking the rhetoric of representational politics. A seemingly sympathetic Bee "feels" the trauma of Asian American men's absence in porn, treating it as a serious social problem: "Dr. Hamamoto has a dream that one day Asian men will be judged not by the color of their skin but by the character of their penis." The conceit of Comedy Central's fake news story is that the absence of Asian men in porn is shocking evidence of discrimination that might be rectified by the professor's visionary, self-produced video featuring "yellow on yellow" sex.²²

The sequence skewers both academic pretentiousness ("It's the worse piece of !%&@ I have ever seen"), Asian American studies itself, and the progressive teleology underlying liberal race activism: exclusion countered with visibility results in greater opportunity. Thus, Bee's call for equality-in-pornography borrows from the rhetoric of the civil rights movement. Concluding on a wistful note of futurity, Bee disingenuously asks former Star Trek actor turned LGBTQ activist George Takei, "Do you think the day will come when your sons and grandsons will be accepted in this country . . . as porn actors?" Hamamoto's attempt to claim one's desire as a heterosexual man of color when faced with an indifferent erotic imaginary validates notions of the injurious effects of sexual fantasy. What is parodied here is its means of redress, the limited script of US racial justice based on the metric of equal representation. As the *Daily Show* questions private fantasy as discriminatory action, it also illuminates the narrow horizon of racial redress.

If the narrative of incrementally progressive racial advancement through greater visibility and equal opportunity represents a core democratic belief, does it likewise apply to pornography? Social movement activism is likewise satirized in filmmaker Greg Pak's independent short *Asian Pride Porn!* (1999), which offers a singular solution to the social "problem" of mainstream pornography's failure to accommodate Asian American desire, a topic likewise broached in his *Machine Love*, discussed in the previous chapter.²³ As in the *Daily Show*, Pak exposes the inadequacies of applying the techniques of liberal politics to redress erotic "injustice." His video features playwright David Henry Hwang calling for an antidote to Asian fetishism based on the assumption that its normative white, male, heterosexual erotic spectatorship forecloses the desire of others. Acknowledging that, for Asian men, phone sex with hot Asian women might do "in a pinch," Hwang goes on to promote a phony video, *Asian Pride Porn XXX*, praising the clip of comedically rendered Asian-on-Asian sex that follows ("Hi. Did you order the *Mongolian beef*?"). Hwang ends with naive sincerity: "From onanism to activism. Asian Pride Porn." An announcer informs us that our porn will arrive discreetly in a box labeled, "Chinese American Voter Turnout in Sacramento Municipal Elections 1972–1976, Volume X," thereby ensuring that no one will open it. Pak's video parallels the realms in which Asian Americans are marginalized: nobody cares about the political power of the Chinese in Sacramento; nobody cares about how Asian Americans get off.

What is held up to parody is not the content of sexual fantasy, but the fallacious belief that sexual representation can be remedied via the same mechanisms that underwrite race activism: visibility and representation as the corrective to grievance. Comedy Central and Greg Pak skewer the notion that racialized sexual fantasy constitutes a rights violation, highlighting the absurdity of counteracting systemic racial structures through the conceit of equivalence. The shorts question assumed reciprocity, the idea that someone *else's* fantasy—here, the white, heterosexual man's Asian fetish—inhibits same race desire or horizontal comradeship in more than one sense. Pak's video, like Comedy Central's fake news story, is a send-up not of Asian fetishism, but of liberal coalitional politics, or more specifically, its limits.

Of Nurses, Sailors, and Pirates: The Fetish of Home

Asian Pride Porn! is good for a laugh. But if race fetishism serves as a conduit for illuminating limited forms of racial legibility, the very opacity of "private" desire can also queer the activist's project. Debuting the same year as *Asian Pride Porn!*, Pak's *Fighting Grandpa* (1999), a documentary featuring his Korean immigrant grandparents, screened at Asian American film festivals. Intending to address cultural misunderstanding among generations, the film engages in the somewhat generic project of Korean American ethnic roots recovery. Yet that narrative is hijacked by a startling postmortem reveal: his grandfather as fetishist.

From the perspective of a third-generation Asian American, the film first ponders how Pak's grandparents managed to have a loving relationship given the context of arranged marriage, long periods spent apart due to migration, and, especially, the unyielding, undemonstrative, parsimonious temperament of his patriarchal grandfather, You Pyung. While his beloved grandmother's devotion to her husband is clear if unfathomable to others, three years after his grandfather's death, Pak is left to speculate on the nature of his grandfather's attachment to his wife, Wechun Pak, and vice versa. To that end, he cycles through conventional explanations of Korean gender conventions and shared immigrant hardship.[24] Nevertheless, the activist's exploration of the collective foundations of intimacy is effectively disrupted by what seems to be unassimilable to that genealogical narrative, the uncertain disclosure of fetishistic desire. *Fighting Grandpa* ends with an earnest voiceover overlaid with images of his deceased grandfather's scrapbook:

> I wanted to believe in grandpa. I wanted to believe he loved her, that he just didn't express it in ways I'd understand. But I can't find the evidence. I look in the scrapbook he kept during the ten years he was in America and grandma was in Korea. But all I find are random photos and clippings. I don't know who these people are, what these pictures meant to him. All these photos of women. Clipped and saved during those years of separation. But then it strikes me. They all look like nurses. Nurses. Just like grandma.

How does this postmortem discovery resolve the grandson's inquiry into his ethnic roots? The revelation, "They all look like nurses" can be read as a romantic gesture made necessary by the trauma of migration and separation, a trauma readily accepted by the film's presumed Asian American audience. In the absence of his beloved, You Pyung settled for images that reminded him of his wife, the clippings a means of keeping her present.

Yet Pak's narration perhaps inadvertently makes the scrapbook discovery equivalent to finding the deceased's porn stash. Even as the film layers photograph after photograph of nurses from his grandfather's collection, the narrator does not state the obvious, that Grandpa, once a respected pastor, entertained a nurse fetish. At the moment in which private desire must be reconciled with the privileged, intended narrative of ethnic recovery and recuperation, the needle skips a groove. The accidental discovery of his grandfather's fetish queers sentimental closure by reframing the grandson's question: not "Did he love his wife?" but "*How* did he love her?"

The anonymous clippings of becapped women—among them, a pilgrim—lend ambiguous insight into the psychosexual desires of Grandpa. The difference in interpretation depends on the narrative's explicit gesture to subordinate these anonymous women to the privileged figure of the wife; the nurses are "just like" Grandma, not vice versa. She is the original that the other women are meant to resemble and recall, the authentic presence for which they substitute. That understanding turns away from fetishistic desire toward a story more befitting to a grandson invested in the projects of ethnic reconciliation privileged by early Asian American history. Such an analysis also depends on collapsing erotic desire into romantic love. Yet Pak's film also suggests that his grandfather found sexual gratification through the figure of the nurse *or her cap*; it follows that grandpa's attachment to his wife was based on her ability to embody that erotic figure. That is, he loved her as a nurse.[25]

Fetishistic desire counters the film's attempt to uncover cultural explanations for intrafamily relations. At one point, the director's aunt testifies that her mother once confided that she didn't enjoy "the physical part of the relationship or the marriage," that she "felt almost dirty" about sex. Pak's narration then intervenes to attribute this to his family's Christian fundamentalism and, by implication of his framing, to the feudalism of arranged marriage. Yet the ending revelation challenges this cultural assessment of sexual repression, opening the second-hand confession to another interpretation: Grandma could not enjoy sex *as* the fetishized object; she could not role play. As if to visualize that resistance, the film depicts the grandmother as invalid, not the caregiver that she had been all her life. The perhaps more startling implication of the film is that while it seeks to restore Wechun Pak to a life beyond her image as loving grandparent, to reconstruct her personal history—and thus her individuality—in an act of feminist and ethnic recovery, the ending actually erases it. "They all look like nurses," the narrator tells us. "Nurses." Wechun was a nurse. To her most intimate companion, everything else may have been irrelevant.

Fetishism thus queers Asian American narratives about ethnic recovery in unanticipated ways. Nguyen Tan Hoang's short video *Pirated!* (2000) at first appears to be a realist documentary account of a refugee's story, depicting his family's 1978 escape from Vietnam by boat, repeated attacks by Thai pirates, and eventual rescue by West German sailors.[26] This historical account quickly dissolves into erotic fantasies and dream sequences of (Asian) pirates and (white) sailors. *Pirated!* locates the origins of refugee fetishism in traumatic migration. Dressed as sailors and pirates, Nguyen's actors perform sex acts within a montage of Hollywood swashbuckling films and campy Vietnamese musicals. The desire to be ravished by these hypermasculine types lies in excess of the refugee story. What is hijacked or "pirated" is the narrative of a Vietnamese American's uncomplicated return to homeland. Queer fetishistic desire enables his critique of Viet Khieu nostalgia as itself a fantasy; *home* is not the good object here. *Fighting Grandpa* likewise points to the excesses of Asian American need for ethnic understanding across generations, what can't be reconciled through, for example, greater awareness of the cultural differences between Koreans and Americans or the disclosure of migration history itself. Homeland and return are merely the displaced objects of refugee desire.

Fighting Grandpa does not hint about the colonial origins of Pak's grandfather's fetish; it does not speculate, for example, on whether his grandfather's religious commitment was tied to an erotic attachment to nuns sent to seek converts on the Korean peninsula or his time at a seminary in the United States, connections suggested by the clipping he saved of a pilgrim couple. But the film ties the fetish to migration by implying that object substitution is a necessary consequence of marital separation and the melancholic recovery of Korea itself. More broadly, memory of homeland is both accessed through and blurred by sexual longing, locating them, in part, as twinned libidinal impulses produced by the diasporic condition. That is, for the Asian American fetishist, migration *forces* erotic object substitution. Yet the film also suggests that the processes of memorialization, as in Nguyen's *Pirated!*, are not wholly distinct from those of erotic gratification. The scrapbook seems to bring Pak closure, providing some proof of his grandfather's attachment to his grandmother, even as it was indeed the deceased's porn stash. But what the film likewise reveals is that culture, history, and context fail to illuminate the complexities of individual desire; they can't account for the paradox of a stern, lawgiving patriarch who yet harbored fantasies of infantilization, of being cared for by a woman in uniform.

Fetishism's structure of substitution may likewise apply to the immigrant story masquerading as object: we prefer a tale in which memory, affection, and intimacy move seamlessly across diasporic space and time, awaiting reunification with loved ones. But we might be left with a story that marks that romantic vision as yet another fantasy. The desire to recover ethnic roots, origins, or homeland may merely serve as a screen for some other animating loss. Pirate hat or nurse's cap: the latent erotics of diasporic migration are essentially fetishistic.

I Love Myself through Asian Women: Academic Object Love

As the blogosphere testifies in colloquial understanding, race fetishism is impolitic: it "stereotypes." Yet "typing" is not only enabling; I would suggest that it is a *requirement* of coalitional politics. The ambivalent structure of fetishistic desire began to cast an uncomfortable focus on my own practice as an Asian

Americanist. It may be clear from this chapter that, much like fetishism itself, my objects of study, art by Simmons, Nakadate, or Pak, are methodologically subordinate to the story they generate. The story here is not a privileged text; it's the discursive frame that renders racial meaning legible in keeping with the field's foundational values of redistributive justice and equality. Ironically, what Linda Williams (2004, 286) has noted about the erotic thrill underlying interracial porn, its encoding of stereotypes on both sides of the color line, illuminates the potentially split feelings underlying critical race practice: "The very taboos that once effectively policed the racial border now work in the service of eroticizing its transgression." At one level, constituting race fetishism as injury might be said to establish a new taboo that polices racial borders with unforeseen affective outcomes. As in chapter 2, I pose this as a halting, self-reflexive question to illuminate the split feeling and perverse spectatorship underlying my own critical practice as an Asian Americanist.

In thinking through how antiracism's academic objects of study enact an erotics of prohibition and transgression, I turn to Kobena Mercer's (1994) seminal essay, "Reading Racial Fetishism: The Photographs of Robert Mapplethorpe," which offers two distinct readings over time. Depicting African American male nudes in homoerotic and aestheticized scenes, Mapplethorpe's 1986 *Black Book* spurred numerous debates on art and obscenity in the US culture wars of the 1980s. Poet and activist Essex Hemphill called Mapplethorpe's photographs "insulting," and the *Village Voice* deemed them to be "ugly, degrading, obscene" (Morrisroe 1995, 253), a viewpoint later shared by conservative senator Jesse Helms, who held Mapplethorpe's work up as a reason to withhold federal funding of "indecent art."[27] Much of the controversy focused on a single image, *Man in Polyester Suit*, which blatantly reinforced the cultural script of Black male hypersexuality by centering on the exposed penis of Mapplethorpe's then partner, Milton Moore, dressed in a suit and cut off at the head.[28] I want to focus here not on the debate over pornography and art, but on the debate the images engendered between Kobena Mercer and himself.

Mercer's 1986 reading of the photographs makes a compelling critique of the fetishistic reduction of Black men, their literalizing of Fanon's "the Negro . . . *is* a penis" (Mercer 1994, 170). But in 1989, he proposed an alternative reading that revised his assumption that "'fetishism' is necessarily a bad thing" (1994, 190). The tension between the two parts of the essay enacts the tensions between identification and disavowal surrounding sexual desire and becomes in part an examination of his own investments as a Black, gay, male spectator, and, I would emphasize, academic. At the heart of his revision lie two competing identifications that provoke seemingly distinct affective responses. His "anger" at the photographs' racial politics of exploitation and objectification secured his position as Black activist, but only at the expense of his homoerotic desire. Mercer's first reading thus served as a cloak for arousal, the feeling that he rejected as a problematic identification with mastery. That is, as a gay desiring subject, the photographs implicated him in a racial fantasy scenario, he notes, in the "same position in the fantasy of mastery that I said was that of the white male subject!" (1994, 193). One can debate whether the viewpoint open to him as a "black gay spectator" is "the same" position of mastery. But his revisionist reading of the racial fetish represents a democratic expansion that defies early feminist theories of the gaze: Mercer makes the case for fetishism as a site of split identifications by arguing that Mapplethorpe's work makes available viewing pleasures for "black spectators as much as anyone else" (193). Acknowledging that Mapplethorpe's photographs can be read at once as homophobic and homoerotic, racist and antiracist, Mercer insists on a broadened field of spectatorship.

What I would highlight here are the assumptions that surround the *academic* production of racial discourse. What is intriguing is not necessarily that Mercer changed his mind—he does not after all repudiate his first reading of the racial fetish as complicit with the Black male stereotype. Rather, the first reading authenticated a specific political identity expected of Black academics; in his condemnation, he reproduced another racial type: not, as in Mapplethorpe's version, Black man as wholly body, but Black man as righteous. Mercer's subsequent analysis of his knowledge production reveals that he had internalized expectations placed on the minority academic to the degree that he would disavow what is perhaps an obvious reading of the photographs. Mercer's responses to the racial stereotype thus reveal the fixity of yet another racial type, the academic of color as condemning watchdog.[29]

The appearance of two options from which to take a stand—as in *Yo, Is This Racist*, a representation is either racist or it is not—effectively masks the expectation that, given the stereotype of the Black academic, there is actually only one: it's racist. The controversies surrounding the politics of the fetish thus become a litmus test of foreclosed flexibility, revealing the degree to which scholarship on race was itself bounded by liberal expectation in the 1980s. That context seemed to disallow the ambivalence underlying fetishistic desire itself; Mercer's (1994, 184) recognition that it "enables understanding of the psychic structure of disavowal, and the splitting of levels of conscious and unconscious belief" applies to his own discourse surrounding the fetish. What is at stake isn't whether, to echo the cliché about pornography, one knows a racial fetish when one sees one, but that the very structure of substitution and disavowal—anger at dehumanization that displaces other identifications or affective responses—unveils the fetishistic structure of early ethnic studies critique. We required the (racist) object in order to create ourselves through the (racist) object. Moreover, Mercer's revision underscores the slightly masochistic nature of our critical enterprise—veiled pleasure in injury—that was and is nonetheless also politically enabling. Obscenity debates in the 1980s obscured the potentially more provocative implication of Mapplethorpe's work, that race circulates not simply as a narrative of violent oppression or white guilt but as a discomfiting source of erotic attraction, of racist love. Foregrounding that ambiguous pleasure, Juliana Chang (2012, 1) acutely flags the "affect of traumatic enjoyment" of Asian American novels, foregrounding the sadomasochist tendencies underlying the consumption of racialized narratives, which, as I suggest in chapter 2, likewise animate people of color's pursuit of racialized tchotchkes. Mercer's double take, intellect versus feeling, demonstrates the ways in which resistance to typing paradoxically creates type.

If I read Mercer's encounter with the image as a metareflection on academic queer of color critical practice, I recognize that this duality applies to my own practice as well. The blur between academic and fetishist became apparent to me after I became interested in a sculpture by Canadian visual artist Elisha Lim entitled *Drag McQueen* (2011). Composed of two wedge boots fashioned from cake, one frosted in chocolate, the piece calls on colloquial understanding of shoe fetishism while suggesting something more (figure 4.8). The chocolate shoe's pink icing reads in loopy script:

Shoes
Oh my god
these shoes
RULE!
let's get
some,
betch[30]

Lim's piece is a clever rift on comedian Liam Kyle Sullivan's video *Shoes*, which repeats the same tag line, campily satirizing an overinvestment in footwear. It highlights queer of color critique of commodity fetishism and the displaced libidinal energy that both announces and screens same-sex desire; "let's get some" is presumably addressed to a woman but invokes shopping through a

FIGURE 4.8 "Oh my god / these shoes / RULE!"; Elisha Lim, *Drag McQueen* cake sculpture (2011); photo credit: Vincent Lim

masculine sexual idiom. The agential top presumes a feminized bottom—being someone's "bitch." The cursive letter *i* written in icing (which looks more like an *e*) can also be misread, "let's get some / butch," a slippage that might be contextualized by Lim's (2010) graphic book, *100 Butches*, consisting of sketches of random women who represent her crushes. The piece plays with multiple forms of substitution invoking both fetishized objects and the various processes of fulfilling desire through them: from chocolate cake to shoe to women, from eating to shopping to sex.³¹

To find out more about the sculpture, I emailed the artist, asking them, for one, what happened to the cake. Unfortunately, I put my query thusly: "I have to ask: did you save it or did you have to throw it out? Better yet, did you *eat* it?" Lim's email response was telling. They replied, "Are you Asian? I'm wondering if you're coming to a place of being subject to the fetish, or of indulging in the fetish? I'm sorry, if this question seems rude, but I just want to make sure I understand everything!" I was mortified: the Asian North American artist thought they were being catfished by a creepy stalker. Which I then came to realize that I was. I *loved* the cake shoe and not simply because I myself have attachment to footwear and, sadly, cake. The exchange speaks to the porousness between the Asian Americanist and Asian fetishist—given my research for this chapter, Google believes that I am in search of a "Filipina lovely." My overinvestment in the object of study mirrored the fetishist's overinvestment in their object substitute. I endowed the sculpture with symbolic importance that legitimizes and confirms my identity, which, for better or worse, is inseparable from my academic identity. I would most certainly consume/buy/make/Instagram those shoe cakes (which, incidentally, are varnished). The artist's query, "Are you Asian?," implies that if I were, I could not then occupy a position of scopophilic mastery over Asian women, underwriting my (unseemly) interest. Mercer's revisionist reading of his own work implies that horizontal lines of affiliation do not resolve the asymmetry intrinsic to fetishistic desire.

The uneasy kinship between the occasions for fetishistic indulgence and academic critique becomes evident in a 2013 online feature in *New York Magazine* entitled, "Nine Sexy College Classes Happening This Fall." The tongue-in-cheek article highlights, for one, an undergraduate course in Asian women's representation offered at MIT with the subtitle, "Fetish fraught":

> Anthropology 21A: "Images of Asian Women: Dragon Ladies and Lotus Blossoms"
>
> Through debates about Orientalism, gender, and power, MIT students will work out the "circumstances that create and perpetuate" the stereotypes of Asian women: "dragon ladies, lotus blossoms, despotic tyrants, desexualized servants, and docile subordinates." Also: probably meet a lot of Asian women.[32]

The idea of the race fetishist showing up and encountering a room full of Asian American feminists is hilarious. But what the feature inadvertently illuminates is the way in which stereotype analysis heralds the "wounded attachment" of coalitional identity. Its humor fails to override the conceit that the presence of Asian women makes a course sexy; the accompanying titillating image of a coy Asian woman in a graduation gown reinforces this. Nevertheless, the parody forces a parallel between the occasion for critiquing the fetish for one audience and the occasion for its indulgence for others; both audiences have differing intents but partake in similar structures of desiring. For the former, the process of self-creation out of differentiation (I'm *not* that image) nonetheless mirrors that of those who might show up, likewise looking for an externalized repository for their narcissism (I love myself through Asian women). (This was indeed operative in the case of Asian fetishist Michael Lohman, a doctoral student at Princeton who stalked, harassed, and violated Asian female students in 2005 in a very specific way.)[33]

This is not to say that the activist enterprise implicit in pedagogy represents a kind of collective pathology: courses like this one, focused on identifying and critiquing the stereotype, validate the productive nature of fantasy and affirm its influence. Rather, I would point to the fetishistic structure of this (pleasurable) means of cultural self-determination: we create ourselves through disidentification with the object that becomes, as in chapter 2's depiction of Black and Asian memorabilia, an obsession. I *do indeed* love myself through Asian women. Inheriting scripts of consciousness raising derived from 1960s movement politics, this solidarity is ritualized in the semi-public forum of the classroom. But in marking Anthropology 21A as the site of two seemingly contradictory pleasures, the article's attempt at humor unwittingly points to a paradox: transgressing a prohibition through a joke may release libidinal energy more efficaciously than the object itself. (As I discuss in the introduction, this backfired on comedian Sarah Silverman when she expressed her love for "Chinks" to skewer people who use the word "Chink.") The very act of marking stereotyping as politically incorrect may succeed in creating not only racial consciousness but erotically charged racial taboos that heighten the pleasures of the end-run around the ethnic joke.[34]

This tension regarding the erotics of transgression surfaces in the context of other activist creative practices. A foundational text in Asian North American feminist media, Helen Lee's 1990 experimental film *Sally's Beauty Spot*, enacts this contradiction in the process of exposing Asian American women's fetishization. The film portrays Sally's awareness of her sexual-racial objectification as symbolized by a black mole on her chest, her "beauty spot." Shot in gorgeous black-and-white, the film's loving focus on the protagonist's body parts recalls Mapplethorpe's aestheticized nudes published a few years prior. Sally, played by the director's sister, obligingly allows the camera to linger on her body's surface—skin, lips, chest—most notably while she is in the bath or shower intent on scrubbing off the offensive blemish. A part of her that can't be erased, the mark represents, the voiceover tells us, a source of shame ("It's always been there," "I had to hide it"). As critic Celine Parreñas Shimizu (2007,

232) notes, the mole "functions as the projection of the Asian women's desirability by others," a projection that is likewise visualized in the film's use of clips of actress Nancy Kwan playing a Chinese prostitute in *The World of Suzie Wong* against white actor William Holden.

Yet the beauty spot is not the fetish object proper: it serves as the fragmented part that is symbolic of Sally's difference to herself. The (implied white, male, heterosexual) viewer is fixated on other body parts—"smooth skin, black hair"—as the visual signs of "Asianness" that incite (his) desire. *Sally's Beauty Spot* acutely depicts the effects of a woman's racial-sexual objectification by applying the structure of fetishistic repudiation to her internalized response: the mole is the object that bears the force of Sally's self-disavowal until she is able to rewrite (or, literally, type) its meaning, a suggestion enforced by shots of a manual typewriter forming the unfinished phrase, "black is . . ." near the end of the film.[35] (As the source of difference to herself, the mole also functions as a *type*writer.) The viewer is asked to fill in what is left dangling, possibly the affirmative movement slogan "Black is beautiful." It is only when Sally understands the impact of the fetishistic gaze on her self-perception, the film implies, that the Asian American woman is able to seek a presumably more egalitarian sexual relationship, here represented by an equally beautiful Black man.[36] Lee's film speaks to the fetish of blackness (rendered in closeups of the skin and lips of Sally's lover) as a form of narcissistic self-love (as in the mole itself), as well as a source of anxious repudiation: here, "black is" both philic and phobic.

Of course, in condemning the sexual objectification of the Asian woman, one could argue that the film likewise objectifies the Asian woman, part by part. Lingering over closeups of Sally's nubile naked body, the film's careful visual aesthetic can't be mistaken for pornography, but like Mapplethorpe's work, it nevertheless blurs the line between inciting aesthetic appreciation and arousal. This is a somewhat obvious point; nevertheless, when the film's erotic objectification of her sister was brought to her attention, Lee confessed, "I was so preoccupied with the concepts of the film that the idea never occurred to me."[37] Yet this frisson contributes to the film's complexity: Lee's film establishes dissonance between viewers' intellectual and affective responses by offering up pleasurable images simultaneous with the message that it's wrong to enjoy them. In this case, the voice of prohibition literally belongs to academics: the filmmaker incorporates citations from feminist and postcolonial critics Tania Modeleski and Homi Bhabha in voiceovers that render the film's political content overt. (This is perhaps one reason I repeatedly mistake the film's title as *Helen's Beauty Spot*.) Academic narration does not simply function as a killjoy to visual pleasure. Rather, the film's intent to mark desire as a site of collective injury may very well incite pleasures of identification by reminding viewers why racial voyeurism is uncool. As in Mercer's first response to *The Black Book*, however, that narration also renders acceptable witnessing the eroticism of aestheticized racial bodies and body parts on the screen. That is, the *story* gives us permission to watch.

My point is not that *Sally's Beauty Spot* is a tease. Rather, it traverses competing racial imaginaries allowing for racial scopophilia as well as its disavowal. This slippage is echoed in my discussion of the critic who recognizes his work as a screen for his own desires, the academic mistaken for the fetishist, or the class exposing Asian stereotypes that inadvertently offers the opportunity for indulging in them. Responding to the Asian fetish unveils the making of *political* fantasy, which likewise engages the ambivalence of fetishistic desire as projects of social justice come to depend on the very objects of their repudiation, what Wendy Brown (1995, 52) deemed "wounded attachment." Such is the potency of that fantasy that I confess to experiencing a bit of a letdown in the knowledge that, as the director informs us about her sister, in real life, Sally Lee harbors no neurosis about her mole whatsoever (H. Lee 2002, 137).

The Erotics of Wounded Attachment

Fantasy carries erotic charge in part because of its distance from "real life." Indeed, this is the point that Judith Butler (2004) affirmed in defending Mapplethorpe's work against the censorship of conservative legislators and pornography against antiporn feminists. She cautioned against assuming a mimetic relationship between fantasy and the real: "In those anti-pornography positions that favor censorship, there is an implicit theory of fantasy that . . . relies upon a representational realism that conflates the signified of fantasy with its (impossible) referent and construes 'depiction' as an injurious act and, in legal terms, a discriminatory action or 'real' effect" ([1990] 2004, 185).[38] That position was echoed by embattled photographer Sally Mann, accused of child pornography after publishing photographs of her partially unclothed children in the 1990s. Mann challenged the correspondence between art and impact: "All too often, nudity, even that of children, is mistaken for sexuality, and images are mistaken for actions."[39] Or as Adrian Tomine's (2006, 29) Asian American protagonist argues in defending his porn stash featuring white women to his Asian girlfriend, "This stuff is just, you know . . . fantasy. It's *supposed* to be different from the reality . . . otherwise, what's the point?" (figure 4.9).

FIGURE 4.9 "This stuff is just, you know ... fantasy": Adrian Tomine, *Shortcomings*, 2006

Race fetishism carries weight as an object of study in Asian American studies precisely because of the awareness that representation has political consequence. The field derives its power from a foundation in social justice, a foundation implicitly tied to ethics. Yet a focus on race fetishism reveals ethics to be a narrow critical frame, a limitation that I am constantly reminded of by students who want to know whether it is okay to have a racial type. In encouraging them to answer ethical questions for themselves, I ask them first to understand the structures that underlie racial desire, as I discuss in the conclusion, structures engaging both feeling and cognition.

While not easily traced or necessarily causal, fantasy's harm might reside in a more abstract set of relations: sexual fantasy *masquerading* as racial knowledge. In reproducing individuals and collectives according to type, that conflation assumes the veneer of truth through repetition. Reflected in this chapter's epigraph, in seeking an interstitial space for sexual fantasy in ways that call to mind Winnicott's notions of play, Linda Williams (2004) suggests a compelling distinction between belief and enactment: "Pornographic and erotic fantasies of interracial lust rely on all viewers, male and female, black and white, *knowing* these stereotypes," she writes. "Although nothing necessarily rules out their also believing them—that is, they can certainly be interpreted in a racist manner—the pleasure taken in pornographic depictions of interracial lust *does not depend on believing* them" (286, emphasis mine). Williams cautions against assuming a mimetic relationship between fantasy and the social; private desire does not equate with public action. The same caution applies to the treatment of Asianized robots in the previous chapter. Nevertheless, the line between a shared material world and psychic reality, the divisions among awareness, belief, and acting on belief are porous and labile. Moreover, "pleasure *taken*" gestures obliquely to the conceptual violence underlying typing: a forcible reduction that enables appropriation. And the more fixed the object, the easier the taking.

If the fetish is "a story masquerading as an object" (Stoller 1985, 155), the story engaged in this chapter is not the content of assigned type. Rather, I suggest that the Asian fetish unveils a different story, the ruptures in *political* fantasy that mark the uneasy oscillation between competing racial imaginaries. The distinction between eroticism and representative politics as incommensurate arenas of power—separate, not equal—might represent a false dichotomy given that *multiculturalism* and *equality* are no less phantasmatic than idealized love; the processes through which we give meaning to that which we desire are not antithetical to the processes through which we imagine ourselves into a community founded on certain principles, including respect for differences. The public text of race is itself a fantasy construction upholding, in Žižek's (1997a, 40–41) terms, the "hegemonic fiction (or even ideal) of multiculturalist tolerance, respect and protection of human rights." To what extent do communally agreed-on rules concerning racial representation in the public sphere contribute to this now tenuous "hegemonic fiction" or, more intriguingly, create the very conditions for eroticizing taboos surrounding racial discourse?

Asian fetishism is a template for understanding a process of desiring. Whose desire and what it produces is the question. I have focused on primarily Asian artists who stage fantasies surrounding their sexualities; the force of their work derives from spectators knowing these fantasies whether or not they also believe them. But the process of fantasizing here is, for better or worse, also my own. My critical and pedagogical practice may inadvertently enforce taboos surrounding race; I was startled by a student who, after a class discussion of race fetishism, requested, "Remind me again why that's wrong?" As a certain racial representation is deemed politically incorrect, its transgression can become eroticized beyond its actual content; as Butler ([1990] 2004, 190) recognizes, "Prohibition is always present in the very position of desire." Moreover, what fissures appear in professing one thing (I am against stereotyping) while desiring another (I am animated by stereotyping)? Ironically, Wendy Brown's (1995) "wounded attachment" not only applies to critical practice seemingly bound to identity politics, but names coalitional politics as fetishistic love. As in chapter 2, this split feeling suggests another context for racist love, the ambivalence that lies at the heart of my own work as part of a collective and the discomfiting awareness that this collective may itself represent a type.

Professional dominatrix Midori (2005, 146) offers us the homily, "Sex without symbolic power inequity can be no sex at all for me." As an Asian Americanist, for me, criticism without symbolic power inequity can be no criticism at all.

CONCLUSION

Racist Hate, Racial Profiling, Pokémon at Auschwitz

Let me conclude with racist hate.

In 2020, the COVID-19 pandemic swept the globe. Arising from a mutated form of a virus able to jump from animals to humans, COVID-19 originated in Wuhan, China, and migrated across continents at a rapid pace. To the outrage of many, the president of the United States deemed it "the Chinese virus." The comment literalized the Yellow Peril as Yellow fever as the virus became personified as Asian and vaguely agential. At the other end of the VAD scale, the anthropomorphized virus adds to this book's archive of cartoon animals, perfume bottles, and robots as yet another example of a nonhuman entity racialized to incite feeling. We watched animated cells replicating themselves, colonizing the lungs, and overrunning their hosts in ways that Rachel Lee

(2014a, 217) has likened to the specter of human migration, the fear of the outsider "now figured as a separate species-being." An infectious disease specialist in the 1980s, Dr. Abraham Verghese (1994), was shocked at how readily apprehension surrounding HIV/AIDS migrated to his patients as a class and then to himself as the doctor who treated them. As he became pathologized by his contiguity to the disease, he became painfully aware of his tenuous racial place in a southern community that likewise positioned him as parasitic "foreign body."[1]

The pandemic witnessed a disturbing rise in hate crimes and microaggressions against Asian Americans, who became its conveniently present and materialized scapegoat. "I am not a virus" became a hashtag for Asians in the United States and around the world ("Je ne suis pas un virus").[2] The metonymic slippage between disease and populations has historical roots. In tracing anti-Chinese rhetoric during San Francisco's cholera epidemic in the 1850s, Nayan Shah (2001, 22) notes the sequence of transference from understanding the spread of disease as a function of high-density tenement living, to Chinatown, to Chinese behaviors, and finally to the Chinese themselves as the "very embodiment of disease." T-shirts sold during the twenty-first-century pandemic shouted, "KEEP CALM: I AM NOT CHINESE," eerily harkening back to Britain's World War II motto and signs then worn by Chinese Americans attempting to disassociate themselves from the Japanese "enemy": "Me CHINESE PLEASE NO JAP."[3] In 2020, "coughing while Asian" became a new form of racial profiling. Deliberately invoking the phrase "driving while Black," the satiric video *Coughing while Asian* depicts the effects of targeting Asian American as carriers of the virus.[4] The video sharply captures the absurdity of overgeneralized logic (if one, then all), the foundation of racial profiling. These echoes of nineteenth- and twentieth-century forms of racial incrimination bring to mind Homi Bhabha's (1994, 77) assertion about the timeless pleasures and terrors derived from the stereotype: "the *same old* stories . . . *must* be told (compulsively) again and afresh, and are differently gratifying and terrifying each time."

The contemporary moment of negative feeling leveraged against Asian Americans lends urgency to the issues at the heart of this book: the latency of racial feeling, how it travels, and its uneven effects. In phobia, fear looks for an object; racialized populations become ready places for fear to land or become enmeshed within a network of anxious feelings that restlessly ping pong across populations made to assume affective resemblance. As Sara Ahmed (2004, 117) astutely notes, emotions do not simply circulate around populations, but produce them through "sticky" affective associations that grow in value (or I would say, truthiness) within an "affective economy": "Emotions play a crucial role in the 'surfacing' of individual and collective bodies through the way in which emotions circulate between bodies and signs. Such an argument clearly challenges any assumption that emotions are a private matter, that they simply belong to individuals, or even that they come from within and *then* move outward toward others." In racist hate, what moves outward might be broken down on the VAD scale as valence, negative; arousal, excited; dominance, loss of control.

This matrix appeared to be in play in March 2021 when Robert Aaron Long opened fire on two Atlanta spas, killing eight people, six of them Asian women: Daoyou Feng, 44; Hyun Jung Grant, 51; Suncha Kim, 69; Soon Chung Park, 74; Xiaojie Tan, 49; and Yong Yue, 63.[5] All were immigrants who worked in a labor-intensive, gendered-ethnic service industry. Long targeted the day spas as a result of his "sex addiction," which led him to associate the site with the hypersexualization of Asian women and its attending faulty logic: if one (Asian woman, the object of desire), then all (Asian women, the objects of rage). Fixated on feelings of lust and guilt, Long's actions appear to be motivated by a lack of control that spawned a desire for domination.[6] Marking this example of racist hate as fetishistic in nature neither wholly explains nor excuses an individual's behavior. But it illuminates why "racist hate" is not simply the inverse of "racist love."

Racial profiling derives from cognitive processes, specifically, transductive logic. This structure underlies Long's targeting as well as the hate crimes against middle-aged and elderly Asian Americans that took place on public streets in broad daylight in 2021: the individual must stand in for all who share their visual markers. The inference that what applies to one member of a group must apply to all members represents part of how young children apply forms of classification. When children use classifications unconventionally, overapplying associations, we find it to be cute, innocent, even funny. Yet when children's overgeneralized perceptions of race and ethnicity reflect those of adults, the effect is less amusing. To illustrate, Patricia G. Ramsey (1987, 62), developmental psychologist studying the acquisition of racial and ethnic biases among the young, recounts the following story: "After one altercation with one of his two Black classmates, a 5-year-old White child told his mother that 'brown people always fight.' This child linked two concrete pieces of information, the fight and his opponent's skin color, and assumed that people who are alike in one respect must be similar in all respects. He was unable to consider at that time that he also had fights with White classmates and that there was a Black child with whom he did not fight." Linking color and violence, the child in Ramsey's study had already absorbed social attitudes of his environment and then applied transductive logic to validate his experience. Not surprisingly, his conclusions converged with those already in circulation, the preexisting associations that harden into racial types. From the point of view of a five-year-old, the belief that "brown people always fight" takes on serious implications when perpetuated by adults, particularly those in positions of institutional power. Racial profiling reflects faulty deductive logic of the sort that children routinely use as a result of their levels of cognitive development: the belief that the attributes of one individual of a group must apply to the group as a whole. This assumed resemblance reveals why combating stereotyping is not simply a matter of correcting ignorance (supplying information heretofore unknown) but involves basic structures of cognition (information processing), particularly in situations of emotional arousal.

Looking at racial profiling from the angle of faulty deductive reasoning produces a startling conclusion about those who rely on overapplied, fixed meaning or stereotypes—racial or otherwise—to order their perceptions of the world: *profiling reflects an inability to process complex pieces of information.* Emotional investment raises the stakes of these cognitive processes of logic, inference, and deduction. We can give children a pass for their racial-ethnic overgeneralizations: their brains are still developing. For adults, not so much. Challenging one's own processes of deduction is one means of "checking privilege." But it means interrogating culturally reinforced ideas about individuals whose visual appearance locates them as part of a group.

The outbreak of anti-Asian bias and violence during the COVID-19 pandemic brings to mind Sartre's anecdote about the irrationality underlying anti-Semitism in Europe prior to the war. As anthropologist Lawrence A. Hirschfeld (1988, 628) recounts, "Sartre (1948) relates the story of a woman who disliked Jews because of her disagreeable encounters with Jewish furriers. Sartre astutely asked 'why did she choose to hate Jews rather than furriers'? The answer evidently involves the realization that the intuitive object of a prejudice is more likely to be a kind of thing rather than a property of that thing." That is, the woman's negative feeling found a ready object in Jews rather than furriers because the former is taken to be the "thing," and the latter, the profession, is merely its attribute. The fixity of "thingness," here ascribed to persons of a *type*, greases the wheels of (negative) feeling. Hirschfeld points to form or logic (or, rather, illogic) here, not history or context. Both are significant: furriers lack a mode of narration, while Jews, to paraphrase Bhabha, are a story told compulsively again and again. Confirmation bias then compounds the truthiness of the narrative already in circulation.

As noted in chapter 2, Hirschfeld goes further to assert that race and ethnicity are "psychologically privileged" (628) forms of classification. Put simply, visual differences beget inferred traits beget affective response beget behaviors. See Asian, assume contagion. As I discussed in the previous chapter, knowing stereotypes does not imply believing them. Yet when the stakes are life and death, who has the wherewithal to check their privilege, confirmation biases, or transductive logic when it is far easier to deflect feeling onto a conveniently "intuitive object of a prejudice"?

Racist love transforms into racist hate with dizzying speed. To echo Bruno Latour's definition of risky objects from chapter 2, racial feeling easily flip-flops its mode of existence. The profiling of Black men that spawned the Black Lives Matter movement took place in the afterglow of "postracial" rhetoric. Smart-Asians-at-Harvard morphs readily into ban-infectious-international-students. For Asian Americans, hard-won taboos against hate speech evaporated overnight ("Bat fried rice" anyone?).[7] The contemporary moment of undisguised anti-Asian bias pulls me full circle: from philic to phobic, from compliment to slur. This book has been concerned with how fantasies of racial abstraction transform anxiety into a source of pleasure; in the shift to racial hatred, what remains operative is racial feeling on a continuum, adoration and animosity as flip sides of the same coin. In this sense, racist love is not simply the opposite of racist hate any more than, for example, the serene, tidy environments advocated by Marie Kondo are simply the opposite of Mari Katayama's impossibly cluttered rooms; both convey a keen sense of reciprocity with nonhuman things that spark joy. As noted in chapter 2, in measuring perception of various groups on two axes, warmth and competence, psychologist Susan Fiske and her colleagues (2002, 878) remind us that "subjectively positive stereotypes on one dimension do not contradict prejudice but often are functionally consistent with unflattering stereotypes on the other dimension." This book thus offers an academic explanation to the often quoted joke from the 1990s sitcom *Seinfeld*. Called out for expressing his love for Chinese women, Jerry responds with an air of self-evident logic, "If I *like* their race, how can that be racist?"

Because racist love derives from the same desiring structure as racist hate, iconicity is not an antidote to profiling. In *On Racial Icons: Blackness and the Public Imagination*, Nicole R. Fleetwood (2015, 4) proposes that celebrities such as Serena Williams and Diana Ross work against a history of degrading Black caricature and "can serve to uplift, literally and symbolically, 'the black race' and the nation." That is absolutely true for Black spectators. Yet I would suggest that for others, these venerated figures are nonetheless also hyperembodied types that counterintuitively work in tandem with earlier representations. Depending on the social location of the venerator, iconicity reflects the foundations of racist love: taking pleasure in a racial type constructed through (positive) symbolism. Asian Americans who have begun to break color barriers and assume a heightened presence within globalized media channels likewise assume this risk: in 2020, Keanu Reeves was the internet's boyfriend; the humorous digital social movements #StarringConstanceWu and #StarringJohnCho aspirationally Photoshop the actors' faces onto mainstream Hollywood movie posters. The gesture is slightly ironic given movies actually starring Constance Wu or John Cho, the actors chosen to represent all Asian Americans. The heightened symbolism of inclusive representation was comically invoked in 2018 by Sandra Oh, the first Asian woman to be nominated for an Emmy for Lead Actress in a Drama Series, who mouthed from her seat in the audience, "It's an honor just to be Asian." In a white-dominated society, iconicity reverses the valence ascribed to Asianness while still functioning as a repository for racial desires that give difference its power. "The fetish or stereotype gives access to an 'identity' which is predicated as much on mastery and pleasure as it is on anxiety and defence," writes Bhabha (1983, 27), "for it is a form of multiple and contradictory belief in its recognition of difference and disavowal of it." As this book suggests, racial feeling is split feeling.

Racist Love situates fantasy as a potent site of racial feeling, one rooted in the reductive pleasures of type. A study of racial affect, it asserts that Asian racialization in the United States is essentially fetishistic: the objects of the preceding chapters unveil pleasure as a means of asserting control over Asian status ambiguity. In this book, I have foregrounded the processes of typing, the repeated overapplication of individual traits to a group that allows the stereotype to masquerade as knowledge. The positive feeling motivating cultural appropriation does not proceed first without its reliability; it represents the "thing" taken. What forms will these conflicted desires assume as the axis of globalization shifts from North-South to East-South in the twenty-first century? At one level, hybridized commodities such as green tea Kit Kat bars and ube ice cream put "getting a bit of the Other" within easy reach (hooks 1992, 21). But globalization also produces awkward collisions.

The news that one could catch Pokémon at Auschwitz was met with outrage in 2016, as twenty-first-century virtual fantasy play collided with the history of twentieth-century trauma. With the aim of collecting and battling cute Japanese "pocket monsters," tourists playing Pokémon GO on their mobile devices were said to disrespect victims of the Holocaust; frivolity at a site of mass death was called out as being wildly inappropriate to the affective demeanor required by the memory of genocide. The Japanese developer Niantic agreed to modify its process of randomly selecting places gleaned from Google Maps and remove virtual Pokéstops and gyms from sites memorializing human suffering. No more Psyduck at the United States Holocaust Memorial Museum in Washington, DC. No Jigglypuff at Japan's Hiroshima Peace Memorial Park. Similarly flagging the ways in which global commodities fail to travel seamlessly, corporate faux pas continue to go viral with increased frequency. Fashion houses and retailers Dolce and Gabbana, Prada, Gucci, Zara, and H & M among others were called out for cultural insensitivity, racism, or anti-Semitism, as their products and advertising landed with a thud in local contexts.[8] Varied sensibilities of what constitutes whimsy, cuteness, style, or beauty reveal the difficulties of *glocalization*, of translating racial and religious meaning across histories, cultures, and geographies. The image of globetrotting Pokémon uniting the world through play represents a specific affront because, in certain places and times, monsters are real.

The COVID-19 panic slipped easily into xenophobia partly because, in the United States, the apocalypse is already Asianized. More broadly, as numerous scholars in Asian American studies have shown, the "Orient" has long served as the "timeless space onto which the West projects its phantasmatic content" (Žižek 1997a, 38). The spread of the virus may well be attributed to globalization as the world gets smaller—the loss of animal habitat, population concentration, ease of travel, the shared precarity of climate change. Yet fear of infection found its object in a people, a *Chinese* virus. How will anxieties concerning the erosion of US dominance in the global economy manifest themselves as anti-Asian bias or, perhaps counterintuitively, as fetishization? During the Cold War, the United States leveraged its soft power (Nye 1990) by selling an attractive American lifestyle—and with it the fantasy of white exceptionalism—through its exports, a phenomenon deemed *Coca-colonization*. Now *hallyu*, the "Korean wave," brands everything from beauty products to televised drama and pop acts with a capital *K*. Will the positive association that envelops hallyu in the United States continue as the nation begins to cede its position as a global hegemon? Will Coca-colonization take a different form to compete with an emerging Asian economic ascendancy? In the 1980s, Japan's international marketing strategy sought to downplay what was Japanese about Japanese commodities, as discussed in chapter 2, an erasure reflecting the philosophy of mukokuseki, something or someone lacking nationality (Iwabuchi 2004).

As part of their appeal, anime characters and mascots such as Hello Kitty and Pokémon deliberately occluded their origins to evoke a deterritorialized, imaginary space enhancing their ability to travel. Hollywood appears to lean in to the spirit of mukokuseki as animated animals, paranormal lovers, and interplanetary superheroes appear to be better positioned to tap Chinese markets; here, the turn to fantasy is a turn to Asia.

And a turn to race. Or more specifically, racial abstraction. Would the presence of Pokémon at Auschwitz represent such a clash of competing sensibilities if pocket monsters were themselves the targets of genocide? That far-fetched profane scenario seems less implausible as scripts of human trauma continue to take fantasy objects. Fantasy genres depend to a certain extent on maintaining the distinction between reality and illusion, on a suspension of disbelief. Highlighting the seductiveness of fantasy literature in 1939, J. R. R. Tolkien ([1939] 1983, 134) affirmed the positive valence associated with the imaginary and, more significantly, its underlying purpose in provoking affective response: "At no time can I remember that the enjoyment of a story was dependent on belief that such things could happen, or had happened, in 'real life,'" he wrote. "Fairy-stories were plainly not primarily concerned with possibility, but with desirability. If they awakened *desire*, satisfying it while often whetting it unbearably, they succeeded." Tolkien's rhetoric marks reading as positively erotic. Freud ([1908] 1959, 421) generalized this heightened affective response as the motivation underlying literary creation: "The creative writer does the same as the child at play. He creates a world of phantasy which he takes very seriously—that is, which he invests with large amounts of emotion—while separating it sharply from reality." "Fairy-stories" have now ceded to other entertainments, including the mundane pleasures of the everyday fantastic, as I have suggested here—coin banks with faces, cats going to kindergarten. I have argued in particular for the ways in which *Asianized* faces and *Japanese* cats enhance that investment, flagging the "stickiness" of Asian association that allows household items and cartoon animals to "spark joy" at the same time that they assume risk.

The archive assembled in this book unfolds pathways through which fanciful things become invested with emotion, the minor affects that likewise awaken desire if not exactly whetting it unbearably. My project thinks through our connection to the nonhuman if with a distinctly different outcome from Donna Haraway's *The Companion Species Manifesto*. Here, she establishes a respectful and hopeful vision of attachment with the domesticated plant and animal life forms that live among us. Expressing new forms of kinship and intimacy that challenge human hubris in the so-called Anthropocene, she writes, "To be in love means to be worldly, to be in connection with significant otherness and signifying others, on many scales, in layers of locals and globals, in ramifying webs" (Haraway 2003, 79). To be in racist love implies a different scale: it reduces worldliness to a consumable fixity, ingestible and small.

In Asian American studies, scholarship on arts and humanities derives its force from an axiomatic belief in the mimetic power of representation, the power of racial discourse to produce, not merely reflect, a cultural terrain. An overtly imaginative archive can appear to be trivial against the concerns of demographics, statistics, and electoral and coalitional politics that govern racial discourse in the public sphere. Yet realism merely conveys "the impression of consequentiality" (Harper 2015, 131). Throughout the preceding chapters, I have marked the veiled politicism underlying the "antirealism" of fantasy by highlighting the substitution of things for people as a potent form of abstraction particularly significant to the study of race. Pandas for orphans and ceramic water-sprinklers for domestic servants (see figure 2.4) rely on metaphoric substitutions predicated on affective resemblance. Whether young, small, and cuddly or subservient and industrious, externalized racial *qualities* suture the original to its substitute; feeling renders the substitution legible. A step removed from the consequentiality of the real, these abstracted relations of affective resemblance nonetheless enable pleasures taken in the nonhuman.

When Robert Stoller speculated that, in fetishistic arousal, the story masquerades as an object, he surmised that the object's power derives from its mode of narration, a point reflected by Laplanche and Pontalis (1986, 26), who noted that fantasy "is not the object of desire, but its setting." The fetish object, Stoller (1985, 155–56) suggested, "serves as a prop in a consciously enacted erotic drama: the whole scene must be played if excitement is to occur." These insights derived from the psychoanalysis of individuals represent critical tools that invite a broadened understanding of social psychology, who or what serves as a prop in political dramas whose end goal is arousal of a different sort. Group categorizations such as international terrorists, asylum seekers, undocumented migrants, and patient zeros serve as collectively defined props in dramas of state surveillance, presidential elections, or pandemic paranoia. Yet with the goal of stoking racist hate, these categories assume heightened political stakes through metaphoric substitution when they are assigned negative valence—infiltrator, rapist, disease carrier—and then again slide readily into psychologically privileged, hypervisible populations, whether Muslim, Mexican, or Chinese. This slippage speaks to the insidious power of affective resemblance in confirming "intuitive objects of a prejudice" (Hirschfeld 1988, 628) and revealing how, in

Ahmed's (2004, 121) words, the "circulation of signs of affect shapes the materialization of collective bodies." That inferential chain is deliberately and dangerously exploited in the service of inciting mass feeling among those unable or unwilling to forgo faulty deductive logic, the *childlike* assumption that "people who are alike in one respect must be similar in all respects" (Ramsey 1987, 62). Racial feeling is a powerful tool; how will it continue to be wielded, by whom, and to what ends?

The "dramas" referenced in this book surrounding parental attachment, ethnic Halloween costumes, or having a "type" may pale in comparison to those that play out as a result of the inflamed emotions surrounding racist hate. Yet these racial scenes likewise structure social reality through the subtle veil of positive feeling, the safety of fantasy's hall pass disclaiming consequentiality. Both transitional objects and fetish objects are repositories of feeling; how they function as collective mechanisms for racial coping reveals the stakes of racist love, as it is counterintuitively bound to xenophobia and profiling. Asian Americans and their object proxies will continue to perform as props in these nuanced racial dramas. Yet what sparks joy at one moment may easily flip-flop its existence in the next. Sometimes, it's an honor just to be Asian.

Until, suddenly, it's not.

Acknowledgments

The pathway to this book has been long and circuitous, but also joyful and surprising. First and foremost, I am indebted to my students in the Asian American Studies Program at the University of Wisconsin, who first inspired this work. Without their willingness to come with me into the dark recesses of fandom and popular culture, this book would not have been written. In robots, pandas, and the cute bric-a-brac of globalization, they saw latent political meaning worthy of our collective attention.

My second debt of gratitude extends to Elena Tajima Creef, whose work in racial visual culture has always been a model for my own. It was her infectious love of the offbeat, the capillaries of significant racial meaning hidden in plain sight, that inspired this book; she is a seer in all senses of the word. I owe a lifelong debt to Cindy I-Fen Cheng, friend and phenomenal colleague, who is always my go-to person and whose political commitment and devotion to Asian American studies and the people in it is a model that kept me moving forward. Ramzi Fawaz motivated me through his incredible positivity and his intellectual example; he taught me a thing or two about fantasy, delight, and hope. I am indebted to Anne McClintock for her astute take on fetishism, belief in this work, and especially for her worldly engagement with ideas.

Mari Yoshihara, Priscilla Wald, Christine Yano, Kate Capshaw-Smith, Malini Johar Schueller, and Rachel Lee supported this work in different ways, all crucial to its foundations. Jennifer Ho, Jigna Desai, erin Khuê Ninh, Josephine Lee, Betsy Huang, Jane Park, Eunjung Kim, Laura Kang, Heidi Kim, and Hye Jin Lee inspired me directly or indirectly and have been my best interlocutors. The seeds of this book were planted long ago by the late Helene Moglen, an extraordinary feminist mentor, who first guided me into thinking rigorously about attachment and intimacy at the University of California–Santa Cruz.

I owe K. T. Horning, director of the Cooperative Children's Book Collective, a special debt of gratitude for her generous, hands-on sharing of her archive. Her knowledge of children's literature is unparalleled. Thanks go to Nina Wright at the Westerly Public Library for her help and able archival stewardship. Phil Yu, Sarah Park Dahlen, Asuka Eguchi, Gene Yang, and Charles Yu all shared their work and time with me, for which I am truly grateful. During the long duration of this book's incubation, Amit Pal and Matt Rothschild at the *Progressive*, Yowei Shaw at NPR, and Louisa Kamps reminded me of the power of public-facing ideas (and how to write a headline).

Thanks go to the extraordinary creative folk who graciously shared their art with me, trusting the anonymous figure at the end of an email: Laurie Simmons, Patty Chang, Elisha Lim, and especially Hong Chun Zhang. Hong's generosity is rivaled only by the genius of her art.

Sue J. Kim, Donna Haraway, Mary Lui, Birgit Rasmussen, and Yuan Shu: I am grateful for your confidence in my ideas. You helped connect me with the audiences for whom this work was intended at MIT, University of California–Santa Cruz, Yale, and Texas Tech. In addition to colleagues at Wellesley College, Edgewood College, Indiana State University, the University of California–Santa Barbara, National Tsing Hua University, and the Chicago Humanities Festival, I am grateful to organizers and audiences in new southern studies at the University of Mississippi, Emory, and the University of South Carolina, who rolled with me even when they were not expecting to hear a talk about the US South and Asianized memorabilia. All these interactions helped me shape this project into the form you see here. Earlier versions of this work appeared as "Racist Cute: Caricature, *Kawaii*-style, and the Asian Thing," *American Quarterly* 71, no. 1 (March 2019): 29–58; and "Racial Abstraction and Species Difference: Anthropomorphic Animals in 'Multicultural' Children's Literature," *American Literature* 91, no. 2 (June 2019): 323–56.

This book would not have existed but for the support of a Race, Ethnicity, and Indigeneity Senior Fellowship at the Institute for Research in the Humanities (IRH) at the University of Wisconsin–Madison. I am especially indebted to Susan Stanford Friedman, the unflappable leader of the IRH, who ran a tight ship and led by her intellectual example: incisive, curious, academically expansive, and welcoming. At the IRH, Louise Young, Lynn Nyhart, Rob Nixon, Richard Goodkin, Tomislav Longinovic, and Ayelet Ben-Yishai especially offered keen advice and feedback, at times unbeknownst to them. I thank Douglas Rosenberg and Henry Drewel, whose casually shared art history references proved to be invaluable to this work. I also want to acknowledge generous funding from the University of Wisconsin–Madison in the form of the Department of English's Dorothy Draheim and Mark and Elisabeth Eccles Professorships; the Office of the Chancellor's Hilldale Award; the Vice Chancellor for Research and Graduate Education's Kellett Mid-Career Award; and the Office of the Provost's Vilas Distinguished Achievement Professor Award. I thank Sue Zaeske, fellow Americanist and associate dean of L&S, for taking Hello Kitty seriously.

I am extremely fortunate to have a wonderful community in Asian American studies at Madison and am grateful for the support of Nhung Nguyen and especially my colleagues Timothy Yu, Lori Kido Lopez, Stacey J. Lee, and Eden Inoway-Ronnie, who are stellar human beings. During the writing of this book, race studies in the English Department blossomed. I want to thank Spring Sherrod, Andrew Leinberger, David Zimmerman, Sara Guyer, Amy Quan Barry, Caroline Levine, and the late Jeffrey Steele for sharing quirky references related to this project, friendship, and/or support in a bureaucracy-heavy institution. Thanks go out to everyone in my Madison intellectual community too numerous to list here: I did not realize how much I depended on our everyday exchanges until they vanished during the pandemic.

Ken Wissoker, Ryan Kendall, and Lisl Hampton shepherded this manuscript through with amazing dispatch, professionalism, and goodwill. Ken's enthusiasm for the project was infectious in the most positive sense of the word and pushed me to live up to expectation. I am grateful to Mel Y. Chen and Jasbir K. Puar for inviting this work into their Anima: Critical Race Studies Otherwise series, which puts me in incredible company.

To the graduate students I have worked with over the duration of this project: you have never failed to inspire me with your own fascinating objects of study, whether bees, dolls, drones, feminist icons, Civil War reenactments, K-beauty, stand-up comedy, or avant-gardist performance art. Your enthusiasm about your archives is infectious, and your ability to tease out complex racial analysis intersecting with animal studies, disability studies, queer of color interpretation, or childhood studies has been key to my own education. To Katie Schaag, Rachel Jane Carroll, Hai-Dang Phan, Heather Swan, Erica Kanesaka Kalnay, Amy Gaeta, Danielle K. Nelson, Iseult Gillespie, Amanda Ong, and Nabiha Mansoor, a hearty dose of ongoing gratitude.

Maya Castronovo and Julian Castronovo helped this project by growing up ... into awesome human beings. Thank you, and you're welcome. To my life partner, Russ Castronovo, without whom this work would never have existed: we did it. And on to the next phase of life together. To the extended Bow family: thank you for who you are—sane, smart, responsible, funny, and kind. Together we have kept alive for the next generation our shared delight in all things adorable. Mom and Dad would approve.

Notes

INTRODUCTION

Stephen Marche, "How to Read a Racist Book to Your Kids," retitled web version of the print essay "Loompaland Is a Complicated Place," *New York Times Magazine*, June 17, 2012, 60. Full references for popular culture and literature, mainstream media, and online sources appear in the notes.

1. In bell hooks's seminal 1992 essay "Eating the Other: Desire and Resistance," she famously defined the dominant culture's enjoyment of difference as a desire for "spice." She begins with the erotic encounter and broadens outward to the romantic fantasy of primitivism and the exotic, which are subject to appropriation and consumption, accessorizing normative white, middle-class life.
2. The postwar period fixed the occupier's vision of Japanese women as childlike and naive; "baby-san" became the generic name for young Japanese women. See Shibusawa 2006, 12.
3. In art, abstraction signifies a mode of nonfigurative representation, one that refuses overt references to material reality. In her definition of abstraction, Ngai (2015, 34) cites Leigh Claire La Berge: abstraction is a "mode of nonfigurative representation" that is "not fully realizable by a particular." For Phillip Brian Harper (2015, 19), abstraction denotes a representation's "remove from ... those real-world phenomena" that it resembles; abstraction conveys a "state of *withdrawal* from some originary point." My own deployment of the term more closely aligns with what Manthia Diawara (1998, 51) has called "transtextuality," the "movement of cultural styles from character to character in film." "Tarantino's discovery," Diawara notes about the film *Pulp Fiction*, was that "black maleness, as embodied in *esthétique du cool*, can be transported through white bodies" (52). That is, abstracted through style, race is transportable as an associative sign system freed from the human body.
4. Marche, "How to Read a Racist Book to Your Kids."

5. The substitution central to the *Cars* franchise, objects for people, taps the child's fascination with the power of machines through the cathected object. Less innocently, Disney harnesses children's desires to its juggernaut of global merchandising: Okuni only bears a name so that she can be marketed as a toy, or, exemplifying the ultimate in commodity fetishism, as a collectible. Dispensing with real bodies, animated films tap global box offices by obviating the need for audiences to identify with human protagonists in real-world settings. Despite mediocre reviews, *Cars* (2006) returned box offices of $441 million USD (domestic) and $551 million (global), enabling a third movie in 2017. As significantly, the first film generated more than $8 billion in retail sales, a figure that prompted Disney to put three hundred toys, Okuni among them, in production prior to the 2011 release of *Cars 2*.
6. In naming an affective structure surrounding Asian American racialization, I am of course drawing on Raymond Williams (1977), who countered the "subjective" nature of feeling and the aesthetic apart from the political. A "structure of feeling" (321) represents a "cultural hypothesis" (132) undertaken to understand affective "connections in a generation or period" (133).
7. In the context of psychoanalysis, *love* signifies complex attachment, not merely romantic feeling. Echoing object relations theory, *racist love* speaks to the admixture of love and hate, ambivalence and anxiety, that underlies (infantile) attachment. The "good" object is entwined with notions of infant libidinal satisfaction against the withholding nature of "bad" objects. See Ainsworth 1969.
8. See Hasan Minhaj's stand-up comedy special *Homecoming King* (dir. Christopher Storer, Prod., Art and Industry, Dist., Netflix, 2017).
9. Silverman delivered the joke on Conan O'Brien's *Late Show* in 2001. When Asian American media watchdog Guy Aoki challenged her use of the slur, she defended the joke as ironic, as skewering her persona as a bigoted "ignoramus." See Lopez 2016 and Sarah Silverman, *The Bedwetter: Stories of Courage, Redemption, and Pee* (New York: Harper Collins, 2010) 146. By 2017, Silverman had renounced her previously defensive stance, noting, "There are jokes I made 15 years ago I would absolutely not make today"; Sophie Heawood, "Sarah Silverman: 'There Are Jokes I Made 15 Years Ago I Would Absolutely Not Make Today,'" *Guardian*, November 19, 2017.
10. For a nuanced account of these metrics, see, for example, Lee and Zhou 2015.
11. In fact, that assessment was inaccurate. Census records reveal that between 2000 and 2010, Asian American populations saw a growth rate of 47 percent in contrast to the growth rate of the Latinx population at 49 percent. Resistance to disaggregating data across Asian ethnic groups allows Asian Americans as a group to avoid being pathologized via conventional forms of race scares of the twentieth century—criminality, drain on social welfare resources, educational achievement gaps. Yet they likewise lack the political power of other groups as an electoral demographic that must be recognized, courted, or empowered. The Pew report's summary was so glibly celebratory that the Asian American Pacific Islander Policy and Research Consortium, an organization of university-based research centers, immediately issued a statement condemning the summary as highly biased, incomplete,

and "implicitly misleading and damaging for Asian American communities" ("Asian American and Pacific Islander Policy Research Consortium Response to Pew Center Report," Asian American/Asian Research Institute, June 25, 2012, https://aaari .info/news6/). The full Pew report, released on June 19, 2012, can be found on Pew Research Center: Social and Demographic Trends, *The Rise of Asian Americans*, updated April 4, 2013, http://www.pewsocialtrends.org/2012/06/19/the-rise-of-asian -americans/.

12. As Stanley Sue and Harry H. L. Kitano (1973) note, Asian Americans were thought to be "patient, clean, courteous, and Americanized" and successful "by virtue of their hard work, thrift, family cohesion, and obedience" (87). The ambiguously positive stereotype famously materialized in 2011 in Amy Chua's coining of the term Tiger Mother, lionizing Asian parenting as a conduit to mimicking the apparent educational and economic achievement of Asian Americans. Six years earlier, the title of a now out-of-print self-help book by Soo Kim Abboud and Jane Y. Kim cheerfully confirmed that Asian achievement was available to all: *Top of the Class: How Asian Parents Raise High Achievers—and How You Can Too* (New York: Berkley, 2005). The Asian American as model minority speaks to the paradox of racial interstitiality as neither Black nor white, but that sense of racial spatialization is likewise neither wholly here (local) nor there (global) as well (Bow 2010). While historians ably document the consolidation of the model minority image during the 1980s, historian Cindy I-Fen Cheng (2013) highlights its oscillation during the Cold War era: lauded as the "first" to break occupational barriers as proof of US meritocracy, Asian Americans were simultaneously represented as communist subversives disloyal to the democratic cause.

13. Public engagement with racial stereotyping relies on repetition as well as contiguity or proximity (Asian/library) and reversed valence (not negative but positive). It also involves cognitive and psychological structures: transductive reasoning and confirmation bias. Transductive reasoning involves overgeneralization: what applies to one applies to all. Gladwell's confirmation bias is also revealed here, as *Asian American* selectively displaces *student* in a narrowed field of vision that might otherwise include all people in a library: rather, he *notices* Asian Americans in that space because it confirms a prior belief. Gladwell's thesis on hard work and practice underlying success also relies on faulty transductive reasoning focused on Asian culture. Arbitrarily, he turns to the complexities of rice paddy farming in south China and the structure of the Chinese language to explain why Chinese Americans are good at math, ignoring restrictive US immigration laws that favored extending visas to those in occupations that require individuals to be *good at math* (Malcom Gladwell, *Outliers: The Story of Success* [New York: Little, Brown, 2008]). For a longer discussion of the structure and content of Asian American stereotyping, see Bow 2017. In explaining the educational attainment of first- and 1.5-generation Chinese and Vietnamese Americans, Jennifer Lee and Min Zhou (2015) point to neoconservatives who likewise turn to essentialist explanations of culture, speculating that "there must be something unique about Asian culture and values that leads to these exceptional

educational outcomes" (67). They note that culture "does play a role, but not in the way that pundits often claim" (67). That is, Asian immigrants rely on ethnic networks for educational resources, import practices such as after-school tutoring, and pool family resources to benefit one member.

14. In *The Erotic Life of Racism*, Sharon Patricia Holland (2012) asserts the primacy of the Black/white binary in US race relations: "I do want to insist stubbornly that the psychic life of racism can best be read in the context of the United States in the space where black and white intersect" (7). "Where black and white intersect" is indeed a potent site for exploring *Asian* racialization (Bow 2010). Yet racism also reveals itself in everyday, less dramatic intersections. Rather than inscribe a competitive framework around race relations, I would assert that the psychic life of racism as racist love is particularly illuminated where "Asian" intersects with the veiled discourses of white supremacy.

15. Freud's "On Narcissism: An Introduction" ([1914] 1957, 122) provides a key insight into racist love as an affective structure illuminating racial attachment writ large. The "neurotic" who is unable to "attain his ego ideal" seeks a way back to self via romantic idealization: "He then seeks a way back to narcissism from his prodigal expenditure of libido upon objects by choosing a sexual ideal after the narcissistic type which shall possess the excellences to which he cannot attain. This is the cure by love." The *model minority* image represents that "cure by love" by refracting back an idealized racial type that "possesses the excellences" that the nation fears it can no longer attain.

16. In "Instincts and Their Vicissitudes" (1915, 117), Freud reads feeling as the nervous system's response to a stimulus that is both mental and somatic. "Feelings," he suggests, "reflect the manner in which the process of mastering stimuli takes place." At the millennium, these triggers have assumed racial form with violent outcomes. The flip sides of the coin that I engage here, racial hatred and racial love, derive from opposing instincts, for Freud, self-preservation and sexual pleasure, that stimulate "unpleasure" and pleasure (136). Psychoanalysis allows for an understanding of both overt and latent feeling prefiguring what would emerge as the field of social psychology. Exploring how feeling produces politicized classes of people lies at the heart of my critical method, one well mined in interdisciplinary Asian American studies.

17. Numerous scholars have remarked on the paradox surrounding the desire for difference in the face of neoliberal globalization's erosion of the local. Philosopher Charles Taylor (2000, 367) noted that in "'traditional' societies, we were very different from each other. But once these earlier horizons have been lost, we shall all be the same." Thus mass culture "publicly declares and perpetuates the idea that there is pleasure to be found in the acknowledgment and enjoyment of difference" (366). See also Harvey 2006 and Žižek 1997.

18. On early American consumption of Chinese imports, Caroline Frank (2011, 12) writes, "According to unanimous consensus among decorative arts scholars, there was one thing all these diverse socioeconomic groups had in common. That was an ignorance of the Chinese significance of the decorations on their dishes." On

Chinese commodities in the eighteenth century, see also D. Jacobson 1993 and Bush 2007. Chi-Ming Yang (2011) argues that eighteenth-century British representations of China were not simply based on Orientalist associations with barbarity, but on ideas of technology and civilization embodied by objects such as the umbrella.

19. On the term *Indo-chic*, see Maira 2007. On the implications surrounding global marketing of Indian style, see Moorti 2003.

20. Around the height of Japan's economic rise in 1995, David Morley and Kevin Robins (1995) coined the term *techno-Orientalism* to describe the underlying anxieties surrounding the projection of an inhuman future ushered in by a technologically advanced world of cybernetics, robotics, artificial intelligence, and simulation. Consistent with earlier iterations of the Yellow Peril, techno-Orientalism denies the East as coeval with the West on both ends of the historical spectrum: it produces the East as archaically feudal yet technologically empowered with the potential to transcend Western modernity.

21. On Asian American status ambiguity, see for example, my *Partly Colored: Asian Americans and Racial Anomaly in the Segregated South* (2010) and Jennifer Ho's *Racial Ambiguity in Asian American Culture* (2015).

22. The portraits evoke the macabre character Cousin Itt from Charles Addams's gothic cartoons. In Zhang's oeuvre as a whole, hair assumes heightened importance. Her drawings of "hairy objects," ordinary things made of hair—book, hamburger, toilet paper—speak to the simultaneity of beauty and repulsion. Elsewhere, twisted strands assume the form of a cyclone, evoking Zhang's connection to her Kansas home. Here, she is not Dorothy transported to a new land by a force of nature, but herself a destructive natural force.

23. Regarding Asian American poetry, Jeon (2012, xxxi) engages "the calculated strangeness of avant-garde art as an occasion to emphasize the physical and visual oddness of racial constructs." My emphasis on "thingness" in the context of abstraction deviates a bit from Jeon's. I focus on mundane objects that not only represent intellectual, conceptual puzzles, but trigger racial feeling. For additional consideration of the relationship between race and abstraction, see also Philip Brian Harper's *Abstractionist Aesthetics: Artistic Form and Social Critique in African American Culture* (2015).

24. As a genre, fantasy is invested in drawing distinctions between mimetic and non-mimetic art, between realism and the imaginary. J. R. R. Tolkien ([1939] 1983, 132) expressed that distance by invoking a distinction between the "Primary World" and fantasy's "Secondary World." Gary Wolfe ([1982] 2004, 222) writes that "whatever we are to call 'fantasy' must first and foremost deal with the impossible." David Sandner (2004, 149) asserts that "what is wanted from fantasy is a *distancing from the ordinary*."

25. Published in 2011 after decades of rampant consumerism in Japan, *The Life-Changing Magic of Tidying Up: The Japanese Art of Decluttering and Organizing* came on the heels of forced downsizing following Japan's financial crisis of 1997 and tsunami in 2011. The translation appearing in the United States in 2014 sold 1.6 million copies in two years and spawned a sequel, manga edition, and, by 2019, the

Netflix series *Tidying Up with Marie Kondo*. Jocelyn McClurg, "Pure 'Magic': Marie Kondo Finally Hits No. 1," *USA Today*, January 14, 2016.

26. A bestseller in Japan, Tatsumi's *The Art of Discarding: How to Get Rid of Clutter and Find Joy* is relentlessly practical, almost hectoring in tone, even as it addresses the psychology of its audience: "Don't think you can't throw something away just because it can still be used. Change your mindset. Think to yourself, I've used it once, so I can throw it away"; Nagisa Tatsumi, *The Art of Discarding: How to Get Rid of Clutter and Find Joy*, trans. Angus Turvill (New York: Hachette, 2017), 126.

27. Of course, Kondo's eager embrace in the United States might be attributed to the fact that she deals only with the symptom of unbridled consumerism, not its cause. Her extensive coverage in the US press (*Atlantic*, *Wall Street Journal*, *New Yorker*, *Slate*, *Vogue*) portrays her on a continuum of strangeness from tiny and childlike to slightly unhinged and mentally unbalanced. She drew the ire of professional organizers for privileging discarding over organizing: one of her chapters is subtitled, "Storage Experts Are Hoarders." Response to the KonMari Method at the National Association of Professional Organizers convention in the United States was apparently laced with racist xenophobia; a *New York Times* reporter conveyed the most mild mannered of these, noting an American organizer's assessment: "It's a book if you're a 20-something Japanese girl and you live at home and you still have a bunch of your Hello Kitty toys and stuff." Quoted in Taffy Brodesser-Akner, "Marie Kondo and the Ruthless War on Stuff," *New York Times Magazine*, July 6, 2016.

28. Stuart Picken (1994, 363) defines *kami* as the "object of reference in Shinto" to avoid extrapolation to "gods" in Western contexts. See also Holtom 1922 and Nakamaki 2003. Kondo (2014) reveals that she worked for years as a "Shinto shrine maiden," or *miko*. The miko is now "most probably a university student collecting a modest wage in this part-time position," whose duties likely involve selling souvenirs and fortunes (cited in Kuly 2003, 201).

29. The relationship between owner and possession is nonetheless hierarchical: items are privileged in relation to proximity to the human body. This philosophy is articulated in Kondo's sequel, *Spark Joy*: "Items such as forks or undergarments, which come in direct contact with delicate parts of our bodies, should be treated as a rank above the rest whenever possible" (2016, 183).

30. For Brown (1998, 942), things serve as the *petit object a*, the third term that mediates self-other relations: "The hybrid object, then, may be figured as a participant in the intersubjective constitution of reality."

31. Cited in "Kara Walker: The Melodrama of 'Gone with the Wind,'" *art21*, November 2011, https://art21.org/read/kara-walker-the-melodrama-of-gone-with-the-wind/.

32. Rachel C. Lee (2014a, 40) aptly summarizes the value assigned to Asian American literature: "Broadly speaking, Asian American texts have been valuable to a revisionist U.S. literary canon precisely because of their testament to the active racial exclusion of Asians. Belying the promise of color-blind political equality, this exclusion occurs through legal bars to immigration, educational segregation, labor

stratification . . . criminalization as enemy aliens and spies, and social and psychic wounding through harmful stereotypes."
33. For an early engagement with concerns surrounding liberal cooptation of the field, see San Juan 1991. For more current assessments, see Chiang 2009; C. Lee 2013; and Ho 2015.
34. This question was more recently posed by Michael Omi in a paper delivered at the 2019 Association for Asian American Studies.

CHAPTER 1. Racial Transitional Objects

Kathleen Horning, personal communication, Madison, WI, September 8, 2016; I extend my deepest gratitude to her for some of the primary sources here. An earlier version of this chapter appeared as "Racial Abstraction and Species Difference: Anthropomorphic Animals in 'Multicultural' Children's Literature," *American Literature* 91, no. 2 (2019): 323–56.

1. For an overview of animal stories in children's literature, see Kimberley Reynolds's *Children's Literature: A Very Short Introduction* (2011), which gives a history by type and use from morality tales such as *Aesop's Fables* to point of view tales such as *Black Beauty*.
2. The characters appear in *Richard Scarry's Storybook Dictionary* (New York: Golden Book, 1966).
3. See Dare Wright, *Edith and Big Bad Bill* (New York: Random House, 1968); Stan Berenstain and Jan Berenstain, *The Berenstain Bears' New Neighbors* (New York: Random House, 1994); and Gary Soto and Susan Guevara, *Chato Goes Cruising* (New York: Putnam, 2005).
4. Mickenberg and Vallone (2011) note other key moments in the emergence of children's literature as a discipline: the creation of a juvenile division at MacMillan in 1919, the establishment of the Newbery Medal in 1922, and the founding of *Horn Book Magazine* in 1924.
5. Cited in *Brown v. Board of Education*, which abolished school segregation in 1954, the Clarks' doll test was hailed as a watershed that established evidence toward the link between segregation and its psychological toll on African American children (Clark and Clark 1947). In the decades following, the doll test was subsequently challenged for its "forced choice" question structure (Holmes 1995; Bernstein 2011). The Clarks' findings could not be replicated under other laboratory conditions; for example, Phyllis A. Katz (1976) questioned whether the doll measure was adequate and found that replicating the test with a choice of four dolls did not produce the same negative self-esteem outcome as the Clarks' original study.
6. Mary Phelps and Margaret Wise Brown, "Lucy Sprague Mitchell," Lucy Sprague Mitchell Papers, 1878–1967, Rare Book and Manuscript Library, Columbia University, New York.
7. Edith Thacher Hurd, eulogy for Lucy Sprague Mitchell, delivered at the New School for Social Research, New York City, December 1, 1967, Sprague Mitchell Papers.

8. Hurd, Mitchell eulogy.
9. Hurd, Mitchell eulogy.
10. For example, Edward Rothstein's review of the 2013 New York Public Library exhibition curated by Leonard S. Marcus, biographer of Margaret Wise Brown, *The ABC of It: Why Children's Books Matter*, disparagingly links the history of Puritan moral education, the idea that books have "an obligation to train the reader in proper moral and political attitudes," to "identity politics" in children's books. Edward Rothstein, "Bedtime with Puritans and Wild Things," *New York Times*, June 20, 2013. This comment is somewhat ironic given that the show underplayed representations of race, something likewise reflected in the book version of the exhibit. Here, the few authors of color mentioned appear in a coda edited by Lisa Von Drasek, curator of the Children's Literature Research Collection at the University of Minnesota Libraries, and did not appear in the show itself (Marcus 2019).
11. The sequel to *Goodnight Moon*, the lesser known *My World* (1949), depicts the animal transitional object self-consciously: "Daddy's boy. / Mother's boy. / My boy is just a toy. / Bear"; Margaret Wise Brown and Clement Hurd, *My World* (New York: HarperCollins, 2001).
12. Keiko Kasza, *A Mother for Choco* (New York: Puffin Books, 1992); David Kirk, *Little Miss Spider* (New York: Scholastic, 1999).
13. Renata Galindo, *My New Mom and Me* (New York: Schwartz and Wade, 2016).
14. The move to understand how children acquire racial biases resulted in various and, at times, contradictory theories (Katz 1976, 144). Aboud's 1993 study takes place in Canada; studies in the United States began with a Black/white binary, which was supplanted by the recognition of a more complicated racial landscape by the 1980s. Katz (1976) provides an overview of academic studies since the 1970s that speculate on how racial biases are learned: direct instruction from parents, innate preferences for light over dark, identification with authority figures. Earlier, Frenkel-Brunswik (1948) suggested that prejudice in children derives from a specific personality type: those who eschew ambiguity and favor categorical fixity. Research focused on the racial attitudes of parents and their parenting styles gave way to a focus on the "cognitive aspects of racial attitudes," exploring how children understand racial and ethnic differences as a reflection of their intellectual development (Katz 1976, 137).
15. Studies focusing on children's biases as a reflection of cognitive development include Katz 1976; Aboud 1987, 1988, 1993; Ramsey 1987; Hirschfeld 1988, 1995; Holmes 1995; and Quintana 1998.
16. The liger, the offspring of a male lion and female tiger, is infertile if male and, if female, experiences low fertility rates. The tigon, the offspring of a female lion and male tiger, can produce offspring.
17. National Association of Black Social Workers (NABSW), "Position Statement on Trans-racial Adoption," National Association of Black Social Workers, New York, 1972, 2.
18. Tanya Valentine and Adam Taylor, *All Bears Need Love* (Lexington, KY: MeeGenius, 2012).
19. NABSW, "Position Statement on Trans-racial Adoption," 2.

20. By 2000, 13 percent of adopted children in US households were foreign born; nearly half of foreign-born adoptees were born in Asia. Rose M. Kreider, *Adopted Children and Stepchildren: 2000* (Census 2000 Special Reports, United States Census 2000; Washington, DC: US Department of Commerce, October 2003).
21. The controversial Operation Babylift evacuated approximately two thousand Vietnamese children at the fall of then-Saigon in April 1975. President Gerald Ford's airlift intended to provide homes for Vietnamese children in the United States and elsewhere but was criticized as a tokenistic media-relations effort to assuage American guilt over the war. More seriously, it was determined that any number of "orphans" destined for adoption were not actually orphans (Bow 2016).
22. In addition, some parents articulated their preference for Asian international adoption by invoking the NABSW position opposing Black/white adoptive families (Brian 2012). As discussed in chapter 4, the desire for Asian children could border on fetishism (H. Jacobson 2008).
23. Dahlen found that such books do "not holistically mirror the experiences of transracially adopted Koreans. Most of the stories were written with the implicitly didactic purpose of describing and explaining adoption." Sarah Park Dahlen, "Representations of Korean Adoption in Children's Literature," Ph.D. diss., University of Illinois at Urbana-Champaign, 2009; abstract cited on https://readingspark.wordpress.com/2009/04/08/dissertation-abstract/.
24. Yet the inadequacies of a color-blind approach were recognized during this period as well. Almost all the children in Frances Koh's 1981 study of Asian adoptees in Minneapolis encountered incidents of racial slurs or name calling (Koh [1981] 1988). Situating these insults as forms of psychic injury, Koh called upon parents and teachers to "confront the name-callers in the child's behalf, as well as to help the adoptee understand the meaning of prejudice and racism" (120). Color-blind discourse surrounding transnational adoption shifted with the International Gathering of the First Generation of Korean Adoptees in 1999, which heightened awareness of their racialization in the west (Brian 2012). NABSW's recognition that adopted Black children need to be taught coping techniques to deal with racism belatedly extended to Asian Americans.
25. Susan E. Lindsley and Tina L. Christiansen, with Wendy M. Cannon, *Maya's Journey Home* (Oakdale, NY: Suitemates, 2008), 22.
26. Kevin Leman and Kevin Leman II, *My Adopted Child, There's No One Like You* (Grand Rapids, MI: Revell, 2007), 14.
27. As in the title of Amy Tan's children's book, *The Chinese Siamese Cat* (1994), regionally derived subspecies nomenclature is uneasily explained away in favor of (human) ethnicity: "You are not Siamese cats but Chinese cats." Whiteness is the default for animals in Marc Brown's world making. One might guess that the cat character, Sue Ellen, is "Asian," as she knows Japanese myth and Chinese words, but her last name is Armstrong.
28. *Big Brother Binky* aired on PBS in 2007, written by Stephanie Simpson (Boston: WGBH Boston and Cookie Jar Entertainment, 2008), DVD, 51 min.

29. The episode does, however, flirt with the "indecent" suggestion of cross-species coupling by portraying a dog and rabbit in the adoption agency's waiting room. Elsewhere, the parallel between interracialism and interspeciesism is embodied by a minor character, Emily, half rabbit, half monkey.
30. While central to the plotline of later films, the first *Kung Fu Panda* never overtly addresses the protagonist's status as adoptee but references a family "secret" obliquely; Mark Osborne and John Stevenson, dirs. (Universal City, CA: Universal Pictures Home Entertainment, 2008), DVD, 92 min. In the final film, the adoption narrative ("Sometimes I can't believe I'm actually your son") is central to the plot's resolution that faith is power: thus, belief in family ties is more powerful than ancestry; Alessandro Carloni and Jennifer Yuh, dirs., *Kung Fu Panda 3* (Beverly Hills, CA: Dreamworks, 2016), DVD, 95 min. The films nevertheless play on an underlying atavism, the idea that biology wins out and destiny is foreordained by lineage.
31. Comment on the PBS webpage for *First Person Plural*, December 17, 2000, http://www.pbs.org/pov/firstpersonplural/.
32. This increased scrutiny was the result of fears of human trafficking, the subject of chapter 3. According to the State Department, in 2013, foreign adoptions dropped 62 percent to 8,668 from a high of 22,991 in 2004. See Rachel L. Swarns, "American Adoptions from Abroad at Their Lowest Level in Years," *New York Times*, January 24, 2013; and *2014 Annual Report on Intercountry Adoption* (Washington, DC: US State Department, March 31, 2015).
33. Realist works dealing with Asian American children as targets of anti-Asian bias include Marjorie Waybill's *Chinese Eyes* (Scottdale, PA: Herald Press, 1974); Soyong Pak and Jung un Kim's *Sumi's First Day of School Ever* (New York: Viking, 2003); and Jan M. Czech, *My American Face* (Washington, DC: Child and Family Press, 2000). While realist picture books visualize physical difference via illustration, the Asian American protagonist's conflict is not often racialized per se; that is, conflict stems from ignorance over some aspect of Asian culture, whether name, language, food, or skill. A happy resolution is achieved via an appreciation of the ethnic sign attached to the Asian child. In this sense, Asian American protagonists in more realist depictions allow for an uncontroversial split between race as a signifier of somatic difference and ethnicity as defined by cultural practices—uncontroversial because children categorize people according to both "how they looked and how they behaved" (Holmes 1995, 41). See, for example, Yangsook Choi, *The Name Jar* (New York: Dell, 2001); Helen Recorvits, *My Name Is Yoon* (New York: Farrar, Straus and Giroux, 2003); and Barnard Ashley, *Cleversticks* (New York: Crown, 1991).
34. According to Aboud (1988, 4), in ascertaining prejudice, "there must be an unfavourable evaluation of a person, elicited by his/her ethnic group membership, and based on an underlying organized predisposition." This adult-oriented definition of prejudice may not be entirely applicable to children because the ability to generalize with consistency requires "cognitive capabilities that are beyond those of a child under seven years of age" (8). Further, in discussing children's biases, Lawrence Hirschfeld (1988, 630) makes a distinction between "prejudice" and racism, the

latter implying behavioral dominance: "I am discussing prejudice and not racism to the extent that racism refers to behavioral dominance. The relationship between attitude and behavior is a hoary question; suffice it to say that it has long been accepted that the identification of an attitudinal complex does not explain a behavioural one, even when the latter 'logically' follows from the former. In terms of the discussion at hand, there are many instances of domination without reference to ethnic or racial affiliation and there are many prejudices that are not associated with socio-economic or political dominance."

35. Fremontmama, comment on "Is the Backyardigans Racist?," forum thread on *Mothering: Home for Natural Family Living*, November 4, 2005, https://www.mothering.com/threads/is-the-backyardigans-racist.364367/page-3.

36. According to federal data, in 2009, 17.8 percent of Asian American students reported being bullied at school or online in comparison to 30.3 percent of whites, 30.3 percent of Blacks, and 26.5 percent of Hispanics. Of course, this may simply imply that Asians are less likely to *report* bullying to authorities; moreover, the 2020 COVID-19 pandemic witnessed a resurgence of informal reports of Asian Americans being bullied; Simone Robers, Jijun Zhang, Jennifer Truman, and Thomas D. Snyder, *Indicators of Crime and Safety: 2011* (National Center for Education Statistics, NCES 2012-002/NCJ 236021; Washington, DC: US Department of Education, and Bureau of Justice Statistics, US Department of Justice, 2012), 130.

37. These include an Eisner Award for Best Graphic Album; ALA Printz Award for Excellence in Young Adult Literature; Reuben Award for Best Graphic Novel; Chinese American Librarians Association Book award; being named Best Book of the Year by Publishers' Weekly, School Library Journal, and the *San Francisco Chronicle*; Booklist Editors' Choice Book; and library media Editor's Choice Award for 2007.

38. In an interview with Yang in 2008, Lan Dong (2011, 237) notes that Yang "perceives the Monkey King's struggle as a stand-in for Asian Americans and anyone else who has been on the minority side of a minority-majority dynamic."

39. That an Asian adolescent might imagine himself as white is somehow *less* plausible here than, say, imagining oneself as a superhero. Ned Vizzini, "High Anxiety," *New York Times*, May 13, 2007.

40. For an excellent overview of the history of eugenics in the context of genetic reproduction, see Subramaniam 2014.

41. As evidence of the mirroring between monkey and man in Japan, Emiko Ohnuki-Tierney (1987, 25) notes that it is the only animal in Japanese (adult) language "addressed and referred to by the use of *san*—the address form used for humans." She writes, "Buddhism recognizes no sharp line between or hierarchy of humans and animals . . . and the line of demarcation is generally more lax" (21). Yet this positive symbolism later shifted; during the early modern period of Japanese history, this animal-human boundary blurring became represented as a threat, fostering representations of monkeys as scapegoats.

42. In the "friendship protection hypothesis," psychologists speculate that having one high-quality friendship mitigates the effects of bullying. In this, books like *ABC*

and *Yoko*, in which belonging is signaled through the recognition of a single figure, model a good-enough integration, marking children's books as a site of pragmatic micropolitics. See Hodges et al. 1999.

43. Kathleen T. Horning, Merri V. Lindgren, and Megan Schliesman, "Observations on Publishing in 2012," Cooperative Children's Book Center, March 1, 2013, https://ccbc.education.wisc.edu/observations-on-publishing-in-2012/.
44. Cited in Roger Sutton, "A Very Good Question," *Read Roger* (blog), Horn Book, July 7, 2013, http://www.hbook.com/2013/07/blogs/read-roger/a-very-good-question/#.
45. This excludes the 23 percent of books whose main characters are animals. See Horning, Lindgren, and Schliesman, "Observations on Publishing in 2012." Nel (2017, 2) references an earlier dataset for establishing the flatlining of multicultural children's books, noting that they never exceed 15 percent of the total. In 2019, the CCBC reported that of books for children and teens they received from US publishers that year, 52 percent were by or about people of color, with Asians composing the highest totals of racial groups. See "Books by and/or about Black, Indigenous and People of Color 2019," Cooperative Children's Book Center, School of Education, University of Wisconsin–Madison, last updated April 16, 2021, https://ccbc.education.wisc.edu/literature-resources/ccbc-diversity-statistics/books-by-and-or-about-poc-2019/.
46. Jaclyn DeForge, "A More Diverse Appendix B," *Open Book Blog*, January 28, 2013, http://blog.leeandlow.com/2013/01/28/a-more-diverse-appendix-b/.
47. Horning, Lindren, and Schliesman, "Observations on Publishing in 2012."
48. Corey Rosen Schwartz, Rebecca Gomez, and Dan Santat, *Hensel and Gretel: Ninja Chicks* (New York: Penguin, 2016).
49. Greater awareness of structural racism following the Black Lives Matter movement in 2020 has extended to awareness of passive and overt racism in children's books. See, for example, Christina Morales, "Scholastic Halts Distribution of Book by 'Captain Underpants' Author," *New York Times*, March 28, 2021. As I discuss in the next chapter, this awareness has also extended to books by Dr. Seuss.
50. Kathleen Horning, personal communication, Madison, WI, September 8, 2016.
51. When asked whether Brown's relationship with Strange was sexual, Brown's friends gave conflicting answers; one simply affirmed, "Oh, of course"; Martha Pichey, "Bunny Dearest," *Vanity Fair* 484 (2000): 176.
52. Quoted in Pichey, "Bunny Dearest," 177.
53. Leonard Marcus (1992) chronicles the long-term relationship between Brown and Strange and cites their love letters yet remains self-consciously opaque as to the sexual nature of their relationship.
54. Bank Street volunteer "Rosie" Bliven to Lucy Sprague, February 21, 1951, Sprague Mitchell Papers.
55. Mock-up, *Home for a Bunny*, Margaret Wise Brown Papers 1929–1952, Westerley Public Library, Westerley, Rhode Island.
56. Since its circulation in 2006, *And Tango Makes Three* appears consistently among the top ten books subject to formal written complaints filed with schools or libraries;

Justin Richardson, Peter Parnell, and Henry Cole, *And Tango Makes Three* (New York: Simon and Schuster, 2005). According to the American Library Association, objections claimed the book "promotes the homosexual agenda"; "Top 10 for 2006," in "Top 10 Most Challenged Books List," Banned and Challenged Books, ALA Office for Intellectual Freedom, accessed April 30, 2021, http://www.ala.org/advocacy/bbooks/frequentlychallengedbooks/top10. See also Karolides 2006.

57. Garth Williams denied political meaning underlying rabbit intimacy ("it is only about a soft furry love") and claimed that his inspiration was the aesthetic representation of color contrast in Chinese painting, not racial difference; quoted in Sollers 1997, 22.
58. Brown's answer came in response to student questions during a visit to the University of Wisconsin–Madison in 2015; Horning pers. comm.
59. Christopher Myers, "Young Dreamers," *Horn Book Magazine*, August 6, 2013, https://www.hbook.com/?detailStory=young-dreamers.
60. See Michael Chabon, "The Unspeakable, in Its Jammies," *Atlantic*, January 12, 2011.

CHAPTER 2. Racist Cute

An earlier version of this chapter appeared as "Racist Cute: Caricature, *Kawaii*-style, and the Asian Thing," *American Quarterly* 71, no. 1 (2019): 29–58.

1. See Mary Roach, "Cute Inc.," *Wired*, July 12, 1999; Yano 2013; and Dale et al. 2017.
2. Ngai's (2012, 92) work engages aesthetic categories as conduits of racialization by situating Blacks through the "ideologeme of racial animatedness." She also acutely connects cuteness to minstrelsy and slavery, noting the ways in which both kinship and ownership are activated by the cute. More recent work gestures to a wider variety of racial effects; see Dale et al. 2017.
3. Latour's (2005, 81) example of one such "risky" object is the space shuttle *Columbia*, which, exploding upon reentering the Earth's atmosphere, suddenly "flip-flopped" its mode of existence.
4. On object-oriented ontology, see for example, Bogost 2012. In contrast, for Latour (2005, 76), proponent of actor-network theory, positing symmetry between humans and nonhumans is "absurd."
5. This correlation between stereotype and psychological harm is documented in Fryberg et al. 2008 and Freng and Willis-Esqueda 2011. Interestingly, few activist groups called for banning American Indian mascots on aesthetic grounds; a 1972 petition advocating for Stanford University's discontinuation of the name Stanford Indians is the exception. Arguing against the sale of Indian figurines and imagery at the Stanford bookstore, students wrote, "These products are physically unattractive. They seem to insist that the race upon which they are fashioned are also unattractive" (quoted in Hirschfelder 1982, 217).
6. For an overview of CRT views on hate speech, see Matsuda 1993, 18.
7. See Ian Sharpira, "Federal Judge Orders Cancellation of Redskins' Trademark Registrations," *Washington Post*, July 8, 2015.

8. In the 1970s, an estimated 80 percent of collectors were white, and 20 percent were Black (Goings 1994, 98); by the 1980s, this was reversed. Michael Harris (2003, 190) notes that at some memorabilia shows, 80 percent of dealers and a majority of consumers are Black. Collectors include Whoopi Goldberg, Anita Baker, Julian Bond, and Oprah Winfrey; Lynell George, "Collecting Controversy: The Curios and Figurines of a Racist Past Are Hot Properties," *Los Angeles Times*, October 19, 1994. On the contemporary manufacture of Black collectibles, see Kelly Kazek, "Mammy and Uncle Mose Figures Sold in Alabama: Historical Collectibles or Offensive Reminder of Racism?" *AL*, March 31, 2014, https://www.al.com/breaking/2014/03/mammy_and_mose_collectibles_so.html.
9. See Frank Wu, "Why I Collect Racism," *Huffington Post*, November 27, 2014.
10. For example, see the painful historical documents reflecting anti-Asian bias in the following anthologies: Tchen and Yeats, *Yellow Peril! An Archive of Anti-Asian Fear* (2014); Ignacio et al., *The Forbidden Book: The Philippine-American War in Political Cartoons* (2004); and Dong, Choy, and Hom, *The Coming Man: 19th Century American Perceptions of the Chinese* (1995).
11. Wu, "Why I Collect Racism."
12. Cited in Stephanie Siek, "q&a: David Pilgrim, Jim Crow Museum of Racist Memorabilia," cnn, May 3, 2012, https://www.cnn.com/2012/05/03/us/qa-david-pilgrim-jim-crow-museum-of-racist-memorabilia-curator/index.html.
13. That is, I am aware that 4 billion people may read these images differently. As evidenced by the highly touted 2012 rollout of a nearly identical Harajuku knock-off, Pan's Ko Lovers perfume in Hong Kong, Asian reception of such objects is not haunted by *racialized* dehumanization. In its "universal" appeal, cuteness becomes an instrument of neoliberal globalization by seeming to erase national resonances, dematerializing history and local specificity.
14. Reflecting brightly colored, natural settings and rounded shapes, the cute aesthetic adopted by Sega, Sony, and Nintendo for video games in the 1980s was said to reflect Osamu Tezuka's pioneering manga designs. See Burrill 2009, 107–18.
15. Of course, positing the baby schema as an innate response naturalizes the affective labor of women; this becomes more evident in a study that suggests that the Kindchenschema is tied to female reproductive hormones. See Lorenz 1971; Glocker et al. 2009; and Sprengelmeyer et al. 2009.
16. See Preston Blair, *Animation 1: Learn to Animate Cartoons Step by Step* (Irvine: Walter Foster, 2003), 18.
17. Eng-Beng Lim (2014, 3) highlights the pedophilic bent of Western paternalism expressed through the dyad white daddy/brown boy and the "queer pedophantasmagoria" underlying colonialism in the Pacific Rim.
18. "Barbara Barry Introduces Indochine Collection for Kravet," Kravet, accessed November 25, 2016, http://www.kravet.com/emails/press/bb-indochine/bb-indo-online-pr.htm.
19. Annie, comment on sumo figurine, cb2, accessed February 15, 2015, http://www.cb2.com/all-accessories/accessories/sumo/s210216.

20. Jana Pijak, "CB2's Sumo Figurine Is a Fun and Artful Home Accent," Trend Hunter, July 15, 2014, http://www.trendhunter.com/trends/sumo-figurine.
21. See Yano 2013 and Ngai 2012. Sanrio takes a different view: designer of Hello Kitty for over nineteen years, Yuuko Yamaguchi asserted that "Kitty has a mouth. . . . It's hidden in the fur" (quoted in Roach, "Cute Inc").
22. "The Chin Family," National Palace Museum, accessed July 14, 2014, http://www.npm.gov.tw/digital/index3_3_5_en.html.
23. "Chin Family."
24. In 2021, Dr. Seuss Enterprises announced that it would cease publication and licensing of *If I Ran the Zoo* and five other titles out of concern that the books "portray people in ways that are hurtful and wrong." Cited in "Statement from Dr. Seuss Enterprises," seussville.com, March 2, 2021, https://www.seussville.com/statement-from-dr-seuss-enterprises/.
25. What some see as the continuing success of Japan's cultural exports, others position as a failure to capitalize on intellectual property, pre- and postrecession (Kelts 2006).
26. For a discussion of mukokuseki, see Iwabuchi 2004. The term *soft power* derives from Joseph Nye Jr. (1990), who emphasized the ways in which, in contrast to threats of coercion, a nation's ability to persuade derives from the attractiveness of its ideals, lifestyle, cultural institutions, and other aspects of civil society.
27. Despite backing from Disney, Pucca merchandise failed to take hold in North America. Cited in Jung Hyung-mo, "How High Will the Pucca Man Fly His Babies?" *Korea JoongAng Daily*, July 25, 2008, https://koreajoongangdaily.joins.com/2008/07/25/features/How-high-will-the-Pucca-man-fly-his-babies/2892805.html.
28. See Kelts 2006. Iwabuchi (2004, 59) nevertheless notes, "The propensity of Japanese animators to make their products appear nonJapanese is evidence that a Western-dominated cultural hierarchy continues to govern transnational cultural flows. But there's more to this story."
29. On cuteness as a soothing response, see Dale et al. 2017.
30. This reaction was one I documented in workshops with Asian American studies classes at the University of Wisconsin–Madison.
31. See Action Ranger Timmy, "Kung Fu Guy," *Why Did I Buy That Toy? Blogging Away Buyer's Remorse*, October 26, 2012, http://whydidibuythat.blogspot.com/2012/10/kung-fu-guy.html.
32. "Kara Walker: The Melodrama of 'Gone with the Wind,'" *art21*, November 2011, http://www.art21.org/texts/kara-walker/interview-kara-walker-the-melodrama-of-gone-with-the-wind.
33. I was surprised that some Asian American student activists deemed the Pucca coin bank (see figure 2.3) to be cute rather than offensive. One woman, in explaining her positive response to what I saw as gross caricature, noted that her emotional connection to this cartoon from childhood could be overridden by her more recently acquired intellectual knowledge. Of those objects shown in figures 2.2, 2.3, and 2.5–2.7, those that solicited the most positive response were associated

with childhood. In contrast, purely decorative objects and those with household functions—pepper grinders, handbags, eggcups—elicited groans. The only time an individual was publicly called out for his evaluation during one of these workshops was an instance in which an Asian American man was teased by his male peers for siding with the cute designation, presumably a sign of femininity.

34. Quoted in Kazek, "Mammy and Uncle Mose Figures Sold in Alabama."
35. See *Stuff Asian People Like*, accessed April 30, 2021, http://stuffasianpeoplelike.com. Its editors explain, "As we're trying to simply explain how and why certain stereotypes about Asians exist through lighthearted humor, we are by no means endorsing them"; "#A Busting the Stereotype: Asians Are Short," *Stuff Asian People Like*, September 10, 2008, http://stuffasianpeoplelike.com/2008/09/10/a-busting-the-stereotype-asians-are-short/.
36. Saper (1993, 82) asserts that in-group ethnic humor does not indicate self-contempt; rather, it allows Jews to "find peaceful strategies for dealing with prejudice and persecution; to take the edge off tragedy; to maintain their dignity, integrity, equilibrium, and sanity and to get along and get ahead."
37. Phil Yu, personal communication, April 15, 2015.
38. For a discussion of the controversy, see Pham and Ono 2008 and Lopez 2016. Pham and Ono's reading of the controversy confirms this viewpoint, reading satire not in the original images but in the "counterrhetoric" of T-shirts subsequently produced by Asian Americans that riffed on the Abercrombie and Fitch imagery, with the subtitle "Ignorance, Racism, Excuses." While they note that the original shirts have become collector's items, they do not say by whom.
39. Quoted in Jenny Strasburg, "Abercrombie & Glitch: Asian Americans Rip Retailer for Stereotypes on T-Shirts," *SFGate*, April 18, 2002, https://www.sfgate.com/news/article/ABERCROMBIE-GLITCH-Asian-Americans-rip-2850702.php.
40. See Leslie Bow, "Snapchat's Messed-Up Racial Filter," *Progressive*, August 15, 2016, https://progressive.org/op-eds/snapchat-s-messed-up-racial-filter/.
41. What constitutes satire was debated regarding the obscenity trial of 2 Live Crew in 1990. Academic Henry Louis Gates testified on behalf of the rappers, defending their depiction of Black hypersexuality as a form of parody. In contrast, law professor Kimberlè Crenshaw (1991, 1292) questioned his defense, which, she argues, "recalls similar efforts on behalf of racist humor, which has sometimes been defended as antiracist—an effort to poke fun at or show the ridiculousness of racism."
42. Jennifer Ho (2015, 28) has suggested that "Asian American studies developed out of a desire for ambiguity, as a way to allow Asians in America to be multiply interpreted and to be read in a richer, more complex manner that moved beyond caricature and stereotype."
43. See *Oxford English Dictionary Online*, s.v. "mascot," accessed May 26, 2021, https://www.oed.com/view/Entry/114553?redirectedFrom=mascot#eid; and *Merriam-Webster Online*, s.v. "fetish," accessed May 26, 2021, https://www.merriam-webster.com/dictionary/mascot#synonyms.

CHAPTER 3. Asian • Female • Robot • Slave

1. NAO was developed in Paris in 2006 by Aldebaran. After the company was purchased by SoftBank Robotics in 2016, the website was revised to be less emotive and exclamatory. The now Japanese multinational company offers three humanoid robots for home, business, and nonprofit use, including Pepper, who can read to children and work as a public greeter, and Romeo, who is designed to assist those with limited mobility. "A-Robots NAO," Aldebaran, accessed August 3, 2015, https://www.aldebaran.com/en/humanoid-robot/nao-robot.
2. PARO Therapeutic Robot was developed by AIST in Japan in 2003 with distributors in the United States, Europe, Hong Kong, and Australia; it occasioned a new professional category: licensed robot therapist.
3. AIBO is homonymous with *pal*, or *partner*, in Japanese. Offered in 1999, it was discontinued in 2014, and owners faced the slow death of their mechanical pets after Sony stopped repairs. A new version of AIBO was resurrected in 2018.
4. This is the view espoused by Robi's inventor, Tomotaka Takahashi, also the developer of the humanoid robot Kirobo for Toyota. "Robi—Just about the Cutest Robot Ever," interview with Tomotaka Takahashi, NHK World, January 3, 2016, video, 11:20, Our Health and Spirit, January 4, 2016, https://www.youtube.com/watch?v=YrTBgqFKSwg.
5. Zaonotto et al. (2020) found that the more humanoid a robot, the greater the sense of likeability, trust, safety, and animacy. They also found, however, that if the more humanoid robot, in this case, NAO, was interacted with first, the nonhumanoid robot was perceived as being more credible.
6. Quoted in the documentary *The Human Robot*, dir. Rob van Hattum, produced by VPRO Backlight, 2015, video, 49:00, June 12, 2015, https://www.youtube.com/watch?v=sXzoboNmwak.
7. Asimov's (1950) directives specifying human mastery (a "robot may not injure a human being"; a "robot must obey the orders given to it by human beings") reflect an anxiety about being surpassed by potentially superior beings.
8. Physicist Stephen Hawking joined a thousand AI and robotics researchers and others in signing a letter likewise opposing the development of lethal autonomous weapons intended for military purposes. See Ben Farmer, "Killer Robots a Small Step Away and Must Be Outlawed, Says UN Official," *Telegraph* (London), August 27, 2014, https://www.telegraph.co.uk/news/uknews/defence/11059391/Killer-robots-a-small-step-away-and-must-be-outlawed-says-top-UN-official.html. The absence of Japanese signatories on the ban had less to do with cultural differences than with history: Japan's Constitution under the directive of the US occupying forces in the postwar period forbids military armament. Article 9 of Japan's 1947 Constitution reads, "The Japanese people forever renounce war as a sovereign right of the nation and the threat or use of force as a means of settling international disputes.... [L]and, sea, and air forces, as well as other war potential, will never be maintained." See Kelts 2006.

9. "Alien/Asian is inextricably tied to science, the future, and technology," writes Stephen Hong Sohn (2008, 6) in a special issue of *MELUS*. See also Roh, Huang, and Niu 2015.
10. Wendy Chun (2003, 18), for example, affirms the Orient as "a privileged example of the virtual" as well as cyberpunk's "orientalizing of the digital landscape" (29).
11. Cited in Gideon Lewis-Kraus, "Check in with the Velociraptor at the World's First Robot Hotel," *Wired*, March 2, 2016, https://www.wired.com/2016/03/robot-henn-na-hotel-japan/.
12. By "strong AI," Searle (1990) refers to machine intelligence that approximates human consciousness, in contrast to weak AI, or *artificial narrow intelligence*.
13. Ryle (1949) invoked the "ghost in the machine" as a critique of Descartes's mind-body opposition and exposed both as mediated through discursivity: idioms, metaphor, definition, human relation. As in his title *The Concept of Mind*, he countered the idea of the mind as mysterious, occult in its unknowability. Appropriated as a popular AI metaphor, the "ghost in the machine" ironically conveys the opposite of what Ryle intended. My take on the embodied AI of this chapter supports his phenomenological challenge of the mind's ineffable nature; the mind, or "ghost," becomes seemingly knowable through the social identity ascribed to the "machine" or materialized body within a network of social relations.

    The popular appropriation of the term *hyperreal* also hinges on a relevant misreading. Jean Baudrillard ([1981] 1994, 122–23) invoked simulacra not in opposition to "the real" but, in effect, as its cloaking device, the hyperreal as the "alibi" of the real: "The imaginary was the alibi of the real, in a world dominated by the reality principle. Today, it is the real that has become the alibi of the model, in a world controlled by the principle of simulation." The fantasy genres engaged in this chapter might also be said to represent the alibi of the real; their pleasure depends on an apartness from the known world. They contribute to a belief in the "realness" of things by preventing us from seeing reality as likewise discursively constructed. For Baudrillard, the very existence of Disneyland, for example, preserves this vital ideological function of containment. The AI narratives of this chapter might be said to perform the same role.
14. I thank Elena Tajima Creef for this reference; viewers can certainly get the gist of Yoshihiro Nishimura's sci-fi B movie *RoboGeisha* (2009) by its trailer, Hans Glock Film Productions, video, 3:20, June 30, 2009, https://www.youtube.com/watch?v=Wo-gGes6qig&has_verified=1.
15. I am aware that there are differences within this list of engineered entities: clones are not machines, and *robot* is not synonymous with *AI*. Nevertheless, I group them together to emphasize the similar ways in which they are situated within modes of emplotment and with the effects implied in note 15 (i.e., strong vs. weak AI). Robots are not simply imagined beings; regardless of such distinctions, they signify through predictable networks of social meaning, in Bhabha's words, the *same old* stories.
16. On the representation of artificial women, see, for example, Wosk 2015; Kakoudaki 2014; Toffoletti 2007; Springer 1996; and Leyda 2017.

17. Reviewing over seven hundred fictional and nonfictional media representations of human-robot sexual intimacy, German researchers found that imagined human-robot relationships lean heavily on normative scripts of human sexuality. The human partner was most typically a heterosexual male adult with some form of social estrangement on the basis of disability, social skills, or attractiveness. Robots were portrayed as having some capacity for emotion and were marked as humanoid in appearance, gendered female, and adult as well as being designated heterosexual (Döring and Poeschl 2019). On the gendered significance of ai, see also West, Kraut, and Chew 2019.
18. Any number of US media featuring female AI (e.g., *The Stepford Wives*, 1975; *Eve of Destruction*, 1991; *Her*, 2013) feature Caucasian leads. I would note that these are less likely to invoke narratives of bondage or trafficking as a single source of narrative framing.
19. According to Kennon (2017), Bell invokes modern accounts of the slave's escape from bondage with particular reference to Margaret Walker's *Jubilee* (1966) and Ernest Gaines's *The Autobiography of Miss Jane Pittman* (1971). I extend the neoslave narrative to encompass a similar mode of emplotment engaging Asian female subjects within speculative literature and visual media that engage technology. Claudia Springer's concepts of "techno-eroticism" and "electronic eros" convey the marriage of technology and sexuality in popular culture paradoxically to predict both "the obsolescence of human beings and a future of heightened erotic fulfillment" (Springer 1996, 8). In contrast, I focus on techno-Orientalist scopophilia, erotic pleasure in viewing speculative futures.
20. For a recent account of the theme of robot slavery, see Kakoudaki 2014.
21. Laura Miller, "The Salon Interview: Dorothy Allison," *Salon*, April 1, 1998, https://www.salon.com/1998/03/31/cov_si_31intb/.
22. For an overview of feminist STS, see, for example, the online mission statement of the journal *Catalyst: Feminism, Theory, Technoscience*, devoted to the interdisciplinary exploration of feminist, queer, crip, postcolonial, and antiracist STS and media studies. "Catalyst: Feminism, Theory, Technoscience," *EASST Review* 35, no. 2 (2016), https://easst.net/article/catalyst-feminism-theory-technoscience/.
23. This multireferentiality was exploited in the film *The Imitation Game* (New York: Elevation Pictures, 2014), whose title refers to Turing's closeted sexuality.
24. Programmer Vladimir Veselov quoted in "Turing Test Success Marks Milestone in Computer History," University of Reading News and Events, June 8, 2014, http://www.reading.ac.uk/news-and-events/releases/PR583836.aspx.
25. Existing AI lack cognitive complexity. As of yet, they can mimic predicting outcomes in the face of variability, but even mechanistically they can only approximate the logic of human agents, who rapidly evolve new desires and wants. According to philosopher John Pollock (1995, 241), "No planning algorithm could actually produce a single plan for the simultaneous satisfaction of all these desires." Similarly, computer scientists Richard E. Neapolitan and Xia Jiang (2013, 2) note that while fictional AI such as the Terminator and HAL "can learn and make decisions in a

complex, changing environment, affect that environment, and communicate their knowledge and choices to humans," as of yet, we "have no such entities." Given this high bar for determining cognition, researchers prefer the term *machine learning* over *artificial intelligence*; Cliff Kuang, "Can AI Be Taught to Explain Itself?" *New York Times Magazine*, November 21, 2017. Reflecting Turing's indifference to the distinction between intelligence as understanding and the simulation of understanding, Neapolitan and Jiang (2013, 4) mildly note, "If the program for all purposes behaves as if it is intelligent, computer scientists have achieved their goal."

26. At the outset, McCarthy envisioned AI research proceeding with the hypothesis that "every aspect of learning or any other feature of intelligence can in principle be so precisely described that a machine can be made to simulate it"; quoted in Andrew Myers, "Stanford's John McCarthy, Seminal Figure of Artificial Intelligence, Dies at 84," *Stanford Report*, October 25, 2011, https://news.stanford.edu/news/2011/october/john-mccarthy-obit-102511.html. Daphne Koller, McCarthy's colleague at Stanford, noted, "He believed in artificial intelligence in terms of building an artifact that could actually replicate human level intelligence, and because of this, he was very unhappy with a lot of AI today, which provides some very useful applications but focuses on machine learning"; quoted in Cade Metz, "John McCarthy—Father of AI and LISP—Dies at 84," *Wired*, October 24, 2011, https://www.wired.com/2011/10/john-mccarthy-father-of-ai-and-lisp-dies-at-84/.

27. This view of task-oriented AI is echoed by the developers of Google Translate. As one researcher working on the project noted, "It's not about what a machine 'knows' or 'understands' but what it 'does,' and—more importantly—what it doesn't do yet"; quoted in Gideon Lewis-Kraus, "The Great A.I. Awakening," *New York Times Magazine*, December 14, 2016, 63.

28. For an overview of the intellectual history of the automaton in the West, see M. Kang 2011.

29. *Ghost in the Shell 2: Innocence*, dir. Mamoru Oshii (Tokyo: Toho Company, 2004), theatrical release, 100 min.

30. *Cloud Atlas*, dir. Lana Wachowski and Lilly Wachowski (Burbank, CA: Warner Bros. Pictures, 2012), DVD, 165 min.

31. Written by Sam Vincent and Jonathan Brackley, the sci-fi drama *Humans*, a joint production between Channel 4 in the UK and AMC in the US, premiered in 2015.

32. *Ex Machina*, dir. Alex Garland (Santa Monica, CA: Lions Gate Entertainment, 2014), videodisc, 108 min.

33. On the controversy surrounding Zhao's *Blood Heir*, see Alexandra Alter, "She Pulled Her Debut Book When Critics Found It Racist: Now She Plans to Publish," *New York Times*, April 29, 2019; and Aja Hoggatt, "An Author Canceled Her Own YA Novel over Accusations of Racism, But Is It Really Anti-Black?" *Slate*, January 31, 2019, https://slate.com/culture/2019/01/blood-heir-ya-book-twitter-controversy.html.

34. On the historical and geographical range of human slavery, see Fynn-Paul and Pargas 2018. In particular, in that volume, see Martinez 2018. Martinez describes

the ways in which Asian women have been subject to enslavement pre-1800s in the context of European colonialism and within the Chinese practices of hereditary slavery and debt bondage. She also focuses on the trafficking in Asian women post-1860s.

35. *Trafficking in Persons Report* (Washington, DC: State Department, 2015), 9. On the controversy surrounding the attribution *slave* to depict trafficking in persons, see, for example, the divided responses to journalist Alex Tizon's essay "My Family's Slave," which tells the story of a domestic worker "bequeathed" to his family in the Philippines who subsequently served his family in the United States. His depiction of diasporic Filipina labor as modern "slavery" incited controversy among readers. Alex Tizon, "My Family's Slave," *Atlantic*, June 2017, https://www.theatlantic.com/magazine/archive/2017/06/lolas-story/524490/.
36. *Trafficking in Persons Report* (Washington, DC: State Department 2016), 6.
37. *Intersections of Human Trafficking, Domestic Violence, and Sexual Assault* (Oakland, CA: Asian Pacific Institute on Gender-Based Violence, 2016), 5.
38. "Trafficking," Asian Pacific Institute on Gender-Based Violence, accessed October 1, 2016, https://www.api-gbv.org/violence/trafficking.php.
39. As reported by the Polaris Project in 2017, 34 percent of those using the hotline were Latina; "Statistics on Trafficking," Asian Pacific Institute on Gender-Based Violence, accessed June 22, 2018, https://www.api-gbv.org/about-gbv/types-of-gbv/trafficking.
40. On Asia as a strategic region during US Cold War military buildup, filmmaker Kyoung Tae Park notes, "The United States has concentrated its forces in Okinawa, Japan, South Korea, and the Philippines. According to 2004 baseline data published by the Department of Defense, despite the shifting geopolitical distribution of the military bases in the post-9/11 era, 66 percent of its 860 overseas bases were still concentrated in three countries, Germany (306 sites), Japan (158 sites), and South Korea (105 sites)"; quoted in Meghan Noé, "South Korea's 'Camptown' Stories," *BU Today*, March 22, 2007, http://www.bu.edu/articles/2007/south-koreas-camptown-stories/. Moreover, as historian Ji-Yeon Yuh (2002) notes, the United States discouraged the establishment of camptowns around German bases, encouraging servicemen to see German women as "girlfriends" in contrast to sanctioning the brothel system in South Korea. On the links between military prostitution and the sex industries in South Korea and Thailand, see also Moon 1997; Bishop and Robinson 1998; and L. Kang 2020. Of course, the traffic in women and girls has a much longer history in Asia. For example, as I discuss later, the Chinese practice of *mui tsai*, girls sold into domestic service, was documented in the seventeenth century and lasted until the revolution in 1949. Contracts specifying the sale of women and girls for this purpose as well as for adoption, future marriage, concubinage, and prostitution (as well as kidnapping for these purposes) were widespread. See Hayes 2003.
41. The Japanese military's brothel system, ironically established to address the rape of civilians, dates to the 1937 Nanjing Massacre in China. There were various means of filling these "comfort stations" during imperial conquest such as recruitment

via civilian labor brokers. More conventionally, women were enlisted through deception, intimidation, arrest, and outright abduction. In Southeast Asia and China, women were more likely to be kidnapped by civilians or arrested by police; in contrast, Japanese military personnel were more likely to be directly involved in women's abduction in the Philippines. On the origins of the comfort women, see Tanaka 1999; and Hicks 1994. The Japanese government acknowledged and apologized for the atrocities in 1993 but did not offer state compensation to South Korean women until 2015. For South Korean activists, however, that action was inadequate; they erected a new statue memorializing the women in front of the Japanese consulate in Busan, ROK, in 2017. See James Sterngold, "Japan Admits Army Forced Women into War Brothels," *New York Times*, August 5, 1993; and "Japan and South Korea Agree WW2 'Comfort Women' Deal," *BBC News*, December 28, 2015, http://www.bbc.com/news/world-asia-35188135.

42. Echoing the more disturbing resonances of the Pygmalion myth, *Ex Machina*'s doppelgänger is *The Stepford Wives*: here, masculine hubris underlying the desire for technological mastery is indistinguishable from mastery over women. The film ignited controversy among feminists who pointed to its underlying misogyny. Maureen Dowd suggested that the film mocks male obsession with "man-pleasing female sex robots" while delivering exactly that spectacle; Maureen Dowd, "Beware Our Mind Children," *New York Times*, April 25, 2015. Reviewers for *Ms.* and *Bitch* magazines invoked Donna Haraway's feminist cyborg with palpable regret. These feminist readings in mainstream media limit their critique of the film's racial politics to its stereotypical imagery or the use of women of color as foils to the film's white female lead. See Manohla Dargis, "Review: in 'Ex Machina,' a Mogul Fashions the Droid of His Dreams," *New York Times*, April 9, 2015; Kjerstin Johnson, "How 'Ex Machina' Toys with Its Female Characters," *Bitch Media*, May 8, 2015, https://www.bitchmedia.org/post/ex-machina-film-review-gender-and-ai-feminism; and Natalie Wilson, "How *Ex Machina* Fails to Be Radical," *Ms.*, April 29, 2015, https://msmagazine.com/2015/04/29/how-ex-machina-fails-to-be-radical/.

43. Johnson, "How 'Ex Machina' Toys with Its Female Characters."

44. Credited to cartoonist and graphic novelist Alison Bechdel from her *Dykes to Watch Out For* comic, the Bechdel test has three requirements for determining a media representation's commitment to gender equality: (1) it must have at least two women in it; (2) who talk to each other; (3) about something other than a man.

45. Lee notes that the women "put themselves in this position of sacrifice." Chang-rae Lee, "On Such a Full Sea," talk at the Chautauqua Institution, Chautauqua, New York, July 3, 2014, video, 57:00, July 6, 2014, https://www.youtube.com/watch?v=j84OAG7mZQ4.

46. *Cyborg* was modeled on Grace Li, an international student attending the University of Houston. Randolph writes, "Haraway's description of Asian women with nimble fingers, working in enterprise zones for very little remuneration stuck in my head"; Lynn Randolph, "Modest Witness: A Painter's Collaboration with Donna Haraway," Lynn Randolph.com, 2009, http://www.lynnrandolph.com/presentations/

?eid=817. Haraway's own image description in part derives from Laura Kang's work for *Compositional Subjects* (2002).
47. Both *Monstress* and *Blood Heir* reflect a standard trope of young adult fantasy fiction in which the protagonists attempt to control their "monster within," speaking directly to the interiority of adolescents in transition, their self-questioning and suspicion of adult authority. On the conventions surrounding fantasy fiction for young adults, see Wilkins 2019.
48. Tzarina T. Prater and Catherine Fung (2015, 206) used software to translate Lai's poem thusly: "*dear mother* / return to languish *that is to say* anguish of foreigner's fodder *otherwise* the boarder pictures a *mixture of* canada wild enough to retrack railway *cn to cnn and rpms to dna* the bend in my corner / love Rachel." They read the poem through the lens of Rachel's racialization, acutely emphasizing its evocations of foreignness, immigration, hybridity, and global markets.
49. The text of Lai's found poem appears in Hayes 2003, 447.
50. Clinton's statement at the Fourth World Conference on Women in Beijing was also reflected in Article 14 of the Beijing Declaration and Platform for Action disseminated by the United Nations, September 15, 1995.
51. Human agency exists in contrast to the "non-cognitive agency" of other lifeforms—viruses, plants—that exhibit instinctual, reflexive reactions to their environments. As Pollock (1995, 8) explains, an "*agent* is any system capable of acting on its environment to render it more congenial to its continued survival," whereas cognitive agents have "both mental representations of the world and likes and dislikes."
52. The program plays with the multiple identificatory positions taken by various family members as it explores the nature of their attachment to or disaffection from synthetic beings. Echoing Asimov's *I, Robot*, one conceit of *Humans* is the fear that the robot nanny, here, ironically also called "dolly," will usurp the maternal caregiving role, the mother's gendered affective labor: the threat is not the child's physical risk before the machine, but her overattachment. In *I, Robot*, Robbie, the robot nanny, is merely the child's transitional object, abandoned as she matures.
53. This racial association is made more evident in the Swedish original, *Real Humans*: when Anita is assessed to be Korean in origin, we are told that "95 to 100 percent of *this type*, if stolen or unregistered, become sex Hub" (emphasis mine). This association references the history of comfort women and camptowns.
54. "Tea and Consent," an animated public service announcement produced by the Thames Valley Police Department in the UK, went viral in 2015. It was both celebrated for its accessible message and critiqued for its lack of nuance surrounding consensual sexual encounters.
55. The jury found Turner, ballyhooed as an athlete from Stanford, guilty of three felonies, but he was sentenced to only six months in prison and probation. The light sentencing spawned calls for Judge Aaron Persky's recall. Chanel Miller, *Know My Name: A Memoir* (New York: Viking, 2019).
56. Miller, *Know My Name*.

57. The boy's father initiates sex with the robot in a scene shot to evoke rape. *Humans* portrays another sentient female AI figure working in a brothel; when she violently rebels, she warns the madam, "Everything your men do to *us*, they want to do to *you*," collapsing the line between sexual fantasy and demeaning action against women.
58. Doug Bolton, "Chinese Researchers Create Jia Jia—A Super-Lifelike 'Robot Goddess,'" *Independent* (London), April 18, 2016, https://www.independent.co.uk/life-style/gadgets-and-tech/news/jia-jia-china-robot-goddess-humanoid-hefei-a6989716.html.
59. While Aiko has the potential to do many things—home tasks, companionship, airport security—as of yet, she actually does nothing. Some of her achievements replicate existing technologies that moved forward without taking android form. But as Trung notes on his website promoting Aiko, "With proper funding a dream can become reality." Project Aiko, last updated June 25, 2013, http://www.projectaiko.com/index.html.
60. Sensor technology conveying degrees of touch has advanced since 2007; by 2014, for example, prosthetic breasts fitted with sensors teach primary care physicians to administer breast exams. These prosthetics are not attached to a humanoid body, which is to say, they are not wholly sexualized. See Thomas M. Johnson, "Sensor Technology Helps Clinicians Improve Breast Exam Skills," National Institute of Biomedical Imaging and Bioengineering, News and Events, April 6, 2015, https://www.nibib.nih.gov/news-events/newsroom/sensor-technology-helps-clinicians-improve-breast-exam-skills-0.
61. "Aiko at Ontario Science Center," Project Aiko, video, 6:16, November 22–23, 2008, http://www.projectaiko.com/video.html.
62. In 2014, the #gamergate movement mounted a campaign of online harassment against women who criticized misogyny in videogames, including Anita Sarkeesian, founder of Feminist Frequency, a website exposing sexism in the media. On the anonymous gamers flaming women, writer Leigh Alexander noted, "They think someone is coming to take their toys away." Quoted in Nick Wingfield, "Intel Pulls Ads from Site after 'Gamergate' Boycott," *New York Times*, October 2, 2014.
63. Aiko's inventor informed the press in an interview posted on his website that "Like a real female, she will react to being touched in certain ways. If you grab or squeeze too hard, she will try to slap you." "About Aiko: Past, Present, and Future," Project Aiko, accessed May 2, 2021, http://www.projectaiko.com/about.html.
64. Cited in FAQ, Project Aiko, accessed May 2, 2021, http://www.projectaiko.com/faq.html.
65. "Aiko the Female Robot: Inventor Le Trung Talks about His Perfect Woman," *Huff Post*, January 10, 2009, updated December 6, 2017, https://www.huffpost.com/entry/aiko-the-female-robot-inv_n_149860.
66. Kwiyeon Ha, "Tokyo Gamers Slapped Down for Virtual Groping," *Reuters*, September 16, 2016.
67. Leah Fessler, "We Tested Bots like Siri and Alexa to See Who Would Stand Up to Sexual Harassment," *Quartz at Work*, February 22, 2017, https://qz.com/911681

/we-tested-apples-siri-amazon-echos-alexa-microsofts-cortana-and-googles-google-home-to-see-which-personal-assistant-bots-stand-up-for-themselves-in-the-face-of-sexual-harassment. See also West, Kraut, and Chew 2019.

68. When asked, Alexa affirms feminism based on a belief in gender equality (Alexa programming, accessed May 30, 2019). For an account of digital assistant responses to sexual harassment, see West, Kraut, and Chew 2019; and Leah Fessler, "Amazon's Alexa Is Now a Feminist, and She's Sorry if That Upsets You," *Quartz at Work*, January 17, 2018, https://qz.com/work/1180607/amazons-alexa-is-now-a-feminist-and-shes-sorry-if-that-upsets-you/. Either inadvertently or deliberately, these digital assistants are raced white. For example, Microsoft's Cortana was named for an (at times) Caucasian-appearing AI from the video game Halo. Imagined in more minute detail by personality designers for Google Assistant, Cortana is a kayak-loving young woman from Colorado and a Northwestern history graduate who works as a personal assistant for a satirical TV host (West, Kraut, and Chew 2019, 95).

69. Modeled on newscasters, actresses, and fashion models, Ishiguro's gynoids have been displayed in numerous public venues, such as cafés, malls, and theaters. See Alex Mar, "Love in the Time of Robots: Are We Ready for Intimacy with Androids?" *Wired*, October 17, 2017, https://www.wired.com/2017/10/hiroshi-ishiguro-when-robots-act-just-like-humans/.

70. Here I am invoking the title of Judith Butler's 1993 book that followed up her theory of gender performativity, one that elicited the persistent query, "What about the body, Judy?" In response, Butler chafed against the overly familiar, infantilizing hailing as well as the implication that she had naïvely discounted the discursivity of materiality.

71. Quoted in Jessi Hempel, "Fei-Fei Li's Quest to Make AI Better for Humanity," *Wired*, November 13, 2018, https://www.wired.com/story/fei-fei-li-artificial-intelligence-humanity/. Li's phrasing echoes the computer science axiom that articulates the relationship between data input and processing, "Garbage in, garbage out." The article in *Wired* opens with Li in black standing behind a white table against a white background, an effect that makes it look as if the lower half of her body has disappeared. It is as if the visual designer could not resist the provocative gender/race inscription I discuss here, in effect rendering the Asian female AI researcher as herself posthuman.

72. Artists portraying these mechanical peoples, notes Gonzalez (2000, 60), "were reflecting a situation in which the relation—and the distinction—between the machine and human became a question of gender and class. Those who had access to certain machines were privileged, those who were expected to behave like certain machines were subjugated. The same is true today."

73. Lisa Stein, "Nobel Scientist Quits in Wake of Scandal," *Scientific American*, October 25, 2007, 5.

74. When employee Joanna Ong brought up the topic of US imperialism, Searle was alleged to have responded, "American imperialism? Oh boy, that sounds great, honey! Let's go to bed and do that right now!" After allegedly groping her, he

informed Ong that he was "going to love her for a long time," echoing the familiar racist-sexist meme. Ong's complaint was filed with the Superior Court of the State of California, County of Alameda, on March 21, 2017, Case RG 17854053, 1–14, quotations on 6 and 5.

75. Tass's comment, April 2, 2016, on "The Human Robot," Top Documentary Films, https://topdocumentaryfilms.com/human-robot/.

76. Hayao Miyazaki's *The Wind Rises* (2013) was criticized for its watered-down pacifism. Korean American critic Inkoo Kang found its depiction of Japanese militarism during World War II overly mild mannered. Similarly, *In This Corner of the World*, a 2016 anime directed by Sunao Katauchi, is set in 1944 but focuses on the horrors of war perpetuated by the United States against Japanese civilians in Hiroshima. Inkoo Kang, "The Trouble with *The Wind Rises*," *Village Voice*, December 11, 2013, https://www.villagevoice.com/2013/12/11/the-trouble-with-the-wind-rises/.

CHAPTER 4. On the Asian Fetish and the Fantasy of Equality

Deemed the "deranged sorority girl," Martinson went viral in 2013 with an expletive-laced email demeaning her fellow sorority sisters at University of Maryland. The leaked email spawned several famous parodies; her sorority, Delta Gamma, accepted her resignation.

1. Contrary to popular belief, academic and informal dating app studies do not confirm yellow fever, (heterosexual) preferences for Asians among other racial groups, for either cismen or ciswomen. OkCupid, summarizing data gleaned from its own dating app, over the course of five years charted attraction based on race preferences. Since 2001, white men revealed a slight preference for Asian women over white women; "Race and Attraction, 2009–2014: What's Changed in Five Years?" OkCupid, September 10, 2014, https://theblog.okcupid.com/race-and-attraction-2009-2014-107dcbb4f060. One academic study of "assortive mating" in the context of racial *exclusion* in internet dating compared data taken from two hundred profiles in four diverse urban areas. Robnett and Feliciano (2011, 816) found, perhaps predictably, that "Asians, Latinos and blacks are more open to dating whites than whites are to dating them." Asian women were *excluded* by a significant percentage of white men ("Of those who state a racial preference, 97 percent of white men exclude black women, 48 percent exclude Latinas, and 53 percent exclude Asian women"). Moreover, Asian men were the group most excluded by white women: "Similarly, 92 percent of white women exclude black men, 77 percent exclude Latinos, and 93 percent exclude Asian men" (816). The data were based on the expression of negative bias rather than preference because, citing the tendency of daters who want to appear open minded, researchers believed it produced greater accuracy: "Thus, we focus our analysis primarily on questions of exclusion—which groups do whites, blacks, Asians and Latinos not want to date?" (816).

2. See the website for the podcast *Yo, Is This Racist?*, hosted by Andrew Ti, accessed May 2, 2021, http://yoisthisracist.com/page/5.

3. Quoted in Rachel L. Swarns, "A Tie That Binds," *New York Times*, April 1, 2012.
4. Ironically, Yau's insistence on the universalism of desire is belied somewhat by the content of his own offering in the collection. His short story "The Chinese Boy Who Lived Up to His Name" explores the source of a white man's masochistic Asian fetish: an adolescent's memory of sexual humiliation at the hands of a Victor, the titular Chinese boy.
5. A key early text is Gayle Rubin's 1984 "Thinking Sex: Notes for a Radical Theory of the Politics of Sexuality." See also A. A. Cheng 2000; Marriott 2000; Nguyen 2014; Nash 2014; E.-B. Lim 2014; and Bow 2014. Nash (2014, 60) calls for an enlarged notion of spectatorship that does not replicate exploitation; she cautions against presuming white male spectatorship that forecloses "the possibility of black *pleasurable* spectatorship, generally, and black pleasurable pornographic spectatorship specifically."
6. Celine Parreñas Shimizu, "Organic Asian American Sexualities," blog essay in response to *They're All So Beautiful*, PBS web series, April 2013, on the They're All So Beautiful website (now defunct).
7. See "Laurie Simmons," *art21*, accessed May 2, 2021, http://www.art21.org/artists/laurie-simmons.
8. The shift between persons and things was particularly evident in Operation Babylift, in which Vietnamese children were at once subjects of international human rights intervention and objects, alternative spoils of war whose legal guardianship was rendered moot. The irony in the latter was not lost on a South Vietnamese army lieutenant commenting on the 1975 crash of the C-5A that attempted to airlift the first planeload of children out of then Saigon, killing 150 children and fifty adults. He was quoted as saying, "It is nice to see you Americans taking home souvenirs of our country as you leave—china elephants and orphans. Too bad some of them broke today, but we have plenty more"; quoted in Gloria Emerson, "Operation Babylift: Collecting Souvenirs," *New Republic* 172, no. 17 (1975): 10.
9. In highlighting the hyperemotionalism that underlies ethnic stereotypes, Ngai (2005, 95) coins the term "racial animatedness." Accounting for this regarding the stereotype of Asian stoicism, she writes, "Animation remains central to the production of the racially marked subject, *even* when his or her difference is signaled by the pathos of emotional suppression rather than emotional excess."
10. See Mari Katayama's CV on her web portfolio, Atelier Shell Kashime, accessed May 2, 2021, http://shell-kashime.com/.
11. I am invoking Rosemarie Garland Thomson's (1997) term *normate* to describe a subject position unmarked by difference, whether by disability, gender, or other nonnormative categories.
12. Katayama's sculptures recall Kusama's *Accumulation No. 1* (1962), a chair made out of what appear to be fabric penises. See Laura Hoptman, "Yayoi Kusama's Return to MoMA," *Inside/Out* (blog), New York Museum of Modern Art, October 9, 2012, https://www.moma.org/explore/inside_out/2012/10/09/yayoi-kusamas-return-to-moma/.

13. Holly Black, "Mari Katayama Celebrates the Body Beautiful," *Elephant*, January 26, 2019, https://elephant.art/mari-katayama-celebrates-the-body-beautiful/.
14. See "Fashion, Art, and Disability—An Interview with Mari Katayama," Accessible Japan, accessed May 3, 2021, https://www.accessible-japan.com/fashion-art-and-disability-an-interview-with-mari-katayama/.
15. Mami Iida, "Mari Katayama 'Broken Heart': Talk Session with Simon Baker," *Real Tokyo*, January 3, 2019, https://www.realtokyo.co.jp/en/interview/mari-katayamabroken-heart-white-rainbow-2019-1-24-3-2/.
16. That is, *racist love* is about the nation, a collective means of self-definition, as Said noted about Orientalism. Freud (1915, 129) notes, "It follows that the preliminary stage of the scopophilic instinct, in which the subject's own body is the object of the scopophilia, must be classed under narcissism, and that we must describe it as a narcissistic formation."
17. Mary Gaitskill, "Beg for Your Life: In the Well with Laurel Nakadate," San Francisco Film Society, SF360, February 24, 2011, http://sf360.org.mytempweb.com/?pageid=13399.
18. Kelly Klaasmeyer, "Bum Fights," Glasstire: Texas Visual Art, April 24, 2010, https://glasstire.com/2010/04/24/bum-fights/.
19. Gaitskill, "Beg for Your Life." Jun Okada (2017, 42) makes a compelling case for Nakadate's work as engaging scopophilia toward the awareness of a loss of connection: "By bottling up possible scenarios of social connection for us to watch, Nakadate's videos create a sense of nostalgia for friendship, which may at first be obscured through her superficial evocation of Lolita, Olympia, and Suzie Wong." This argument, however, is predicated on enlarging notions of connection to encompass sado-masochist friendship.
20. "They So Horny?" with Samantha Bee aired on *The Daily Show with Jon Stewart*, Comedy Central, November 19, 2003.
21. For Mura (2003, 297), whiteness is the fetish that compensates for his lack of phallic power as an Asian man in the United States: "If I were with a white woman, I thought, then I would be as 'good' as a white guy." He analyzes his addiction to pornography as stemming from white ideation, going further to note how it was fueled by racial taboos and the excitation surrounding the threat of violence.
22. Hamamoto's (1998) academic article does not comment on the politics of *women*'s presence in porn or the possibility that they might take pleasure in their fetishization. His discussion of the pornographic film *The World's Biggest Gang Bang* is notably silent on this point; while the object of the "world's biggest gang bang" is an Asian American woman, he chooses to focus not on the symbolic meanings that accrue here, but on the figure of the lone and marginalized Asian male participant and the actress's seeming indifference to her role. While the article celebrates (white) feminists claiming their own desire through pornography, Hamamoto has little to say about how this project might cross racial lines. The pornographic film referred to in the comedy news report is *Yellowcaust: A Patriot Act* (2003), the shooting of

which was later depicted in the documentary *Masters of the Pillow*, dir. James Hou (Orem, UT: Avenue Films, 2003).

23. *Asian Pride Porn!*, written, directed, produced, and edited by Greg Pak (New York: Pak Man Productions, 1999), DVD, 3 min.

24. Pak's project of genealogical recovery reveals a Korean American history of war, migration, and immigrant class struggle. Tellingly, Grandpa avoided conscription in the Japanese Imperial Army by attending a seminary in Dubuque, Iowa, and ended up being separated from his wife for ten years. While betrothed, he "allowed" his fiancée to complete her training as a nurse in Korea ("He just let me go to school"), something that came in handy when she opened a practice in midwifery to support herself and their children in Korea in his absence.

25. Ironically, the testimony of Pak's grandparents' marital devotion is voiced early in the film by the nurse who has attended his dying grandfather in the hospital and who attests to his wife's devotion to her husband, not vice versa. Her testimony is the one that the film subsequently unravels as slightly incomprehensible: How could the unlovable be loved or return love? But the nurse's interview is significant not only for the structure it provides the narrative, but as a framing device. The film's conclusion disclosing a potential nurse fetish gives greater meaning to one of the few nonfamily members appearing in the film.

26. *Pirated!*, dir. Nguyen Tan Hoang (Vancouver, BC: Video Out, 2000), DVD, 11 min. In recounting his goal with the short film, Nguyen writes, "Working against the nostalgic notion of *finding oneself by going back*, the restaging of my formation of identity takes place not back there in the motherland, but on the high seas, during the journey in-between a space-time not to be found or recaptured, but only re-imagined and re-looped." Quoted in DVD liner notes of *Nguyen Tan Hoang, Videos: 1999–2002* (Philadelphia, PA: Kimchi Chige Productions, 2006).

27. After the furor over sexually explicit content in the traveling Mapplethorpe retrospective show *Robert Mapplethorpe: The Perfect Moment* in 1989, Senator Jesse Helms sponsored a bill seeking to withhold National Endowment of the Arts funding for art deemed "obscene or indecent." While the Senate passed the bill, the House refused to ratify it.

28. Mapplethorpe's attitude was both celebratory and demeaning: he acknowledged that the dynamic "has to be racist. I'm white and they are black." Emphasizing Mapplethorpe's race fetish, domination as a source of the erotic, his biographer depicts him as clarifying that he was not saying the N-word "all the time. Only during sex" (cited in Morrisroe 1995, 288).

29. Mercer (1994, 203) recognized the convergence between the disapproving, "angry tone" of his first reading of Mapplethorpe and the strident voices of sexual conservatism: "I do not want a black gay critique to be appropriated to the purposes of the New Right's antidemocratic cultural offensive." That is, he was aware that the affective valence of his stance risked creating an imagined coalition with Jesse Helms and antiporn feminists.

30. Elisha Lim, *Drag McQueen*, cake, icing, lacquer, leather, wood, shown in *Gender: An Exhibit of Epic Proportions*, the Raging Spoon, Toronto, July 2011.
31. As Barbara Johnson (2010, 143) notes, shopping "is a desire structure, not just an economic structure."
32. Kat Stoeffel, "Nine Sexy College Classes Happening This Fall," *New York Magazine*, September 6, 2013, https://www.thecut.com/2013/09/nine-sexy-college-classes-happening-this-fall.html. Thanks go to Ramzi Fawaz for pointing out this reference.
33. Lohman was accused of placing his semen and urine in the drinks of fellow students on campus, all of them Asian and female. Having victimized as many as one hundred women over time, he literalized the dynamics of the fetish by requiring his targets to ingest a part of himself, symbolically binding the objects of his fantasy to him. A classic example of Asian fetishism, what is striking about Lohman's case is that it was not cast as a hate crime; Princeton University's public service alert to the campus community did not identify Asian women as his targets. See Lisa Wong Macabasco, "Princeton Incident Shows Extreme Case of Asian Fetish," *Asian Week*, April 29, 2005, http://www.asianweek.com/2005/04/29/princeton-incident-shows-extreme-case-of-asian-fetish/.
34. Humor is a means of circumventing repression. Yet the very attempts to uphold taboos surrounding race, the gestures of repression, can themselves be sources of eroticism. This is parallel to, as Žižek (1997a, 34) notes, "the case of the obsessional neurotic who gets libidinal satisfaction out of the very compulsive rituals destined to keep at bay the traumatic *jouissance*."
35. Thanks go to Elena Tajima Creef for noting the significance of the phrase "black is" to the work of *Sally's Beauty Spot*.
36. The film's ending perhaps anticipates this effect. *Sally's Beauty Spot* closes with footage that attempts to restore Sally to multifaceted personhood: she playfully crosses her eyes and mugs for the camera, displaying her sense of humor. Lee's strategy—Sally is more than her body—seems to echo that of numerous Asian American women who respond to reductive racial-sexual objectification by asserting a "real" subject against erotic fantasy. I would argue that this shot does not function as an outtake; it counters the film's sensuous aesthetic by momentarily gesturing outside it. Helen Lee, dir., *Sally's Beauty Spot* (New York: Women Make Movies, 1990), VHS, 12 min.
37. Lee argues for the film's depiction of "a sexualization that comes from a self-possessed self-actualization rather than objectification" (quoted in Hoolboom 2008, 24).
38. Yet Butler (1997) argued somewhat differently in regard to racial hate speech, confirming, for example, that burning crosses represents discriminatory action.
39. Soon after an article on her book of photographs, *Immediate Family*, appeared in a mainstream publication in 1992, Mann became enmeshed in controversy. Known thereafter as "the woman who made pictures of her naked kids," Mann was accused of everything from bad parenting to obscenity, pedophilia, and incest. In defending

art as representation distinct from its material referent or effects, Mann recounts the story of her daughter Jessie, aged nine or ten, who dismissed a dress for a gallery opening of *Immediate Family* because its sleeve gap showed her chest. A friend countered, "Why on earth would you care if someone can see your chest through the armholes when you are going to be in a room with a bunch of pictures that show that same bare chest?" Jessie replied, "Yes, but that is not my chest. Those are photographs"; Sally Mann, "Sally Mann's Exposure," *New York Times Magazine*, April 16, 2015, 52.

CONCLUSION

1. For a longer discussion of the doctor's parallel between the HIV/AIDS epidemic's migration and his own, see Bow 2010.
2. I am indebted to Elena Tajima Creef for bringing to my attention visuals surrounding COVID-derived anti-Asian bias as well as flagging artistic responses to hate speech.
3. This image of a Chinese American industrial worker during World War II appears in "Chinese Americans Labeling Themselves to Avoid Being Confused with the Hated Japanese Americans, 1941," Rare Historical Photos, May 17, 2017, https://rarehistoricalphotos.com/chinese-americans-during-ww2-1941/. See also Elena Tajima Creef's (2004, 147) discussion of the Chinese American reporter who pinned a sign to his lapel reading, "Chinese Reporter—NOT Japanese—please."
4. *Coughing while Asian*, dir. Michael Tow and Teja Arboleda, Tow-Arboleda Films, video, 0:59, February 2, 2020, https://www.youtube.com/watch?v=HZq7fwUywR4.
5. Also killed in the mass shooting were Delaina Ashley Yaun González and Paul Andre Michels. A ninth person, Elcias Hernandez-Ortiz, was shot, but survived. Media outlets were slow to report the names of the victims; moreover, the rallying cry of the Black Lives Matter movement, "Say Their Names," was not invoked here, perhaps because Americans found it hard to recall or pronounce Asian American names.
6. Captain Jay Baker of the Sheriff's office in Cherokee County issued early statements that discounted a connection between racialization and sexual targeting and appeared to minimize the perpetrator's actions as a result of his having a "bad day." In May 2021, President Biden signed a bill to address hate crimes against Asian Americans.
7. This example of hate speech during the COVID-19 pandemic appeared on a T-shirt designed by California-based Jess Sluder depicting bat wings on the take-out box associated with diasporic Chinese restaurants. Negative response to the shirt went viral after an art director for Lululemon, a popular manufacturer of women's yoga apparel, shared the link on his personal Instagram account. See Iliana Magra and Christine Hauser, "Lululemon Fires Employee Over 'Bat Fried Rice' Shirt," *New York Times*, April 22, 2020.
8. Examples of corporate insensitivity in global fashion are too numerous to detail here, but I would note that controversy seemed to surround Italian-based luxury houses in particular. In an unusual move, in 2018, Prada was ordered by the New York City Commission on Human Rights to undergo corporate sensitivity training for its US employees and executives in Milan after the promotion of Pradamalia figurines that

resembled monkeys in blackface. The same year, Dolce and Gabbana stoked outrage in China with its tone-deaf advertising depicting a Chinese model attempting to eat pizza and other Italian foods with chopsticks. Cofounder Stefano Gabbana incited further controversy by allegedly posting anti-Chinese comments on his personal Instagram account, which he subsequently claimed had been hacked. My point here is not to parse intentionality or degree of offense in any one case, but to raise questions about how the very reduction of objects, signs, and narratives producing racial meaning trigger varied affective responses across global contexts. As in chapter 2, such "risky" objects resist glocalization. In these corporate faux pas, racial shorthands were taken to be indicators of scorn, aggression, or provincialism antithetical to international business success.

References

Aboud, Frances E. 1987. "The Development of Ethnic Self-Identification and Attitudes." In *Children's Ethnic Socialization: Pluralism and Development*, edited by Jean S. Phinney and Mary Jane Rotherman, 32–55. Newbury Park, CA: Sage.
Aboud, Frances E. 1988. *Children and Prejudice*. New York: Basil Blackwell.
Aboud, Frances E. 1993. "The Developmental Psychology of Racial Prejudice." *Transcultural Psychiatric Review* 30 (3): 229–42.
Ahmed, Sara. 2004. "Affective Economies." *Social Text* 22 (2): 117–37.
Ainsworth, Mary D. Salter. 1969. "Object Relations, Dependency, and Attachment: A Theoretical Review of the Infant-Mother Relationship." *Child Development* 40, no. 4: 969–1025.
Allison, Anne. 2004. "Cuteness as Japan's Millennial Product." In *Pikachu's Global Adventure: The Rise and Fall of Pokémon*, edited by Joseph Tobin, 34–49. Durham, NC: Duke University Press.
Andrijasevic, Rutvica, and Nicola Mai. 2016. "Editorial: Trafficking (in) Representations: Understanding the Recurring Appeal of Victimhood and Slavery in Neoliberal Times." *Anti-Trafficking Review* 7:1–10.
Aristotle. 2011. *The Philosophy of Aristotle*. Edited by Renford Bambrough. Translated by J. L. Creed and A. E. Wardman. New York: Signet.
Asimov, Isaac. 1950. *I, Robot*. Garden City, NY: Doubleday.
Baciagalupi, Paolo. (2009) 2015. *The Windup Girl*. New York: Night Shade Books.
Barthes, Roland. (1970) 1982. *Empire of the Signs*. Translated by Richard Howard. New York: Hill and Wang.
Baudrillard, Jean. (1981) 1994. *Simulacra and Simulation*. Ann Arbor: University of Michigan Press.
Benjamin, Walter. (1929) 1999. "Children's Literature." In *Selected Writings*, vol. 2, *1927–1934*, edited by Michael W. Jennings, Howard Eiland, and Gary Smith, 250–56. Translated by Rodney Livingstone. Cambridge, MA: Belknap Press of Harvard University Press.

Berlant, Lauren. 2011. *Cruel Optimism*. Durham, NC: Duke University Press.
Berlant, Lauren, and Sianne Ngai. 2017. "Comedy Has Issues." *Critical Inquiry* 43, no. 2: 233–49.
Bernstein, Robin. 2011. *Racial Innocence: Performing American Childhood from Slavery to Civil Rights*. New York: New York University Press.
Bettelheim, Bruno. (1975) 2010. *The Uses of Enchantment: The Meaning and Importance of Fairy Tales*. New York: Vintage.
Bhabha, Homi K. 1983. "The Other Question: Homi K. Bhabha Reconsiders the Stereotype and Colonial Discourse." *Screen* 24 (6): 18–36.
Bhabha, Homi K. 1994. *The Location of Culture*. London: Routledge.
Bishop, Ryan, and Lillian Robinson. 1998. *Night Market: Sexual Cultures and the Thai Economic Miracle*. New York: Routledge.
Bogost, Ian. 2012. *Alien Phenomenology, or What It's Like to Be a Thing*. Minneapolis: University of Minnesota Press.
Bonilla-Silva, Eduardo. 2003. *Racism without Racists: Color-Blind Racism and the Persistence of Racial Inequality in the United States*. New York: Rowman and Littlefield.
Bow, Leslie. 2001. *Betrayal and Other Acts of Subversion: Feminism, Sexual Politics, Asian American Women's Literature*. Princeton, NJ: Princeton University Press.
Bow, Leslie. 2010. *Partly Colored: Asian Americans and Racial Anomaly in the Segregated South*. New York: New York University Press.
Bow, Leslie. 2014. "Fetish." In *A Companion to Asian American Literature and Culture*, edited by Rachel Lee, 122–31. New York: Routledge.
Bow, Leslie. 2016. "Asian Americans, Racial Latency, Southern Traces." In *Oxford Handbook to the Literature of the U.S. South*, edited by Barbara Ladd and Fred Hobson, 493–513. Oxford: Oxford University Press.
Bow, Leslie. 2017. "On Racial Stereotyping." In *Routledge Handbook of Asian American Studies*, edited by Cindy I-Fen Cheng, 21–38. New York: Routledge.
Brian, Kristi. 2012. *Reframing Transnational Adoption: Adopted Koreans, White Parents, and the Politics of Kinship*. Philadelphia: Temple University Press.
Brown, Bill. 1998. "How to Do Things with Things (A Toy Story)." *Critical Inquiry*, no. 24, 935–64.
Brown, Bill. 2001. "Thing Theory." *Critical Inquiry* 28 (1): 1–22.
Brown, Bill. 2006. "Reification, Reanimation, and the American Uncanny." *Critical Inquiry* 32 (2): 175–207.
Brown, Wendy. 1995. *States of Injury: Power and Freedom in Late Modernity*. Princeton, NJ: Princeton University Press.
Bukatman, Scott. 2012. *The Poetics of Slumberland: Animated Spirits and the Animating Spirit*. Berkeley: University of California Press.
Burrill, Derek A. 2009. "Jet-Set Kids: Mutation/Seduction/Hybridization." In *The Japanification of Children's Popular Culture from Godzilla to Miyasaki*, edited by Mark I. West, 107–118. Lanham, MD: Scarecrow Press.
Bush, Christopher. 2007. "The Ethnicity of Things in America's Lacquered Age." *Representations* 99 (1): 74–98.

Butler, Judith. (1990) 2004. "The Force of Fantasy: Feminism, Mapplethorpe, and Discursive Excess." In *The Judith Butler Reader*, edited by Sara Salih, 183–203. Oxford: Blackwell.

Butler, Judith. 1993. *Bodies that Matter: On the Discursive Limits of "Sex."* New York: Routledge.

Butler, Judith. 1997. *Excitable Speech: A Politics of the Performative*. New York: Routledge.

Chang, Juliana. 2012. *Inhuman Citizenship: Traumatic Enjoyment and Asian American Literature*. Minneapolis: University of Minnesota Press.

Chang, Yoonmee. 2010. *Writing the Ghetto: Class, Authorship, and the Asian American Ethnic Enclave*. New Brunswick, NJ: Rutgers University Press.

Cheng, Anne Anlin. 2000. "Wounded Beauty: An Exploratory Essay on Race, Feminism, and the Aesthetic Question." *Tulsa Studies in Women's Literature* 19 (2): 191–217.

Cheng, Anne Anlin. 2001. *The Melancholy of Race: Psychoanalysis, Assimilation, and Hidden Grief*. Oxford: Oxford University Press.

Cheng, Anne Anlin. 2019. *Ornamentalism*. New York: Oxford University Press.

Cheng, Cindy I-Fen. 2013. *Citizens from Asian America: Democracy and Race during the Cold War*. New York: New York University Press.

Chiang, Mark. 2009. *The Cultural Capital of Asian American Studies: Autonomy and Representation in the University*. New York: New York University Press.

Chin, Frank, and Jeffery Paul Chan. 1972. "Racist Love." In *Seeing through Shuck*, edited by Richard Kostelanetz, 65–79. New York: Ballantine.

Choi, Franny. 2019. *Soft Science*. Farmington, ME: Alice James.

Choy, Catherine Cenzia. 2013. *Global Families: A History of Asian International Adoption in America*. New York: New York University Press.

Chuh, Kandice. 2003. *Imagine Otherwise: On Asian American Critique*. Durham, NC: Duke University Press.

Chun, Wendy Hui Kyong. 2003. "Orienting Orientalism, or How to Map Cyberspace." In *Asian America.Net: Ethnicity, Nationalism, and Cyberspace*, edited by Rachel Lee and Sau-ling Cynthia Wong, 3–36. New York: Routledge.

Clark, Kenneth B., and Mamie Clark. 1947. "Racial Identification and Preference in Negro Children." In *Readings in Social Psychology*, edited by Theodore M. Newcombe and Eugene L. Hartley, 169–78. New York: Henry Holt.

Creef, Elena Tajima. 2004. *Imaging Japanese America: The Visual Construction of Citizenship, Nation, and the Body*. New York: New York University Press.

Crenshaw, Kimberlè. 1991. "Mapping the Margins: Intersectionality, Identity Politics, and Violence against Women of Color." *Stanford Law Review* 43 (6): 1241–99.

Dale, Joshua Paul, Joyce Goggin, Julia Leyda, Anthony P. McIntyre, and Diane Negra, eds. 2017. *The Aesthetics and Affects of Cuteness*. New York: Routledge.

de Manuel, Dolores, and Rocio G. Davis. 2006. "Editors' Introduction: Critical Perspectives on Asian American Children's Literature." *Lion and the Unicorn* 2 (30): v–xv.

Diawara, Manthia, and Silvia Kolbowski. 1998. "Homeboy Cosmopolitan." *October*, no. 83: 51–70.

Dong, Lan. 2011. "Reimagining the Monkey King in Comics: Gene Luen Yang's *American Born Chinese*." In *Oxford Handbook of Children's Literature*, edited by Julia L. Mickenberg and Lynne Vallone, 231–54. Oxford: Oxford University Press.

Dong, Lorraine, Philip P. Choy, and Marlon K. Hom, eds. 1995. *The Coming Man: 19th Century American Perceptions of the Chinese*. Seattle: University of Washington Press.

Döring, Nicola, and Sandra Poeschl. 2019. "Love and Sex with Robots: A Content Analysis of Media Representations." *International Journal of Social Robotics* 11:665–77. https://doi.org/10.1007/s12369-019-00517-y.

Dorow, Sara K. 2006. *Transnational Adoption: A Cultural Economy of Race, Gender, and Kinship*. New York: New York University Press.

Dubey, Madhu. 2010. "Speculative Fictions of Slavery." *American Literature* 82 (4): 779–805.

Durbin, Steve C. 1987. "Symbolic Slavery: Black Representations in Popular Culture." *Social Problems* 34 (2): 122–40.

Eng, David L. 2001. *Racial Castration: Managing Masculinity in Asian America*. Durham, NC: Duke University Press.

Fanon, Frantz. (1952) 1991. *Black Skin, White Masks*. Translated by Charles Lam Markmann. New York: Grove Weidenfeld.

Feng, Peter X. 2000. "Recuperating Suzie Wong: A Fan's Nancy Kwan-dary." In *Countervisions: Asian American Film Criticism*, edited by Darrell Hamamoto and Sandra Liu, 40–56. Philadelphia: Temple University Press.

Fiedler, Leslie. (1948) 1955. *An End to Innocence: Essays on Culture and Politics*. Boston: Beacon.

Fiske, Susan T., Amy J. Cuddy, Peter Glick, and Jun Xu. 2002. "A Model of (Often Mixed) Stereotype Content: Competence and Warmth Respectively Follow from Perceived Status and Competition." *Journal of Personality and Social Psychology* 82 (6): 878–902.

Fleetwood, Nicole R. 2015. *On Racial Icons: Blackness and the Public Imagination*. New Brunswick, NJ: Rutgers University Press.

Frank, Caroline. 2011. *Objectifying China, Imagining America: Chinese Commodities in Early America*. Chicago: Chicago University Press.

Freng, Scott, and Cynthia Willis-Esqueda. 2011. "A Question of Honor: Chief Wahoo and American Indian Stereotype Activation among a University-Based Sample." *Journal of Social Psychology* 151 (5): 577–91.

Frenkel-Brunswik, Else. 1948. "A Study of Prejudice in Children." *Human Relations; Studies Towards the Integration of the Social Sciences* (1): 295-306.

Freud, Sigmund. (1905) 1989. *Jokes and Their Relation to the Unconscious*. Translated by James Strachey. New York: Norton.

Freud, Sigmund. (1908) 1959. "Creative Writers and Day-Dreaming." In *The Standard Edition of the Complete Psychological Works of Sigmund Freud*, vol. 9, 419–28. Translated by James Strachey. London: Hogarth Press and the Institute of Psycho-analysis.

Freud, Sigmund. (1914) 1957. "On Narcissism: An Introduction." In *A General Selection from the Works of Sigmund Freud*, edited by John Rickman, 105–23. New York: Doubleday.

Freud, Sigmund. (1915) 1961. "Instincts and Their Vicissitudes." In *The Standard Edition of the Complete Psychological Works*, vol. 14, *1914–16*, translated by James Strachey, 113–38. London: Hogarth Press and the Institute of Psycho-analysis.

Freud, Sigmund. (1919) 1964. "The Uncanny." In *The Standard Edition of the Complete Psychological Works of Sigmund Freud*, vol. 17, *1917–19*, translated by James Strachey, 217–56. London: Hogarth Press and the Institute of Psycho-analysis.

Freud, Sigmund. (1921) 1959. *Group Psychology and the Analysis of the Ego*. Edited by John D. Sutherland. Translated by James Strachey. International Psycho-analytical Library, no. 6. London: Hogarth Press and the Institute of Psycho-analysis.

Freud, Sigmund. (1927) 1961. "Fetishism." In *The Standard Edition of the Complete Psychological Works of Sigmund Freud*, vol. 21, *1927–31*. Translated by James Strachey, 152–57. London: Hogarth Press and the Institute of Psycho-analysis.

Fromm, Erich. 1955. *The Sane Society*. New York: Rinehart.

Fryberg, Stephanie A., Hazel Rose Markus, Daphna Oyserman, and Joseph M. Stone. 2008. "Of Warrior Chiefs and Indian Princesses: The Psychological Consequences of American Indian Mascots." *Basic and Applied Social Psychology* 30 (3): 208–18.

Fulbeck, Kip. 2006. *Part Asian/100% Hapa*. San Francisco: Chronicle.

Fung, Richard. (1991) 2012. "Looking for My Penis: The Eroticized Asian in Gay Video Porn." In *The Gender and Media Reader*, edited by M. C. Kearney, 380–87. New York: Routledge.

Fynn-Paul, Jeff, and Damian Alan Pargas, eds. 2018. *Slaving Zones: Cultural Identities, Ideologies, and Institutions in the Evolution of Global Slavery*. Leiden: Brill.

Gilmore, Ruth Wilson. 2006. *Golden Gulag: Prisons, Surplus, Crisis, and Opposition in Globalizing California*. Berkeley: University of California Press.

Glocker, Melanie L., Daniel D. Langleben, Kosha Ruparel, James W. Loughead, Ruben C. Gur, and Norbert Sachser. 2009. "Baby Schema in Infant Faces Induces Cuteness Perception and Motivation for Caretaking in Adults." *Ethology* 115 (3): 257–63.

Goings, Kenneth W. 1994. *Mammy and Uncle Mose: Black Collectibles and American Stereotyping*. Bloomington: Indiana University Press.

Gonzalez, Jennifer. 2000. "Envisioning Cyborg Bodies: Notes from Current Research." In *The Gendered Cyborg: A Reader*, edited by Gill Kirkup, Linda James, Kath Woodard, and Fiona Hovenden, 58–73. London: Routledge.

Greene, Carol. 1993. *Margaret Wise Brown: Author of "Goodnight Moon."* Chicago: Children's Press.

Grusin, Richard. 2015. Introduction to *The Nonhuman Turn*, edited by Richard Grusin, vii–xxix. Minneapolis: University of Minnesota Press.

Hamamoto, Darrell. 1998. "The Joy Fuck Club: Prolegomenon to an Asian American Porno Practice." *New Political Science* 20 (3): 323–45.

Haraway, Donna J. 1991. "A Cyborg Manifesto: Science, Technology, and Socialist-Feminism in the Late Twentieth Century." In *Simians, Cyborgs, and Women: The Reinvention of Nature*, 149–82. New York: Routledge.

Haraway, Donna J. 2003. *The Companion Species Manifesto: Dogs, People, and Significant Otherness*. Chicago: Prickly Paradigm.

Harman, Graham. 2002. *Tool-Being: Heidegger and the Metaphysics of Objects*. Chicago: Open Court.

Harper, Phillip Brian. 2015. *Abstractionist Aesthetics: Artistic Form and Social Critique in African American Culture*. New York: New York University Press.

Harris, Daniel. 2000. *Cute, Quaint, Hungry and Romantic*. New York: Basic Books.

Harris, Michael D. 2003. *Colored Pictures: Race and Visual Representation*. Chapel Hill: University of North Carolina Press.

Harvey, David. 2006. *Spaces of Global Capitalism: Towards a Theory of Uneven Geographical Development*. London: Verso.

Hasegawa, Yuko. 2002. "Post-identity Kawaii: Commerce, Gender and Contemporary Japanese Art." In *Consuming Bodies: Sex and Contemporary Japanese Art*, edited by Fran Lloyd, 127–41. London: Reaktion.

Havens, John C. 2016. *Heartificial Intelligence: Embracing Our Humanity to Maximize Machines*. New York: Penguin.

Hayes, James. 2003. "Women and Female Children in Hong Kong and South China to 1949: Documents of Sale and Transfer." In *Hong Kong: A Reader in Social History*, edited by David Faure, 426–62. Oxford: Oxford University Press.

Hayles, N. Katherine. 1999. *How We Became Posthuman: Virtual Bodies in Cybernetics, Literature, and Informatics*. Chicago: University of Chicago Press.

Hicks, George. 1994. *The Comfort Women: Japan's Brutal Regime of Enforced Prostitution in the Second World War*. New York: Norton.

Hirschfeld, Lawrence A. 1988. "On Acquiring Social Categories: Cognitive Development and Anthropological Wisdom." *Man* 23 (4): 611–38.

Hirschfeld, Lawrence A. 1995. "Do Children Have a Theory of Race?" *Cognition* 54:209–52.

Hirschfelder, Arlene B. 1982. *American Indian Stereotypes in the World of Children: A Reader and Bibliography*. Metuchen, NJ: Scarecrow.

Ho, Jennifer Ann. 2015. *Racial Ambiguity in Asian American Culture*. New Brunswick, NJ: Rutgers University Press.

Hodges, Ernest, Michel Boivin, Frank Vitaro, William M. Bukowski. 1999. "The Power of Friendship: Protection Against an Escalating Cycle of Peer Victimization." *Developmental Psychology* 35 (1): 94–101.

Holland, Sharon Patricia. 2012. *The Erotic Life of Racism*. Durham, NC: Duke University Press.

Holmes, Robyn M. 1995. *How Young Children Perceive Race*. Thousand Oaks, CA: Sage.

Holtom, Daniel Clarence. 1922. "The Political Philosophy of Modern Shinto: A Study of the State Religion of Japan." PhD diss., University of Chicago.

hooks, bell. 1992. *Black Looks: Race and Representation*. Boston: South End.

Hoolboom, Mike. 2008. "Helen Lee: Priceless." In *Practical Dreamers: Conversations with Movie Artists*, 21–34. Toronto: Coach House Books.

Horning, Kathleen T. 2014. "Children's Books: Still an All-White World?" *School Library Journal*, May 1, 2014. https://www.slj.com/?detailStory=childrens-books-still-an-all-white-world.

Hwang, David Henry. 1989. *M. Butterfly*. New York: Plume.

Ignacio, Abe, Enrique de la Cruz, Jorge Emmanuel, and Helen Torbio, eds. 2004. *The Forbidden Book: The Philippine-American War in Political Cartoons*. Ann Arbor, MI: T'Boli.

Iwabuchi, Koichi. 2004. "How 'Japanese' Is Pokémon?" In *Pikachu's Global Adventure: The Rise and Fall of Pokémon*, edited by Joseph Tobin, 53–79. Durham, NC: Duke University Press.

Jacobson, Dawn. 1993. *Chinoiserie*. London: Phaidon.

Jacobson, Heather. 2008. *Culture Keeping: White Mothers, International Adoption, and the Negotiation of Family Difference*. Nashville, TN: Vanderbilt University Press.

Jentsch, Ernst. (1906) 1995. "On the Psychology of the Uncanny." *Angelaki* 2 (1): 12–33.

Jeon, Joseph Jonghyun. 2012. *Racial Things, Racial Forms: Objecthood in Avant-Garde Asian American Poetry*. Iowa City: University of Iowa Press.

Johnson, Barbara. 2010. *Persons and Things*. Cambridge, MA: Harvard University Press.

Kakoudaki, Despina. 2014. *Anatomy of a Robot: Literature, Cinema, and the Cultural Work of Artificial People*. New Brunswick, NJ: Rutgers University Press.

Kang, Laura Hyun Yi. 2002. *Compositional Subjects: Enfiguring Asian/American Women*. Durham, NC: Duke University Press.

Kang, Laura Hyun Yi. 2020. *Traffic in Asian Women*. Durham, NC: Duke University Press.

Kang, Minsoo. 2011. *Sublime Dreams of Living Machines: The Automaton in the European Imagination*. Cambridge, MA: Harvard University Press.

Karolides, Nicholas J. 2006. *Banned Books: Literature Suppressed on Political Grounds*. Rev. ed. New York: Facts on File.

Katz, Phyllis A. 1976. "The Acquisition of Racial Attitudes in Children." In *Towards the Elimination of Racism*, edited by Phyllis Katz, 125–54. New York: Pergamon.

Kelts, Roland. 2006. *Japanamerica: How Japanese Pop Culture Invaded the U.S.* New York: Palgrave Macmillan.

Kennon, Raquel. 2017. "Neo-slave Narratives." *Oxford Bibliographies*, July 26, 2017. DOI: 10.1093/OBO/9780190221911-0017.

Khanna, Ranjana. 2003. *Dark Continents: Psychoanalysis and Colonialism*. Durham, NC: Duke University Press.

Kim, Eunjung. 2015. "Unbecoming Human: An Ethics of Objects." *GLQ* 21 (2–3): 295–320.

King, William Davies. 2008. *Collections of Nothing*. Chicago: University of Chicago Press.

Kinsella, Sharon. 1995. "Cuties in Japan." In *Women, Media, and Consumption in Japan*, edited by Lise Skov and Brian Moeran, 220–54. Honolulu: University of Hawaii Press.

Klein, Melanie. (1955) 1975. "The Psycho-analytic Play Technique: Its History and Significance." In *The Writings of Melanie Klein*, vol. 3, *Envy and Gratitude and Other Works, 1946–1963*, 122–40. New York: Free Press.

Koh, Frances M. (1981) 1988. *Oriental Children in American Homes*. Minneapolis: East-West Press, 2nd ed.

Kondo, Marie. 2014. *The Life-Changing Magic of Tidying Up: The Japanese Art of Decluttering and Organizing*. Translated by Cathy Hirano. Berkeley: Ten Speed.

Kondo, Marie. 2016. *Spark Joy: An Illustrated Master Class on the Art of Organizing and Tidying Up*. Translated by Cathy Hirano. Berkeley: Ten Speed.

Kuly, Lisa. 2003. "Locating Transcendence in Japanese Minzoku Geinô: Yamabushi and Miko Kagura." *Ethnologies* 25 (1): 191–208.

Lai, Larissa. 2009. *Automaton Biographies*. Vancouver, BC: Arsenal Pulp.

Laplanche, Jean, and J. B. Pontalis. 1986. "Fantasy and the Origins of Sexuality." In *Formations of Fantasy*, edited by Victor Burgin, James Donald, and Cora Kaplan, 5–34. London: Methuen.

Laplanche, Jean and J. B. Pontalis. 1988. *The Language of Psychoanalysis*. Translated by Donald Nicholson-Smith. London: Karnac.

Larrick, Nancy. 1965. "The All-White World of Children's Books." *Saturday Review* 48 (37): 63–65, 84–85.

Larsen, Nicole E., Kang Lee, and Patricia A. Ganea. 2018. "Do Storybooks with Anthropomorphized Animal Characters Promote Prosocial Behaviors in Young Children?" *Developmental Science* 21 (3): 1–9.

Latour, Bruno. 2005. *Reassembling the Social: An Introduction to Actor-Network-Theory*. Oxford: Oxford University Press.

Lee, Christopher. 2013. *The Semblance of Identity: Aesthetic Mediation in Asian American Literature*. Stanford, CA: Stanford University Press.

Lee, Helen. 2002. "A Peculiar Sensation: A Personal Genealogy of Korean American Women's Cinema." In *Screening Asian Americans*, edited by Peter X. Feng, 133–55. New Brunswick, NJ: Rutgers University Press.

Lee, Jennifer, and Min Zhou. 2015. *The Asian American Achievement Paradox*. New York: Sage.

Lee, Josephine. 2010. *The Japan of Pure Invention: Gilbert and Sullivan's "The Mikado."* Minneapolis: University of Minnesota Press.

Lee, Josephine. 2021. "Decorative Orientalism." In *Asian American Literature in Transition, 1850–1930: Volume 1*, edited by Josephine Lee and Julia H. Lee, 187–204. Cambridge: Cambridge University Press.

Lee, Rachel C. 2014a. *The Exquisite Corpse of Asian America: Biopolitics, Biosociality, and Posthuman Ecologies*. New York: New York University Press.

Lee, Rachel C. 2014b. Introduction to *A Companion to Asian American Literature and Culture*, edited by Rachel C. Lee, 1-18. New York: Routledge.

Le Guin, Ursula K. 1989. *The Language of the Night: Essays on Fantasy and Science Fiction*. Edited by Susan Wood with Ursula K. Le Guin. London: Women's Press.

Leyda, Julia. 2017. "Cute Twenty-First-Century Post-fembots." In *The Aesthetics and Affects of Cuteness*, edited by Joshua Paul Dale, Joyce Goggin, Julia Leyda, Anthony P. McIntyre, and Diane Negra, 151–74. Durham, NC: Duke University Press.

Lim, Elisha. 2010. *100 Butches*. Minneapolis, MN: Consortium.

Lim, Eng-Beng. 2014. *Brown Boys and Rice Queens: Spellbinding Performance in the Asias*. New York: New York University Press.

Lopez, Lori Kido. 2016. *Asian American Media Activism*. New York: New York University Press.

Lorenz, Konrad. 1971. *Studies in Animal and Human Behavior*. Cambridge, MA: Harvard University Press.

Lott, Eric. 1993. *Love and Theft: Blackface Minstrelsy and the American Working Class*. New York: Oxford University Press.

Low, Jason T. 2013. "Why Hasn't the Number of Multicultural Books Increased in Eighteen Years?" *Open Book Blog*, June 17, 2013. https://blog.leeandlow.com/2013/06/17/why-hasnt-the-number-of-multicultural-books-increased-in-eighteen-years/.

MacCann, Donnarae. 2001. "Editor's Introduction—Racism and Antiracism: Forty Years of Theories and Debates." *Lion and the Unicorn* 25 (3): 337–52.

Maira, Sunaina. 2007. "Indo-Chic: Late Capitalist Orientalism and Imperial Culture." In *Alien Encounters: Popular Culture in Asian America*, edited by Mimi Thi Nguyen and Thuy Linh Nguyen Tu, 220–41. Durham, NC: Duke University Press.

Marcus, Leonard S. 1992. *Margaret Wise Brown: Awakened by the Moon*. Boston: Beacon.

Marcus, Leonard S. 2019. *The ABC of It: Why Children's Books Matter*. Minneapolis: University of Minnesota Press.

Marriott, David. 2000. *On Black Men*. New York: Columbia University Press.

Martinez, Julia. 2018. "A Female Slaving Zone? Historical Constructions of the Traffic in Asian Women." In *Slaving Zones: Cultural Identities, Ideologies, and Institutions in the Evolution of Global Slavery*, edited by Jeff Fynn-Paul and Damian Alan Pargas, 309–35. Leiden: Brill.

Marx, Karl. (1859) 1990. *Capital*. Vol. 1. Translated by Ben Fowkes. New York: Penguin.

Massumi, Brian. 1995. "The Autonomy of Affect." *Cultural Critique*, no. 31, 83–109.

Matsuda, Mari J. 1993. "Public Response to Racist Speech: Considering the Victim's Story." In *Words that Wound: Critical Race Theory, Assaultive Speech, and the First Amendment*, edited by Mari J. Matsuda, Charles R. Lawrence III, Richard Delgado, and Kimberlè Williams Crenshaw, 17–51. Boulder, CO: Westview.

McClintock, Anne. 1995. *Imperial Leather: Race, Gender, and Sexuality in the Colonial Conquest*. New York: Routledge.

McClintock, Anne. 2009. "Paranoid Empire: Specters from Guantánamo and Abu Ghraib." *Small Axe* 13 (1): 50–74.

McGray, Douglas M. 2002. "Japan's Gross National Cool." *Foreign Policy*, May/June, 44–54.

Mercer, Kobena. 1994. "Reading Racial Fetishism: The Photographs of Robert Mapplethorpe." In *Welcome to the Jungle: New Positions in Black Cultural Studies*, 171–220. New York: Routledge.

Merish, Lori. 1996. "Cuteness and Commodity Aesthetics: Tom Thumb and Shirley Temple." In *Freakery: Cultural Spectacles of the Extraordinary Body*, edited by Rosemarie Garland Thomson, 185–203. New York: New York University Press.

Mickenberg, Julia L., and Lynne Vallone. 2011. Introduction to the *Oxford Handbook of Children's Literature*, edited by Julia L. Mickenburg and Lynne Vallone, 3-21. Oxford: Oxford University Press.

Midori. 2005. *Wild Side Sex: The Book of Kink: Educational, Sensual, and Entertaining Essays*. Los Angeles: Daedalus.

Mitchell, David, and Sharon Snyder. 2000. *Narrative Prosthesis: Disability and the Dependencies of Discourse*. Ann Arbor: University of Michigan Press.

Mitchell, Lucy Sprague. 1921. *Here and Now Story Book*. New York: Dutton.

Moon, Katherine. 1997. *Sex among Allies: Military Prostitution in U.S.-Korea Relations*. New York: Columbia University Press.

Moore, Annie Carroll. 1920. *Roads to Childhood: Views and Reviews of Children's Books*. New York: Doran.

Moorti, Sujata. 2003. "Out of India: Fashion Culture and the Marketing of Ethnic Style." In *Companion to Media Studies*, edited by Angharad N. Valdivia, 293–308. London: Blackwell.

Mori, Masahiro. 1970. "The Uncanny Valley." Translated by Karl F. MacDorman and Takashi Minato. *Energy* 7 (4): 33–35.

Morley, David, and Kevin Robins. 1995. *Spaces of Identity: Global Media, Electronic Landscapes and Cultural Boundaries*. London: Routledge.

Morrison, Toni. 1992. *Playing in the Dark: Whiteness and the Literary Imagination*. Cambridge, MA: Harvard University Press.

Morrisroe, Patricia. 1995. *Mapplethorpe: A Biography*. New York: Random House.

Morrow, Robert W. 2006. *"Sesame Street" and the Reform of Children's Television*. Baltimore, MD: Johns Hopkins University Press.

Moy, James. 1993. *Marginal Sights: Staging the Chinese in America*. Iowa City: University of Iowa Press.

Mura, David. 2003. "Fargo and the Asian American Male." In *Screaming Monkeys: Critiques of Asian American Images*, edited by M. Evelina Galang, 295–97. Minneapolis, MN: Coffee House Press.

Murakami, Takashi. 2005. *Little Boy: The Arts of Japan's Exploding Subculture*. New Haven, CT: Yale University Press.

Nakamaki, Hirochika. 2003. *Japanese Religions at Home and Abroad: Anthropological Perspectives*. London: Routledge.

Nash, Jennifer C. 2014. *The Black Body in Ecstasy: Reading Race, Reading Pornography*. Durham, NC: Duke University Press.

Neapolitan, Richard E., and Xia Jiang. 2013. *Contemporary Artificial Intelligence*. Boca Raton, FL: CRC Press.

Nel, Philip. 2017. *Was the Cat in the Hat Black? The Hidden Racism of Children's Literature and the Need for Diverse Books*. Oxford: Oxford University Press.

Ngai, Sianne. 2005. *Ugly Feelings*. Cambridge, MA: Harvard University Press.

Ngai, Sianne. 2012. *Our Aesthetic Categories: Zany, Cute, Interesting.* Cambridge, MA: Harvard University Press.

Ngai, Sianne. 2015. "Visceral Abstractions." *GLQ* 21 (1): 34–63.

Nguyen Tan Hoang. 2014. *A View from the Bottom: Asian American Masculinity and Sexual Representation.* Durham, NC: Duke University Press.

Nye, Joseph S., Jr. 1990. "Soft Power." *Foreign Policy* 80:153–71.

Nyong'o, Tavia. 2002. "Racial Kitsch and Black Performance." *Yale Journal of Criticism* 15 (2): 371–91.

Ohnuki-Tierney, Emiko. 1987. *The Monkey as Mirror: Symbolic Transformations in Japanese History and Ritual.* Princeton, NJ: Princeton University Press.

Oishi, Eve. 2006. "Visual Perversions: Race, Sex, and Cinematic Pleasure." *Signs* 31 (3): 641–74.

Okada, Jun. 2017. "Collectivity and Loneliness in Laurel Nakadate's Postracial Identity Aesthetics." In *Routledge Companion to Asian American Media*, edited by Lori Kido Lopez and Vincent N. Pham, 37–48. New York: Routledge.

Ong, Anthony D., Anthony L. Burrow, Thomas E. Fuller-Rowell, Nicole M. Ja, and Derald Wing Sue. 2013. "Racial Microaggressions and Daily Well-Being among Asian Americans." *Journal of Counseling Psychology* 60 (2): 188–99.

Ong, Paul, and John M. Liu. 1994. "U.S. Immigration Policies and Asian Migration." In *The New Asian Immigration in Los Angeles and Global Restructuring*, edited by Paul Ong, Edna Bonacich, and Lucie Cheng, 45–73. Philadelphia: Temple University Press.

Ono, Kent A., and Vincent N. Pham. 2009. *Asian Americans and the Media.* Cambridge: Polity.

Pak, Greg. 2005. *Robot Stories and More Screenplays.* San Francisco: Immedium.

Pak, Susie J., and Elda E. Tsou. 2011. "Introduction." *Journal of Asian American Studies* 14 (2): 171–91.

Park, Jane Chi Hyun. 2010. *Yellow Future: Oriental Style in Hollywood Cinema.* Minneapolis: University of Minnesota Press.

Parreñas, Celine Shimizu. 2007. *The Hypersexuality of Race: Performing Asian/American Women on Screen and Scene.* Durham, NC: Duke University Press.

Pham, Vincent N., and Kent A. Ono. 2008. "'Artful Bigotry and Kitsch': A Study of Stereotype, Mimicry, and Satire in Asian American T-Shirt Rhetoric." In *Asian American Rhetorics*, edited by Luming Mao and Morris Young, 175–96. Salt Lake City: University of Utah Press.

Picken, Stuart D. B. 1994. *Essentials of Shinto: An Analytic Guide to Principal Teachings.* Westport, CT: Greenwood.

Pilgrim, David. 2005. "The Garbage Man: Why I Collect Racist Objects." Jim Crow Museum of Racist Memorabilia, Ferris State University, February. https://www.ferris.edu/HTMLS/news/jimcrow/collect.htm.

Pollock, John L. 1995. *Cognitive Carpentry: A Blueprint for How to Build a Person.* Cambridge, MA: MIT Press.

Prater, Tzarina T., and Catherine Fung. 2015. "'How Does It Not Know What It Is?': The Techno-Orientalized Body in Ridley Scott's *Blade Runner* and Larissa Lai's

Automaton Biographies." In *Techno-Orientalism: Imagining Asia in Speculative Fiction, History, and Media*, edited by David S. Roh, Betsy Huang, and Greta A. Nui, 193–208. New Brunswick, NJ: Rutgers University Press.

Quintana, Stephen M. 1998. "Children's Developmental Understanding of Ethnicity and Race." *Applied and Preventive Psychology* 7:27–45.

Ramsey, Patricia G. 1987. "Young Children's Thinking about Ethnic Differences." In *Children's Ethnic Socialization: Pluralism and Development*, edited by Jean S. Phinney and Mary Jane Rotherman, 56–72. Newbury Park, CA: Sage.

Reynolds, Kimberley. 2011. *Children's Literature: A Very Short Introduction*. Oxford: Oxford University Press.

Rhee, Margaret. 2017. *Love, Robot*. Brooklyn: Operating System.

Rivinus, T. M., and Lisa Audet. 1992. "The Psychological Genius of Margaret Wise Brown." *Children's Literature in Education* 23 (1): 1–14.

Robnett, Belinda, and Cynthia Feliciano. 2011. "Patterns of Racial-Ethnic Exclusion by Internet Daters." *Social Forces* 89 (3): 807–28.

Roh, David S., Betsy Huang, and Greta A. Niu, eds. 2015. *Techno-Orientalism: Imagining Asia in Speculative Fiction, History, and Media*. New Brunswick, NJ: Rutgers University Press.

Rubin, Gayle. [1984] 1993. "Thinking Sex: Notes for a Radical Theory of the Politics of Sexuality." In *The Lesbian and Gay Studies Reader*, edited by Henry Abelove, Michele Aina Barale, and David M. Halperin, 3–44. New York: Routledge.

Ryle, Gilbert. 1949. *The Concept of Mind*. Chicago: University of Chicago Press.

Said, Edward W. 1978. *Orientalism*. New York: Random House.

San Juan, E., Jr. 1991. "Beyond Identity Politics: The Predicament of the Asian American Writer in Late Capitalism." *American Literary History* 3 (3): 542–65.

Sandner, David. 2004. Introduction to *Fantastic Literature: A Critical Reader*, edited by David Sandner, 1–13. Westport, CT: Praeger.

Saper, Bernard. 1993. "Since When Is Jewish Humor Not Anti-Semitic?" In *Semites and Stereotypes: Characteristics of Jewish Humor*, edited by Avner Ziv and Anat Zajdman, 71–86. Westport, CT: Greenwood, 1993.

Sartre, Jean-Paul. (1946) 1970. *Anti-Semite and Jew*. New York: Schocken.

Searle, John R. 1990. "Is the Brain's Mind a Computer Program?" *Scientific American* 262 (1): 26–31.

Sedgwick, Eve Kosofsky. 1997. "Paranoid Reading and Reparative Reading; or, You're So Paranoid, You Probably Think This Introduction Is about You." In *Novel Gazing: Queer Readings in Fiction*, edited by Eve Kosofsky Sedgwick, 1–37. Durham, NC: Duke University Press.

Shah, Nayan. 2001. *Contagious Divides: Epidemics and Race in San Francisco's Chinatown*. Berkeley: University of California Press.

Shibusawa, Naoko. 2006. *America's Geisha Ally: Reimagining the Japanese Enemy*. Cambridge, MA: Harvard University Press.

Shiokawa, Kanako. 1999. "Cute but Deadly: Women and Violence in Japanese Comics." In *Themes and Issues in Asian Cartooning: Cute, Cheap, Mad, and Sexy*, edited by

John A. Lent, 93–125. Bowling Green, OH: Bowling Green State University Popular Press.
Smith, Katharine Capshaw. 2002. "Introduction: The Landscape of Ethnic American Children's Literature." *MELUS* 27 (2): 3–8.
Smith, Katharine Capshaw. 2014. *Civil Rights Childhood: Picturing Liberation in African American Photobooks*. Minneapolis: University of Minnesota Press.
Sohn, Stephen Hong. 2008. "Introduction—Alien/Asian: Imagining the Racialized Future." *MELUS* 33 (4): 5–22.
Sollors, Werner. 1997. *Neither Black Nor White Yet Both: Thematic Explorations of Interracial Literature*. Cambridge, MA: Harvard University Press.
Spiegelman, Art. 2011. *MetaMaus*. New York: Pantheon.
Spivak, Gayatri Chakravorty. 1988. "Can the Subaltern Speak?" In *Marxism and the Interpretation of Culture*, edited by Cary Nelson and Lawrence Grossberg, 271–313. Urbana: University of Illinois Press.
Spivak, Gayatri Chakravorty. 1990. "Poststructuralism, Marginality, Post-coloniality and Value." In *Literary Theory Today*, edited by Peter Collier and Helga Geyer-Ryan, 219–44. Ithaca, NY: Cornell University Press.
Sprengelmeyer, R., D. I. Perrett, E. C. Fagan, R. E. Cornwell, J. S. Lobmaier, A. Sprengelmeyer, H. B. M. Aasheim, I. M. Black, L. M. Cameron, S. Crow, N. Milne, E. C. Rhodes, and A. W. Young. 2009. "The Cutest Little Baby Face: A Hormonal Link to Sensitivity to Cuteness in Infant Faces." *Psychological Science* 20 (2): 149–54.
Springer, Claudia. 1996. *Electronic Eros: Bodies and Desire in the Postindustrial Age*. London: Athlone.
Stoller, Robert J. 1985. *Observing the Erotic Imagination*. New Haven, CT: Yale University Press.
Subramaniam, Banu. 2014. *Ghost Stories for Darwin: The Science of Variation and the Politics of Diversity*. Urbana: University of Illinois Press.
Sue, Derald Wing, Jennifer Bucceri, Annie I. Lin, Kevin L. Nadal, and Gina C. Torino. 2007. "Racial Microaggressions and the Asian American Experience." *Cultural Diversity and Ethnic Minority Psychology* 13 (1): 72–81.
Sue, Stanley, and Harry H. L. Kitano. 1973. "Stereotypes as a Measure of Success." *Journal of Social Issues* 29 (2): 83–98.
Tanaka, Yuki. 1999. Introduction to *Comfort Woman: A Filipina's Story of Prostitution and Slavery under the Japanese Military*, by Maria Rosa Henson, ix–xxi. Lanham, MD: Rowman and Littlefield.
Taylor, Charles. 1994. *Multiculturalism: Examining the Politics of Recognition*. Edited by Amy Gutmann. Princeton, NJ: Princeton University Press.
Taylor, Charles. 2000. "Modernity and Difference." In *Without Guarantees: In Honour of Stuart Hall*, edited by Paul Gilroy, Lawrence Grossberg, and Angela McRobbie, 364–74. London: Verso.
Tchen, John, and Dylan Yeats. 2014. *Yellow Peril! An Archive of Anti-Asian Fear*. London: Verso.

Thomson, Rosemarie Garland. 1997. *Extraordinary Bodies: Figuring Physical Disability in American Culture and Literature*. New York: Columbia University Press.

Toffoletti, Kim. 2007. *Cyborgs and Barbie Dolls: Feminism, Popular Culture, and the Posthuman Body*. London: I. B. Tauris.

Tolkien, J. R. R. (1939) 1983. *The Monsters and the Critics and Other Essays*. Edited by Christopher Tolkien. London: Allen and Unwin.

Tomine, Adrian. 2006. *Shortcomings*. Montreal: Drawn and Quarterly.

Turing, A. M. 1950. "Computing Machinery and Intelligence." *Mind: A Quarterly Review of Psychology and Philosophy* 59 (236): 433–60.

Turkle, Sherry. 1991. "Romantic Reactions: Paradoxical Responses to the Computer Presence." In *Boundaries of Humanity: Humans, Animals, Machines*, edited by James J. Sheehan and Morton Sosna, 224–52. Berkeley: University of California Press.

Turkle, Sherry. 2011. *Alone Together: Why We Expect More from Technology and Less from Each Other*. New York: Basic Books.

Verghese, Abraham. 1994. *My Own Country: A Doctor's Story of a Town and Its People in the Age of AIDS*. New York: Vintage.

Warriner, Amy Beth, Victor Kuperman, and Marc Brysbaert. 2013. "Norms of Valence, Arousal, and Dominance for 13,915 English Lemmas." *Behaviour Research and Therapy* 45:1191–1207.

Weise, Jillian. 2018. "Common Cyborg." *Granta*, no. 144. https://granta.com/common-cyborg/.

West, Mark, Rebecca Kraut, and Han Ei Chew. 2019. *I'd Blush if I Could: Closing Gender Divides in Digital Skills through Education*. Paris: UNESCO, EQUALS.

Wilkins, Kim. 2019. *Young Adult Fantasy Fiction: Conventions, Originality, Reproducibility*. Cambridge: Cambridge University Press.

Williams, Linda. 1995. "Corporealized Observers: Visual Pornographies and the 'Carnal Density of Vision.'" In *Fugitive Images: From Photography to Video*, edited by Patrice Petro, 3–41. Bloomington: Indiana University Press.

Williams, Linda. 2004. "Skin Flicks on the Racial Border: Porn, Exploitation, and Interracial Lust." In *Porn Studies*, edited by Linda Williams, 271–308. Durham, NC: Duke University Press.

Williams, Patricia J. 1998. *Seeing a Color-Blind Future: The Paradox of Race*. New York: Farrar, Straus and Giroux.

Williams, Raymond. 1977. *Marxism and Literature*. Oxford: Oxford University Press.

Winnicott, D. W. (1971) 1991. *Playing and Reality*. London: Routledge.

Wolfe, Gary. (1982) 2004. "The Encounter with Fantasy." In *Fantastic Literature: A Critical Reader*, edited by David Sandner, 222–273. Westport, CT: Praeger.

Wool-Rim Sjöblom, Lisa. 2019. *Palimpsest: Documents from a Korean Adoption*. Montreal: Drawn and Quarterly.

Wosk, Julie. 1992. *Breaking Frame: Technology and the Visual Arts in the Nineteenth Century*. New Brunswick, NJ: Rutgers University Press.

Wosk, Julie. 2015. *My Fair Ladies: Female Robots, Androids, and Other Artificial Eves*. New Brunswick, NJ: Rutgers University Press.

Wu Chʻêng-ên. 1994. *Monkey: Folk Novel of China [Journey to the West]*. Translated by Arthur Waley. New York: Grove.

Yang, Chi-Ming. 2011. *Performing China: Virtue, Commerce, and Orientalism in Eighteenth-Century England, 1660–1760*. Baltimore, MD: Johns Hopkins University Press.

Yang, Gene Luen. 2006. *American Born Chinese*. New York: First Second.

Yano, Christine R. 2013. *Pink Globalization: Hello Kitty's Trek across the Pacific*. Durham, NC: Duke University Press.

Yau, John. 1998. Introduction to *Fetish: An Anthology of Fetish Fiction*, edited by John Yau, i–xi. New York: Four Walls Eight Windows.

Yuh, Ji-Yeon. 2002. *Beyond the Shadow of Camptown*. New York: New York University Press.

Yung, Judy. 1995. *Unbound Feet: A Social History of Chinese Women in San Francisco*. Berkeley: University of California Press.

Zaonotto, Debora, Massimiliano Patacchiola, Angelo Cangelosi, and Jeremy Goslin. 2020. "Generalisation of Anthropomorphic Stereotype." *International Journal of Social Robotics* 12:163–72. https://doi.org/10.1007/s12369-019-00549-4.

Žižek, Slavoj. 1989. *The Sublime Object of Ideology*. London: Verso.

Žižek, Slavoj. 1997a. "Multiculturalism, or, The Cultural Logic of Multinational Capitalism." *New Left Review*, no. 225: 28–51.

Žižek, Slavoj. 1997b. *The Plague of Fantasies*. London: Verso.

Index

ABC of It: Why Children's Books Matter, The (Marcus), 212n10
Abercrombie and Fitch, 103, 105, 220n38
Aboud, Frances, 39, 50–51, 212n14, 214n34
abstraction. *See* racial abstraction
activism, ironic spectatorship and, 100–104
adolescent graphic novels, racial themes in, 30, 33, 53–59
adoption: of Asian children, 42–47, 214n32; in children's literature, 37–42; racial anxieties over, 40–41. *See also* transnational adoption; transracial adoption; transspecies adoption
Adventures of Huckleberry Finn (Twain), 66–67
aesthetics: of kawaii style, 82–90; racist kitsch and, 70–75
affect theory: kawaii aesthetic and, 86–87; racism and, 8–9; racist kitsch and, 72–75; techno-Orientalism and, 111–16
African Americans: Black celebrityhood and, 195–96; collections of racist kitsch by, 79–82, 98–100, 218n8; Mapplethorpe's photographs of, 180; neoslave literature of, 113–14, 120–26, 129; racial profiling of, 105; racist caricatures of, 71–72, 74–82, 87, 90–91; under-representation in children's literature of, 59–62
Afro-American Novel and Its Tradition, The (Bell), 114

agency: relationality and, 17; robotics and, 132–36, 227n51
Ahmed, Sara, 72, 192–93, 199–200
AIBO mechanical dog robot, 109, 221n3; object-oriented ontology and, 112
Aiko female-embodied robot, 137–41, 147–49, 228n59, 228n63
Air Doll (film), 159
Alessi Mandarin juicer, 104; as Asian caricature, 70–71, 73–75, 87–88
Alexa digital assistant, 113, 141, 147, 229n68
All Bears Need Love (Valentine and Taylor), 41–42
Allison, Dorothy, 114
Altered Carbon (film), 113
American Asiaphilia, 10–15
American Born Chinese (Yang), 19, 33, 53–59, 64
American Indians. *See* Native Americans
American Psychological Association, 75
Andrijasevic, Rutvica, 125–26
And Tango Makes Three (Richardson, Parnell, and Cole), 63–64, 216n56
Angry Asian Man website, 101–4
animals: as anthropomorphic objects, 25–37; as educational tools, 37–42, 52–53; foundling stories of, 37; humanals and racial abstraction and, 48–53; racial representation in children's literature and, 59–62; in transracial adoption stories, 42–47; in Yang's *American Born Chinese*, 53–59

animated objects, fantasy of, 2–5
anthropomorphic objects: animals as, 25–34; caricature and, 73–82; children's perceptions of, 52–53; cuteness aesthetic and, 85–90, 92–95; humanals and micropolitics of abstraction, 48–53; political consequences of, 104–7; racism and, 2–5; social robotics and, 109–16; transspecies/transracial adoption, 37–42; in Yang's *American Born Chinese*, 53–59
anti-Asian bias: in children's literature, 214n33; COVID-19 pandemic and, 191–200, 235n2; cuteness aesthetic and, 74–75, 85; repulsion and attraction and, 5–7; techno-Orientalism and, 111–16
anti-Semitism, 101, 194, 196–98, 220n36
Aristotle, 76; on pleasure, 4
Arthur (television show), 45–46, 48
artificial intelligence (AI): Asian women as symbols of, 136–41, 146–50; consenting AI, 132–36; diversity and bias in, 147–50; in film, 113; limitations of, 223n25; origins of, 117–18; social robotics and, 110–16; speculative narratives of, 118–26; Turing test of, 116–17
Art of Discarding, The (*Suteru Gigyutsu*) (Tatsumi), 15, 210n26
Asian Americans: accumulation of caricature by, 79–82; art by, 12–14; attraction as anti-Asian bias, 5–7; bullying in school of, 215n36; caricatures of, 66, 69–75; in children's literature, 31, 42–47, 214n33; COVID-19 pandemic and racialization of, 23–24; creative practices of, 173–74; fetishism and, 7–9, 153–58; hate speech and crimes against, 192–200; imaginaries surrounding, 18–21; intergenerational misunderstandings among, 176–79; literature of, 210n32; nonhuman proxies for, 2–5, 10–15, 48–53; personhood status of, 134–35; perverse scholarship on, 21–23; population statistics for, 206n11; racialization of, 5–7, 206n6; racist hate/love for, 142–45, 191–200; sexuality, representation of, 174–75; spectatorship of racist cute by, 95–100; speculative literature of, 129–32; split spectatorship for, 21–22; stereotyping of, 5–7, 207nn12–13; transitional objects associated with, 30–31; visual representations of, 2–5

Asian American Studies Association, 21
Asianized female-embodied robots, 136–41
Asian Pacific Institute on Gender-Based Violence, 121
Asian Pride Porn! (film), 175–76
Asiatic Barred Zone, 10
Asimov, Isaac, 110–11, 145, 221n7
Astro Boy, 112
attachment, fetishism and proclamations of, 8–9
attraction, in anti-Asian bias, 5–7
Audet, Lisa, 52
Aunt Jemima caricature, 77, 100
Auschwitz, Pokémon at, 196–98
automata, 113
Automaton Biographies (Lai), 129–31
autonomous personhood, liberal fantasy of, 128

Babbage, Charles, 147
Bacigalupi, Paolo, 113, 126
Backyardigans, The (television series), 48, 53
Baker, Jay, 235n6
Baker, Simon, 168
Bambi (film), 84
Bamboozled (film), 100
Bank Street College of Education, 31, 34
Bank Street Writer's Laboratory, 31, 33–36
Barbie dolls, feminist attachment to, 100–104
Barry, Barbara, 85
Barthes, Roland, 10, 87
Battlestar Galactica (film), 113
Baudrillard, Jean, 66–67, 117, 222n13
Bayarsaikhan, Gana, 123
Bear Called Paddington, A (Bond), 37
bears, anthropomorphization in children's literature of, 27–34, 41–42, 44
Bechdel, Alison, 125, 226n44
Bechdel test, 125, 226n44
Bee, Samantha, 175
Beg for Your Life (Nakadate video), 171
Bell, Bernard, 114, 223n19
Benjamin, Walter, 26, 35, 170
Berenstain Bears series, 27–28, 30
Bernstein, Robin, 32, 67
Best Word Book Ever (Scarry), 27
Bettelheim, Bruno, 19, 29, 33, 36–37, 41–42
Bhabha, Homi, 5–7, 79, 95, 186, 192, 196

biodiversity, race as, 48–49
biological parents, adoptees' search for, 46–47
Bitch magazine, 124
Black Book, The (Mapplethorpe), 180–82, 187
Black Lives Matter, 76–77, 105, 195, 216n49
Black memorabilia, racist caricatures as, 79–82
Black Skin, White Masks (Fanon), 55
Black women's spectatorship, 97
Blade Runner (film), 130
Blair, Preston, 84
Blood Heir (Zhao), 120, 129, 227n47
Bonilla-Silva, Eduardo, 53
boycotts, racist stereotypes and, 103–7
Brian, Kristi, 43, 44, 46
Bringing Asha Home (Krishnaswami), 44
Broken Heart exhibition (Katayama), 168
Brown, Bill: "American uncanny" concept of, 114, 142–43, 161–62; cuteness aesthetic and, 85, 91; on neoslavery narrative, 114, 126–27; on racial scopophilia, 17; on racist kitsch, 74, 100; on things, 139–40, 154
Brown, Marc, 45–46, 48, 64
Brown, Margaret Wise, 18–19, 31–33, 35–36, 47, 52, 62–64, 212n10, 216n51, 216n53
Brown, Michael, 105
Brown, Wendy, 98, 156, 174, 187
Brown v. Board of Education, 75
Buck, Pearl S., 42
Buddhism, in Yang's *American Born Chinese*, 54–59
Bullfrog and Gertrude Go Camping (Dauer), 37
Busy, Busy World (Scarry), 27, 44
Butler, Judith, 18, 117, 148, 187, 189–90, 229n70

Cabaret (film), 167
Cambodia, transracial adoption from, 47
camptowns, sex trafficking in, 121–22, 149
capitalism, human life under, 115–16, 127–28
caricature: censuring of, 107; as microaggression, 75–82; racist kitsch and, 70–75
caricatures of Asian Americans, 66, 69–75
Cars 2 (film), 2–5, 206n5
CB2 retailer, 85–86
Chabon, Michael, 66–67
Chan, Gemma, 133, 136–37, 151
Chan, Jeffery Paul, 5–6, 9
Chanel Take Away bag, 93–95

Chang, Juliana, 24, 182
Chang, Patty, 170
Chang, Yoonmee, 23–24
Charlie Hebdo terrorist attack, 69–70
Chato book series (Soto and Guevara), 28, 31–32
Cheng, Anne Anlin, 10, 14, 85, 173
Cheng, Cindy I-Fen, 207n12
Chen Xiaoping, 137
Chief Wahoo mascot, 76
Ch'ieng-lung (Emperor), 87–88
Child Magazine, 44
children and childhood: kawaii aesthetic and, 91–92; racial perceptions of, 18–19, 38–39, 193–94, 212n14
children's literature: anti-Asian bias in, 214n33; conflicting theories about, 34–36; humanals and micropolitics of abstraction in, 48–53; politicization of abstraction in, 62–67; power of, 25–34; racism in, 26–36, 53, 216n49; transracial adoption in, 42–47; transspecies characters in, 37–42
Child Welfare League of America, 40–41
Chin, Frank, 5–6, 9
China: luxury market in, 93–94; transnational adoption from, 42–47
Chinese Americans, 93–94, 120; anti-Asian bias against, 191–200, 235n2
"The Chinese Boy Who Lived Up to His Name" (Yau), 231n4
Chinese culture, American embrace of, 10–15
Chinese Exclusion Act, 10
Chinese imports, American consumption of, 10, 208n18
Chinese room experiment (Searle), 116–18
Chinese Siamese Cat, The (Tan), 213n27
Chin Family kitchen goods, 87–88, 104
chinoiserie, 10, 85, 208n18
Cho, John, 196
Cho, Margaret, 104
Choi, Franny, 131–32, 146
Choo-Choo Cherry caricature, 76
Choy, Catherine Cenzia, 42
Chua, Amy, 207n12
Chuh, Kandice, 23
Clark, Kenneth, 32, 65, 75, 99, 211n5
Clark, Mamie, 32, 65, 75, 99, 211n5

class politics: in dystopian Pacific Rim fiction, 127–32; kitsch and, 77–79, 94–95
Cleveland Indians, 76
Clinton, Hillary Rodham, 132
Cloud Atlas (film), 118–19, 127
Cloud Atlas (Mitchell), 113, 127
Coca-colonization, 92–94, 197–98
Colbert, Stephen, 104
Cole, Henry, 63–64
Colgate-Palmolive, 77
collecting: African American collections of racist kitsch, 79–82, 218n8; by Asian Americans, 97–100
colonialism: cuteness aesthetic and, 84–85, 98–99, 218n17; fantasy and, 21–22, 163; melancholia of, 170
color-blind rhetoric, in children's literature, 49–53, 213n24
Comedy Central, 174–76
comfort women, 121–22, 149, 225n41
comic-grotesque, racial kitsch and, 76–82
Common Core Standards, 61
community expectations, racial imagery and, 99–100
Companion Species Manifesto, The (Haraway), 198–99
Concept of Mind, The (Ryle), 222n13
consent, artificial intelligence and, 133–36
consumer narcissism, thingness and, 85
contiguity, stereotyping and, 207n13
"Cool Japan" campaign, 73
Cooperative Children's Book Center (CCBC), 61
corporate culture: racist caricatures and, 76–77, 103, 196–200, 235n8; Sanrio marketing and, 83–84
Coty Corporation, 81–82, 84, 92–93
Coughing while Asian (video), 192
Council on Interracial Books for Children, 31, 35
COVID-19 pandemic, anti-Asian activism and, 23–24, 191–200, 235n7
Crate and Barrel, 85–86
Crazy Rich Asians (film), 21
Cream of Wheat, Rastus caricature on, 77
Creef, Elena Tajima, 21, 235n2
Crenshaw, Kimberlè, 220n41

critical race theory: caricature and, 76, 79–80; psychoanalysis and, 15; structure of feeling and, 106–7
Cruise, Tom, 157
cultural appropriation, as racist love, 7–9
cultural difference: caricatures and, 76–77; children's literature and, 26–34, 51; kawaii aesthetic in Japan and, 83–90, 92–95; racial difference vs., 49–53; racist love and, 7–9; techno-Orientalism and, 116–26
Cunanan, Andrew, 157
cuteness: Asian American spectatorship and, 95–100; gender anxiety and, 91; kawaii aesthetic and, 83–90; as microaggression, 75–82; passivity of, 93; pathos of, 104–7; racist kitsch and, 73–75; social robotics and, 112–16
cyberpunk, robotics and, 112–13
cyborg: Asianization of, 10–12, 147; disability activism and, 167; feminist discussion of, 226n42; gender and, 14–15; neoliberal norms and, 129–32; social robotics and, 112–16
Cyborg (Randolph), 127, 226n46
"A Cyborg Manifesto: Science, Technology, and Socialist-Feminism in the Late Twentieth Century" (Haraway), 114–15, 127

Dahlen, Sarah Park, 43–44
Daily Show, The (television series), 174–76
Darkie toothpaste, 77
dating apps, 230n1
Daughter from Danang (film), 46
dehumanization, of caricature, 80–82
developmental psychology: children's literature and, 32, 35–36; prejudice research in, 50; transspecies/transracial adoption and, 38–39
Dick, Philip K., 130
difference: cultural vs. racial difference, 49–53; desire for, 208n17; erotic charge of, 117; kawaii aesthetic and, 89–90; nonhuman proxies and, 18–19, 48–53; normate concept of, 231n11; racist caricature and, 73–75; in transspecies stories, 40
digital assistants, feminization of, 133, 138, 141, 147, 229n68
digital social movements, 196
diminutive in cuteness aesthetic, 87–90

disability, objectification of, 165–68
discriminatory action, 4, 74–75, 95–96, 175, 187, 234n38
Disney animation, cuteness aesthetic and, 84
diversity, positive framing of, 2
Divine Endurance (Jones), 112–13
Dixie Souvenir, 100
Do Androids Dream of Electric Sheep? (Dick), 130
doll study (Clark), self-esteem assessment and, 32, 65, 75, 99, 211n5
dominance, as kawaii aesthetic, 82–90
Dorow, Sara K., 43
Drag McQueen (Lim), 182–84
Dubey, Madhu, 120, 125, 129
dystopian Pacific Rim fiction, 127–32

"Eating the Other" (hooks), 205n1
Edith and Big Bad Bill (Wright), 27–29
education: children's literature and, 30–32; emotional growth and, 25–26; imagination vs., 32–34; racist caricature in, 79–82
emotion: kawaii aesthetic and absence of, 86–87; racial profiling and, 105–7, 193–200
Eng, David, 156–57
Engle, Margarita, 60
eroticism: Asian fetishism and, 156–58, 162–66; in Asian-themed film, 21–22; human-machine interface, 12; power dynamics of, 170; race and, 2; of wounded attachment, 187–90
ethnographic imperative, 23–24
eugenics, 56
evangelical Christians, transracial adoption and, 43
Ex Machina (film), 113, 119, 122–26, 145, 150, 226n42

fabricants, 113, 118–19
fairy tales: children's anxieties and role of, 41–42; darkness of, 27–28; educational theories on, 34–36
Fairy Tale Wars, 18–19, 34–37, 60
families: intergenerational misunderstanding in, 176–79; transspecies/transracial adoption and, 37–42
Fanon, Frantz, 7, 55

Fantasia (film), 90
fantasy: Asian American attachment to, 22; Asian fetish and, 154–58; for children, 19, 35, 65–67; as literary genre, 25–26; mimetic and non-mimetic in, 148–50, 209n24; objectification and, 163–64; Orient and, 10, 14–15; parodies of, 174–76; play and, 32–33; posthuman discourse and, 15–18; racial profiling and, 196–200; scrutable objects, 18–21; social robotics and, 114–16; Tolkien on, 149, 198
feminism: nonhuman rights and, 127; Pygmalion myth and, 226n42; social robotics and, 114–16
Feng, Daoyou, 193
Feng, Peter X., 21
Fetish: An Anthology of Fetish Fiction (Yau), 155
fetishism: in academic racial discourse, 180–87; of Asian Americans, 7–9; Asian photography, video and media, 22–23; of Black masculinity, 180–82; disability and, 165–68; intergenerational misunderstanding and, 176–79; kawaii aesthetic and, 83–90; in *Love Doll* photographic exhibit, 159–65; migration and, 178–79; Nakadate's photographic exploration of, 169–74; Oriental thingness and, 10–15; parody and, 174–76; race and, 153–58; of racist caricature, 71–75, 80–82; as wounded attachment, 187–90
Fiedler, Leslie, 7
Fighting Grandpa (documentary), 176–79, 233n24–25
Film No. 4: Bottoms (film), 13–14
First Amendment, caricature and, 76
First Generation of Korean Adoptees, 213n24
First Person Plural (documentary), 46–47
Fiske, Susan, 88–89, 195
Five Chinese Brothers, The (Bishop), 66
Fleetwood, Nicole R., 195–96
Flower Drum Song (musical), 173
Floyd, George, 105
forced choice test, 32, 65, 75, 99, 211n5
Ford, Christine Blasey, 139
Forever Bottom! (video), 170
foundling stories, 37–42
Franco, Vincente, 46
Frank, Caroline, 10, 208n18

Freud, Sigmund: affect theory and, 8–9; on castration anxiety, 160; on emotion, 87; on identification, 98; on jokes and caricature, 73, 76, 107; on objects, 18, 208nn15–16; on scopophilia, 232n16
friendship protection hypothesis, 215n42
Fromm, Erich, 115–16
Fung, Richard, 170

#gamergate movement, 228n62
"The Garbage Man: Why I Collect Racist Objects" (Pilgrim), 79–81
Gardner, Eric, 105
Garland, Alex, 119, 122
Gates, Henry Louis, 220n41
Geisel, Theodor (Dr. Seuss), 89–90, 219n24
geisha car, 2–5, 206n5
Geminoid F female-embodied robot, 137, 141–45, 148–49
gender: Asianized female-embodied robots, 136–41, 146–50; Black masculinity stereotype and, 105–7, 180–82, 220n41; children's perceptions of, 39; kawaii aesthetic and, 83–92; "Kindchenschema" (baby schema) and, 84, 218n15; robotics and, 112–16, 145–50; techno-Orientalist neoslave narrative and, 116–26
genetics, race and, 56
geopolitics, kawaii aesthetic and, 91–92
ghost in the machine, 112, 222n13
Ghost in the Shell 2: Innocence (Oshii), 113, 118, 149
Gilmore, Ruth Wilson, 105
Giovannoni, Stefano, 87
Gladwell, Malcolm, 6–7, 207n13
globalization: anxiety about, 9; cuteness aesthetic and, 85–90; gender and, 127–32; Indo-chic and, 10; kawaii aesthetic and, 91–95; racist caricaturing and, 196–200, 235n8
Goings, Kenneth, 77–78, 87, 91, 99–100, 104
Gone with the Wind (Mitchell), 97
Gonzalez, Jennifer, 147
Goodnight Moon (Brown), 35–36
Goostman, Eugene (chatbot), 117
graphic novels, race and anthropomorphism in, 53–59
Great Society initiatives, 31–32

Guevara, Susan, 28, 31
guilt, pleasure and, 22, 96
gynoids, 20–21, 112–13, 126, 133–36, 146–50

hair, Asian stereotypes concerning, 12–14, 24, 209n22
Halloween costumes, ethnic costume controversy, 27, 76, 105
hallucinatory Whiteness, 55–56
hallyu (Korean wave), 197–98
Hamamoto, Darrell, 157, 174–75, 232n22
Happy Birthday (Nakadate video), 171
Harajuku Lovers perfume bottle, 81–82, 84–85, 92–93, 104, 218n13
Haraway, Donna, 114, 127, 147, 198–99, 226n42
Harman, Graham, 125
Harris, Daniel, 84
Harris, Michael, 103
Harvey, David, 91, 128
Hasbro corporation, 101–2
Hasegawa, Yuko, 83–84
hate speech and hate crimes: caricature as, 4, 70–76; COVID-19 pandemic and, 192–200, 235n7
hawaiiana, 85
Hawking, Stephen, 221n8
Hayles, N. Katherine, 112, 114–15, 147
Head Start program, 31
Hello Kitty, 70–71, 83, 86–87, 92; ironic spectatorship and, 100–104
Helms, Jesse, 180–82, 186–87, 233nn27–29
Hemphill, Essex, 180
Hensel and Gretel: Ninja Chicks (Schwartz, Gomez, Santat), 61–62
Here and Now Story Book (Mitchell), 34
Hernandez-Ortiz, Elcias, 235n5
heterosexual norms, framing of robots through, 147–50
hierarchies of race, *American Born Chinese* and, 56–59
"High Heel Project" (Katayama), 167
Hirschfeld, Lawrence, 52, 107, 194–95
Ho, Jennifer, 47, 220n42
Holland, Sharon Patricia, 208n14
Holt, Bertha and Harry, 43
Holt International Children's Services (Holt Adoption Program), 43

Home for a Bunny (Brown), 35, 63–64
Homo sapiens, eugenics hierarchies and research on, 56
homosexuality, in children's literature, 62–67
Hong Kong, 91
hooks, bell, 2, 8, 97, 153, 205n1
Hop Low (Disney character), 90
Horn Book magazine, 60
Horning, Kathleen, 25, 61–62, 211, 216n43, 216n47, 216n50, 217n58
household goods, Asian caricature in, 70–71
How to Attract Asian Women, 155
How to Build a Human (documentary), 136–41
How We Became Posthuman: Virtual Bodies in Cybernetics, Literature, and Informatics (Hayles), 114–15
Huang, Eddie, 69, 83
humanals, micropolitics of abstraction and, 48–53
human-machine interface: Asianization of, 20–21; as erotic encounter, 12, 144; rights of nonhumans and, 126–32; robotics and, 110–16, 136–45; sexual intimacy with robots, 223n17
humanoid robots: development of, 109–16, 221n5; female-embodiment of, 137–41
Humans (television series), 113, 119, 127, 133–36, 145, 151, 227n52, 228n57
Human Robot, The (documentary), 112, 141–45
human trafficking: futurist anti trafficking narratives and, 132–33; neoslave narratives and, 120–22, 125–26, 149–50, 225n35
humor, repression and, 234n34
Hurd, Edith Thacher, 32, 34–35
Hwang, David Henry, 170, 175–76
hybridity: social robotics and, 113–16; transspecies adoption stories and, 40

I, Robot (Asimov), 227n52
identification, with cuteness aesthetic, 97–98
identity politics, fetishism and, 155–58
"I Enjoy Being a Girl" (song), 173
If I Ran the Zoo (Seuss), 90, 219n24
I Have Child's Feet (Katayama), 168–69
I Love You Like Crazy Cakes (Lewis), 44
I'm a Cyborg, but That's OK (film), 129

imagination: education vs., 35–36; play and, 26–34
Immediate Family (Mann), 234n39
immigration laws, 10
I'm Wearing Little High Heels (Katayama), 167–68
Indian Child Welfare Act, 41
Indo-chic, 10, 85
infantilization of Asians: kawaii aesthetic and, 83–92; racist kitsch and, 73–75; transracial adoption and, 47
inscrutability: Asian stereotype of, 116–17, 124–25; kawaii aesthetic and, 86–87; techno-Orientalism and, 111–16
intergenerational misunderstanding, fetishism, 176–79
International Social Services–USA, 43
interracial dating, 230n1
interspecies cooperation: in children's literature, 28–29, 31–34, 44; transspecies/transracial adoption and, 37–42
In This Corner of the World (anime), 230n76
intimacy, sexual intimacy with robots, 112–16, 223n17
IQ tests, 32
ironic spectatorship, activism and, 100–104
Ishiguro, Hiroshi, 137, 141–45, 148, 159
Ishiguro, Kazuo, 113
Iwabuchi, Koichi, 92
I Want to Be the One Who Walks in the Sun (Nakadate video), 170–71

Jacobson, Heather, 162
Japan: comfort women, 121–22, 149, 225n41; economic rise of, 3, 91–95, 209n20; kawaii style in, 72–75, 81–82; monkeys and man in, 215n41; politics of kawaii in, 82–90; robotics in, 110–16, 221n8; US occupation of, 91–92
japonisme, 10, 85
Jentsch, Ernst, 123, 160
Jeon, Joseph Jonghyun, 13, 75, 209n23
Jeong, Ken, 104
Jia Jia female-embodied robot, 137–41, 145, 147
Jim Crow laws, 55–56
Jim Crow Museum of Racist Memorabilia, 79–81
Johnson, Barbara, 163–64

Jokes and Their Relation to the Unconscious (Freud), 76
Jolly Olly Orange caricature, 76
Jones, Gwyneth, 112–13
Journey to the West (Wu Cheng'en), 33, 53–55, 57–58
"The Joy Fuck Club: Prolegomenon to an Asian American Porno Practice" (Hamamoto), 174–75
Just Add One Chinese Sister, 44

Kang, Laura, 122, 149
Kasza, Keiko, 37–38
Katauchi, Sunao, 230n76
Katayama, Mari, 157, 165–69, 173–74, 195
Katz, Phyllis A., 211n5, 212n14
Kavanaugh, Brett, 139
kawaii aesthetic: Asian American spectatorship of, 95–100; cultural erasure and, 106–7; emergence in Japan of, 81–82; gender and, 83–92; globalization of, 72–75, 92–95; Japanese perceptions of, 93–95; politics of, 82–90; as racial kitsch, 19–20; threatening competence stereotype and, 91–95
Kennon, Raquel, 113–14
Khanna, Ranjana, 14, 98, 170
Kim, Eunjung, 129, 168
Kim, Suncha, 193
Kimchi and Calamari (Kent), 44
"Kindchenschema" (baby schema), 84, 218n15
King, Rodney, 28
King, William Davies, 98
King and I, The (musical), 21
Kinsella, Sharon, 91
kinship, nonnormative concepts of, 37–38, 40
Kirk, David, 38
Kirobo anthropomorphic machine, 110
Kitano, Harry, 6, 207n12
Kitano, Naho, 112
kitsch: activism and ironic spectatorship and, 100–104; global circulation of, 91–95; kawaii aesthetic and, 83–90; racial stereotyping in, 73–82; racist caricatures and, 70–75
Klara and the Sun (Ishiguro), 113
Klein, Melanie, 26, 29, 66
Know My Name (Miller), 134–35

Know Your Filipina Handbook: Your Best Guide for Dating Filipinas, 154
Koh, Frances, 213n24
Ko Lovers perfume, 218n13
Kondo, Marie: cuteness aesthetic and, 86, 107; ironic spectatorship and, 104; KonMari Method and, 15–18, 195, 208n25, 209n27; on possession, 112, 210n29
koneko ji (kitten writing), 83
KonMari Method, 15–18, 209n25
Korean Americans, intergenerational misunderstanding among, 176–79
Kravet home decor company, 85
Kung Fu Panda (film trilogy), 46, 214n30
Kusama, Yayoi, 166
Kuu Kuu Harajuku series, 92–93
Kwan, Kevin, 90
Kwan, Nancy, 21, 173, 186

Lagerfeld, Karl, 93–95
Lai, Larissa, 113, 127, 129–31
Lamb-a-Roo, The (Kimpton), 37
Land O'Lakes Indian maiden, 77
Lanham Act, 76–77
Laplanche, Jean, 18, 199
Latinx men, racial profiling of, 105
Latour, Bruno, 17, 74, 85, 95, 106–7, 195, 217nn3–4
laundry products, Asian stereotypes and, 77–78, 103
"Laurie Simmons: My Daughter the Sex Doll" (Robinson), 162
Lee, Bruce, 101
Lee, Chang-rae, 127
Lee, Helen, 185–87
Lee, Jennifer, 207n13
Lee, Josephine, 10, 85
Lee, Rachel, 191–92, 210n32
Lee, Spike, 100
Le Guin, Ursula, 25–26, 35
Lessons 1–10 (Nakadate video), 171
Li, Fei-Fei, 146–47, 229n71
Liem, Deann Borshay, 46–47
Lim, Elisha, 157, 182–84
Lim, Eng-Beng, 218n17
Little Chicken (Brown), 35–36
Little Miss Spider (Kirk), 38, 40

Little Raccoon Learns to Share (Packard), 52
Little Fur Family, The (Brown), 35
Little Green Goose, The (Sansone), 37
Liu, Marjorie, 113, 129
Lohman, Michael, 185, 234n33
"Looking for My Penis" (Fung), 170
Lopez, Lori Kido, 103–4
Lorenz, Konrad, 84
Lott, Eric, 9
Love, Robot (Rhee), 129–30
love and theft, 9
Lovelace, Ada (Lady), 147
Love Doll, The (photographic series), 155, 159–65, 168
Lucky Tiger (Nakadate photo series), 171–74
Lum, Debbie, 170

MacCann, Donnarae, 35
Machine Love (film), 147, 175
Made in China: A Story of Adoption (Oelschlager), 44
Mai, Nicola, 125–26
Maira, Sunaina, 10, 85
"Making Of" (Choi), 131–32
Mammy and Uncle Mose: Black Collectibles and American Stereotyping (Goings), 99–100
manga: cuteness aesthetic and, 84, 91; racial themes in, 30, 33, 53–59; robotics in, 118; video gaming and, 218n14
Man in Polyester Suit (Mapplethorpe), 180
Mann, Sally, 187, 234n39
Mapplethorpe, Robert, 180–82, 186–87, 233nn27–29
Marche, Stephen, 1
Marcus, Leonard, 32–33, 35, 212n10
Marley, Bob, 103
Martin, Trayvon, 105
Martinson, Rebecca, 153
Mary Poppins (film), 16
Masamune, Shirow, 118
mascots, as racist kitsch, 76–77, 87–88, 217n5
Massumi, Brian, 17
maternal pleasure, transracial adoption and, 162
Matsuda, Mari, 76
Mattel Corporation, 93
Maus (Spiegelman), 64, 66

Maya's Journey Home (Lindsley, Christiansen, and Cannon), 44, 46
M. Butterfly (Hwang), 170, 172
McCarthy, John, 117–18, 224n26
McClintock, Anne, 8, 14, 158
McGray, Douglas, 92
Media Action Network for Asian Americans, 104
melancholic loss, 9
Mercer, Kobena, 180–82, 187, 233n29
metonymy, cultural appropriation and, 94
#MeToo, 21, 115–16; robotics and, 133–36, 139–45
Michels, Paul Andre, 235n5
microaggression, caricature as, 75–82
Midori, Fetish Diva, 155–56, 190
migration: COVID-19 pandemic and, 191–92; fetishism and, 178–79
Miller, Chantal, 134
mimetic effect, 22, 26, 32
mind-body dualism, social robotics and, 112, 222n13
Minhaj, Hasan, 5–6
Miss Bindergarten (Slate and Wolff), 48
Mitchell, David, 113, 167
Mitchell, Lucy Sprague, 26, 30–36, 38
mixed-race children, adoption of, 42–47
Miyasaki, Hayao, 230n76
Mizuno, Sonoyo, 123–24
Modeleski, Tania, 186
model minority label, 6, 207n12; cuteness aesthetic and, 88–90; Freud and, 208n15
Modern Family (television program), 146
Monkey King, in Yang's *American Born Chinese*, 53–59
monkeys, Chinese Americans linked to, 54–56
Monstress comic series (Liu and Takeda), 113, 129, 227n47
Moon, Kathy, 149
Moore, Anne Carroll, 34–35, 40, 60
Moore, Milton, 180
Mori, Masahiro, 142–43, 161
Morley, David, 10, 111
A Mother for Choco (Kasza), 37–38, 40
Moy, James, 10
mukokuseki (cultural erasure), 92–95
Mulberry Bird: Story of an Adoption, The (Brodzinsky and Stanley), 37

multicultural children's literature, 26, 31–34, 50–53, 60–67, 216n45
multicultural rhetoric, fetishism and, 155–58
Murakami, Takashi, 91–92
My Adopted Child, There's No One Like You (Leman), 44–45
Myers, Christopher, 64–65
My German Boyfriend (film), 169–70
My New Mom and Me (Galindo), 37–40

Nakadate, Laurel, 157, 165–68, 169–74, 232n19
NAO humanoid robot, 109–16, 145, 221n1
narcissism, Freud on, 208n15
National Association of Black Social Workers (NABSW), 40–41
National Palace Museum of Taiwan, 71, 73, 87
Native Americans: adoption among, 41; racist caricatures of, 75–77, 217n5; in Scarry's children's books, 27
nativism, exclusion of Asians and, 10
Nel, Philip, 61, 63
neoliberalism: cuteness aesthetic and, 87–90, 93–95; for-profit value of humans under, 126–27; globalization and, 9; threatening competence stereotype and, 91–95
neoslave narrative: in *Humans*, 133–36; techno-Orientalism and, 113–26, 129, 223n19
new materialism: KonMari method and, 17; racist kitsch and, 74–75
New York Magazine, 184
Ngai, Sianne: on automatism, 162–63; on caricature, 73–74, 91–93, 217n2; on cuteness, 84, 96; on object-oriented ontology, 17–18; racial animatedness concept of, 231n9
Nguyen Tan Hoang, 156–58, 169–70, 178–79
Nickelodeon network, 48, 92–93
"Nine Sexy College Classes Happening This Fall" (*New York Magazine*), 184–85
Nintendo, 92
nonhuman proxies: for Asians, 2–5, 10–15, 48–53; in children's literature, 26–34, 49–53, 62–67; Haraway on, 198–99; kawaii aesthetic and, 92–95; racial prejudice and, 18–19; representation imperative and, 59–62; rights of, 126–32; robotics and, 110–16
Nutcracker Suite, The (Tchaikovsky), 90
Nyong'o, Tavia, 72

object-oriented ontology, 15–18; academic antiracism and, 179–87; Asian caricature and, 71–75; cuteness aesthetic and, 85–90; fetishism and, 156–58, 162–63; robotics and, 112–16; scrutable objects, 18–21
Oelrichs, Blanche, 62
Oh, Sandra, 196
Ohnuki-Tierney, Emiko, 57
Oishi, Eve, 21, 97, 156–57
OkCupid dating app, 230n1
Okuni (geisha car), 2–5, 22, 206n5
one-friend hypothesis, 215n42; adolescent integration and, 58
100 Butches (Lim), 183
Ono, Yoko, 13–14
On Racial Icons: Blackness and the Public Imagination (Fleetwood), 195–96
On Such a Full Sea (Lee), 127
Operation Babylift, 43, 213n21, 231n8
Orient, thingness of, 10–15; cuteness aesthetic and, 85–90
Orientalism, 10; racist caricature and, 73–75, 77–78; xenophobia and, 197–200. *See also* techno-Orientalism
ornamentalism, kitsch and, 85
Oshii, Mamoru, 118
Our Baby from China: An Adoption Story (D'Antonio), 44
Outliers: The Story of Success (Gladwell), 6–7

Page Act, 10
Pak, Greg, 147, 157–58, 175–79, 233nn24–25
pandas, in transracial adoption stories, 44–47
Park, Jane, 10
Park, Soon Chung, 193
Parnell, Peter, 63–64
parodies of racism, 104; fetishism and, 174–76
PARO therapy robot, 109–16, 221n2
Parreñas, Celine Shimizu, 157, 185–86
passing (racial), 55–56
pathos, cuteness and, 104–7
Peace Constitution (Japan), 91–92
Pearl S. Buck International, 42
peer groups, race and, 58–59
People v. Brock Allen Turner, 134–35, 247n55
Pepper humanoid robot, 221n1
personhood, cultural appropriation and, 94

perverse spectatorship, 21–22, 97, 156–57, 180–87
Pew Research Center, 6, 206n11
phantasmatic, 18
Philippines, sex trafficking and, 121–22
Pikachu, 92
Pilgrim, David, 79–81, 98
Pillsbury, caricatures used by, 76–77
Pink Globalization (Yano), 83
Pirated! (video), 178–79, 233n26
play, imagination and, 26–34, 66–67
pleasure: Asianness as, 12–14; of Black women's spectatorship, 97; in childhood, 29–30; cuteness aesthetic and, 88–90, 96–100, 107; of erotic spectatorship, 154, 172, 181–82, 189; in exhibitionism, 173; Freud on, 208n16; geisha car as form of, 3–5; race and, 1–5; racist kitsch and, 73–75
poetry, by Asian Americans, 209n23
Pokémon GO, 196–98
politicization of abstraction: in children's literature, 62–67; fetishism and, 156–58, 180–82, 187
Pontalis, J. B., 18, 199
possession: erotic, 8, 17; ownership and, 210n29
posthumanism: nonhumans and, 126–27; techno-Orientalism and, 111–16, 147–50
power asymmetry: cuteness aesthetic and, 85, 87–90; eroticism and, 189–90; fetishism and, 158, 162–63, 170; robotics and, 148–50
prejudice in children, 50–51, 212n14, 214n34
Produce Love, The (*Die Ware Liebe*), 170
progressive pedagogy: in children's literature, 27–28, 32–34; transspecies adoption stories and, 40–42
proximity, stereotyping and, 4, 207n13
psychic violence, in Yang's *American Born Chinese*, 55
psychoanalysis: children's literature and, 33, 36; colonialism of, 14–15; harm of racial images in, 75–82; object relations theory, 206n7; racism and, 8–9, 59
Pucca character, 70–72, 92, 104, 219n27, 219n33
Pygmalion myth, 113, 226n42

Quick Kick cartoon character, 101–4

Rabbits' Wedding, The (Williams), 64
race: "American uncanny" and, 114, 142–43, 161–62; Black/white binary in, 208n14; caricatures based on, 70–82; in children's literature, 26–36, 53, 216n49; children's perceptions of, 18–19, 38–39, 212n14; color-blind racism, 53; COVID-19 pandemic and, 23–24; cuteness aesthetic and, 84–90; fetishism and, 153–58, 163–64; Freud on, 18, 208nn15–16; gender and, 124; negative framing of, 2; Orientalism and, 10–15; parodies of rights and, 174; pleasure and, 1–5; robotics technology and, 111–16; structure of feeling and, 106–7; transspecies/transracial adoption stories and, 38–42; in Yang's *American Born Chinese*, 53–59
race fetishism. *See* fetishism
racial abstraction: ambivalent stereotyping and, 5–7; in children's literature, 32–34; cuteness aesthetic and, 86–90; general process of, 205n3; kitsch and, 70–75; KonMari Method and, 16; micropolitics of, 48–53; pleasure and, 4–5; politicization of, 62–67; social robotics and, 113–16; transracial adoption and, 43–47
Racial Innocence: Performing American Childhood from Slavery to Civil Rights (Bernstein), 32
racial kitsch, 19–20
racial profiling, 191–200; cuteness and, 104–7
racial scopophilia, 2, 18, 20, 22, 113–14, 157, 165, 169, 174, 187; nonhumans and, 17–18
Racial Things, Racial Forms: Objecthood in Avant-Garde Asian American Poetry (Jeon), 13
racist hate, 5, 7, 191–200
racist love: ambivalent stereotyping and, 5–7; Asian fetishism as, 153–58; Asian gynoids as objects of, 146–50; Asian racialization and, 24; in children's literature, 26–34; cultural appropriation as, 7–9; kawaii spectatorship as, 96–100; nationalism and, 232n16; pathos of things and, 104–7; as racist hate, 195–200; self-affirmation and, 170–74; techno-Orientalism and, 111–16
Ramsey, Patricia G., 38–39, 193
Randolph, Lynn, 127
Rastus caricature, 77

"Reading Racial Fetishism: The Photographs of Robert Mapplethorpe" (Mercer), 180
Real Humans (television series), 133, 227n53
Rebecca's Journey Home (Sugarman), 44
Reconstruction era, Black racist kitsch emergence during, 91
Reeves, Keanu, 157, 196
repetition, stereotyping and, 207n13
representation: caricature and, 75–82; nonhuman proxies and, 59–62; racial abstraction and, 2–5, 205n3
reproduction, transspecies adoption stories and, 40
resilience, in children's literature, 52–53
Rhee, Margaret, 129–30
Richardson, Justin, 63–64
rights of nonhumans, 126–32
Rise of Asian Americans, The (Pew Research), 6
risky objects: kitsch as, 74, 95, 217n3; racist hate and, 195
rituals, in children's literature, 35–36
Rivinus, T. M., 52
Robert Mapplethorpe: The Perfect Moment (exhibition), 233n27
Robi anthropomorphic machine, 109, 145, 221n4
Robins, Kevin, 10, 111
Robinson, Tony, 105
Robinson, Walter, 162
RoboGeisha (film), 113
RoboHon anthropomorphic machine, 110
robotics: Asianized female-embodied robots, 136–41, 146–50; definitions of, 222n15; killer robot development, 110–16, 221n8; passing fiction in, 124–25
robots: Asianization of, 12, 20–21; as companions, 109–10; "robot gap," 110–11; therapeutic, 109
Robot Series (film anthology), 147
Rosie's Family: An Adoption Story (Rosove), 37
Rothstein, Edward, 212n10
Runaway Bunny, The (Brown), 35
Russia, transnational adoption from, 47
Ryle, Gilbert, 112, 222n13

Saga (Vaughn and Staples), 113
Said, Edward, 10

Sally's Beauty Spot (film), 185–87, 234n36
Salt Fish Girl (Lai), 113, 127
Sanrio, 70, 72–73, 75, 83, 92
Santat, Dan, 61–62
Saper, Bernard, 101, 220n36
Sartre, Jean-Paul, 194
satire, 220n41
Savage, Dan, 155
Scarry, Richard, 27, 32, 48
Scopes Monkey Trial, 56
Scott, Ridley, 130
Searle, John R., 112, 116–18, 146, 148, 222n12, 229n74
Sedgwick, Eve Kosofsky, 64
Seeking Asian Female (documentary), 170
segregation, racist kitsch in era of, 55–56, 75–82
Seinfeld (television series), 195
self-enhancement, cultural appropriation and, 9
self-esteem, race and, 32, 65, 75, 211n5
September 11, 2001 attacks, anti-Arab feelings after, 5–6
servant caricature, 77–78
Sesame Street (television program), 31
sex tourism industry, 121–22
sexuality: Asianized female-embodied robots and, 136–41, 146–50; Asian women stereotypes of, 193–200; Black masculinity stereotype, 105–7, 180–82, 220n41; children's perceptions of, 39; intergenerational misunderstandings about, 176–79; kawaii aesthetic and, 83–92; in neoslave narrative, 116–26; parodies of, 174–76; race fetishism and, 153–58; robotics and, 112–16, 145–50
Shell (Katayama), 166–67
Shinto, 16–17, 210n28; robotics and influence of, 112
Shiokawa, Kanako, 83–84, 89, 91
Shoes (video), 182–83
Shortcomings (Tomine), 187–88
Silverman, Sarah, 6, 104, 185, 206n9
Simmons, Laurie, 20–21, 155, 159–65
Sinette, Elinor, 61
Singapore, 91
Siri digital assistant, 113, 138, 141, 147, 229n68
slavery: agency and, 132–33; "American uncanny" and, 114, 142–43, 161–62; neoslave

literature and film, 113–14, 120–22; thingness of, 85, 91, 217n2
Smith, Katharine Capshaw, 32
Snapchat, racist stereotypes on, 103
social change, in children's literature, 35–36
social power: machine intelligence and, 117; positive asymmetries in, 5–7
social realism, fantasy and, 18–19
social robotics, racial feeling and, 109–16
SoftBank Robotics, 221n1
Soft Science (Choi), 131–32
Soto, Gary, 28, 31
South Korea: kawaii aesthetic and, 93; kitsch production in, 70–72, 91–92; sex trafficking and, 121–22, 225n41; transracial adoption from, 43–47
species difference: racial diversity and, 19, 26–34; segregation and, 57–59; transspecies/transracial adoption and, 37–42
spectatorship: activism and irony in, 100–104; of Black women, 97; cuteness and, 95–100; exploitation and, 231n5; in Katayama's exhibits, 165–68; kawaii aesthetic and, 84–90; racist kitsch and, 74–75
speculative fiction: artificial intelligence and, 118–26; of Asian Americans, 129–32; robotics and, 113–16; slavery and violation in, 125–26
speculative realism, KonMari method and, 17
Spiegelman, Art, 25, 64
Spivak, Gayatri, 154, 163
Springer, Claudia, 223n19
Sprinkle Plenty laundry aid, 77–78
Staples, Fiona, 113
Stefani, Gwen, 81–82, 84, 92–93
Stepford Wives, The (film), 113, 226n42
stereotyping: activism and ironic spectatorship about, 101–4; of Black masculinity, 105–7, 180–82, 220n41; corporate culture and, 103–4; cuteness aesthetic and, 87–90; harm of, 75–82, 217n5; hyperemotionalism of, 231n9; as microaggression, 75–82; mobilization against, 95–100; race fetishism and, 153–58; racial abstraction and ambivalence of, 5–7, 207nn12–13; racial profiling and, 191–200; in racist kitsch, 74–75; thought experiments in, 116–17
stoicism, as Oriental stereotype, 86–87

Stoller, Robert, 22, 199
Story of Babar, The (de Brunhoff), 37
Strange, Michael, 62–63, 216n51, 216n53
structural racism, 216n49
Stuart Little (White), 37, 40
Stuff Asian People Like (blog), 101
A Subtlety, or the Marvelous Sugar Baby (Walker sculpture), 101–2
Sue, Stanley, 6, 207n12
Sullivan, Liam Kyle, 182–83
sumo figure, cuteness aesthetic and, 85–86, 104
Sutton, Roger, 60
Symbiotic Human-Robot Interaction Project, 141–45
synths, 113, 119, 133–36

Taiwan, 71, 73, 87, 91
Takeda, Sana, 113, 129
Takei, George, 175
Tan, Amy, 213n27
Tan, Xiaojie, 193
Target, cuteness aesthetic at, 84–85, 92–93
Tatsumi, Nagisa, 15, 210n26
Taylor, Charles, 59–60, 208n17
techno-eroticism, 223n19
techno-Orientalism, 10–15, 20, 209n20; neo-slave narratives and, 116–26, 147–50; social robotics and, 109–16; trafficking narrative of, 127–28
Tezuka, Osamu, 84, 112
Life-Changing Magic of Tidying Up: The Japanese Art of Decluttering and Organizing, The (Kondo), 15–18
thing theory: body difference and, 168–69; cuteness aesthetic and, 85; fetishism and, 159–65; in Katayama's exhibitions, 165–68; pathos of, 104–7; racist kitsch and, 74–75; relationality and, 17; self-objectification and, 170–74; threatening competence stereotype and, 91–95
Thirteenth Amendment, 120–21
Thomson, Rosemarie Garland, 231n11
threatening competence stereotype: globalization and, 91–95; kawaii aesthetic and, 88–90
Three Graces (Zhang), 12–14, 154, 174
"Three Laws of Robotics" (Asimov), 110–11
Ti, Andrew, 154–56

Tiger Mother stereotype, 207n12
Tikki Tikki Tembo (Mosel), 66
Tiny Rabbit's Big Wish (Engle), 60
tolerance: in children's literature, 52–53; of hate speech, 76
Tolkien, J. R. R., 26, 35, 149, 198
Tomine, Adrian, 187–88
Toyota, robotics and, 112
trademarks, racist caricatures in, 76–77
transitional objects: children's play and, 15, 26, 30–31; racist kitsch and, 75
transnational adoption, dominance of Asian adoptees in, 42–47
transnational capitalism: cuteness aesthetic and, 87–90; dematerialization of, 93–95
transracial adoption: "American uncanny" and, 162; in children's literature, 37–42; growth of, 42–47
transspecies adoption, 19; in children's literature, 37–42, 48–53
Travels of Ching, The (Bright), 66
Trump, Donald, 107
Trung, Le, 137–40
Tsou, Elda, 23
Turing, Alan, 116–17
Turing test, 116–17, 122, 125
Turkle, Sherry, 139, 145
2 Live Crew, 220n41

Unbound Feet: A Social History of Chinese Women in San Francisco (Yung), 155
uncanny feeling theory: Brown's "American uncanny" and, 114, 142–43; fetishism and, 160–65
Uncle Mose caricature, 100
United Nations, autonomous weapons and, 111
United States: artificial intelligence weaponization in, 110; Asia as strategic region for, 225n40; Asian adoption in, 42–53; Asian American spectatorship in, 95–100; Asian fetish in, 153–58; caricature and hate speech in, 105, 107; Chinese labor in, 93–94; critical race theory in, 106; cuteness as microaggression in, 69–79, 93; global hegemony and human rights and, 128; ironic spectatorship in, 100–101; kawaii aesthetic in, 81–82; 87–88; racialization of Asians in, 2, 23–25; racial profiling in, 191–200; robotics in, 110–16; slavery and human trafficking legislation in, 120–22; techno-Orientalism in, 111–16; threatening competency stereotypes in, 55–56, 88–89
US Constitution, 122
US Trafficking Victims Protection Act, 121

VAD (valence, arousal, dominance) scale, stereotyping and, 73, 76, 89–90
van Hattum, Rob, 141–45
Vaughn, Brian K., 113
ventriloquism, object-oriented ontology and, 17–18
Verghese, Abraham, 192
Viacom, 92–93
Vietnam: fetishism and migration in, 178–79; sex trafficking and, 121–22; transracial adoption from, 42–43, 47, 213n21, 231n8
Village Voice, 180
violence: in cuteness, 84; gender-based violence, 120–22; racial profiling and, 105, 193–94
virtual women, techno-Orientalist neoslave narrative and, 116–26
visibility, race and, 59–62
Visibly_Smart advertisement, 10–12
VISTA program, 31
visual media: racist caricatures in, 69–75; social robotics and, 113

Waiting for May (Stoeke), 44
Waley, Arthur, 55
Walker, Kara, 22, 97, 101–2
Washington Redskins, 76
Was the Cat in the Hat Black? (Nel), 63–64
Watson, James D., 146, 148
We Adopted You, Benjamin Koo (Girard), 44
Weise, Jillian, 14, 167
Weisgard, Leonard, 36
Wells, Rosemary, 48, 50
Westworld (television series), 113
White Citizens' Council, 64
Whiteness: Asian fetishism and, 154, 157–58, 230n1; fetishism of, 232n21; framing of robots through, 147–50; iconicity of, 22; in parenting, 42; racist kitsch and, 74–75

Why Did I Buy That Toy? Blogging Away Buyer's Remorse (blog), 96–98, 101
"Why I Collect Racism" (Wu), 79–80
Williams, Garth, 64, 217n57
Williams, Linda, 153–54, 180, 188–89
Williams, Patricia, 53
Williams, Raymond, 206n6
Wind Rises, The (Miyasaki), 230n76
Windup Girl, The (Bacigalupi), 113, 126
Winnicott, D. W., 15, 26, 29, 36, 75, 148, 188
Wolff, Ashley, 48
Wolfie the Bunny (Dyckman and OHora), 37
women: infantilization of Japanese women, 205n2; robotics images of, 20–21, 112–16; techno-Orientalist neoslave narrative, virtual women and, 116–26; trafficking of, 121, 126
Wong, Anna May, 170
Wool-Rim Sjöblom, Lisa, 47
wordless speech, caricature as, 76
World of Suzie Wong, The (film), 21, 186
wounded attachment: Brown's concept of, 98, 156, 174, 187; erotics of, 187–90
"Wounded Beauty: An Exploratory Essay on Race, Feminism, and the Aesthetic Question" (Cheng), 173
Wright, Dare, 27, 29

"Write, Robot" (Rhee), 129–30
Wu, Constance, 196
Wu, Frank, 79–80
Wu Cheng'en, 53–54

Yang, Chi-Ming, 208n18
Yang, Gene Luen, 19, 33, 53–59, 215n38
Yano, Christine, 83
Yau, John, 155, 231n4
Yaun González, Ashley, 235n5
Yellow Room (Katayama), 168
Yo, Is This Racist? website, 154, 181
Yoko (Wells), 48–51, 57
YOMYOMF ("You offend me, you offend my family") blog, 101
Yu, Phil, 101–4
Yue, Yong, 193
Yuh, Ji-Yeon, 121–22, 149
Yung, Judy, 155
Yung, Wayne, 169–70

Zhang, Hong Chun, 12–14, 154, 209n22
Zhao, Amelie Wen, 120, 129
Zhou, Min, 207n13
Žižek, Slavoj, 1, 14, 107
Zootopia (film), 28–29

www.ingramcontent.com/pod-product-compliance
Lightning Source LLC
Chambersburg PA
CBHW050213240426
43671CB00013B/2317